COUNTERREVOLUTION

U.S. Foreign Policy

COUNTER REVOLUTION:

U.S. FOREIGN POLICY

Edward and Regula Boorstein

International Publishers   *New York*

Library of Congress Cataloging-in-Publication Data

Boorstein, Edward, 1915-
    Counterrevolution: U.S. foreign policy / Edward and Regula
Boorstein
        p.   cm.
    Includes bibliographical references and index.
    ISBN 0-7178-0684-7 : $8.95
    1. United States — Foreign relations — 20th century.
2. Counterrevolutions — History — 20th century. 3. Revolutions
— History — 20th century. 4. World politics — 20th century.
I. Boorstein, Regula. II. Title.
[E744.B665 1990]
327.73 — dc20

                                        90-40845
                                        CIP

CONTENTS

COUNTERREVOLUTION

U.S. Foreign Policy

Introduction

Many people know from current experience about U.S. efforts to kill the Nicaraguan Revolution but are too young to have witnessed what the United States did when revolution erupted in Cuba. Others from a previous generation remember the effort to snuff out the Cuban Revolution, while U.S. support of Chiang Kai-shek against the Chinese revolutionaries happened before their time. Almost nobody who observed day-to-day the actions of the United States against the Russian Revolution is still around.

We attempt in this book to provide a broad perspective on the longstanding, worldwide U.S. campaign of counterrevolution by examining United States actions against revolutions in a number of countries, starting with Russia and China and coming down to Nicaragua and southern Africa.

The effort to put down revolution has been a central focus of U.S. foreign policy in the 20th century, especially since World War II. Not only did the United States work to keep revolutions in Russia, China, Cuba, Vietnam, Angola, Nicaragua, and other countries from winning, but it maintained a strong hostility for years, even decades, after they had won. Many writers trace the beginning of the cold war from 1945 without considering what went before. Actually, the cold war was in good part a continuation of the deep hostility of the United States to the 1917 Russian Revolution and the socialist state it created—a hostility only partially interrupted by World War II.

The U.S. posture toward revolution remains one of the world's crucial questions. In opposing revolution, the United States is opposing the striving of peoples around the world to free themselves from poverty, oppression, and exploitation. For many of these peoples there is no solution except to break out by revolution from the social, economic, and political conditions which hem in their societies. And the United States' hostility to revolution creates a permanent threat of U.S. military intervention in one place or another.

The situation is not unchanging. The end of the 1980s marked the beginning of what President George Bush referred to as "a brand-new era of U.S.-Soviet relations." Although no one can foretell all the manifold consequences of this change, the world will not be the same.

Yet some things remain the same. While the United States softened its policy toward the Soviet Union, it maintained the old hard line toward many other countries including Cuba, Vietnam, and Angola. It was still poised to act against any country that sought to overthrow the established capitalist-imperialist order. And even toward the Soviet Union elements of the old hard line remained.

Key questions remain to be answered. What explains the difference between the softer policy toward the Soviet Union and the hard line toward the other countries? What will it take to get the United States to change its policy toward these countries as well? How will the United States respond if a new revolution seems about to win, say in the Philippines or in Brazil? We hope that a historical analysis of the U.S. reaction to revolutions will shed light on such questions and give an inkling of what the future may hold.

Our interest in U.S. counterrevolution stems in good part from our personal experience. We lived and worked in Cuba during the early years of the Revolution—during the Bay of Pigs invasion and the October missile crisis—and in Chile at the time of the 1973 coup against the Popular Unity government. We had a chance to see close up what it means to a country and its people to be the target of the implacable U.S. hostility to radical change. One of us—Edward—has written a book, *Allende's Chile*, which details the U.S. assault on the legally elected Allende government.[1]

1. Russia/Soviet Union:

1917-1946

It was the first World War with its senseless slaughter, from which Russia suffered far more than any other country, that set off the Russian revolution. In the first ten months of war, Russia lost 3.8 million men.[1] By the end of 1916, the government had called up 16 million. With each new call-up, people asked, "What does this mean, do they want to bury us all...?"[2] The draft left a third of the peasant households without labor and the output of grains declined. The government poured out printing-press money and prices soared. Goods became scarce. Disorganization spread.

To maintain the army became impossible. Badly fed, led by incompetent and corrupt officers, often sent into battle poorly armed, the soldiers deserted in droves. The army introduced flogging for breaches of discipline and the death penalty for self-inflicted wounds, but this only made matters worse.

By the beginning of 1917, the economy was in chaos. The railroads had broken down, almost completely ending the flow of foodstuffs to Petrograd, Moscow, and other cities. Food riots spread. One factory after another shut down, and unemployment shot up.[3]

Lenin explained the connection between the war and the revolution:

> Russia had no alternative. The war had caused such destruction and starvation everywhere, made the people and soldiers so weary, they realized they had been tricked for so long, and that the only way out for Russia was revolution.[4]

The revolution had, of course, been building up for a long time before the war. There had been a forerunner as far back as 1825—the uprising of the Decembrists, revolutionary army officers from the nobility, against the Czar. There was a major revolution in 1905, an overture to the revolution in 1917.

The 1917 revolution had other causes besides the war—the combination of capitalism, an oppressive autocracy, and a semi-feudal land and agricultural system; the general backwardness; the cruel conditions under which Russia's workers and peasants had to live. Of course, the war itself was not an accident, but the result of capitalist rivalries. Still it was the war, bringing things to a head, which brought the revolution.

The revolution came in two phases. In the first, in March (February by the old Russian calendar), the people overthrew the Czar. But the new Kerensky government couldn't cope with the food problem, didn't distribute land to the peasantry, and —above all—didn't end the war. In November (October) came the second, socialist phase of the revolution in which the Bolsheviks took power.

The Bolshevik government moved swiftly to establish peace. On November 8, one day after taking power, it issued a "Decree on Peace," calling "upon all the belligerent peoples and their governments to start immediate negotiations for a just, democratic peace." This was the first foreign policy act, the first major act of any kind, of the new government.

The decree expressed the government's readiness to conclude peace "at once, without the least delay," proposing an immediate armistice. It explained that by "a just, democratic peace," it meant a peace "without annexations and without indemnities." The Russian government, it said, "considers it the greatest of crimes against humanity to continue this war over the issue of how to divide among the strong and rich nations the weak nationalities they have conquered...." The Decree made a point of addressing itself to people as well as governments and appealing in particular to the workers of Great Britain, France, and Germany.[5]

On November 21, the Soviet government sent notes to the ambassadors of the United States and the other Allied governments asking them to consider the Decree on Peace "a formal proposal for an immediate armistice on all fronts and the immediate opening of peace negotiations."[6] The United States, like the other Allied governments, ignored the note.

On November 22, Lenin, Chairman of the Council of People's Commissars, sent a wireless message to the army and fleet on the problem of peace, stating:

> Soldiers, the cause of peace is in your hands! Do not allow the counter-revolutionary generals to frustrate the great cause of peace.... Let the regiments at the front immediately elect representatives to start formal negotiations for an armistice with the enemy.[7]

On November 27, an armistice was concluded on the northern front, and a little later on the others.[8]

WHAT WAS THE REACTION of the United States to the Bolshevik victory?

The U.S. ambassador in Petrograd, David R. Francis, reacted the next day in a letter to the U.S. Consul General in Moscow:

> It is reported that the Petrograd Council of Workmen and Soldiers has named a cabinet with Lenin as Premier, Trotzky as Minister of Foreign Affairs, and Madame or Mlle Kollontai as Minister of Education. Disgusting! —but I hope such effort will be made [sic], as the more ridiculous the situation the sooner the remedy.[9]

Secretary of State Robert Lansing gave his reaction five weeks later, on December 10, in a memorandum to President Woodrow Wilson:

> My Dear Mr. President: I have been considering the Russian situation and, although our information is meager and to an extent confusing, I have reached the following conclusions:
>
> That the Bolsheviki are determined to prevent Russia from taking further part in the war.
>
> That the longer they continue in power the more will authority in Russia be disorganized and the more will the armies disintegrate, and the harder it will become to restore order and military efficiency.
>
> That the elimination of Russia as a fighting force will prolong the war for two or three years, with a corresponding demand upon this country for men and money.
>
> That with Bolsheviki domination broken the Russian armies might be reorganized and become an important factor in the war by next spring or summer.
>
> That the hope of a stable Russian Government lies for the present in a military dictatorship backed by loyal, disciplined troops.

That the only apparent nucleus for an organized movement sufficiently strong to supplant the Bolsheviki and establish a government would seem to be the group of general officers with General Kaledin, the hetman [chief] of the Don Cossacks.

Lansing then presented the idea of getting

a message through to Kaledin...telling [of our] non-recognition of the Bolsheviki and our readiness to give recognition to a government which exhibits strength enough to restore order.... It seems to me that nothing is to be gained by inaction, that it is simply playing into the Bolsheviki's hands, and that the situation may be saved by a few words of encouragement....

Finally, Lansing presented a list of counterrevolutionary generals available for the struggle against the Bolsheviks.

Kaledin is a man of ponderous determination....He radiates force and mastery....
Alexieff is a modest, quiet man, but the most skilful strategist in Russia....
Brousiloff is the most brilliant general in the Russian armies....
Korniloff is not the equal of any of the three other generals in military skill.... He has, however, considerable influence with soldiers recruited in Siberia and Turkestan.[10]

Wilson approved Lansing's line and the proposal to "encourage" Kaledin. Action began quickly. The day after Lansing submitted his memorandum, he had a talk with the President. The next day he asked for the President's approval of a telegram which he explained he had prepared "in line with our talk." The telegram was to be sent to the U.S. Treasury Delegate to the Inter-Allied Council on War Purchases and Finance in London. It stated that "the Russian situation has been carefully considered and the conclusion has been reached" that the movement under Kaledin and Korniloff "offers... the greatest hope for the reestablishment of a stable government." But "it would seem unwise for this Government to support [Kaledin] openly....Without actually recognizing his group as a *de facto* government..., [the United States] cannot under the law loan money to him...." The telegram, accordingly, requested the Treasury Delegate to take up with the proper authorities the possibility of having the British and French Governments finance "the Kaledin enterprise," with the United States lending them the money to do so. Wilson promptly gave the telegram his "entire approval."[11]

Another Lansing memorandum further clarifies his views and concerns. He is commenting on a Bolshevik peace appeal, which stated that if the Allied governments refused to enter into peace negotiations, the working class would have to take power:

> This document is an appeal to the proletariat of all countries, to the ignorant and mentally deficient, who by their numbers are urged to become masters. Here seems to me to lie a very real danger in view of the present social unrest throughout the world.[12]

Lansing's public communications took a different line from his private ones. In a statement in which he tried to justify the United States' unwillingness to recognize the Bolshevik government, he said:

> The Government of the United States awaits the full manifestation of the will of the Russian people because it is convinced that it is its imperative duty to avoid any interference or any appearance of interference with the domestic affairs of Russia....
>
> The United States has only the kindliest feelings for Russia. Its policy as to recognition or non-recognition of a government at the present time is founded on the principle that the Russian people are sovereign and have the right to determine their own domestic organization without interference or influence by other nations....[13]

Wilson came out with more rhetoric in his famous Fourteen Point peace program. This program was an answer to the peace initiatives of the Bolsheviks. British Foreign Secretary David Balfour had written the State Department that "in view of the appeal made to the peoples of the world by the Bolsheviki," a presidential statement would be desirable. Edgar Sisson, director of the U.S. propaganda program in Russia, had cabled that he could use in Russia and "feed into Germany" a presidential statement of "anti-imperialist war aims and democratic peace requisites of America, thousand words or less, short almost placard paragraphs, short sentences."[14] Wilson laid out his program in an address to Congress on January 8, 1918. Point VI called for:

> The evacuation of all Russian territory and such a settlement of all questions affecting Russia as will secure the best and freest cooperation of the other nations of the world in obtaining for her an unhampered and unembarrassed opportunity for the independent determination of her own political development and national

policy, and assure her of a sincere welcome into the society of free nations under institutions of her own choosing; and, more than a welcome, assistance also of every kind that she may need and may herself desire. The treatment accorded Russia by her sister nations in the months to come will be the acid test of their good-will, of their comprehension of her needs as distinguished from their own interests, and of their intelligent and unselfish sympathy.[15]

Thus, within a few weeks of the socialist revolution, the United States had fixed a policy toward the new regime: promotion of action by counterrevolutionary generals to replace the new government with a military dictatorship, combined with sanctimonious rhetoric about the duty of avoiding interference in Russia's domestic affairs.

THE UNITED STATES ALSO began early to consider the possibility of intervention in Russia with U.S. troops but held back, for several reasons, from deciding immediately to undertake such action. Intervention would divert troops badly wanted for the western front in France. It could turn out to be counter-productive, stirring up patriotic feelings in Russia and strengthening the Revolution. And as a February 8, 1918 memorandum from the State Department to the British Embassy explained: The U.S. Government had "not lost hope of a change for the better to be brought about without foreign intervention."

But this same memorandum also shows that the United States was considering intervention, analyzing how it might be done:

> Should such intervention unfortunately become necessary in the future, the American Government is disposed at present to believe that any military expedition to Siberia or the occupation of the whole or of a part of the Trans-Siberian Railway should be undertaken by international cooperation....[16]

Many other State Department communications refer to intervention. A telegram from the Consul at Vladivostok to the Secretary of State on January 1, 1918 reported:

> I am receiving numerous requests from better-class Russians for foreign intervention and protection to enable them to organize.[17]

Ambassador Francis stated in a telegram to the Secretary of State on May 11, 1918:

I trust sincerely we have been making all possible preparations for Allied intervention as I have recommended for months past, and that active negotiations have begun among Allies therefor....[18]

Francis' trust was justified. The Allied military planners at the Supreme War Council at Versailles had prepared a plan for intervention which called for invasion via North Russia and Siberia. It proposed to use, along with Allied and Japanese forces, the so-called Czechoslovak Corps, consisting of war prisoners who were travelling along the Trans-Siberian railway to Vladivostok, supposedly to leave Russia.[19] And the United States was indeed negotiating different aspects of the plan with the British, French, and Japanese.[20]

At the end of May, the Czechoslovak Corps, encouraged by British, French, and U.S. agents, revolted against the Soviet government. Lansing sent a memorandum to Wilson:

> The situation of the Czecho-Slovak forces in western Siberia seems to me to create a new condition which should receive careful consideration.... There are, it seems, between 10,000 and 15,000 at Vladivostok and some 40,000 to 60,000 in western Siberia. In the latter territory Omsk and Tomsk are reported to be in their hands. Is it not possible that in this body of capable and loyal troops may be found a nucleus for military occupation of the Siberian railway?[21]

Meanwhile, the Russian government was working to establish peaceful relations with the United States. It prepared a "Plan for the Development of Economic Relations Between Soviet Russia and the United States" which Lenin transmitted to Washington in May 1918. The plan, supported by detailed statistical tables, presented concrete recommendations. Soviet Russia could pay for imports with raw material exports—grain, forestry products, oil, etc. It needed to import agricultural implements, railroad equipment, mining machinery. Russia's economic policy did not permit special concessions to individual countries, but it could give the United States, on equal terms with other countries, concessions for railroad and canal construction, the development of the coal industry, the exploitation of Siberian water resources.[22]

The U.S. Government did not respond to the Russian plan. Instead, it was carrying out a disguised embargo on trade with Russia. Twelve days after the victory of the revolution, the U.S. War Trade Board had passed a resolution which read:

For the time being and until further action by the Board to withhold all licenses for exportation of controlled commodities to Russia....[23]

But the Government tried to hide what it was doing and this created confusion, even among some U.S. officials, about whether there was an embargo. When the U.S. ambassador to Britain asked for clarification, Lansing sent a telegram, explaining:

This resolution has not been made public and because a few shipments have been allowed to proceed to outlying Russian territory, publicity has been given to the statement by War Trade Board that shipments to Russia are not being held up.[24]

Later, concerned about the public reaction as people in Russia and elsewhere began to understand that an embargo existed, Lansing responded to an inquiry from the U.S. ambassador to Japan by saying:

No embargo.... Two ships on Pacific.... Shipments also being made via Kola, Murmansk.... For the present it is important an impression should not be created in the minds of the Russian people that they are being abandoned by the Allies or the United States Government.[25]

The system was clever. By denying most applications for export licenses, the U.S. could maintain an embargo. By occasionally granting a few licenses, it could allow shipments in which it had an interest—those destined to areas not controlled by the Bolsheviks—and then blandly declare that there was no embargo.

Still later, Assistant Secretary of State William Phillips clarified:

So far as the United States is concerned, no blockade exists. It is the present policy of this Government, however, to refuse export licenses for shipments to Russian territory under Bolshevik control and to refuse clearance papers to American vessels seeking to depart for Petrograd, the only remaining Bolshevik port.[26]

The U.S. Government took the decision to intervene with troops at a White House meeting on July 6, 1918. Lansing had thought up the pretext: the Czech seizure of Vladivostok and parts of western Siberia had introduced "a sentimental element into the question of our duty."[27] According to Lansing's memorandum on the meeting, it was decided:

> That the present situation of the Czecho-Slovaks requires this Government and other governments to make an effort to aid those at Vladivostok in forming a junction with their compatriots in western Siberia; and that this Government on sentimental grounds and because of the effect upon the friendly Slavs everywhere would be subject to criticism if it did not make this effort....[28]

The Wilson administration ran true to form in its announcement of the intervention. It began by denouncing intervention, and then referred to what it was doing as "military action" that was "admissible."

> In the judgment of the Government of the United States...military intervention in Russia would be more likely to add to the present sad confusion there than to cure it....Therefore, military action is admissible in Russia now only to render such protection and help as is possible to the Czecho-Slovaks against the armed Austrian and German prisoners who are attacking them, and to steady any efforts at self-government or self-defense in which the Russians themselves may be willing to accept assistance....
>
> The Government of the United States wishes to announce to the people of Russia in the most public and solemn manner that it contemplates no interference with the political sovereignty of Russia, no intervention in her internal affairs...but that what we are about to do has as its single and only object the rendering of such aid as shall be acceptable to the Russian people themselves in their endeavors to regain control of their own affairs, their own territory and their own destiny.[29]

The need to protect the Czechs from Austrian and German prisoners supposedly attacking them was fiction. A few months earlier, when the Allies professed alarm over rumors that Lenin was turning Siberia over to Germany by arming tens of thousands of these prisoners, the Russian government had suggested that they send an investigator. The United States and Britain each sent an army officer who in all Siberia discovered only 1,200 armed prisoners, mostly former Hungarians, Czechs, and Yugoslavs who had assumed Russian citizenship and been incorporated into Soviet forces to help guard the Manchurian frontier. The Czech Corps was fighting not armed war prisoners, but the Soviet army. As Frederick L. Schuman puts it, "Aid to the Czechs could have no meaning except war on Soviet Russia."[30]

Two U.S. regiments from the Philippines arrived at Vladivostok in mid-August. Forty-seven hundred U.S. troops disembarked at Archangel in early September.[31]

The U.S. action was part of a larger intervention in which Britain, France, Japan, and other countries—eventually fourteen—took part. The imperialists forged a chain around Russia, with U.S., British, and French troops invading the North (through Archangel), U.S., Japanese, British, and French the Far East (through Vladivostok), the British the Southeast (through Batumi, Baku and Ashkhabad), and the French and British the South (through Odessa). To boot, Germany in mid-1918 invaded from the West.

The intervention with foreign forces was part of a still broader operation in which the Allies and Germany encouraged Russian counterrevolutionaries to rebel against the Bolshevik government. The British engineered a coup d'état against the Bolshevik Soviet in Archangel and then, together with the U.S. forces, worked to raise a local anti-Bolshevik army. The United States, Britain, and France supported Admiral Kolchak who was proposing to set up an anti-Bolshevik government in Siberia. Japan had its own favored counterrevolutionary military leader there, Semenov. Britain and France provided munitions and money to General Denikin's army in the Caucasus and the Ukraine. In the West, Germany helped General Krasnov and in the Northwest, on the approaches to Petrograd, the British helped General Yudenich.

The Allies meant, in the ugly metaphor of Winston Churchill, to strangle the Bolshevik infant in the cradle. Russia, exhausted and bloody from three years of world war, was condemned to further years of devastating civil war.

How did U.S. policy appear to the Russians? A few weeks after U.S. troops invaded, Georgi Chicherin, the Soviet foreign minister, sent a note to Wilson. After noting how Wilson had said in his Fourteen Points that "the treatment accorded Russia by her sister nations" would be "the acid test of their good will," he went on:

> Since that time six months have gone by and the Russian people have had sufficient time to experience in practice the good will of your government.... This expressed itself, to begin with, in the Czech conspiracy, organized on Russian territory with the financial support of your French ally and your diplomatic assistance.... [The] counter-revolutionary mutiny [of the Czechs], making impossible

the movement of grains and oil by the Volga, cutting off the workers and peasants of Russia from the grains and other supplies of Siberia and condemning them to hunger—that's what first of all the workers and peasants of Russia have experienced in practice from your government and your allies....

Next they experienced... the attack on north Russia with the participation of American troops, their encroachment upon Russian borders without excuse and without a declaration of war, the seizure of Russian cities and villages, the shooting of Soviet officials, and all sorts of acts of violence against the peaceful Russian population.

You promised, Mr. President, to assist Russia in obtaining the independent determination of its own political development...; in practice, this assistance has expressed itself in [an attempt] to impose on the Russian people by violence those oppressors and those exploiting classes, whose domination the workers and peasants of Russia overthrew in October of last year....[32]

The Bolshevik soldiers knew what they were fighting for. The domestic counterrevolutionaries had no real strength of their own; without foreign money, they could have done nothing. The interventionist governments could give their soldiers no good motive for attacking Russia, only transparent lies about dangers from German prisoners and not even these after the war with Germany ended. One after the other, Russia beat back the counterrevolutionary forces. Churchill, a leading strategist against what he called "the foul baboonery of Bolshevism," gives an example of what happened in his description of the French invasion of the south:

The foreign occupation offended the inhabitants: the Bolsheviks profited by their discontents. Their propaganda...spread far and wide through the Ukraine. On February 6, 1919, they reoccupied Kiev, and the population of the surrounding districts rose against the foreigners and the capitalists. The French troops were themselves affected by the Communist propaganda, and practically the whole of the fleet mutinied. Why should they fight now that the war was over? Why should they interfere in Russian affairs? Why should they not go home? Why should they not indeed assist those Russian movements which sought to level all national authority and establish the universal regime of soldiers, sailors, and workmen?[33]

What about the north? George F. Kennan, the U.S. diplomat and historian, writes:

The lack of any respected anti-Communist political authority in the area, and of any sort of domestic-political appeal to the Russian people, was an insuperable barrier to the successful recruitment of a Russian armed force.... The workers were hostile, the peasantry apathetic.... Such Russian units as were eventually scraped together out of this skeptical and disaffected populace proved to be quite unreliable; many eventually revolted and went over to the Bolsheviki.[34]

How about the U.S. soldiers?

Very soon the terrible Arctic winter set in, with temperatures of fifty degrees below zero.... For the Americans, this was a particularly excruciating ordeal. Homesick and bewildered, devoid of any plausible knowledge of why they were there...,these unfortunate men clung on through the seemingly endless winter....It is no wonder...that morale began to disintegrate. Disciplinary troubles, bordering in some instances on mutiny, occurred in a number of Allied units.[35]

Frederick L. Schuman tells of a near mutiny on March 30, 1919 when

Company I of the 339th United States Infantry refused to obey orders to proceed to the front from Archangel. The men soon yielded to appeals and threats and agreed to advance on condition that one of their number who had been arrested be released. The incident...was symptomatic of increasing unrest which created considerable apprehension in Washington. Fear of a general mutiny was expressed....The dissatisfaction of the soldiers was ascribed to Bolshevist propaganda....[36]

Meanwhile, in the United States, a struggle over intervention was taking place. This struggle started shortly after the Bolshevik victory. The establishment press and the Government, aided by Russian emigrés in various parts of the world, worked to poison public opinion against the revolution with a steady flow of horror stories. First came a repetition of earlier stories that the Bolsheviks were paid agents of the Kaiser. Then came "the nationalization of women:" the Soviets had supposedly made all women over eighteen property of the state and had instituted a system of compulsory marriages. On October 31, 1918, the *New York Times* carried the headline: GREAT MASSACRE PLANNED BY REDS—NIGHT OF NOVEMBER 10 FIXED FOR A ST. BARTHOLOMEW OF THE RUSSIAN BOURGEOISIE—WILD PANIC IN PETROGRAD. The next day, an editorial described the Bolsheviks as "ravening beasts of prey, a large part of them actual criminals, all of them mad with the raging passions of the class struggle."[37]

At the same time, "the formation of the first Socialist government thrilled and inspired the American radicals," according to the historian Philip S. Foner. The Socialist Party, whose candidate, Eugene V. Debs, had won 900,000 votes in the 1912 presidential election, proclaimed support of the revolution. The IWW and several other trade unions, many individual unionists and other workers, many recent immigrants, and a number of publications, including the newspaper *Jewish Daily Forward* and the African-American Socialist magazine *The Messenger*, hailed the revolution.[38]

As the intervention and civil war got under way, they became a focus of public discussion. Agents of the Russian Embassy, the old one which the United States still treated as the representative of Russia, inserted full-page advertisements in leading newspapers proclaiming the duty of the allies to recognize the Kolchak government. A group of prominent people, including Elihu Root, Nicholas Murray Butler, and Samuel Gompers, expressed support for Kolchak in *Struggling Russia*, a magazine put out by the Embassy. All were agreed, writes Schuman, that "Bolshevism must be destroyed."[39]

But, at the same time, a broad movement against intervention developed. The Socialist Party demanded, "Withdraw the troops from Russia!" Delegates to the Central Labor Council of Seattle declared that "Pacific Coast longshoremen will tie up the coast from Seattle to San Diego before they will load rifles or munitions for Siberia...." William Randolph Hearst's *New York American* editorialized: "The United States troops have no business in Russia....If the Democratic party in Congress had any regard for true democracy...they would take the necessary steps to bring these American troops home at once...."[40]

Several members of Congress spoke out against intervention. Senator William E. Borah of Idaho wondered

> Why it is that Admiral Kolchak and others claiming to represent the Russian people can get no support from the Russian people themselves, but depend entirely for their support upon people from abroad?[41]

Senator Hiram Johnson of California said:

I warn you of the policy, which God forbid this nation ever should enter upon, of endeavoring to impose by military force upon the various peoples of the earth the kind of government we desire for them and that they do not desire for themselves.[42]

Congressman William E. Mason of Illinois sent a telegram to a mass meeting of 15,000 at New York's Madison Square Garden:

The blockade which will starve women and children of Russia this winter is a crime against humanity. The American troops in Siberia without a declaration of war by Congress is a violation of the Constitution of the United States.[43]

Fearful of mutiny by the troops, worried about the opposition at home, the Wilson administration began to consider withdrawal. In February 1919, Wilson sent William C. Bullitt, a member of the U.S. peace delegation in Paris, to Russia to explore Soviet peace terms. Bullitt brought back very favorable terms — terms that would have left huge territories in the hands of Kolchak and Denikin. Lenin later explained that "although the terms were extremely unfavorable, we were prepared to accept them because we were convinced that the forces of Kolchak and Denikin would disintegrate from within."[44] Bullitt's report concluded:

No government save a socialist government can be set up in Russia today except by foreign bayonets, and any government so set up will fall the moment such support is withdrawn.... The proposal of the Soviet Government presents an opportunity to make peace with the revolution on a just and reasonable basis....[45]

Wilson refused to even hear Bullitt, who resigned in disgust. Bullitt later explained that the main reason for the rejection of his recommendations was the rapid progress of Kolchak's spring offensive from Siberia.[46]

In the north, however, the situation looked bad and the administration felt compelled to pull out. A few days after the near mutiny at Archangel, General March, the Army Chief of Staff, pledged withdrawal of U.S. forces there by June, and by June 30 they were gone.[47]

Moreover, the Bolsheviks soon ended Kolchak's offensive and were chasing him across Siberia. Almost everyone greeted the Red troops as liberators. The nobles and tsarist officers who dominated the Kolchak government evoked fierce enmity among the people, not only with their reactionary land and economic policies, but with their oppression and terror. The very Czechs who had started the anti-Bolshevik uprising in Siberia revolted against Kolchak and stated in a memorandum to the Allied representatives in Vladivostok:

> The military authorities of the government of Omsk are permitting criminal actions that will stagger the entire world. The burning of villages, the murder of masses of peaceful inhabitants, and the shooting of hundreds of persons of democratic convictions and also those only suspected of political disloyalty occurs daily.[48]

On November 15, the Bolsheviks took Omsk. On Christmas Day, Kolchak gave up his command. By the end of the year, the policymakers in Washington had decided to pull out of Siberia. The last U.S. troops left Vladivostok on April 1, 1920.

The Allied effort to kill the revolution inflicted incalculable damage on Russia. A Soviet commission later concluded that the damage was equal to the loss of three years of pre-war national income. But how can one measure the cost in human terms—the value of the people who died in the fighting or in epidemics of typhus that could not be controlled because the embargo had created a shortage of medicine?

The imperialists greeted socialism at its birth with deadly enmity. There could be no talk then of "Soviet aggression" or a "world-wide communist conspiracy." There could be no question of a Soviet military threat. The imperialists didn't like the loss of their Russian properties and the prospective profits from them. They didn't like the removal of Russia from the imperialist system. They were afraid that the idea of socialism might spread.

ALTHOUGH THE UNITED STATES felt compelled to end military intervention, its hostility to the Bolshevik government continued, manifesting itself openly in a refusal to extend recognition. Lansing's successor, Bainbridge Colby, stated the policy in a letter to the Italian ambassador on August 10, 1920:

> We cannot recognize, hold official relations with, or give friendly reception to the agents of a government which is determined and bound to conspire against our institutions....[49]

In his first message to Congress on December 6, 1923, President Coolidge declared that he would not enter into relations with another regime which refuses to recognize the sanctity of international obligations.... Encouraging evidences of returning to the ancient ways of society can be detected. But more are needed.... Whenever there appear works meet for repentance, our country ought to be the first to go to the economic and moral rescue of Russia.[50]

Within ten days, Soviet Foreign Minister Chicherin sent Coolidge a telegram:

After reading your message to Congress Soviet Government sincerely anxious to establish at last firm friendship with people and government United States informs you of its complete readiness to discuss with your government all problems mentioned in your message, these negotiations being based on principle non-intervention internal affairs.[51]

Two days later Secretary of State Hughes replied:

There would seem to be at this time no reason for negotiations.... If the Soviet authorities are ready to restore the confiscated property of American citizens or make effective compensation, they can do so. If the Soviet authorities are ready to repeal their decree repudiating Russia's obligations to this country and appropriately recognize them, they can do so.... Most serious is the continued propaganda to overthrow the institutions of this country. This Government can enter into no negotiations until these efforts directed from Moscow are abandoned.[52]

Meanwhile, part of the press, including newspapers with large circulation, continued wild reporting on the Soviet Union. Here are some *Chicago Tribune* headlines collected by Schuman:

CLAIM STARVING POOR THREATEN DOOM OF SOVIET (June 15, 1925)

RUSSIANS FREE! TO ROB, STARVE, MURDER, AND DIE (November 15, 1925)

SECRET REPORT SHOWS RUSSIA NEAR COLLAPSE (March 20, 1926)

ODESSA TROOPS MUTINY AGAINST MOSCOW REGIME (August 9, 1926)

REDS REINFORCE KREMLIN FORT AS MUTINY GROWS (August 13, 1926)

ECONOMY REGIME IN RUSSIA FAILS; CRISIS IMPENDS (August 21, 1926)

INDUSTRY FACES SWIFT DISASTER IN RED RUSSIA (October 23, 1927)

HUNDREDS DIE IN UKRAINE RIOTS, RUMANIA HEARS (November 26, 1927)

Schuman comments that "all of the reports of mutinies, revolts, and uprisings were wholly without foundation, so far as the writer has been able to ascertain, and...the remaining headlines differed only in the degree of their inaccuracy."[53]

During the 1920s, the State Department developed a new Soviet Service. The Department felt that it needed Russian experts, and it began to send young Foreign Service officers to Europe for training. George F. Kennan went to Riga, Latvia, which had a large Russian emigré population. Kennan later wrote: "To live in Riga was...in many respects to live in Tsarist Russia...."[54] Charles Bohlen went to Paris, but spent summers in Estonia at a Russian pension run by two sisters who "lived in the hope that someday the nightmare would pass away and they would return to old Russia, complete with Czar and aristocracy."[55]

The father of the training program, Robert F. Kelley, chief of the Division of Russian and East European Affairs, stood out even in the State Department for his antipathy to the Bolsheviks. Throughout the 1920s, his Division regularly turned out memoranda against recognition. Kelley encouraged the students to identify with Russia's past. When Kennan wrote him asking whether to take courses in Soviet finance, Soviet political structure, etc., the answer was no. The purpose of the program, Kennan learned, was to provide

> a background in Russian language and culture not dissimilar to that which would normally have been assumed on the part of a well-educated Russian of the old, prerevolutionary school.[56]

Kennan later recalled an activity of the students:

> We used to practice our Russian and sharpen our wits by drafting *Pravda* editorials in which we announced the reinstatement of capitalism in Russia....[57]

Kennan's political view of the Soviet Union echoed Kelley's:

> Never—neither then nor at any later date—did I consider the Soviet Union a fit ally or associate, actual or potential, for this country.[58]

The absence of recognition held down U.S.-Soviet trade during the 1920s; trade grew, but not nearly as much as it might have. The United States eliminated the embargo in 1920, but when businessmen sought assurances about transactions with the Soviets, the State Department responded: "We have not considered that government safe enough for us to extend recognition to it, but if you wish to trade with them we have no objection whatever."[59] Soviet ability to import from the United States was restricted by a State Department ruling that since the gold held by the Soviet government had been confiscated from its rightful owners, it could not be accepted here. Credits could have filled the gap, but nonrecognition kept credits down. The Soviet Union's ability to pay for imports with exports was limited at first by the devastation that had been inflicted on its economy; when exports did start flowing, accusations of dumping were made and special levies imposed on various goods.

With the inauguration of the Soviet Union's first Five Year Plan in 1928 and the descent of the capitalist world into the Great Depression in 1929, the interest of U.S. businessmen in Soviet trade surged. U.S. exports to the Soviet Union rose from $74 million in 1928 to $114 million in 1930. The United States replaced Germany as the leading source of Soviet imports. The Soviet Union became the largest purchaser of U.S. agricultural and industrial equipment. With other markets collapsing as the Depression took hold, the Soviet market took on added significance.[60]

Companies doing business with the Soviet Union demanded that the long-standing policy of nonrecognition be scrapped. James D. Mooney, vice president of General Motors, told the American Automobile Club in Paris in October 1930 that to obtain full advantage of the commercial possibilities of the Soviet Union, diplomatic relations were necessary. Newspapers, such as the *Brooklyn Eagle*, called for recognition. Senator Hiram Johnson declared:

> There are billions of dollars worth of future orders in Russia for American workers to fill, and in these times it is simply economic idiocy for America, by its policies, to preclude Americans from trade and commerce which so readily could be obtained.[61]

But there were opposing forces. Father Edmund A. Walsh, vice president of Georgetown University, led a fight by the Roman Catholic Church against recognition. Hamilton Fish, a

New York Republican Congressman who headed a House committee on subversive activities, also stood in the forefront of the
opposition. The *Chicago Tribune* and the American Federation
of Labor were opposed. President Herbert Hoover, who as
Food Administrator in Europe during and after the war had used
food to try to contain communism, felt that recognition would
clear the way for Communist agitators and propaganda.[62]

The Japanese invasion of Manchuria in 1931 gave new impetus to the movement for recognition: Congressmen and
others saw in the Soviet Union a potential collaborator against
Japanese aggression. Hitler's accession to power in Germany
had a similar result: many felt that the Soviet Union might be
useful in coping with him.

Franklin D. Roosevelt, a realist, could see that the policy of
getting rid of socialism in Russia had failed and he was sensitive
to the threatening international situation. Several months after
becoming president, he asked Secretary of State Cordell Hull for
his judgment on recognition. Hull said:

> I favor recognizing Russia.... The world is moving into a dangerous
> period both in Europe and in Asia. Russia could be a great help in
> stabilizing this situation as time goes on and peace becomes more
> and more threatened.

Hull reports that the President, "without a moment's hesitation, replied, 'I agree entirely.'"[63]

Because of the State Department bureaucracy's opposition to
recognition, Roosevelt relied on others in the negotiations that
led to resumption of relations. He used Henry Morgenthau, then
Farm Credit Administrator, and William C. Bullitt, newly appointed Special Assistant to the Secretary of State, for the initial discussions with the Soviets, then carried out the final talks himself.
On November 17, 1933, he announced recognition.

Nonrecognition had lasted 16 years. The United States had
held on to it long after the other big powers had given it up.

THE LETTERS EXCHANGED between
Roosevelt and Soviet Foreign Minister Maxim Litvinov establishing recognition expressed in largely identical language the hope
"that our nations henceforth may cooperate for their mutual
benefit and for the preservation of the peace of the world."[64]
This was more than just diplomatic rhetoric. Given the growing
danger of war created by German and Italian fascism and

Japanese militarism, cooperation in "stabilizing the situation"—
to use Hull's phrase—could have been a key element in relations between the two countries.

But now the U.S. side of U.S.-Soviet relations was in the hands
not of Roosevelt and two or three assistants working directly
under him, but of the State Department bureaucracy that had
lived for so long in an atmosphere of anti-Sovietism. Those who
had written countless memoranda against recognition, who had
become Russian experts studying with emigrés from the revolution, who (in the language of a Roosevelt biographer) belonged
to the small, cliquish "striped pants set" with its "narrow class
loyalties" were now in charge of the day-to-day management of
relations.[65]

In its management, the State Department brought to the fore
not the question of cooperation for peace, but a series of lesser,
often routine and even petty problems. There were conversations and negotiations on such things as the pre-October debt
repudiated by the Bolsheviks, the cost of erecting a new Embassy building in Moscow, the rate of exchange at which U.S. diplomats could obtain rubles, the Soviet practice of levying export
taxes when diplomats took out valuable antiques, delays by the
Soviets in granting visas. On all these problems the State
Department raised complaints.

On one occasion, Litvinov, having studied a U.S. memorandum of complaints, commented that with the exception of the
debt the matters were all "trivial" or had been "disposed of to
the satisfaction of the United States."[66] Litvinov was being
diplomatic in making an exception of the debt. The amount at
issue was small—$100-125 million. Many other countries, includ-
ing Britain and France, whose debts to the United States were
enormous compared to that of the Soviet Union, were also not
paying them. Even Kennan, who himself had written some of
the complaint memoranda, later commented that Roosevelt did
not attach much importance to the debt and "was right not to do
so."[67]

Soon after recognition, U.S.-Soviet relations began to cool.
Sumner Welles, then Undersecretary of State, who enjoyed the
confidence of Roosevelt, later commented:

Unfortunately, the supervision of Soviet-American relations in both
Washington and Moscow was largely entrusted by this govern-

ment to men who proved incapable and unsympathetic to the task of bettering the ties between the two countries.[68]

MEANWHILE, WHAT WAS HAPPENING with the problem of war and peace? The danger of war was growing—not just because of the growing aggressiveness of Germany, Japan, and Italy, but also because there were forces in Britain, France, and the United States trying to push these countries into war against the Soviet Union. The desire to "destroy communism" had not died with the end of intervention. It had merely slumbered, only to waken again when the emergence of fascism in Germany seemed to present a new opportunity for achieving the goal.

Again Sumner Welles:

> In those prewar years, great financial and commercial interests of the Western democracies, including many in the United States, were firm in the belief that war between the Soviet Union and Hitlerite Germany could only be favorable to their own interests. They maintained that Russia would necessarily be defeated, and with this defeat Communism would be destroyed; also that Germany would be so weakened as a result of the conflict that for many years thereafter she would be incapable of any real threat to the rest of the world.[69]

What was the best way of dealing with the expansionist drive of the fascist powers? The best way was through a system of collective security. At first, Britain, France, and the Soviet Union enjoyed military superiority over Germany and Italy. With united, firm action, they could probably have prevented aggression from even being attempted and been in a strong position to deal with it if it did occur. Had the United States joined in collective security, Japanese aggression also could have been stopped.

Appeasing the aggressors would not stop them. It would only make them stronger and whet their appetites. It would not prevent war. It meant war later, under far worse conditions.

But the governments of Britain and France couldn't stomach an alliance with the Soviet Union in a possible war against the fascist states. They had their eye on the chance of wiping out socialism. As Stanley Baldwin, Britain's prime minister from 1935 to 1937, put it in briefing a select group from the House of Commons:

We all know [Hitler's] desire as he has come out with in his book [*Mein Kampf*] to move East, and if he moves East, I shall not break my heart.... I do not believe he wants to move West, because West would be a very difficult programme for him....If there is any fighting in Europe to be done, I should like to see the Bolsheviks and Nazis doing it.[70]

Neville Chamberlain, who took over as prime minister in 1937, carried further the policy of channelling Hitler's expansionism eastward. Churchill writes that "Mr. Chamberlain was imbued with a sense of a special and personal mission to come to friendly terms with the Dictators of Italy and Germany...." He was against an alliance with the Soviet Union because this would establish "exclusive groups of nations."[71] But he did want an agreement among Britain, France, Germany, and Italy. These four countries would somehow not constitute "an exclusive group."

France tended to follow the British lead on policy toward Hitler Germany. Most French leaders held views similar to those of Baldwin and Chamberlain. Edouard Daladier, premier when Hitler first came to power and also from 1938 to 1940, felt that an understanding with Hitler could solve two problems: free France from the threat of invasion and strengthen defenses against communism.[72] Pierre Laval, both premier and foreign minister in 1935 and 1936, was even stronger for appeasement than Daladier. Many in the propertied classes viewed the French Left as a greater menace than Hitler.

The aggressor countries committed one transgression after another. In violation of the Versailles treaty, Germany began to rearm, and then remilitarized the Rhineland; Italy invaded Ethiopia; Germany and Italy intervened militarily on the fascist side in the Spanish Civil War; Germany seized Austria; Germany dismembered Czechoslovakia, then swallowed it up entirely.

At every stage in the march toward war, it would have been possible to mount collective action against the dictators through a coalition stronger than they were. But Britain and France refused to join in collective action. When Hitler began the buildup of his military forces, Britain didn't try to halt him, but instead signed a naval treaty with Germany which recognized its right to rearm. When Hitler remilitarized the Rhineland, Britain and France sent mild, meaningless protests. When Hitler moved against Czechoslovakia, Britain and France refused to join the

Soviet Union in collective action to defend it; instead they betrayed it.

Churchill reacted immediately to the settlement on Czechoslovakia accepted by Prime Minister Neville Chamberlain at Munich. He warned that "it will open up for the triumphant Nazis the road to the Black Sea."[73]

The Italian historian Gaetano Salvemini writes that the "sins" of British policy during the whole prewar period were the consequences of a basic assumption that Hitler would go east. "If one ignores that assumption, British policy after 1934 becomes a succession of absurd muddles. If one bears it in mind, the policies of the British Tories become clear and consistent."[74]

WHAT WAS THE SOVIET POLICY for meeting fascist aggression and the threat of war? Soviet policy was collective security. "Peace is indivisible," said Litvinov again and again—a phrase that rang through the world during the 1930s. "We must recognize that at the present time there is not one State, large or small, that is not open to aggression...." Litvinov argued that "the League of Nations is strong enough to bridle the aggressor.... There are no States nor any *bloc* of States that could defy the united forces of the members of the League...."[75]

In every one of the crises that led to the war, the Soviet Union called for collective action. It called Hitler's move to rearm "a menace to peace" to which the League of Nations could not close its eyes. It appealed for aid to Ethiopia against the Italian attack. It declared itself ready to take part in League action against the remilitarization of the Rhineland. Right after Hitler's seizure of Austria, Litvinov warned that Czechoslovakia was in danger and declared the readiness of the Soviet Union to "join in collective actions which...would have the purpose of arresting the further development of aggression and removing the accentuated danger of a new world shambles."[76]

We can recapture a little of the impact of Soviet policy from comments by Hull and Welles in their memoirs. According to Hull, Litvinov became "a world figure by reason of his constructive support of peace at Geneva." And Welles wrote:

> As one today looks back,...Maxim Litvinov must be recognized as the only outstanding European statesman who was consistently right during the years between the wars. It was Litvinov's constant appeal that "peace is indivisible"; that the purpose of the Covenant of the League of Nations could be achieved if the European

powers complied with its provisions; and that in the increasing welter and turmoil, disaster was inevitable unless the powers of Europe were willing to see that the sanctions set forth in the Covenant were enforced.[77]

HOW DID THE UNITED STATES fit into the struggle over war or peace?The initial U.S. answer to the fascist war threat was a neutrality act requiring the President to embargo the sale of arms to all belligerents in a war. Roosevelt wanted the power to apply the embargo only to the aggressor which would have enabled him to support collective sanctions by other countries. But the isolationists in Congress refused to give him this power.

When Italy invaded Ethiopia, the United States refused to support even the ineffective sanctions of the League of Nations and instead imposed an embargo on both belligerents. During the Spanish civil war, the United States again applied a neutrality act which, combined with a British and French policy of "non-intervention," cut the Loyalists off from arms, while the fascist insurgents got them from Germany and Italy. When Hitler remilitarized the Rhineland, Roosevelt took a grave view of the action, but the United States did nothing.

Finally in 1937 Roosevelt spoke out strongly for collective action against aggression. Three months after Japan attacked China, he declared in a major speech in Chicago:

> The peace-loving nations must make a concerted effort in opposition to those violations of treaties and those ignorings of humane instincts which today are creating a state of international anarchy and instability from which there is no escape through mere isolation or neutrality.... When an epidemic of physical disease starts to spread, the community approves and joins in a quarantine of the patients in order to protect the health of the community against the spread of the disease.[78]

The "quarantine speech" provoked a violent negative reaction. A *Philadelphia Inquirer* poll of Congress showed more than two to one against common action with the League in the Far East. Two Congressmen threatened to have the President impeached. Secretary of State Hull and other leading Democrats remained quiet instead of supporting the President. Roosevelt later commented, "It's a terrible thing to look over your shoulder when you are trying to lead—and to find no one there."[79]

In 1936, Roosevelt appointed as ambassador to the Soviet Union Joseph E. Davies, a capitalist who believed communism "cannot work on this earth," but who made up his mind to be "free from prejudice" and send back objective reports.[80] Roosevelt asked him—as Davies recorded in his diary—"to make every effort to get all the firsthand information, from personal observation where possible, bearing upon the strength of the regime, from a military and economic point of view...."[81] Davies visited steel, aluminum, and tractor plants, oil fields, dams, collective farms, and hospitals, and sent home reports which Roosevelt told him "were very valuable...in assessing the actual and potential strength of the Russian situation."[82] Davies' estimate of Soviet military strength, made at a time when it was fashionable to pooh-pooh it, was proved right by the war. He wrote in 1938: "The military strength of the U.S.S.R. is impressive.... It would be exceedingly difficult to conquer or annihilate these forces, with their ally the Russian winter."[83]

Sumner Welles later wrote:

> I doubt whether people in this country as yet realize sufficiently the concrete value of the work accomplished by Ambassador Davies during his relatively brief mission to the Soviet Union.... Above all else, he was governed by a deep-seated conviction that, in view of the increasingly dark international horizon, a way must be found to remove every unnecessary obstacle to the establishment of a closer understanding between the two peoples.[84]

But how did the anti-Soviet experts of the State Department react to Davies? Kennan describes the reaction at the Moscow Embassy:

> He drew from the first instant our distrust and dislike, not so much personally (that was not of importance) but from the standpoint of his fitness for the office and of his motivation in accepting it. We doubted his seriousness.... At the end of Mr. Davies's first day in Moscow, a number of us assembled in Henderson's rooms and solemnly considered whether we should resign in a body from the service.[85]

Davies was the ambassador to the Soviet Union for only a year and a half. The Government transferred him to Belgium in mid-1938, leaving the Moscow Embassy to be headed for many months by only a chargé d'affaires.

The quarantine speech and the appointment of Davies as ambassador to the Soviet Union reflected Roosevelt's interest in collective security. But with the adverse reaction to the speech and the ever clearer tendency of the British and French governments toward appeasement rather than collective security, Roosevelt retreated. The transfer of Davies to Belgium was part of the retreat. Another part was the appointment of Joseph P. Kennedy to the key post of ambassador to Britain.

Kennedy did not believe in collective security. Shortly after becoming ambassador, he wrote, "The more I see of things here, the more convinced I am that we must exert all our intelligence and effort toward keeping clear of any kind of involvement."[86] He impressed the German ambassador as having sympathies for Hitler's Reich and felt that "the democracies and dictators should cooperate for the common good rather than emphasize self-apparent differences."[87] He became a visitor to Cliveden, the country home of Lord and Lady Astor, where highly placed British reactionaries, known as the "Cliveden set," met on weekends and talked about turning Hitler eastward. He strongly supported Chamberlain's appeasement policy and publicly identified himself with it.

William Bullitt, now U.S. ambassador to France, another key post, also favored appeasement. In May 1938, as the Czech crisis was building up, he cabled Roosevelt:

> I feel that it would be an unspeakable tragedy if France, to support Czechoslovakia, should attack the "Siegfried Line".... The war would be a long one.... There could be only one possible result: the complete destruction of Western Europe and Bolshevism from one end of the continent to the other.... If you believe as I believe that it is not in the interest of either the United States or civilization as a whole to have the continent of Europe devastated I think we should attempt to find some way which will let the French out of their moral commitment.[88]

Roosevelt cannot be equated with Kennedy and Bullitt. He spoke out often against international lawlessness—meaning fascist aggression. To the extent he felt he could, he came out for international cooperation to control lawlessness. He ridiculed Kennedy's identification with the Cliveden set and with Chamberlain.

Still, that Roosevelt placed two such people as Kennedy and Bullitt in the key ambassadorial posts of Britain and France is significant. He may have done so only because political realities, as he saw them, made impossible a strong U.S. stance for

collective action to stop the aggressors. But whatever the reason, Roosevelt's policy during the Czech crisis was to go along
with the British and French appeasers.

When President Benes of Czechoslovakia appealed to him to
urge Britain and France not to desert the Czechs, he did not
respond. When he received a copy of Chamberlain's cable to
Hitler saying, "I feel more strongly than ever that your demands
can be satisfied within a comparatively short time...." and proposing the meeting that took place in Munich, Roosevelt sent
the Prime Minister a two-word message: "Good man."[89] When
the Munich agreement was reached, Roosevelt sent Chamberlain another message: "I fully share your hope and belief that
there exists today the greatest opportunity in years for the establishment of a new order based on justice and on law."[90]

Roosevelt was "divided" at the time of Munich, says his biographer, James MacGregor Burns. He had "deep misgivings as to
Chamberlain's appeasement policy and its implications."[91] Although his misgivings foreshadowed a different U.S. policy, in
the Munich episode he tagged along with Chamberlain, in effect
acquiescing in the policy of trying to turn Hitler eastward.

This policy was bound to produce a reaction from Moscow.
The Soviet Union was in mortal danger. Hitler had written in
Mein Kampf that Germany needed "living space" which "could
be obtained by and large only at the expense of Russia...."[92]
Britain and France were refusing to join in collective action
against Hitler but rather nudging him eastward. If the Soviet
Union did not do something drastic, it might find itself not only
attacked by Hitler, but with the western countries helping him,
trying once again to wipe out the first socialist state. This threat
led to the German-Soviet nonaggression pact.

The democracies were aware of the possibility of such a pact.
Hull writes that "the prospect of a German-Russian pact had
long been in our minds."[93] In January 1939, six months before
the pact, Davies wrote from Brussels to Harry Hopkins, Roosevelt's confidant and assistant:

> The Chamberlain policy of throwing Italy, Poland, and Hungary
> into the arms of Hitler may be completed by so disgusting the
> Soviets that it will drive Russia into an economic agreement and an
> ideological truce with Hitler.[94]

A few weeks later Stalin declared in a speech to a Party Congress that among the tasks of Soviet foreign policy were:

1) To continue the policy of peace and of strengthening business relations with all countries;

2) To be cautious and not allow our country to be drawn into conflict by war mongers who are accustomed to have others pull the chestnuts out of the fire for them....[95]

In April 1939, Moscow made an offer for a mutual assistance treaty between Britain, France, and the U.S.S.R. Churchill immediately argued for acceptance, telling the House of Commons, "Here is an offer, a fair offer, and a better offer, in my opinion, than the terms which the government seek to get for themselves; a more simple, a more direct, and a more effective offer. Let it not be put aside...." But Chamberlain's reception of the offer, writes Churchill in his memoirs, was "cool, and indeed disdainful."[96]

For the treaty talks in Moscow, Britain sent William Strang, a lower-ranking official of the Foreign Office. "This was another mistake," writes Churchill. "The sending of so subordinate a figure gave actual offense."[97]

Why did Britain react to the Soviet offer with disdain, send subordinate officials, and drag out the negotiations in every way possible? Because it did not want to cooperate in collective security with the Soviet Union, because it preferred to try for a deal with Hitler, because it hoped to the end to turn him eastward. The Soviets moved to protect themselves in the only way left. In August came the German-Soviet pact. Churchill writes in his memoirs:

> The fact that such an agreement could be made marks the culminating failure of British and French foreign policy and diplomacy over several years.[98]

WHEN GERMANY ATTACKED the Soviet Union in June 1941, Roosevelt conferred with Sumner Welles, who then read an announcement to the press. Asserting that both communism and fascism were "alien" to Americans, the announcement added:

> But the immediate issue that presents itself to the people of the United States is whether the plan for universal conquest...which Hitler is now desperately trying to carry out, is to be successfully halted and defeated.... In the opinion of this Government, any defense against Hitlerism, any rallying of the forces opposing Hitlerism, from whatever source these forces may spring, will hasten

the eventual downfall of the present German leaders, and will therefore redound to the benefit of our own defense and security.[99]

But the isolationists took a different position. As Robert E. Sherwood, who worked in the White House, puts it in his book, *Roosevelt and Hopkins,* "Now they were free to go berserk with the original Nazi party line that Hitler represented the only bulwark against Bolshevism."[100]

Charles A. Lindbergh, who had earlier promoted British and French appeasement, spoke out again:

I would a hundred times rather see my country ally herself with England, or even with Germany with all her faults, than with the cruelty, the godlessness and the barbarism that exist in Soviet Russia.[101]

The *Chicago Tribune* said that the German-Russian conflict was the only war for a century that civilized men could regard with complete approval.[102]

Senator Harry S. Truman said:

If we see that Germany is winning we ought to help Russia and if Russia is winning we ought to help Germany and that way let them kill as many as possible, although I don't want to see Hitler victorious under any circumstances....[103]

Although Roosevelt told reporters that "of course, we are going to give all the aid we possibly can to Russia," he proceeded cautiously. He was wary of clashing with the isolationists. He wanted to know how long the Soviets would be able to hold out against the Germans.

He became less concerned about isolationist opposition to aid upon receiving a summary of public opinion polls shortly after the German attack. The overwhelming majority of Americans wanted the Soviet Union to win the war. They were in favor of aid to the Soviets so long as it was not at the expense of aid to Britain.[104]

But on the question of how long the Soviets would hold out, Roosevelt received mostly discouraging judgments. Almost everyone talked of the imminent collapse of the Soviet forces. War Department intelligence estimated that the campaign would last one to three months.[105] British military authorities talked of the occupation of the Ukraine and Moscow in three to six weeks.[106] The *New York Times* thought it probable that

Hitler would achieve his objectives within a few weeks. Only a few people—former Ambassador Davies, his military attaché in Moscow, Philip Faymonville, and Harry Hopkins, who was in charge of Lend-Lease aid—provided different views.[107]

Hopkins got Roosevelt to send him to Moscow so he could make a firsthand judgment on how long the Soviet Union could hold out. The *Wall Street Journal* criticized the trip, saying that to give aid to the Soviet Union was "to fly in the face of morals."[108]

What Hopkins learned gave him confidence in the Soviets' power of resistance. His trip was, in the words of Sherwood, a "turning point in the wartime relations of Britain and the United States with the Soviet Union. No longer would all Anglo-American calculations be based on the probability of early Russian collapse...."[109]

Roosevelt and Hopkins both worked to speed up the shipment of aid to the Soviets. But for weeks, the bureaucratic quagmire in Washington and anti-Soviet attitudes in the War and other government departments kept the aid from reaching significant levels. The U.S. military attaché in Moscow, for example, was harshly critical of the Soviets and kept talking of the end of their resistance and the possibility that equipment shipped by the United States might be captured by the Germans.

Hopkins appointed as Lend-Lease representative in Moscow an officer sympathetic to the Soviets—Colonel Philip R. Faymonville. Faymonville was confident of the Soviet ability to hold out and events were proving him right. But the appointment, writes Sherwood, "led to a great deal of controversy between Hopkins and the War Department...."[110]

The anti-Soviet people in the Government did not limit themselves to dragging their feet on Lend-Lease shipments or attacking Faymonville and Hopkins. They also questioned Soviet good faith. Again Sherwood: "There was always a faction, and it was strongly represented in the State Department, which was sure that the Russians would make a separate peace with Germany...." Roosevelt received "repeated warnings of possible Russian perfidy...in 1941 and throughout the years that followed...."[111]

U.S. entry into the war brought to the fore a new question—the opening by the United States and Britain of a second front against Germany. This was by far the most important question in U.S.-Soviet relations during the war.

Even before U.S. entry, the question of a second front had been under discussion in Britain. Lord Beaverbrook, the British minister of supply, was already asking in October 1941 for a second front. There is today, he argued, one military problem — how to help Russia. Russian resistance has provided new opportunities, by denuding western Europe of German troops. But it has also created a new peril. Russia may collapse, and then Hitler will concentrate all his forces against us.[112]

Once the United States entered the war, its leaders began to think through their grand strategy. Secretary of War Henry L. Stimson commented in his memoirs about the political aspect of the problem:

> The central political decision of World War II was that it must be fought in an alliance as close as possible with Great Britain and Soviet Russia. Not once during the war was this decision questioned or any modification of it seriously considered by Stimson or by any man whose views he knew among the leaders of the administration.... Together, with or without welcome and helpful accessions of strength from smaller nations, [these three] could not lose. Apart, or at cross-purposes, or with any one of them defeated, they could hardly win.[113]

Stimson argued that the proper policy was not to divert forces to other fronts, but to send

> "an overwhelming force to the British Isles and [threaten] an attack on the Germans in France...." His objective was to secure a decision to invade Europe from the British base at the earliest practicable moment....[114]

Army Chief of Staff General George C. Marshall, in a memorandum to President Roosevelt, gave the basic military argument for a second front in Western Europe:

> Western Europe has been selected as the theatre in which to stage the first great offensive of the United Powers because:
> It is the only place in which a powerful offensive can be prepared and executed by the United Powers in the near future....
> Successful attack in this area will afford the maximum of support to the Russian front.[115]

In May-June 1942, Soviet Foreign Minister Vyacheslav Molotov visited the United States for talks with Roosevelt. He argued for a second front in 1942 and "requested a straight answer" as to whether Britain and the United States would establish one.

Here from the interpreter's record is the answer:

> The President then put to General Marshall the query whether developments were clear enough so that we could say to Mr. Stalin that we are preparing a second front. "Yes," replied the General. The President then authorized Mr. Molotov to inform Mr. Stalin that we expect the formation of a second front this year.[116]

Molotov proposed a sentence for inclusion in a communique to be released in Washington and his proposal was accepted. The sentence read:

> In the course of the conversations full understanding was reached with regard to the urgent tasks of creating a second front in Europe in 1942.[117]

But the United States and Britain did not open a second front in 1942. Instead, disregarding the warnings of Marshall and Stimson against diverting forces into secondary theatres, they mounted a campaign in Africa which was the forerunner of a further diversionary campaign in Italy. These campaigns absorbed resources needed for a second front and served repeatedly as an excuse to postpone it.

In January 1943, Roosevelt and Churchill met at Casablanca and sent a message to Stalin saying that U.S. and British forces in Britain would "prepare themselves to re-enter the continent of Europe as soon as practicable." Stalin thanked them for the message and added: "I should be grateful if you would inform me of the concrete operations planned and of their timing."[118] To this, Churchill, saying that he was speaking for both himself and Roosevelt, responded:

> We are also pushing preparations to the limit of our resources for a cross-Channel operation in August.... If the operation is delayed by the weather or other reasons, it will be prepared with stronger forces for September.[119]

But in May, three months before the promised operation, Roosevelt and Churchill met again and again postponed it, this time to the spring of 1944.

In his message to Roosevelt responding to this decision, Stalin said:

> Your decision creates exceptional difficulties for the Soviet Union, which, straining all its resources, for the past two years, has been engaged against the main forces of Germany and her satellites,

and leaves the Soviet Army, which is fighting not only for its country, but also for its Allies, to do the job alone, almost single-handed, against an enemy that is still very strong and formidable.

Need I speak of the disheartening negative impression that this fresh postponement of the second front and the withholding from our Army, which has sacrificed so much, of the anticipated substantial support by the Anglo-American armies, will produce in the Soviet Union—both among the people and in the Army?[120]

Many Americans appreciated Soviet feelings about a second front. Stimson's memoirs state that his own

concern for a proper second front led him to a certain sympathy with Russian suspicion of Western motives; not to open promptly a strong western front in France, he felt, would be to leave the real fighting to Russia.[121]

General John R. Deane, chief of the wartime U.S. Military Mission to Moscow, writes:

The Russians had some reason to question the sincerity of our intentions in this matter [of the second front].[122]

James MacGregor Burns comments:

The second front delay far more than any other factor aroused Soviet anger and cynicism.... Was not this evidence that the West, whatever its protestations, was following a strategy of letting Russia and Germany bleed each other to death?[123]

What lay behind the repeated postponements of a second front? The leader in promoting the postponements was Churchill. Churchill had more than one motive. When, for example, he pressed for operations in Africa and the Mediterranean he had in mind, among other things, strengthening the British imperialist position in those areas. But the basic reason for the second front delays was the old, underlying hostility to the Soviet Union. Churchill was the same person he had been during the intervention he helped lead twenty-five years earlier. He was still—as far as he could, given the presence of a bigger enemy— fighting communism.

Roosevelt didn't share Churchill's extreme hostility to the Soviet Union. But there were people in the United States, representing powerful interests, who did. Roosevelt acted the same way he had at the time of Munich: He vacillated, but at bottom, followed the British lead.

The resultant British-American policy was indeed to let the Soviet Union and Germany bleed each other. The second front was delayed as long as it could have been without running the risk of having Soviet troops liberate all of Germany and march on to the Atlantic.

Some American writers have listed grievances against Soviet conduct as an ally during the war. General Deane writes about Soviet "suspicion of foreign motives;" Soviet officials did not give enough publicity to U.S. aid; were not sufficiently cooperative in establishing coordination of air operations to avoid accidents; etc.[124] But leaving aside a discussion of the merits of these grievances, one thing is clear: the biggest grievance during the war, the one that overshadows all the Western grievances taken together, was a Soviet grievance—the delay in establishing a second front.

Along with Deane's grievances, we have Stimson's judgment:

> As they continued to fight effectively long beyond the most optimistic early estimates of most American intelligence officers, and as gradually a narrow but significant bridge of cooperation was constructed, it became clear that in their own strange way the Russians were magnificent allies. They fought as they promised, and they made no separate peace.[125]

Thus, along with the frictions, there was also cooperation, an alliance that achieved its purpose.

THE HIGH TIDE OF U.S.-British-Soviet unity came during the Yalta conference in February 1945. The Allies arrived at a number of agreements—on the democratization and demilitarization of Germany, occupation zones, reparations, the Polish problem. The Soviet Union agreed to enter the war against Japan within two or three months after the surrender of Germany.

Several Americans who attended have written of Soviet reasonableness at the conference and of the optimism that the U.S. delegation felt when it ended. Secretary of State Edward Stettinius later wrote that "the record of the Conference shows clearly that the Soviet Union made greater concessions at Yalta to the United States and Britain than were made to the Soviets."[126] Roosevelt's Chief of Staff, Admiral William D. Leahy, wrote that at the end of the Conference "the American delegation, including Roosevelt and most of his staff, was weary but in a high mood. They felt the foundations of world peace had been laid...."[127] Harry Hopkins told Robert E. Sherwood:

We were absolutely certain that we had won the first great victory of the peace.... The Russians had proved that they could be reasonable and farseeing and there wasn't any doubt in the minds of the President or any of us that we could live with them and get along with them peacefully for as far into the future as any of us could imagine.[128]

But within a few weeks, as the German armies began to collapse, the tide of Allied unity began to recede. Churchill describes his evaluation of the situation:

The destruction of German military power had brought with it a fundamental change in the relations between Communist Russia and the Western democracies. They had lost their common enemy, which was almost their sole bond of union.[129]

He adds some "practical points of strategy and policy:"

First, that Soviet Russia had become a mortal danger to the free world.
Secondly, that a new front must be immediately created against her onward sweep.
Thirdly, that this front in Europe should be as far east as possible....[130]

Churchill explains further what had changed in the few weeks since Yalta to bring forth the shift in his line. Responding in his memoirs to criticisms of his position at Yalta by a few members of Parliament, he asked:

What would have happened if we had quarrelled with Russia while the Germans still had three or four hundred divisions on the fighting front?[131]

But now German military power was no longer a threat and Churchill felt that Britain did not need the Soviets any more.

Churchill wasn't thinking of the need for an accommodation with the Soviets to establish a firm basis for peace. He wasn't thinking of democracy. A few months earlier, working to reestablish prewar British domination of Greece, he had used British troops in a bloody intervention in a Greek civil war to put down EAM/ELAS, the mass-supported wartime resistance movement; as Fleming puts it, "the last thing Churchill would have permitted in Greece was a free election, for he knew that the EAM would win it."[132]

Churchill was simply thinking like the hard-bitten British imperialist he was. It was legitimate for him to use the presence of British and American armies to try to reestablish monarchies in Belgium, Italy, and Greece. But the Soviets—they must be kept "as far east as possible."

While Churchill now felt free to quarrel with the Soviets, he didn't want Britain to do so alone. He began in his messages to Roosevelt to work for a joint U.S.-British front against the Soviets. He felt that "we have been deceived" on Poland and that once this became known, "there would come an open rift between us and Russia." When Stalin sent Roosevelt a sharp message in a dispute over whether U.S. and British officials were engaging in separate surrender negotiations with the Germans in Bern, Switzerland, Churchill commented: "I am astounded that Stalin should have addressed to you a message so insulting to the honour of the United States and also of Great Britain."[133]

Roosevelt's focus was different from Churchill's. He too understood that the disappearance of the common enemy would bring difficulties for the alliance, but he drew a different conclusion—not that quarrelling was now justified, but that an extra effort in the interests of unity and peace was all the more important. He occasionally agreed with Churchill on specific difficulties with the Soviets, but did not let Churchill maneuver him. Rather he restrained Churchill and kept coming back from each specific difficulty to his general focus—unity and peace.

At the 1943 Casablanca conference, long before the end of the war, Roosevelt told his son Elliott:

> The unity we have made for war is nothing to the unity we will have to build for peace. After the war—that's when the cry will come that our unity is no longer necessary. *That's* when the job will begin... in earnest.[134]

Roosevelt stressed that unity and cooperation would be necessary despite the differences between the United States and the Soviet Union. In his last State of the Union message on January 6, 1945, he said:

> In our disillusionment after the last war we preferred international anarchy to international cooperation with nations which did not see and think exactly as we did.... We must not let that happen

again, or we shall follow the same tragic road again—the road to a third world war.[135]

In his inauguration speech on January 20, 1945, he said:

The only way to have a friend is to be one. We can gain no lasting peace if we approach it with suspicion and mistrust—or with fear.[136]

Roosevelt was suspicious of Churchill's campaign against the Soviet Union. The *Forrestal Diaries* contain the following entry for a Cabinet meeting on March 16, 1945, when this campaign was already well under way:

The President indicated considerable difficulty with British relations. In a semi-jocular manner of speaking, he stated that the British were perfectly willing for the United States to have a war with Russia at any time and that, in his opinion, to follow the British program would be to proceed toward that end.[137]

Some writers assert, citing one or two harsh comments Roosevelt made at the height of the Bern incident, that toward the end he was changing his mind about the Soviets. But the day before he died, in his last cable to Churchill, Roosevelt said:

I would minimize the general Soviet problem as much as possible because these problems, in one form or another, seem to arise every day and most of them straighten out as in the case of the Bern meeting.[138]

And in the last speech he dictated, which he never got to deliver, he said:

The work, my friends, is peace. More than an end of this war—an end to the beginnings of all wars.... I ask you to keep up your faith.[139]

MANY IN POSITIONS OF POWER and influence in the United States had a different focus. Republican Senator Arthur H. Vandenberg, of Michigan, a state with many people of Polish origin, rejected Roosevelt's argument for Allied unity and proclaimed his disagreement with "the palpably unjust decisions made at Yalta" on Poland.[140] Averell Harriman, the former international banker now ambassador to the Soviet Union, was sending home a barrage of cables and letters hostile to the Soviets: "Time has come when we must make clear what we expect of them as the price of our goodwill."[141] There were countless anti-Soviet officials in the State, War, and other government departments.

But among the American people there had been a great upsurge of admiration and good will toward the Soviet Union as a result of its heroic fight against the Fascists. Although Roosevelt had to maneuver to deal with the problems posed by the Soviets, the British, U.S. officials, and domestic political pressures, he was able to maintain his basic focus on unity and peace until his death.

As soon as Truman became president, various people rushed to advise him. Churchill, striving for a joint U.S.-British position against the Soviet Union on the Polish question, told Truman in a cable: "It is important to strike the note of our unity of outlook and of action at the earliest moment."[142] He had his foreign minister, Anthony Eden, stop in Washington on the way to the opening conference of the United Nations in San Francisco, to present to Truman "our impressions of what is actually happening in Moscow and Warsaw."[143] Harriman hurried back to Washington to tell Truman of the difficulties he was encountering in Moscow and the need to "stand firm."[144]

Leahy, now Truman's Chief of Staff, states that he had to work harder briefing Truman than Roosevelt. "Everyone, including Truman himself, knew that in the field of international relations he had much to learn...."[145] The limitations of Truman's knowledge and experience didn't stop him from forming judgments quickly. While Harriman was telling him of the "deterioration" of the Soviet attitude since Yalta, he interrupted

> to say that I was not afraid of the Russians and that I intended to be firm. I would be fair, of course, and anyway the Russians needed us more than we needed them.[146]

Molotov, also on his way to the San Francisco conference, met with Truman on April 23. Just before his talk with Molotov, Truman held a conference with his chief advisers. Stettinius reported difficulties with the Soviets over the Polish question. Truman asked the advisers for their views, but only after first stating that "our agreements with the Soviet Union had so far been a one-way street and that this could not continue."[147] Stimson said "we ought to be very careful and see whether we couldn't get ironed out on the situation without getting into a head-on collision."[148] On the big military matters, the Soviet government had kept its word and often done far better than it had promised. "The Russians [in their position on Poland] perhaps were being more realistic than we were in regard to their own security."[149] Marshall agreed with Stimson that a break with the Soviet Union would be serious; the Soviets had it within their power to delay their entry into the war against Japan.[150] But Secretary of the Navy Forrestal argued: "If the Russians were to be rigid in their attitude we had better have a showdown with them now than later...."[151] Harriman also defended "firmness." Leahy sums up the consensus: "The time had arrived to take a strong American attitude toward the Soviet Union and that no particular harm could be done to our war prospects if Russia should slow down or even stop its war effort in Europe and Asia."[152]

Armed with the judgment that the Soviets were no longer needed militarily, Truman was cocky and combative in his meeting with Molotov. Leahy says that he used "language that was not at all diplomatic."[153] His basic line was simple: The Soviet Union must carry out the Yalta agreement on Poland. Leahy, who had been present at Yalta, had stated at the advisers' conference a little earlier that the agreement was susceptible of two interpretations, but Truman disregarded this. The Soviets must carry it out according to the U.S. interpretation. Along with this demand went a threat: Failure to live up to Yalta would endanger big three unity and continued collaboration.[154]

Molotov replied that the Soviet Union wished to abide by the Yalta agreements, and was abiding by them. The Soviet Union wished to continue to collaborate. It would be unfortunate if anything should interfere with postwar collaboration, but the only acceptable basis for collaboration was equality. He was convinced that all difficulties could be overcome.[155]

Truman records that he "replied sharply that an agreement had been reached on Poland and there was only one thing to do and that was for Marshal Stalin to carry out that agreement in accordance with his word." Molotov protested against Truman's scolding: "I have never been talked to like that in my life." Truman shot back, "Carry out your agreements and you won't get talked to like that."[156]

Harriman recalled, "I was a little taken aback, frankly, when the President attacked Molotov so vigorously.... I [regretted] that Truman went at it so hard because his behavior gave Molotov an excuse to tell Stalin that the Roosevelt policy was being abandoned.... I think it was a mistake...."[157] But more than just a "mistake" was involved.   After all of eleven days in office, Truman was beginning the abandonment of the Roosevelt policy.   He was beginning to apply the Churchill strategy of creating "a new front" against the Soviets "as far east as possible."

While Truman's cockiness lay partly in his character, it also reflected the surging power of the United States.   The United States was coming out of the war unscathed, enriched, with an economy practically equal to that of the rest of the world combined, with the atom bomb scheduled to enter into its possession within a few months.   Truman felt he could lay down the law to Molotov, without accepting backtalk.

Although in appearance Truman concentrated on the Polish question, he was really talking about all of Eastern Europe and U.S.-Soviet relations in general.   He and his advisers had selected Poland as the best case for a showdown.   As he told Molotov, he saw the Polish question as a symbol—a "symbol of the future development of our international relations."[158]

What were the issues in dispute over Poland?   The key issue was the government Poland would have.   A Polish government in exile had been established in London in 1940 with Churchill's help.   Harriman describes this government as

> predominantly a group of aristocrats, looking to the Americans and the British to restore their position and landed properties and the feudalistic system.... They think the only future of Poland lies in Great Britain and the United States fighting Russia to protect Poland.[159]

Britain, under Churchill, would have set up the London Poles as the government of Poland had British armies been the ones liberating that country.   But could one expect the Soviet Union to accept an unfriendly government—a government that could form part of a belt of hostile countries along its borders, such as was set up against it after World War I?

Early in 1944, representatives of the Polish Workers (Communist) Party and other antifascist parties and organizations formed a Polish National Council within Poland. When Soviet troops arrived, this Council formed a National Liberation Committee in Lublin which developed into a full-scale government, recognized by the Soviets as the Polish Provisional Government.

Even Churchill had trouble with the London Poles, who lacked all sense of reality.   He urged them at the beginning of 1944 to come to agreement with the Soviets, but they refused.   He later reproached Mikolajczyk, their Premier: "If you had come to an agreement with the Russians at that time, you would not have today those Lublin people."[160] When Churchill pleaded with them to moderate their positions so that they could at least participate with the Lublin Poles in the postwar Polish government, they remained adamant. At one point Churchill became so exasperated that he told Mikolajczyk:

> If you want to conquer Russia, we shall let you go your own way. You ought to be in a lunatic asylum![161]

At Yalta, Churchill worked—with support from Roosevelt—to have the Lublin government replaced by a new one and, failing that, to get as many London Poles as possible included in the Lublin government. Poland, said Churchill, was for Britain a question of "honor." Stalin responded that for the Soviet Union Poland was

> not only a question of honor, but also a question of security. Throughout history, Poland has been the corridor through which the enemy has passed into Russia.[162]

After lengthy discussion, the Big Three arrived at a compromise agreement that the Lublin government should be "reorganized on a broader democratic basis with the inclusion of democratic leaders from Poland itself and from Poles abroad."[163] Leahy remarked to Roosevelt: "This [agreement] is so elastic that the Russians can stretch it all the way from Yalta to Washington without ever technically breaking it." The President replied, "I know, Bill."[164]

Thus Truman began his policy of moving from the wartime alliance to hostility on the issue of Poland, which is far from the United States, but borders on the Soviet Union and was vital to its security, and on the basis of the Yalta agreement, which according to his own Chief of Staff was subject to two interpretations.

The shift away from the Roosevelt policy showed in other things, for example, the cutting off of Lend-Lease aid. As the war in Germany drew to a close, many U.S. officials, including Harriman, advocated limiting Lend-Lease to the Soviets; if the United States did want to provide assistance, it could get greater "leverage" with ordinary economic aid or credits than with Lend-Lease. On the very day Germany surrendered, Truman signed an order stopping Lend-Lease.[165] Ships already on the high seas received instructions to turn back. The order applied to other European countries as well as the Soviet Union, but as the historian Gar Alperovitz has pointed out, "there can be no doubt that the abrupt...cutoff was designed primarily with the Russians in mind."[166]

As a result of protests from all sides, including Stettinius, who complained that "the order was issued without any warning whatsoever,"[167] Truman "modified" it. Later, Stalin remarked to Harry Hopkins about the "unfortunate and even brutal" manner in which Lend-Lease had been cut off. If, said Stalin, the refusal to continue Lend-Lease was designed to put pressure on the Soviets and soften them up, then it was a fundamental mistake. If the Soviets were approached frankly on a friendly basis, much could be done, but pressure would bring about the exact opposite effect.[168] On September 22, 1945, eight days after the Japanese surrender, the United States again cut off Lend-Lease — this time for good.

Another example of movement away from the Roosevelt policy is the abandonment of the agreement on reparations entered into by the United States at Yalta. Roosevelt himself had proposed the language of the agreement:

> The Moscow Reparation Commission should take in its initial studies as a basis for discussion the suggestion of the Soviet Government that the total sum of the reparation...should be 20 billion dollars and that 50% of it should go to the Union of Soviet Socialist Republics.[169]

This agreement not only committed the United States to the principle that the Soviet Union should receive reparations, but indicated the order of magnitude.

Truman's advisers decided to discard the $20 billion figure and to insist on the principle that German exports would first be used to pay for imports, and only after that go for reparations — the so-called First Charge Principle. Truman wanted as head of the U.S. delegation to the Allied Reparations Commission "someone who could throw his weight around," so he replaced the statistician, Dr. Isador Lubin, with the tough oil operator, Edwin C. Pauley. Pauley pressed the U.S. position in the Commission and a deadlock resulted. The Soviets argued for the $20 billion figure and against the First Charge Principle which meant that reparations would be a leftover; they insisted on a definite figure so they would know how much they would be getting. At the Potsdam conference of the three Allied leaders, Stalin and Molotov continued to press for a definite figure, but got nowhere. Secretary of State James Byrnes writes: "We finally succeeded in eliminating from the agreed declaration any mention of a total amount...."[170]

Underlying the U.S. action on reparations were far-reaching plans beginning to form in the minds of U.S. policymakers about the future organization of Europe and Germany's role in it. The Yalta agreement rested on the assumptions that the United States and the Soviet Union would remain friendly and that the problem was to create arrangements that would prevent the resurgence of a militaristic Germany. On these assumptions, the United States could agree to a high level of reparations. They would help the Soviet Union and weaken Germany—both consequences were acceptable.

But when U.S. policymakers began to think of the Soviet Union as the problem, and of how to organize Western Europe against communism, reparations took on a different aspect. Now reparations would be strengthening the Soviet Union at the expense of Germany and the West. The U.S. actions on reparations were first steps in bringing West Germany into what eventually became a full-scale political, economic, and military alliance against the Soviet Union.

Truman and his advisers were thinking of the Soviet Union as "the problem" from the beginning of his administration. By the end of the Potsdam conference, less than four months later, Truman had reached a momentous conclusion: The Soviets were planning to conquer the world. "How he arrived at this startling conclusion is not evident from his account of the conference," writes Fleming in his monumental book, *The Cold War and its Origins*.[171] According to Truman:

> The persistent way in which Stalin blocked one of the war-preventative measures I had proposed showed how his mind worked and what he was after. I had proposed the internationalization of all the principal waterways. Stalin did not want this. What Stalin wanted was control of the Black Sea straits and the Danube. The Russians were planning world conquest.[172]

The Black Sea straits control the passage between the Mediterranean and the Black Sea, where the Soviet Union has its only warm water ports. Internationalization of these straits would have included the United States and Britain in the control of a waterway close to the Soviet Union and vital to her. Similarly, internationalization of the Danube would have included them in the control of that waterway. Although Truman speaks here of "all the principal waterways," he didn't really mean all. His plan didn't propose internationalization of the Panama and Suez canals. The Soviets rejected his one-sided proposal, arguing instead for a joint Soviet-Turkish guarantee of free passage through the Black Sea straits and that control of the Danube was the business of the Danubian countries themselves. How does the disagreement with Truman's waterway proposal indicate — even remotely — that the Soviets were planning world conquest?

Also by the time of the Potsdam conference, two other factors had begun to affect Truman's Soviet policy: the weakening of Japan and the acquisition of the atomic bomb.   When Truman took office, the collapse of Germany had provided the basis for his shift from the Roosevelt policy.   But most of his advisers felt that the United States still needed the Soviet Union against Japan. In the weeks that followed, Japan's position deteriorated sharply, and the day when the United States would have the bomb moved close. Various advisers worried about the disadvantages of Soviet entry into the war and wondered whether the United States might not be able to end it at an acceptable cost without the Soviet Union.   By the time of Potsdam, Japan was all but defeated, and during the course of the conference the United States successfully exploded the first bomb in the New Mexican desert. U.S. policy on Soviet entry completed a 180-degree turn from Yalta. Now the United States didn't want the Soviets in the war.

Churchill records his thoughts upon hearing of the successful explosion of the bomb:

> We should not need the Russians. The end of the Japanese war no longer depended upon the pouring in of their armies.... A few days later I minuted to Mr. Eden: "It is quite clear that the United States do not at the present time desire Russian participation in the war against Japan." The array of European problems could therefore be faced on their merits....[173]

Churchill helped influence Truman to use the bomb. Truman writes that

> I regarded the bomb as a military weapon and never had any doubt that it should be used. The top military advisers to the President recommended its use, and when I talked to Churchill he

unhesitatingly told me that he favored the use of the atomic bomb if it might aid to end the war.[174]

But in dropping atomic bombs on Hiroshima and Nagasaki, the United States was pursuing more far-reaching aims than simply ending the war. The first was to end the war *quickly*, before the Soviet Union entered, or if it did, before the Red Army got too far into Manchuria. A further, parallel aim, was to demonstrate the power of the bomb to the Soviet Union.

Several high-ranking U.S. military officials have recorded their view that the use of the bomb was unnecessary. Eisenhower writes that when Stimson told him that the United States was preparing to drop an atomic bomb on Japan,

> I voiced to him my grave misgivings, first on the basis of my belief that Japan was already defeated and that dropping the bomb was completely unnecessary, and secondly because I thought that our country should avoid shocking world opinion by the use of a weapon whose employment was, I thought, no longer mandatory as a measure to save American lives.[175]

Admiral Leahy writes:

> It is my opinion that the use of this barbarous weapon at Hiroshima and Nagasaki was of no material assistance in our war against Japan. The Japanese were already defeated and ready to surrender....[176]

U.S. officials have also expressed their clear understanding of the potential political value of the bomb. Truman reports an April conversation with Stimson: "If expectations were to be realized, he told me, the atomic bomb would be certain to have a decisive influence on our relations with other countries."[177] That same month Byrnes told him that "the bomb might well put us in a position to dictate our own terms at the end of the war."[178] Byrnes also told the nuclear scientist, Leo Szilard, a month later that he thought the atomic bomb would "render the Russians more manageable in Europe."[179]

Truman and Churchill reacted jubilantly at Potsdam upon receiving the news that the United States had successfully exploded an atomic bomb. Truman, according to Churchill, "was a changed man. He told the Russians just where they got on and off and generally bossed the whole meeting."[180] Churchill himself, according to Alan Brooke, the British commander-in-chief, was "completely carried away," saying that "We now had something in our hands which would redress the balance with the Russians."[181]

Three weeks later, Churchill stated to the House of Commons that the West now had powers "which were irresistible."

> The United States stand at this moment at the summit of the world.... Let them act up to the level of their power....[182]

The United States followed Churchill's counsel. On the way home from Potsdam, Truman decided that "I would not allow the Russians any part in the control of Japan."[183] At the same time, the United States mounted a campaign to extend its own influence in areas liberated by the Soviets. In an effort to get the governments of Rumania, Bulgaria, and Hungary reorganized to its liking, it threatened to withhold diplomatic recognition and clandestinely conspired with opposition parties.

The bomb was present at the Council of Foreign Ministers meeting in London in September, at which the problems of these countries were discussed. Two days before sailing, Byrnes discussed the role of the bomb with Stimson, who recorded in his diary:

> I found that Byrnes was very much against any attempt to co-operate with Russia....He looks to having the presence of the bomb in his pocket, so to speak, as a great weapon to get through the thing.[184]

At a London reception, Molotov asked Byrnes whether he had an atomic bomb in his pocket and expressed doubts about whether the United States was interested in seeing governments friendly to the Soviet Union in countries adjacent to it. The former Radescu government in Rumania, Molotov said, "was hostile to the Soviet Union and yet received British and American support but when the Groza government, which was friendly, had been established, both the United States and Britain had withdrawn support."[185]

The United States was pressing to expand its influence and control, not just in Japan and Eastern Europe, but throughout the world. It had its traditional empire in Latin America. Now it was taking over islands in the Pacific, had troops and air bases in China, was moving in economically and politically as the old European colonial empires in Asia and Africa crumbled, was grabbing for control of Middle East oil, and was acquiring strong positions in West Germany and the rest of Western Europe.

Backing the U.S. expansion was the strength of its economy in a war-torn world and the atomic bomb.

One member of Truman's cabinet, Stimson, came to disagree with the rush to exploit the bomb without thinking of the longer-run consequences. Nobody could dismiss Stimson as an impractical idealist. He was finishing his second stint as Secretary of War, and had been Secretary of State, Governor General of the Philippines,and a corporation lawyer. He had been among the first to appreciate the military and diplomatic powers offered by the bomb and had explained them to Truman. But mulling over the meaning of the bomb, he had moved away from his own initial positions and concluded that the United States should strive for an agreement with the Soviet Union to control it. On September 11, 1945, he presented this proposal in a memorandum to Truman. He made several key points:

> Unless the Soviets are voluntarily invited into [a] partnership upon a basis of cooperation and trust, we are going to maintain the Anglo-Saxon bloc over against the Soviet in the possession of this weapon. Such a condition will almost certainly stimulate feverish activity on the part of the Soviet toward the development of this bomb in what will in effect be a secret armament race of a rather desperate character....
>
> *Relations may perhaps be irretrievably embittered by the way in which we approach the solution of the bomb with Russia. For if we fail to approach them now and merely continue to negotiate with them, having this weapon rather ostentatiously on our hip, their suspicions and their distrust of our purposes and motives will increase....* (Italics in original.)
>
> If the atomic bomb were merely another though more devastating military weapon..., it would be one thing.... But I think the bomb instead constitutes merely a first step in a new control by man over the forces of nature too revolutionary and dangerous to fit into the old concepts....

Stimson suggested an approach that might

> lead to the proposal that we would stop work on the further improvement in, or manufacture of, the bomb as a military weapon, provided the Russians and the British would agree to do likewise. It might also provide that we would be willing to impound the bombs we now have in the United States provided the Russians and British would agree with us that in no event will they or we use the bomb as an instrument of war unless all three governments agree to that use....[186]

The scientists who worked on the bomb had been warning Stimson what it meant. In a report submitted to him two months before the bombing of Hiroshima, they had written that the atomic bomb is "fraught with infinitely greater dangers than were all the inventions of the past...."[187] They had stressed the impossibility of the United States maintaining a monopoly of the bomb. "We cannot hope to avoid a nuclear armament race, either by keeping secret from competing nations the basic scientific facts of nuclear power, or by cornering the raw materials required for such a race."[188]

Stimson presented his view to the cabinet at the last meeting he attended, on September 21. Dean Acheson writes that "the discussion was unworthy of the subject."[189] Stimson seemed to win the support of several present, including Acheson, Robert Patterson, and Henry Wallace. But others such as James Forrestal argued that the bomb and the knowledge that produced it were "the property of the American people...." and that "the Russians, like the Japanese, are essentially Oriental in their thinking, and until we have a longer record of experience with them on the validity of engagements...it seems doubtful that we should endeavor to buy their understanding and sympathy."[190] Truman and his cabinet rejected Stimson's recommendations.

Stimson had stressed the importance of a direct approach to the Soviets; an approach through the United Nations where the United States commanded a steamroller majority would not "be taken seriously" by them. But the United States took the problem to the U.N. Stimson had spoken of stopping the manufacture of the bomb, impounding the existing U.S. stock, and agreeing never to use the weapon except by agreement with Britain and the Soviet Union. But the United States moved in the opposite direction. Soon after the Cabinet meeting, Vannevar Bush, head of the Office of Research and Scientific Development, stated in a memorandum to the Secretary of State that "our program toward international understanding should involve no premature 'outlawing of the bomb,' which is a dangerous phrase."[191]

The United States adopted a simple strategy: to prevent the bomb from being outlawed; to propose a system of control that appeared international but, given U.S. domination of the U.N., would be run by the United States; and then, when the Soviets rejected the U.S. proposals, to advance the argument that so long as there was no international control, the United States had no choice but, as Byrnes put it, "to develop better bombs and more of them."[192]

Truman expressed the opinion in a newspaper interview that only the United States had the resources and organizational skill to make atomic bombs. To the reporter's question whether an armament race was on, Truman replied: "Yes, but I think we will stay ahead."[193]

By the beginning of 1946, what became known as the Cold War had been under way, largely behind the scenes, for many months. But while the U.S. Government had turned away from the Roosevelt policy of cooperation with the Soviet Union, the people of the United States had not. Among the people, there still remained a great reservoir of admiration and good will toward the Soviet Union, generated during the war. The people wanted peace. But a cold war, like any war, requires that public opinion be mobilized behind it.

Truman selected Churchill to fire the first salvo of the mobilization campaign. When the president of Westminster College in Fulton, Missouri wrote Churchill inviting him to speak there, Truman added a note saying, "If you'll come out and make them a speech I'll take you out and introduce you."[194] Churchill went over his proposed speech with Truman, Byrnes, and Leahy. In his opening, he noted that "The president has travelled a thousand miles to dignify and magnify our meeting here today...."[195]

Churchill's speech called openly for a cold war against the Soviet Union and, in thinly veiled language, threatened a hot war. Basic to his argument was his estimate of the power of the United States:

> The United States stands at this time at the pinnacle of world power.... With primacy in power is also joined an awe-inspiring accountability to the future....Opportunity is here now, clear and shining....[196]

Since United States power depended so greatly upon the bomb, Churchill came out squarely against entering into any international agreements to control it. Instead, he gave his blessing to the nuclear arms race, counting on the United States to stay ahead:

> We have at least a breathing space before this peril [Soviet possession of the bomb] has to be encountered, and even then..., we should still possess so formidable [a] superiority as to impose

effective deterrents upon its employment or threat of employment by others.

Referring to Eastern Europe, Churchill said: "It is not our duty *at this time, when difficulties are so numerous,* to interfere forcibly in the internal affairs of countries whom we have not conquered in war...." (Italics added.) In other words, although conditions were not then propitious for using force to change the situation in Eastern Europe, they might become so.

Churchill proposed a "fraternal association of the English-speaking peoples." He was precise about what this meant militarily: "the joint use of all naval and air-force bases in the possession of either country," etc.

Then Churchill turned to his key task of stoking up fear and hatred of the Soviet Union.

From Stettin in the Baltic to Trieste in the Adriatic, an iron curtain has descended .... The future of Italy hangs in the balance.... Except in the British Commonwealth and in this United States... the Communist parties or fifth columns constitute a growing challenge and peril to Christian civilization.

Many people spoke out against the speech. Senator Claude Pepper of Florida accused Churchill of "aligning himself with the old Chamberlain Tories who strengthened the Nazis as part of their anti-Soviet crusade." Senator Glen Taylor of Idaho asserted that the proposed alliance with Britain would "cut the throat" of the U.N. and "destroy the unity of the Big Three." Former Secretary of the Interior, Harold Ickes, pointed out that "without Russia we would still be fighting the war." Mrs. Roosevelt warned that "we should not have our vision clouded by thinking the English-speaking peoples, in spite of their strength, can get along without the far greater number of people who are not English-speaking." James Roosevelt, FDR's eldest son, said: "It is up to us and to every peace-loving man and woman in the entire world to stand up now and repudiate the words, the schemes, and the political allies of the Hon. Winston Churchill."[197]

The *St. Louis Post Dispatch* found Churchill's case "not convincing." The *Boston Globe* said that Churchill had invited the United States "to become the heir to the evils of collapsing colonialism...." The *Chicago Sun* declared: "To follow the standard raised by this great but blinded aristocrat would be to march to the world's most ghastly war."[198]

But the *New York Times* hailed Churchill as "the towering leader" of "our whole civilization." The *Wall Street Journal* supported him and attacked the "criminal decision of Yalta." The "isolationist" Hearst and Patterson newspapers ignored Churchill's suggestion of an alliance with Britain, but otherwise were enthusiastic. *Time* magazine gave a big play to the speech, and its owner, Henry Luce, gave a dinner in honor of Churchill.[199]

In the struggle for public opinion, the greater, more powerful part of the press backed Churchill. Fleming writes that "a first poll of public opinion showed that of those who had heard of Churchill's proposal...only 18 percent approved..., yet another poll a month later showed 85 percent approving the idea." Polls being what they are, one can question what exactly the supposed 85 percent were approving. But there can be little doubt that the Churchill-Truman initiative, as Fleming calls it, succeeded in setting off a tremendous shift in public opinion.[200]

The Cold War was now official and out in the open. The United States had reverted to the hostility that began with the October Revolution. But the hostility didn't just resume. Aggravated by the struggle over the postwar organization of eastern Europe; by the fear of the "spread of communism;" and by U.S. reluctance to accept one of the chief consequences of the war—a far stronger and more influential Soviet Union—the hostility came back with redoubled strength.

2. China

The first great revolution after World War II was the Chinese Revolution. Any honest study will show that it was a natural outgrowth of Chinese history and circumstances. China had been in turmoil, in the throes of a developing revolutionary process, for over a hundred years. The imperialist countries — Great Britain, Japan, Russia, Germany, France, the United States — had inflicted countless humiliations on China and had turned it into a semi-colony, enjoying little real independence. The peasants, the bulk of the population, suffered under an age-old feudal landholding system; they had to turn over a large part of what they produced to landlords. Even when there were no special calamities, the people of China did not get enough to eat, and periodically widespread famines struck. The Chinese government was corrupt, incompetent, repressive, unable to command the loyalty of not only the people but its own armies. On top of everything else came World War II, which aggravated the crisis and speeded up its development.

Faced after the War with the developing Chinese revolution, the U.S. Government didn't ask itself whether a revolution was necessary, or which side represented the Chinese people, or what U.S. policy would be in the best interests of its own people. It was promoting imperialist interests and automatically supported the Chiang Kai-shek side that was defending the rotten social system and government against the people. It intervened, providing money, arms, advice, and political and moral support. When the revolution triumphed, a coalition of the China Lobby and right wing Republicans raised the question "Who lost China?" and the cry of treason.

Seldom, if ever, in U.S. history has separation from reality gone so far. Here was a revolutionary process that had gathered hurricane force in a country containing a fourth of the world's population. There were the China Lobby and right wing Republicans arguing that the result could have been avoided except for the actions of a handful of U.S. officials who "sold China down the river."

THE MORE THAN HUNDRED-YEAR turmoil in China began with the Opium War of 1840-1842, which ushered in the domination of China by imperialism. The war added a new, basic antagonism to Chinese society: the antagonism between the Chinese people and the imperialists. The imperialists committed repeated aggressions against China, and the Chinese people resisted.

Imperialism also sharpened existing antagonisms. Wars brought higher taxes which the landowners shifted to the peasants, strengthening the already acute contradiction between these two classes. The helplessness of the government in the face of foreign aggression, its collaboration with the foreigners, increased the hostility of the people toward it.

At the time of the Opium War, British merchants were the leading foreign traders in China. With British industry growing rapidly, they eagerly sought to expand what they saw as the potentially vast Chinese market. Restrictions on trade imposed by the Chinese government were the main obstacles to expansion. Britain used a conflict over opium as a pretext for a war that it could use to get rid of the restrictions.

For several decades, British as well as U.S. merchants had been shipping opium into China in large quantities, even though the Chinese government had prohibited its import. A group of Chinese officials and scholars demanded that this smuggling be stopped. Not only was the use of opium destructive for the people, but the unproductive opium imports were a severe economic burden.

In 1839, the Emperor of China appointed Lin Zexu High Commissioner to fight the opium trade. Lin Zexu took strong measures. He ordered the confiscation against compensation in tea leaves of the opium held by foreign smugglers and had it dumped into pits filled with salt water or publicly burned. He required foreign merchants to sign a pledge that they would not bring opium into China.

The British merchants pressed their government to intervene and Britain sent an expeditionary force. The war continued on and off for two years.

Under the peace treaty, signed aboard the British warship *Cornwallis,* China was forced to cede Hongkong to Britain "in perpetuity;" to open five ports where the British could trade, settle, and come and go without hindrance; to fix tariff rates on British goods only by mutual agreement; to pay an indemnity of 21 million silver dollars, including 6 million for the destroyed opium.

A Supplementary Treaty established the rudiments of "extra-territoriality," which exempted British subjects in China from Chinese law. It also assured Britain of "most favored nation" treatment: "Should the emperor ... grant additional privileges or immunities to any of the subjects or citizens of ... foreign countries, the same privileges and immunities will be extended to and enjoyed by British subjects."[1]

The treaty with Britain was the first of a series of Unequal Treaties, as they are known. The United States and France followed close behind Britain, demanding similar treaties, and other countries came later. The United States obtained even wider extraterritorial privileges as well as additional rights for U.S. ships on China's waterways. But the British didn't mind. Under the "most favored nation" clause they, too, got the additional benefits.

The Unequal Treaties started the process by which China became a semi-colony. Deprived of control over its own tariffs, China was helpless to protect its industries against the competition of foreign goods. The establishment of open ports with extraterritoriality was the first step in the creation of foreign enclaves along China's coasts and waterways.

NINE YEARS AFTER THE OPIUM WAR, a peasant uprising known as the Taiping Rebellion broke out. The war had let loose the forces that brought about this rebellion—rising prices, rising taxes, the destruction of the prestige of the government. The rebellion was not just another of the countless peasant wars that had been hitting China for centuries, but a profound upheaval. The rebels overran most of the south, set up a separate state, and for a time controlled more than half the population of China. The rebellion lasted fourteen years.

As the Taipings advanced, they burned land deeds and loan contracts and confiscated the property of many landlords, government officials, and rich people, turning over land to tenants and food and clothing to the poor. They prosecuted profiteering and established a monopoly to make salt available at low prices. They banned the binding of women's feet and the sale of brides and opened civil service examinations to women.

The imperialist powers didn't care a whit about the meaning of the Taiping Rebellion for the Chinese people; they examined it from the point of view of their own interests. The United States asked itself whether the Taipings would recognize the unequal treaties. In a report to the State Department, Robert McLane, the U.S. minister to China, expressed the opinion that they would not.[2] The Taipings would also fight harder against the opium trade, which they prohibited in the areas they controlled. On the other hand, they were not isolationist like the old government and would probably open up China more fully to general foreign trade.

Like Britain and France, the United States at first proclaimed a policy of "neutrality." But neutrality was just a cover for the real policy which was to wait and see how best to squeeze advantage from the situation; in particular, how to use the government's difficulties to blackmail it into further concessions. A high Chinese official reported that McLane presented him with a demand for revision of the treaties and quoted him as saying:

> If the requests are granted, the United States will come to the aid of China in putting down the rebellion. Otherwise, I will report everything to my government and we shall deal with the situation as we see fit.[3]

The United States, along with Britain and France, reneged on the neutrality policy early on. In 1853, an uprising erupted in Shanghai; its leaders hoped to make it part of the Taiping Rebellion. The three powers helped the government put down the insurgents, with French troops playing the most active role. Then they used the occasion to gain complete control of the Shanghai customs and to set up an Anglo-French-U.S. administration in the Shanghai foreign settlement with its own police, judges, and tax office—thus removing the area from Chinese jurisdiction.

During the Taiping Rebellion, a second Opium War broke out: Britain wanted still more rights and privileges and used a minor incident—a Chinese search of a vessel of disputed registry—as a pretext for launching another war. A second round of unequal treaties with Britain, France, the United States, and Russia followed. These treaties opened up still more Chinese cities to foreign trade and foreign warships, further restricted Chinese authority to tax foreign goods, further extended extraterritoriality.

With the end of the Second Opium War, Britain and France openly helped the Manchu government against the rebels, while the United States gave covert aid. British and French warships defended Shanghai from attack by a Taiping army and dislodged Taiping forces from other cities. An American adventurer named F. T. Ward, acting with the behind-the-scenes collusion of U.S. authorities, built a mercenary force from foreigners in Shanghai and attacked Taiping cities.

Anson Burlingame, the U.S. minister to China, reported to Secretary of State William H. Seward about an interview he had with Prince Kung of the royal family. "We discoursed of the rebellion in China, and of the means of overcoming it; of the success of General Ward, an American...." Already in those days, the United States was giving advice to a reactionary regime on how to combat revolution. "I recommended," wrote Burlingame, "that they should abandon the old style of fighting, and that they should organize a smaller, but more efficient, force against the rebellion, and, above all, that they should adopt a more liberal policy towards all but the leaders of it."[4]

When Ward was killed in battle, Burlingame, in a special report, expressed his high esteem. "Indeed, he taught the Chinese their strength, and laid the foundations of the only force with which their government can hope to defeat the rebellion."[5] Seward in turn wrote Burlingame that "your proceedings in regard to the appointment of a successor to General Ward are approved of."

The foreign intervention enabled the Manchu government to put down the Taiping Rebellion. In 1864, the Taiping state fell. The rebellion showed in embryonic form the two basic revolutionary forces that were to gather great strength in China across the years: anti-feudalism and anti-imperialism. The Taipings started with a revolt against feudalism, but found themselves forced into a struggle against imperialism as well. Feudalism and imperialism were linked. The feudal local government and the landholding class that supported it had entered into an alliance with foreign imperialism to put down a revolution by their own people. Like all great revolutions, even those that fail, the Taiping Rebellion would inspire future revolutionaries, including the leader of the first big Chinese revolution of the 20th century, Sun Yat-sen.

THE FALL OF THE TAIPINGS did not end the turmoil in China. Other uprisings as well as foreign aggressions and wars followed one another in a seemingly endless succession. It took the Imperial government another ten years to suppress a series of smaller uprisings by peasants or ethnic minorities. Then in 1884, France declared war on China and invaded several provinces. A long series of aggressions by Japan culminated in the Sino-Japanese war in 1895.

In the years that followed, the main imperialist powers, other than the United States, scrambled to grab "spheres of influence" in China: Britain, France, Japan, Russia, and Germany each carved out a large area in which it claimed special powers and privileges. Sixteen of China's twenty-one provinces came under the sway of these powers. The danger arose that China would be completely partitioned, like Africa. The United States was busy, first fighting a war with Spain and then putting down an insurrection in the Philippines, and did not participate.

The U.S. imperialists, however, did not like being cut off from the immense profit-making potential of China. So in 1899, Secretary of State John Hay sent a note to the other imperialist powers proclaiming the "Open Door" policy. As the State Department later put it, "Hay asked the Powers involved in the struggle over China to give guarantees that in their respective 'spheres of influence or interest' they would not interfere with the equality of rights of nationals of other countries in matters of tariffs, railroad charges, and harbor dues."[6]

The United States did not bother to inform the Chinese government of the Hay note. It was not rejecting the other powers' encroachments on Chinese sovereignty, just demanding for itself equal access to the spoils. No one of these powers felt strong enough to defend an exclusive sphere of interest, so they all went along with the open door policy—a policy that amounted to an arrangement for the joint control and exploitation of China.

The growing imperialist penetration of China brought with it a large rise in the number of foreign nationals there, most of whom considered the Chinese an inferior people. Americans referred to Chinese as "boy" or "Chinaman" and were quick to deprecate the "strange" customs of China. A U.S. missionary wrote that the Chinese could endure greater amounts of pain than others because they had a less highly developed nervous system.[7]

Americans, exempted from Chinese law by the Unequal Treaties, dealt with Chinese in a high-handed manner. Robert McClellan, in a study of American attitudes toward China, writes: "Acts of violence against the Chinese by Americans in China were common enough so as to attract little notice. When an American seaman on shore leave wrecked the British consulate, threw several Chinese in the river, and beat up two Chinese police who tried to control him, he was fined ten dollars." A U.S. bank teller described how he travelled the streets outside the foreign compound. "If a Chinaman does not at once make room for me in the street I would strike him forcibly with my cane in the face." When asked whether such an act would go unpunished, he replied: "Should I break his nose or kill him, the worst that can happen would be that he or his people would make complaints to the Consul, who might impose the fine of a dollar for the misdemeanor, but I could always prove that I had just cause to beat him."[8]

Missionaries were the foreigners with whom ordinary Chinese came most into contact so they became a special object of anger. They enjoyed the same exemption from Chinese law as other foreigners and, by and large, shared the attitudes and prejudices about China of most of them. In acquiring land and buildings for churches, they resorted to unlawful practices, relying on their home government to protect them against the Chinese authorities. They were disdainful of Chinese customs and critical of Chinese religion. They made comparatively few converts, but these they protected, and the converts, taking advantage of the protection, often refused to pay taxes, violated Chinese law, and disobeyed local officials. Ordinary Chinese felt that because of the missionaries' ties to the imperialist governments both they and their converts enjoyed a special status in Chinese society.[9]

The growing imperialist aggressiveness, the economic disruptions caused by the influx of foreign goods and investments, and an accumulation of grievances against the missionaries led to the anti-foreign Yi He Tuan Uprising, known in the West as the

Boxer Rebellion. The Yi He Tuans demonstrated, rioted, destroyed railways and telegraph lines, burned churches, and attacked foreign missionaries and Chinese Christians.

It was often difficult to tell what was happening, and exaggerated and distorted accounts appeared. U.S. Minister E.H. Conger wrote Secretary Hay that

> The reports of the missionaries are necessarily based upon information which they received from their excited, frightened, and ignorant converts, who generally believe that they can of right call upon the missionaries in every case of trouble of whatever sort, and are continuously expecting and clamoring for foreign protection.... In no case as yet have the "Boxers" attacked any American mission or disturbed any property in the towns or villages where they are stationed.[10]

That U.S. citizens had not been attacked did not prevent the Minister from demanding of the Chinese authorities that they "punish the ringleaders" in "antiforeign cases." He

> impress[ed] upon the Chinese Government that the Government of the United States is firmly determined that the treaty stipulations as to the rights of all American citizens and their work shall be faithfully carried out, not only for their benefit but for that of China as well.[11]

The "treaty stipulations" had, of course, been extorted from China in the wake of the Opium Wars and other aggressions.

On one occasion, the Minister saw some "antiforeign" booklets being sold in the streets of Beijing. As he reported to Hay:

> By my request many copies, together with the blocks on which they were printed, have been seized and destroyed.[12]

The uprising spread rapidly and by June 1900, the Yi He Tuan had gained virtual control of Beijing and were laying siege to the foreign legations there. Eight foreign powers, including the United States, created a joint military force to suppress the "bandits."

The intervention was a classical imperialist operation, with the foreign soldiers shooting people indiscriminately, setting fire to buildings, raping and looting. Peter Fleming writes in his account of the capture of Beijing by the interventionists that looting "went on squalidly for months with each nationality blaming some other for setting a bad example and claiming that its own hands were clean. It was common knowledge that the highest as well as the lowest plundered."[13]

A new Unequal Treaty imposed new humiliations on China. The Chinese government had to pay an indemnity. The imperialist powers received control of the Legation Quarter in Beijing along with the right to fortify it and to station troops at key points along the communications line between Beijing and the coast.

IN 1911, ELEVEN YEARS after the Yi He Tuan rebellion, a new, far stronger uprising broke out. By that time foreign investments in China totalled $1.5 billion and foreigners controlled the pig iron industry, more than half the coal industry, a large part of the textile industry, as well as wharves, railroads, power stations, and mines. The foreign corporations had turned China into an appendage of the imperialist countries, a supplier of cheap raw materials—cotton, silk, tea, bristles—and an outlet for finished goods. Imported manufactures were swamping Chinese markets, destroying existing local industries and holding back the development of new ones. To be able to pay the Boxer indemnity, the Manchu government had increased taxes. Growing overpopulation in the countryside had made the food problem critical. Floods and droughts brought famine to many provinces. The years 1900-1910 saw a new wave of boycotts and strikes against imperialism, peasant attacks against tax collectors, riots by the urban poor against high food prices, as well as a series of revolutionary attempts to overthrow the Manchu government. The 1911 attempt succeeded.

The United States had been following with anxiety the events that led up to the 1911 revolution. In June, six months before it broke out, the U.S. minister to China, W. J. Calhoun, reported to the State Department that "there are not lacking signs of a renewed and somewhat widespread discontent among the Chinese toward their Manchu rulers" and that "the situation can easily become critical...." To help forestall trouble, Calhoun had instructed U.S. consuls to

> impress upon all the local authorities with whom they came in contact the urgent necessity, for China's own sake, that the public peace be preserved, and that with this end in view they might find it beneficial to join with their colleagues in the event of its being decided by the local consular body to take concerted action in

adopting necessary measures to suppress effectually the circulation of any inflammatory literature and bring to an end this foolish movement, which is only calculated to deceive ignorant people to instigate riots and disturbances, thus endangering the lives and property of all foreigners, Americans included.[14]

When the revolution broke out, the imperialist powers cast about for someone who could fight it effectively and settled upon Yuan Shikai, a former Manchu military commander. The day the revolutionaries took their first city, Calhoun called on Prince Zai Li, the regent who ruled in the name of the boy-emperor, and advised him to summon Yuan as "counsellor and executive of the emperor's will." Britain immediately backed the U.S. move; soon the other imperialist powers followed. Yuan had helped suppress the Ye Hi Tuan to protect the foreigners. He had always been friendly to the imperialists. He was the "strong man" they felt they now needed.[15]

The government quickly appointed Yuan commander of its armies and prime minister. Yuan hoped that, backed as he was by the imperialists, he could end the revolution by negotiations. While he was organizing his forces, his government entered into peace talks with the revolutionaries. To support him the United States and the other leading imperialist powers, acting in concert, sent identical notes to the negotiators, which read:

> The _____ Government considers that the continuation of the present struggle in China seriously affects not only the country itself but also the material interests and the security of foreigners. While maintaining the attitude of strict neutrality adopted by it up to the present time, the _____ Government considers that it is its duty in an unofficial manner to call the attention of the two delegations to the necessity of arriving as soon as possible at an understanding capable of putting an end to the present conflict....[16]

Pinning its hopes on Yuan Shikai, the United States was not actively planning direct intervention in China. But a note from the Secretary of State to the German ambassador to the United States shows that it held in reserve the possibility of such intervention in the form of joint action with the other imperialist countries:

> There happily has thus far been no reason for interference on the part of the foreign powers, inasmuch as both Imperialists [those acting in the name of the emperor] and Republicans have guaranteed the life and property of the foreign population....If, however,

contrary to all expectations, any further steps should prove necessary, this Government is firm in the conviction that the policy of
concerted action after full consultation by the powers should and
would be maintained....[17]

Yuan's government operated in Beijing, the seat of the old
government. The revolutionaries established a government in
Nanjing with Sun Yat-sen, a thoroughgoing democrat, as provisional president. The revolution developed into a struggle between the two governments. The imperialists supported Beijing,
giving it advice and financial help, while refusing to recognize
the Nanjing government.

Yuan saw that he could strike a deal with Nanjing if he sacrificed the Manchu dynasty, and the imperialists, feeling that the
dynasty was no longer useful to them, supported him. Yuan
demanded that he be given the post of president once the
Manchus were out. Sun agreed, fearing imperialist intervention
if he did not go along. Shortly after Yuan became president, the
U.S. House of Representatives passed a resolution congratulat-
ing "the people of China on their assumption of the powers,
duties and responsibilities of self-government."[18]

The 1911 revolution had profound historical significance—it
was part of a world revolutionary process, it attracted large masses of people to the revolutionary struggle, it toppled the more
than 2000-year-old Chinese monarchical system. But otherwise
the 1911 revolution was a failure—it didn't get rid of feudalism in
the countryside, it didn't free China from the imperialist strangle-
hold. By awakening people while leaving a large part of the job
required in China undone, it set the stage for further revolution.

The essence of Yuan Shikai's position vis-a-vis the imperialist
countries shows in his inaugural address:

> The attitude of the foreign powers towards us has always been that
> of peace and fairness, and whenever occasion therefor has arisen
> they have rendered us cordial assistance.... I hereby declare, there-
> fore, that all treaties, conventions and other engagements entered
> into by the former Manchu and the Provisional Republican Govern-
> ments with foreign governments shall be strictly observed, and...
> further that all rights, privileges and immunities enjoyed by foreign-
> ers in China by virtue of international engagements, national en-
> actments and established usages are hereby confirmed.[19]

Yuan was servile enough toward the imperialists, but he was
unable to provide the rest of what they wanted—a strong, stable

government. He had difficulty controlling peasant uprisings and workers' demonstrations, Nanjing republicans who engaged in guerrilla operations against him, and ambitious generals in his own armies. Claiming a national crisis, he created a military dictatorship and began to move toward reestablishing the monarchy with himself as emperor.

A nationwide anti-monarchic movement erupted. In South China a rebellion broke out. Various generals proclaimed their opposition to Yuan and several provinces declared their independence of the central government. Yuan failed to make himself emperor. In 1916 he died.

With Yuan's death, the weakening of the central government became even more pronounced. Power fell into the hands of warlords — military chieftains — who became the independent rulers of different parts of China. The United States and Britain supported one clique of warlords, Japan another, using them to strengthen their positions in China. The warlords maintained large military forces and fought endless wars with each other.

BY THIS TIME, THE UNITED STATES and Japan had become the main rivals in the imperialist struggle over China. The rivalry was fierce, though partly controlled by agreement between the two countries. In 1917, the Lansing-Ishi agreement embodied the longstanding strategy of the United States toward China. The United States recognized Japan's "special interests in China" (as though it had the right to grant such recognition), and in return Japan agreed to the U.S. policy of the "open door."[20]

The imperialist powers also dealt with the fate of China at the Versailles peace conference which distributed the spoils of World War I. The conference decided to turn over former German concessions in Shandong to Japan. This action sparked a mass student protest meeting in Beijing on May 4, 1919 and a May 4th Movement which spread like wildfire. Seventy thousand workers in Shanghai and other cities went out on strike.[21] A nationwide boycott of Japanese goods broke out that was to last three years. Anti-imperialist sentiment, which had played almost no role in the 1911 revolution, was high and rising.

In 1922, the United States, having become the richest and most powerful country in the world, obtained an international agreement on China even more to its liking than the Lansing-Ishi agreement. Nine countries, including the United States, Japan, Britain, France, Italy, several smaller countries, and

China, signed a treaty in Washington committing themselves "not to support any agreements...designed to create Spheres of Influence...."[22] Japan gave up the special rights in China it had obtained as a result of the war. As against spheres of influence, the open door arrangement for the joint control and exploitation of China under U.S. leadership had prevailed.

The same year the Soviet government, which had been proposing to China that diplomatic relations be reestablished, sent a representative to Beijing. The U.S., Japanese, British, and French envoys sent notes to the Beijing government asserting that the Soviet representative was propagating "radicalism" in China and that such activity should be kept under surveillance. But in November, mass meetings in Beijing and other cities celebrated the anniversary of the October Revolution.[23] In 1924, the Beijing government, giving way before popular pressure, agreed to the resumption of relations. The Soviet Union renounced extraterritorial rights, port concessions, and the receipt of indemnity payments.

The period from 1919 through 1925 saw a rising revolutionary ferment in China. One wave of strikes followed another. In 1925, negotiations over a strike at Japanese cotton mills ended in a clash in which the Japanese killed one labor delegate and wounded several others. On May 30, during a protest demonstration by students and workers, police at the Shanghai international settlement commanded by the British fired into the demonstrators, killing ten.[24] A gigantic anti-imperialist movement flared up across the country, with strikes by workers and students, the closing of shops by merchants, demonstrations in the villages by peasants, as well as anti-Japanese and anti-British boycotts. In many places, clashes with police and troops occurred. Britain, Japan, the United States, France, and Italy brought warships and marines to Shanghai.

The ferment culminated in a revolutionary civil war during 1926 and 1927. Sun Yat-sen had begun several years earlier to revitalize the revolutionary movement, reorganizing his political party—the Kuomintang, forming a united front with the recently formed Communist Party, and setting up a new revolutionary government in Guangzhou (Canton). Reflecting the influence of the Russian Revolution, Sun himself had become radicalized. Going beyond his earlier goals of getting rid of the Manchus and establishing a democratic republic, he adopted the anti-feudal and anti-imperialist policy advanced by the Communists. The

Kuomintang decided to create a revolutionary army and announced a "northern expedition" to wipe out warlord control of central and north China. Sun proclaimed that the aim of the expedition was "not only to overthrow warlordism, but also to drive out imperialism upon which the warlords in China depend for their existence...."[25] He appointed a young officer named Chiang Kai-shek to lead the revolutionary army.

In 1925, Sun died. Chiang continued preparations for the expedition, which he launched in mid-1926. Carrying out anti-feudal and anti-imperialist agitation, the Kuomintang army fought a revolutionary war against the imperialist-backed warlords. Workers supported the revolutionary army with strikes. In several provinces, peasant uprisings occurred. The Communists mounted insurrections in Shanghai. The expeditionary army advanced rapidly and in areas it captured the workers and peasants movements swelled. In Hankou and Jiujiang, workers occupied the ports and drove the British out.

The imperialist powers nervously watched the advance of the revolution and increased their forces in China. Forty thousand foreign troops moved into Shanghai—U.S. Marines, British, Japanese, and other soldiers. The U.S. Navy announced that its Asiatic Fleet was proceeding to China to ensure the protection of U.S. nationals. Asserting that Chinese mobs had attacked foreign nationals and consulates, U.S., British, and other foreign warships bombarded Nanjing. The American Chamber of Commerce in China came out for "unified action by the Powers to suppress disorder and to restore conditions favorable to the formation of a responsible Government."[26]

But the U.S. Government was cautious about getting too involved militarily in a country as huge as China. President Coolidge declared in a memorandum to his Cabinet that "for us at the present to send a large force of regular soldiers, outside of the Navy, would be very strongly condemned publicly here, in Congress and out, and would inflame China."[27]

Nevertheless, the possibility of a larger U.S. intervention remained. Wilson had also started out cautious about intervention and had ended up sending U.S. troops to northern Russia and Siberia. Professor C.P. FitzGerald of the Australian National University, who knew the China of the 1920s firsthand, wrote: "It can hardly be doubted that at this point, February 1927, war with the West, undeclared, but probably most destructive and

prolonged, was imminent.   Had the revolutionary parties held
together it was inevitable."[28]

But the revolutionary parties did not hold together.   The business interests in China, foreign and Chinese, found in Chiang
Kai-shek the solution to the problem of revolution.   He was
having disagreements with the revolutionary government and
was showing signs of fearing the upsurge of the people.   Agents
of the business interests converged on him, promising money
and arms if he broke with the Communists and suppressed the
rebellious workers and peasants.   Israel Epstein writes that
"Shanghai's comprador bankers, acting for the foreigners and
themselves, got Chiang to agree and made promises of immediate financial backing."   An American lawyer named Stirling Fes-
senden, chairman of the Council of Shanghai's International Settlement, sanctioned the deal "on behalf of Anglo-American business."[29]

In March 1927, the Communists led the workers of Shanghai
in an insurrection designed to clear the way for the Kuomintang
troops that were approaching the city.   The insurrection was
successful.   But within three weeks Chiang—using Shanghai
gangsters and Kuomintang troops—turned on his allies, the
workers and Communists, and massacred them.   His forces carried out a counterrevolutionary coup d'état.   Similar coups took
place in other cities, such as Guangzhou, Nanjing, and
Hangzhou.

The U.S. minister to China, J.V.A. MacMurray, reported to the
State Department:

> On April 15th a move against the communists occurred at Canton
> [Guangzhou] which Mr. Jenkins reported to be the most encourag-
> ing development of its sort during the past two years. Although
> definite figures were not available it was conservatively estimated
> that more than two thousand communists were arrested that day
> in Canton by soldiers and police acting under instructions from
> Chiang Kai-shek and Li Chi-ch'en. The number of casualties inci-
> dent to the action was not given out but it was thought that be-
> tween fifty and one hundred people were killed, most of them
> being members of railway unions who resisted arrest. Mr. Jenkins
> reported that the Government's forces acted with energy and
> skill....[30]

The State Department White Paper on China, published years
later, after the triumph of the Revolution, tells us that

Following the capture of Shanghai in March 1927 [Chiang] carried out a purge of the Communists in Shanghai, and somewhat later conducted a similar one in Canton. These purges involved several hundred thousand deaths.[31]

The imperialists had once again found a "strong man." Chiang went on to consolidate his position, but he faced long years of revolutionary civil war with the Communists.

FOR CHINA, WORLD WAR II BEGAN in 1931 when Japan invaded Manchuria. The local warlord asked Chiang what to do. Chiang, engaged in a "pacification" campaign against the Communist "bandits," replied: "In order to avoid any enlargement of the incident, it is necessary to resolutely maintain the principle of non-resistance."[32] The Communist Party, in contrast, quickly raised the slogan of resistance and began to organize for it. The invasion produced anti-Japanese strikes, rallies, and demonstrations and a nationwide boycott of Japanese goods. In 1932, Japan set up a puppet regime in Manchuria. It also attacked Shanghai.

Chiang's non-resistance policy was unpopular not only among the people, but among many of his own supporters. In 1936, a Kuomintang general and a warlord had Chiang kidnapped and forced him into negotiations with the Communists in which he agreed to cooperate with them in resisting Japanese aggression.

In 1937, Japan began a massive invasion of China, the first step in an attempt to conquer the whole country. Chiang ordered the mobilization of his armies. But he was more interested in preserving his troops for use against the Communists than in fighting the Japanese. He regarded territory liberated and held by the Communists as a threat to his control and placed his own troops along the borders of such territory so they could strike when the opportunity arose. They struck often. Chiang felt that he did not have to go all out against the Japanese: the United States and other Western powers would in a not distant future also be at war with Japan and they would take care of it.

Chiang's reluctance to fight the Japanese continued throughout the war. In September 1944, General Joseph Stilwell, sent by the United States to work with Chiang, reported to the U.S. Army Chief of Staff:

Chiang Kai-shek has no intention of making further efforts to pro-
secute the war.... He believes the war in the Pacific is nearly over,
and that by delaying tactics, he can throw the entire burden on
us.... He himself is the main obstacle to the unification of China
and her cooperation in a real effort against Japan....[33]

AT THE END OF WORLD WAR II, China was theoretically a
"great power," a status conferred by her powerful allies at the
insistence of the United States. But, in fact, she remained what
she had been during the previous hundred years—a feudal,
semi-colonial country.

Landlords and rich peasants, constituting ten percent of the
population, owned 55 to 65 percent of the land. "In Honan...,"
writes Jack Belden, "one might ride a donkey cart past scores of
villages for a whole day and still be on the same family's land."[34]
At the other extreme, hundreds of millions of people had to eke
out a living on minuscule plots. Many Chinese peasants worked
plots consisting of partly their own and partly rented land. A fifth
were tenant farmers, pure and simple.[35]

Rents ran at 50 percent of the crop, though the landlord often
demanded and received more. What was left was hardly
enough to keep the peasant family alive. Land taxes added to
the burden, and on top of them came usurious interest rates
paid to the money-lenders who advanced funds necessary to
pay rents and taxes and to buy things the peasant family could
not produce itself. "The most massive and best-built houses in
the villages and small towns were always the pawnshops,"
writes Belden.[36]

The feudalism was a matter not just of economics, but also of
landlord political power. Landlord power was greatest in the
interior; along the seacoast, it often had to be shared with city
merchants. But, writes Belden:

Even in northern Kiangsu, along the seacoast and not far from
Shanghai, landlords lived like feudal barons in mud castles, surrounded by armed guards and controlling tenants in fifteen or
twenty villages. Such castles acted as a trading center for tenants
who were completely at the mercy of the landlord or his bailiffs.
Not only had the tenant to bring 50 per cent of his crops to the
manor, but also his personal and family problems. In Shansi, I
found that landlords often governed all wedding ceremonies and
funerals, so that no one could get married or be buried without the

approval of these feudal lords. The power of the landlords gave them control over village women, especially the wives of their tenants, with whom they could have whatever relations pleased them. Very often, the tenant and his wife acquiesced in these relations out of fear, but if the tenant should protest, he had little chance to make his protest effective. In a village in western Shantung I came across a landlord whose common practice was to make his tenant go out into the fields and work while he took his pleasure of the tenant's wife....The institutions of slave girls, concubinage and forced marriage were also irrevocably tied to the landlord system.[37]

The counterpart of China's feudalism was its semi-colonial status, manifested in both its economic structure and its lack of true political independence. Imperialism, for all its boasting about bringing modern ways to China, had not brought it modern industry. Graham Peck writes:

Modern industry had so far touched only the surface of China, around its outer edges.... Nine out of every ten modern factories were in Shanghai and the rest were in a handful of other coastal or river cities. Taken together, they represented less industrial power than a small Western country like Belgium had.[38]

The pattern was typical for many imperialist-dominated countries: a few foreign enclaves plus general stagnation.

China was also a semi-colony politically. It was free of Japan. The unequal treaties and concessions held by the other imperialist powers had ended during the war. But instead of becoming truly independent, China had become a client state of the United States.

The U.S. ambassador to China was a sort of proconsul. He kept up a steady flow of "advice" to the Kuomintang government. He threw his weight around. Theodore White and Annalee Jacoby recount that "within a few months of [Ambassador Hurley's] arrival all Chungking knew that he had excoriated [Foreign Minister] T.V. Soong in the presence of a handful of Chinese officials."[39] Can one imagine a Chinese ambassador excoriating a U.S. Secretary of State?

The very look of China reflected its client status. Graham Peck writes:

Even the ignorant could see that they were living in an American-influenced time. Former U.S. Army vehicles, uniforms, and arms became most conspicuous all over China. There were American military advisors in the Kuomintang capital—moved back to Nanking in early 1946—while American warships from our naval base at Tsingtao patrolled the Chinese seacoast, and American military planes flew about widely over the interior.[40]

China's semi-colonial status included a form of extraterritoriality. The United States had given up extraterritoriality during the war. But almost immediately after doing so, it wrung an agreement from China removing U.S. military personnel from the jurisdiction of Chinese courts.

The Chiang Kai-shek government was a type found often in U.S. client states—a reactionary dictatorship. Here is a description of the makeup of that government by *U.S. News & World Report:*

> The Kuomintang Party Government of Chiang consists exclusively of landlords, propertied war-lords and generals of one military clique or another, bankers who profit from wartime speculation and professional politicians vying for power.[41]

The secret police of the Chiang government were everywhere. C.P. FitzGerald writes that "the Chinese people groaned under a régime Fascist in every quality except efficiency."[42]

Corruption afflicted the government from top to bottom. White and Jacoby tell about Madame Kung, sister-in-law of Chiang:

> She is a woman with a highly developed money sense. One or two of her financial operations, like her whispered activities in the Shanghai textile market, were normal commercial flyers. But many of her deals, such as her transactions in foreign exchange, made commercial history and involved a manipulation based on facts that only the wife of the Minister of Finance would know.[43]

Warlords often had their own private ways of making money, such as opium running, which Chiang let them pursue so long as they fulfilled his demands for army recruits and rice. An army divisional commander received money for 10,000 men; if his division was below strength and he only had to pay 7,000 or 5,000, he could pocket the difference. Potential army conscripts with money did not have to serve: local officials sold exemptions at standard prices.[44]

The army was not only corrupt, but inhumanly backward, reflecting the inhumanity of the regime and the whole social system. "The attitude of the officer toward the soldier," writes Jack Belden, "was that of landlord toward peasant."

> Officers considered it their privilege and right to beat soldiers. During both the Japanese war and the civil war, I saw soldiers beaten on station platforms with bamboo rods, on highways with automobile crank handles, in rooms with iron bars. I once saw a colonel who had been a... consular official in New York City slap a soldier several times across the face because he couldn't find a pack of cards. When I protested, the colonel said: "That's all these dumb beasts understand."[45]

The army's treatment of the peasant civilian population was no better. The officers requisitioned grain, animals, and carts with little concern for what this meant for the impoverished peasants.

To top it all came the economic effects of the war, in particular the enormous inflation. During the first seven months of 1945, with the inflation still only picking up speed, the price level rose 250 percent.[46] Agricultural laborers, urban workers, government employees, university professors suffered, while grain merchants, speculators, black marketeers, all who were able to engage in "deals," made fabulous profits. Corruption proliferated.

Everything fed the revolution. Only by revolution could China's peasants get land, get out from under landlord control, and get rid of the grain merchant, the tax collector, and the voracious Kuomintang army. Only by revolution could China's miserably poor workers—farm laborers, urban workers in the foreign enterprises—free themselves from exploitation. Without revolution, China would have remained in the grip of imperialism, a semi-colony, dominated and exploited by the United States. The rottenness of the Chiang regime helped bring on the revolution. The inflation was the last straw. It broadened the opposition, causing the middle class and even many from the upper class to repudiate Chiang.

By the end of World War II, a mighty revolutionary force had built up in China. This force did not just arise by itself: conscious action and organization by the Communist Party helped to build it. But conscious action and organization that wins the support of masses of people is not conspiracy. The fundamental reason for the revolution in China was that China needed revolution. As Graham Peck puts it: "In a society like China's, revolution can be a fundamental and entirely natural fact of life, as hard to slow up as a pregnancy."[47]

EVEN AS WORLD WAR II was ending, the United States was carrying out a clear, massive intervention in China's revolutionary struggle. It was acting to have control of the Japanese-held territory pass to the Kuomintang and not to the Communists.

When Japan surrendered, General Douglas MacArthur, Supreme Commander for the Allied Powers, designated Chiang's forces as the sole agent to receive the surrender of the Japanese in China. Then the United States transported Chiang's forces into the areas where the Japanese troops were located. Some areas the United States occupied for the Kuomintang government with U.S. Marines.

The following quotation from the State Department White Paper on China indicates the scope of the U.S. operation:

> In order to assist the Government in reoccupying Japanese-held areas and opening lines of communication, the United States immediately after V-J Day transported three Nationalist armies by air to key sectors of East and North China, including Shanghai, Nanking and Peiping, and likewise during the ensuing months provided water transport for an additional large number of troops until, according to Department of the Army figures, between 400,000 and 500,000 Chinese soldiers had been moved to new positions.... In order to assist the Government further in maintaining control of certain key areas of North China and in repatriating the Japanese, and at the request of the National Government, over 50,000 United States Marines were landed in North China and occupied Peiping, Tientsin, and the coal mines to the north, together with the essential railroads in the area. With such American assistance, forces of the Generalissimo, who had been designated by SCAP [Supreme Commander for the Allied Powers] as the sole agent to receive the surrender of Japanese forces in China proper, were able to effect the surrender of the great majority of the 1,200,000 Japanese troops stationed there, together with their equipment and stocks of military materiel.[48]

The United States had strange allies in this operation. Jointly guarding railroads against the Chinese Communists were U.S. Marines, Kuomintang soldiers, former puppet collaborators of the Japanese, and the Japanese Army. Now held to be enemies were Chinese villagers who had risked their lives to smuggle to safety American flyers who bailed out over China.[49]

President Truman has explained the significance of the U.S. action. "It was perfectly clear to us that if we told the Japanese to lay down their arms immediately and march to the seaboard the entire country would be taken over by the Communists."[50] What the United States did prevented an early Communist victory, swung the balance temporarily toward the Kuomintang, and inflicted several additional years of civil war on China.

Besides transporting Chiang's troops and having U.S. Marines occupy key areas and guard railroads vital for the Kuomintang redeployment and military operations, the United States was giving the Chiang government other forms of help. It was providing equipment to build a 39-division army and an 8-and-one-third-group air force, and it was transferring naval vessels. According to the White Paper, the aid eventually reached a total of $2 billion, a huge sum equivalent, during the period it covered, to more than half the total expenditures of the Chinese government.[51]

Why was the U.S. Government intervening in favor of Chiang and against the revolution? Did it believe that the Chiang government was what the Chinese people wanted, what was in their best interest? This cannot be. A number of its own foreign service officers had reported clearly what the Chiang government represented. Here are a few examples:

> The Kuomintang is a congerie of conservative political cliques interested primarily in the preservation of their own power against all outsiders and in jockeying for position among themselves.
>
> John S. Service

> The governmental and military structure is being permeated and demoralized from top to bottom by corruption, unprecedented in scale and openness.
>
> Service

> The Kuomintang and Chiang Kai-shek recognize that the Communists, with the popular support which they enjoy and their reputation for administrative reform and honesty, represent a challenge to the Central Government and its spoils system. The Generalissimo cannot admit the seemingly innocent demands of the Communists that their party be legalized and democratic processes be put into practice. To do so would probably mean the abdication of the Kuomintang....
>
> John Patton Davies

Communist growth since 1937 has been almost geometric in progression.... The reason for this phenomenal vitality and strength is
simple and fundamental. It is mass support, mass participation.
The Communist governments and armies are the first governments and armies in modern Chinese history to have positive and
widespread popular support.

Davies[52]

But for those determining U.S. policy, neither the rottenness
of the Chiang regime nor the desires of the Chinese people
were relevant in the decision whether to intervene or not. The
U.S. policymakers were interested in one thing: defending U.S.
imperialist interests. The decision to support Chiang against the
Communists was practically automatic.

The foreign service officers who sent in the harsh criticisms of
Chiang were also defending imperialism. The main difference
between them and the top policymakers lay in their firsthand
knowledge of China and their greater realism. They were willing, despite their criticisms, to support Chiang so long as there
was any hope for his regime. But because of their firsthand
knowledge, they saw that Chiang was outliving his usefulness.

The same John Patton Davies who reported on the "widespread popular support" of the Communists also wrote:

We should not now abandon Chiang Kai-shek. To do so at this
juncture would be to lose more than we could gain.... But we must
be realistic. We must not indefinitely underwrite a politically
bankrupt regime.[53]

In one crucial respect, the top policymakers also were realistic: They ruled out full-scale intervention with U.S. troops in the
Chinese civil war. As Truman put it, such intervention was "impracticable.... The American people would never stand for such
an undertaking."[54]

There were also other obstacles. China was too big: it could
swallow up enormous amounts of men and resources. How the
Soviets would react was uncertain. So the United States decided—in the words of Truman—"to support the Generalissimo
politically, economically, and, within limits, militarily."[55]

As part of its effort to preserve the Kuomintang government,
the United States pressed Chiang to make reforms. Those recommended by a Mission headed by General Albert C. Wedemeyer are an example. Wedemeyer spoke of the need to do
something about corruption, abuses by the secret police, and

the bad relationship between the army and the civilian population. He even mentioned the need for land reform.[56]

But how is a government dominated by landholders going to carry out a land reform? Why would Chiang want to reform the secret police when he felt that only with a tough secret police could he maintain himself in power? How could you get rid of corruption when those being asked to carry out the job were themselves the most corrupt? How could a people's army be built without changing the whole rotten society?

The proposals for reform went into high-sounding reports, but even those who were arguing for these proposals didn't really expect them to be carried out. They couldn't be carried out. They were in contradiction with the nature of Chinese society and government and required revolution to be carried out.

SEVERAL MONTHS AFTER the end of World War II, the United States sent a more high-powered mission to China, headed by the former Army Chief of Staff, George C. Marshall. The officially stated purpose of the mission was "to bring about the unification of China and, concurrently, effect a cessation of hostilities"[57] between the Kuomintang government and the Communists. To achieve these ends, General Marshall was to mediate impartially between the two sides.

U.S. public relations hype, including a rash of stories about Marshall's probity, tried to mask the true nature of the mission. Actually, U.S. "good offices" could not possibly be impartial; the United States was a party to the dispute, strongly supporting one side. Marshall, regardless of his personal probity, was a representative of the U.S. Government. He might, to promote his position as mediator, try to be impartial on some specific questions. But basically, he was working to attain United States policy goals, which meant strengthening the Kuomintang and weakening the Communists.

Within the U.S. Government, the partiality was clear from the beginning. As the instructions to Marshall were being drawn up, the question arose whether the U.S. transport of Kuomintang troops to north China and Manchuria would interfere with his ability to mediate the negotiations. The instructions, as finally agreed upon, gave Marshall discretion to determine when Kuomintang troops might be moved. Dean Acheson writes that Marshall discussed the problem with Truman and Secretary of State

Byrnes. "He favored supporting the Generalissimo and moving the troops. The President and Secretary agreed."[58]

Even while Marshall was mediating between the Kuomintang and the Communists he was approving the movement of troops to reestablish Chiang's hold on China. Zhou Enlai, the chief Communist negotiator, later stated that the United States not only transported Chiang's troops to Manchuria and north and central China before a cease-fire agreement was reached, but that afterward, in violation of the agreement, it transported nine Kuomintang armies to various parts of China.[59]

There was also the military and economic aid that the United States was providing Chiang. Even the White Paper noted that "General Marshall was being placed in the untenable position of mediating on the one hand between the two Chinese groups while on the other the United States Government was continuing to supply arms and ammunition to one of the two groups, namely, the National Government." The State Department felt it necessary to make this admission because it was defending the administration against the charge that it had not done enough for Chiang's government.[60]

Marshall's mediation and the resulting truce served to gain time to complete the arming and training of the divisions the United States was equipping and to carry forward their redeployment. At the beginning of 1946 when the mediation began, the divisions were neither fully trained and supplied nor suitably deployed, so that the Kuomintang was not yet prepared for all-out civil war. The preparedness advanced greatly under cover of the mediation.

While building up the Kuomintang for civil war, the United States hoped that the mediation might result in a satisfactory solution without war. A satisfactory solution would be a coalition government with the Communists occupying a position of little power and a general political and economic situation in which the Kuomintang could fight the Communists successfully by political means.

In working for this sort of solution, Marshall tried to get the reactionary Chiang regime to give itself a liberal veneer. He hoped, says the White Paper, for the "organization of a patriotic liberal group under the indirect sponsorship of the Generalissimo." Such a group would "exercise a leavening influence upon the absolutist control wielded by the reactionaries and the militarists."[61]

Marshall's purpose was severalfold: to reduce the reactionary rigidity of the regime and make it easier to negotiate a deal with the Communists; to improve the regime's international image; and, finally, by making the regime appear more liberal and democratic, to remove a strong argument for the revolution and undercut the appeal of the Communists. With a negotiated end to the civil war and a regime that remained firmly under Chiang's control but had a liberal veneer and included Communists, the United States could pour in economic aid. The improvement in the economic situation would help dampen the fires of revolution and bring the problem of the Communists under control.

But this strategy didn't work. Marshall explained: "There is a dominant group of [Kuomintang] reactionaries who have been opposed, in my opinion, to almost every effort I have made to influence the formation of a genuine coalition government." A Political Consultation Conference, called at Marshall's urging, arrived at various agreements on liberalization. "However," says Marshall, "irreconcilable groups within the Kuomintang... evidently had no real intention of implementing them."[62] The Kuomintang simply did not want to give up its dictatorship. Dean Acheson explains why: "More and more the Kuomintang evinced the conviction that pursuit of a united and democratic China meant that they would lose all."[63]

Truman writes of the position of the Kuomintang and the Communists in the negotiations:

> In the early stages the Communist representatives appeared more tractable to Marshall than the leaders of the Central Government.... And it was also his impression that the Communists were more ready to take their chances in the struggle conducted in the political arena than were the Nationalists. The Nationalists, so it seemed to Marshall, appeared to be determined to pursue a policy of force....[64]

What the Nationalists did was try to satisfy Marshall with a few democratic trimmings, while continuing their long-standing policy of rule by terror. The regime suppressed newspapers and periodicals, banned books, put out police dragnets to haul in opponents, and imprisoned not just Communists, but also liberals and democrats. In a letter to Chiang in August 1946, Truman referred to "evidence of the increasing trend to suppress the expression of liberal views" and added that "the assassinations of distinguished Chinese liberals at Kunming recently have not been ignored" in the United States.[65]

During the course of Marshall's mediation, the military balance between the Kuomintang and the Communists kept shifting in favor of the former as a result of the arms, training, and help with redeployment provided by the United States. After a while, Kuomintang forces began to attack the Communists, using periods of truce as convenient pauses in which to receive supplies, be transported to new positions, and prepare new attacks. The White Paper states that Marshall "often felt that the National Government had desired American mediation as a shield for its military campaigns...."[66] It does not say that Marshall ever did anything to prevent U.S. mediation from being used this way.

In fact, while Marshall and other U.S. officials voiced many complaints about the Chiang regime, they never backed their complaints with action. If Marshall and Truman were really eager for a negotiated settlement and thought that the Kuomintang was determined on a policy of force, why didn't they hold back on U.S. military aid to dampen the Kuomintang's belligerence? Arming the side that is looking for a fight is not the way to achieve a peaceful solution to a quarrel.

In mid-1946, Chiang launched an all-out offensive against the Communists, a civil war on a scale unprecedented in China. Chiang boasted that "the Communist problem can be settled by military means within five months."[67] His armies, equipped by the United States, enjoyed a monopoly of heavy weapons and airpower, along with great numerical superiority. U.S. experts advised them. The U.S. Army and Navy helped with troop transport.

The continuation of U.S. aid despite Chiang's offensive gave the final blow to the dying mediation process. The Communist Party issued a statement on July 7, calling on the United States to end its "armed intervention" in China's internal affairs, to stop fostering civil war, to stop sending military supplies and advisors, and to withdraw all its military forces immediately.

O. Edmund Clubb, former U.S. consul general in Beijing, writes:

> The coffin-lid was nailed down on American mediation on August 30 when the United States sold to the National Government, at bargain prices, war surplus with a procurement value of $900

million. Although stocked originally for the use of the American armed forces, the supplies were designated as "civilian-type." General Marshall went to some pains to explain to Zhou En-lai that the supplies did not include combat material but (in the words of the *China White Paper*) "consisted of machinery, motor vehicles, communications equipment, rations, medical supplies and various other items which would be of considerable value in the rehabilitation of the Chinese economy." The United States Government could hardly expect the Chinese Communists to rest assured, however, that the Nationalists would not use military trucks and communications equipment in the war that was being fought.[68]

At the end of the year, Marshall went home. Truman issued a statement asserting that "we are pledged not to interfere in the internal affairs of China."[69] But the interference continued. Although Truman, under pressure from public opinion, withdrew the bulk of the U.S. military forces, a U.S. Military Advisory Group remained.

FOR MONTHS AFTER THEY STARTED their offensive, Chiang's armies seemed to do well, making big territorial gains. But the gains were illusory. The Kuomintang armies were suffering big losses in personnel, while the Communist forces were expanding by converting prisoners of war to their cause. Furthermore, Chiang's armies were overextending themselves, making themselves dependent on long communications lines they could not protect without weakening their fighting forces. By the spring of 1947, the Kuomintang offensive had ended, and by the summer, the Communists had moved to the offensive and begun to win victory after victory.

Much of the Kuomintang's U.S. equipment ended up with the Communists. A U.S. military attaché estimated after the fall of Manchuria that "at least 75 per cent exclusive of ammunition has been captured by the Communists."[70]

Massive defections took place. Belden writes:

To beat the Communists, Chiang had to attack them, but every time he did so, his troops became infected with the revolutionary mood of the 8th Route [Communist] soldiers.[71]

Officers, including generals, went over. One general, who was also governor of Shandong province, got on the radio after being captured and urged the Shandong troops to mutiny or surrender en masse. Three division commanders in other areas surrendered without fighting.

On the civilian front, the Kuomintang's position was also disintegrating. In December 1946, a general strike paralyzed Shanghai. Later that month, two U.S. Marines raped a young woman at Beijing University, and a student strike against U.S. imperialism flared across China. According to a dispatch of the U.S. consul general at Beijing, the students carried banners with the slogan, "Drive all American armed forces out of China."[72] In May 1947, students began another wave of strikes and demonstrations, demanding an end to the civil war and action to improve economic conditions. In many cities, crowds angered by a big increase in the price of rice broke into rice shops. More and more of even the minority that had supported Chiang turned against him. By early 1948, the Kuomintang itself was beginning to come apart.[73]

As the Kuomintang regime moved into its final months, U.S. officials both in Washington and China anxiously kept tabs on the situation. "Present regime has lost confidence of people," said a telegram by Ambassador Stuart to the Secretary of State on October 22, 1948. But what should the United States do? "We cannot give will to fight and desire [to] become good soldiers," said a telegram from the Acting Secretary of State to the Ambassador, two weeks later.[74] The United States could increase its aid. But there were "weighty considerations" against this, said a State Department Policy Statement.

> Our own resources are limited; to underwrite unreservedly the National Government would commit our resources to an unpredictable but doubtless extremely high degree in a struggle, the outcome of which would still be dubious, to the detriment of programs in more vital areas in which it is probable that our resources could be decisive.[75]

The United States considered the possibility of an alternative to the Chiang regime. "But as yet," said the Policy Statement,

> non-Communist forces of opposition to the National Government have not coalesced under leadership which would give reasonable promise of being determined and able to marshal the remaining strength of Nationalist China effectively against the Communist threat. Until this occurs, to aid and encourage any opposition movements would be to weaken the National Government and to

hasten its disintegration without assurance that a more effective instrument would take its place.[76]

In contradistinction to the policy when Marshall's Mission was in China, the United States was now against the establishment of a coalition government. To quote the Policy Statement:

A coalition government including the Communists would...be un-suitable as an instrument for achieving American objectives in China. The Communists have now increased their strength to a point where they would probably insist upon decisive participation in the executive branch of the government rather than mere recognition as a legal party.[77]

The United States was now also, therefore, against mediation of the Chinese conflict. There were reports of "Soviet overtures...looking toward Soviet or joint Soviet-U.S. mediation...." Should such overtures be made formally and be viewed favorably by "important groups in the war-weary Chinese Government," the United States "would be placed in a difficult position." It did not want mediation, yet "open opposition to the move would place upon the U.S., particularly in the eyes of the Chinese people, a large measure of onus for continuing hostilities."[78]

So the Revolution moved on. Alternately flaring and smoldering for over one hundred years, it had gathered irresistible sweep and power. In 1949, it triumphed.

THE UNITED STATES CONTINUED to intervene against the Chinese Revolution even after its triumph on the mainland. The U.S. Navy evacuated Chiang and his followers to Taiwan, where the United States continued to support him.

On Taiwan, also, Kuomintang rule was dictatorial and bloody. The White Paper contains a memorandum by U.S. Ambassador Leighton Stuart which tells of an outbreak of "spontaneous protest and unorganized riots" in February 1947 and the government's reaction:

Martial law was invoked.... Armed military patrols began to appear in the city [Taipei], firing at random wherever they went.... Beginning March 9, there was widespread and indiscriminate killing. Soldiers were seen bayonetting coolies without apparent provocation.... Looting began wherever the soldiers saw something desirable. In the Manka area,...a general sacking by soldiers took place on March 10; many shopkeepers are believed to have been

shot.... A reliable estimate was made that about 700 students had
been seized in Taipei by March 13.... Fifty are reported to have
been killed at Matsuyama and thirty at Kokuto (suburbs of Taipei)
on the night of March 9.... After three days in Taipei streets, government forces began to push out into suburban and rural areas.
Mounted machine gun patrols were observed along the highroads
15 to 20 miles from Taipei shooting at random in village streets in
what appeared to be an effort to break any spirit of resistance....
Foreigners saw bodies in the streets of Tamsui.... The continuing
presence of fresh bodies in Keelung Harbor and other evidence
indicate that the elimination of the informed opposition is continuing.[79]

In the spring of 1950, Communist forces concentrated for an
assault on Taiwan. According to O. Edmund Clubb, "it was the
current estimate of the American government that the Nationalist regime's days were numbered."[80] But then, upon the outbreak of the Korean War, Truman declared that he had "ordered the Seventh Fleet to prevent any attack upon Formosa
[Taiwan]."[81] Clubb comments that "as a result the rump
Nationalist regime, which previously had been hardly breathing,
acquired a new lease on life."[82]

The Korean War sharpened the hostility between the United
States and the new People's Republic of China and several
times, both during the war and afterward, the danger arose of a
full-scale U.S.-Chinese conflict. "General MacArthur," writes
Truman, "repeatedly advised the Joint Chiefs of Staff that in his
opinion the war should be expanded by attacks on airfields in
Manchuria, by a blockade of the China coast, and by the utiliza-
tion of the Formosa Chinese."[83]

When Eisenhower became president, he did not reject Mac-
Arthur's proposals, but rather considered them as a possible
way to break the stalemate in the war. He writes:

In the light of my unwillingness to accept the status quo, several
other moves were considered in the event that the Chinese Communists refused to accede to an armistice in a reasonable time....
First, it was obvious that if we were to go over to a major offensive,
the war would have to be expanded outside of Korea—with strikes
against the supporting Chinese airfields in Manchuria, a blockade
of the Chinese coast, and similar measures.... To keep the attack
from becoming overly costly, it was clear that we would have to
use atomic weapons. This necessity was suggested to me by
General MacArthur....[84]

Eisenhower used the threat of expanding the war and employing atomic weapons as a means of coercion at the truce negotiations.

> One possibility was to let the Communist authorities understand that, in the absence of satisfactory progress, we intended to move decisively without inhibition in our use of weapons, and would no longer be responsible for confining hostilities to the Korean peninsula.... In India and in the Formosa Straits area, and at the truce negotiations at Panmunjom, we dropped the word, discreetly, of our intention. We felt quite sure it would reach Soviet and Chinese Communist ears.[85]

Twice after the Korean War had ended, crises erupted over the offshore Quemoy and Matsu islands, which had remained in Kuomintang hands when the mainland fell. The Quemoys blocked the port of Amoy only two miles away; the Matsus blocked Foochow ten miles away. Chiang used the islands to harass the Communists—to harry shipping, to shell the mainland, to mount commando raids. Chiang also saw the islands as useful symbols of his promise to return to the mainland and as stepping-stones for invasion. He could not, of course, even dream of invasion by his own forces alone, but he hoped for a U.S.-Chinese war that would enable him to return.

The first crisis occurred in 1954-1955. In his 1954 New Year's message, Chiang had pledged an attack on the mainland "in the not distant future;" his Easter message had called for a "holy war." In August, the South Korean dictator, Syngman Rhee, speaking before a joint session of the U.S. Congress, proposed that the United States join him and Chiang in a war on China. "As if in reply," writes Eisenhower, Zhou Enlai called two weeks later for "the liberation of Formosa." On September 3, Communist artillery batteries near Amoy began shelling Quemoy.[86]

The administration considered how to respond. Many in the United States spoke against flirting with war over insignificant little islands so close to China. British Foreign Minister Anthony Eden "had no enthusiasm," says Eisenhower, "for risking a war over Quemoy and Matsu." But the United States would not give up the idea of defending the islands and the crisis dragged on.[87]

When the Communists seized Ichiang, another offshore island, on January 10, 1955, Eisenhower decided that "the time had come to draw the line." In a special message to Congress he asked for authority to "protect Formosa and the Pescadores and related positions, if necessary, in defense of the principal islands." Zhou Enlai called it a "war message."[88]

Churchill wrote Eisenhower that he did not see why the United States should hold "bridgeheads for a Nationalist invasion of Communist China" at the risk of a world war. But Eisenhower wrote him explaining "why we would not abandon the offshore islands.... At all costs, I said: '... We must not lose Chiang's army and we must maintain its strength, efficiency and morale.'" Giving up Quemoy and Matsu "would so undermine the morale and loyalty of the non-Communist forces on Formosa that they could not be counted on."[89]

At a White House meeting, Secretary of State John Foster Dulles said, "If we defend Quemoy and Matsu we'll have to use atomic weapons. They alone will be effective against the mainland airfields." He added that "before this problem is solved, I believe there is at least an even chance that the United States will have to go to war." To this, says Eisenhower, "I merely observed that if this proved to be true it would certainly be recognized that the war would not be of our seeking." Several days later, a reporter asked him whether the United States would use tactical atomic weapons in a general war in Asia. "Against a strictly military target, I replied, the answer would be 'yes.' I hoped this answer would have some effect in persuading the Chinese Communists of the strength of our determination."[90]

After continuing for eight months, the crisis, in Eisenhower's words, "began to dissolve." By April 23, the United States received reports that Zhou Enlai was saying that "China had no intention of going to war with the United States, and that it was ready to negotiate with us over Formosa and the Far East." On April 26, Dulles declared that the United States was "willing to talk with the Chinese Communists about a cease fire." By May 22, newspapers were reporting that an informal cease fire was in effect.[91]

Some months later, in an interview with *Life* magazine, Dulles expounded his policy of confrontation:

> You have to take chances for peace, just as you must take chances in war. Some say we were brought to the verge of war. Of course we were brought to the verge of war. The ability to get to the verge without getting into war is the necessary art. If you cannot master it, you inevitably get into war.... We walked to the brink and we looked it in the face. We took strong action.[92]

In 1958, a new crisis erupted over Quemoy and Matsu and Dulles got another chance to practice brinkmanship.   The Nationalists had been concentrating increasing troop strength on Quemoy and the United States had stationed twenty military advisors there.   The chief political officer of the Nationalist command on Quemoy had stated in 1957 that the island was being changed from a defense outpost to a forward command post for offensive operations.   Hostile incursions from Quemoy and Matsu—commando raids, the landing of subversive agents, flights to drop propaganda leaflets—had become, said Zhou Enlai, "more unbridled."   In August 1958, mainland batteries again began to shell Quemoy.[93]

The United States intervened at once. A group of U.S. military leaders arrived in Formosa.   U.S. forces in the area went on a "readiness alert," prepared for "immediate operations." Washington announced that the aircraft carrier *Essex* and four destroyers from the Sixth Fleet in the Mediterranean were en route to reinforce the Seventh Fleet. The Seventh Fleet began to escort supply convoys to Quemoy.

A memorandum prepared by the Pentagon, the CIA, and the State Department that Eisenhower says he and Dulles "studied, edited, and agreed on," presents U.S. policy. The memorandum ascribed earth-shaking significance to Quemoy.   "If Quemoy were lost" a long chain of disasters would follow.   Formosa would probably go too.   This would "jeopardize the anti-Communist barrier...in the Western Pacific; e.g., Japan, Republic of Korea, Republic of China, Republic of the Philippines, Thailand and Vietnam.   Other governments in Southeast Asia such as those of Indonesia, Malaya, Cambodia, Laos and Burma would probably come fully under Communist influence.... Japan with its great industrial potential would probably fall within the Sino-Soviet orbit.... The consequences in the Far East would be even more far-reaching and catastrophic than those which followed when the United States allowed the Chinese mainland to be taken over by the Chinese Communists...."[94]

The memorandum also asserts that "saving" Quemoy might require the use of nuclear weapons. "There would be a strong popular revulsion against the U.S...." But "if relatively small detonations were used ...and if the matter were quickly closed, the revulsion might not be long-lived or entail consequences as far-reaching and permanent" as those that would flow from the loss of Quemoy. Still, "it is not certain... that the operation could be thus limited in scope or time, and the risk of a more extensive use of nuclear weapons, and even a risk of general war, would have to be accepted."[95]

But throughout the world, opposition arose to running the risk of nuclear war over a couple of minute islands in China's coastal waters. British Prime Minister Harold Macmillan, in a letter to Dulles, quoted Churchill's statement during the 1954-1955 crisis: "A war to keep the coastal islands for Chiang would not be defensible" in Britain.[96] The State Department received thousands of letters on the crisis, eighty percent of them critical.[97] Former Secretary of State Dean Acheson spoke out:

> We seem to be drifting, either dazed or indifferent, toward war with China, a war without friends or allies, and over issues which the administration has not presented to the people, and which are not worth a single American life.[98]

The pressure on the administration had its effect. When Zhou Enlai proposed that U.S.-Chinese ambassadorial talks in Warsaw be resumed—they had begun in 1955 but were suspended on June 30, 1958—the United States promptly accepted. Then at a press conference on September 30, Dulles shifted position on China. If there were a cease fire, he said, "it would be foolish" to keep large forces on the offshore islands. Asked about the return of the Nationalist Chinese to the mainland, he replied, "I don't think that just by their own steam they are going to get there" and added that "there is no commitment of any kind" by the United States to help them do so. Within days, the People's Republic announced a partial cease fire. Soon Dulles visited Chiang and the two issued a communique with the following key point: "The principal means" for the Nationalist government to achieve its "sacred mission," the "restoration of freedom" to the mainland, is the "implementation of Dr. Sun Yatsen's three people's principles (nationalism, democracy, and social well-being) and not the use of force...."[99] The crisis ended.

BESIDES SUPPORTING CHIANG'S REGIME on Taiwan, the United States used the CIA against the new China. The CIA's activities were varied. It supported anti-Communist armies, tried to develop "resistance movements," carried out commando raids, and engaged in propaganda and spying.

Ralph McGehee, who spent twenty-five years with the CIA, is one of several who tell of a CIA-supported Kuomintang army in

Burma. The army fled into Burma from Yunnan when the Revolution triumphed in 1949. The CIA supported it with "massive supply operations" by air. In 1951 this army invaded Yunnan. The CIA predicted that the Yunnan peasants would rise to support it, but they didn't and Mao's forces quickly drove the invaders out. The CIA reinforced the army with troops from Taiwan and, in 1952, it invaded again. But again it got no peasant support and suffered quick defeat.[100]

In 1959, several thousand troops and other followers of Tibet's Dalai Lama escaped to India after they had failed in an uprising against the revolutionary government. Victor Marchetti, a former CIA official and John D. Marks, a former State Department intelligence expert, write that "special [CIA] ops officers began secretly training and reequipping the Dalai Lama's troops—fearsome Khamba horsemen—in preparation for eventual clandestine forays into Tibet.... Although the CIA officers led their Tibetan trainees to believe that they were being readied for the reconquering of their homeland, even within the agency few saw any real chance that this could happen." The Dalai Lama's troops did make guerrilla raids into Tibet, "supported and covered by 'private' planes of the Civil Air Transport complex, a CIA proprietary...."[101]

The CIA also tried during the 1950's to develop "resistance movements" inside China, but it got nowhere. Along with other U.S. intelligence agencies, it ringed China with listening posts and sent out spy planes to collect information.[102]

Marchetti and Marks tell of some CIA propaganda operations against China in 1967:

> The agency took its balloons out of storage, shipping them to a secret base on Taiwan. There they were loaded with a variety of carefully prepared propaganda materials—leaflets, pamphlets, newspapers—and, when the winds were right, launched to float over the mainland provinces due west of the island.... [Then] a decision was...made to install on Taiwan a pair of clandestine radio transmitters which would broadcast propaganda—and disinformation—of the same nature as that disseminated by the balloon drops.[103]

THE UNITED STATES MAINTAINED its hostility against China till the end of the 1960s. For twenty years, it refused to recognize the People's Republic and used its diplomatic power to maintain the fiction at the U.N. that the government in Taiwan represented China.

The hostility began to melt only in 1969 when the newly elected Richard Nixon and his National Security Advisor Henry Kissinger decided that the United States might be able to draw benefit from the rift between China and the Soviet Union. Kissinger, as he mentions in his memoirs, had written in 1961 of "the possibility of a rift" and argued that if it occurred, "we should take advantage of it."[104] Nixon, according to Kissinger, saw in an opening to China an opportunity to "squeeze the Soviet Union into short-term help" in ending the Vietnam War on advantageous terms.

For many months, the United States and China exchanged messages which indicated ever more explicitly, says Kissinger, "a willingness to bring about a fundamental change in our relationship."[105] Talks followed. Kissinger visited China in 1971 to negotiate the change with the Chinese leaders. In 1972, Nixon visited China to put the final touches on the negotiations and extract the maximum political benefit from the affair.

The media immediately signalled to the people of the United States that China was no longer the menace of earlier years. As Kissinger writes, the banquets in China, "televised live on the morning shows in America, performed a deadly serious purpose. They communicated rapidly and dramatically to the peoples of both countries that a new relationship was being forged."[106]

Kissinger has given his assessment of the possible future of U.S.-Chinese ties.

> For our part, we did not have any illusions about the permanence of the new relationship. Peking and Washington were entering a marriage of convenience.... Once China becomes strong enough to stand alone, it might discard us. A little later it might even turn against us, if its perception of its interests requires it.... But whatever China's long-term policy, our medium-term interest was to cooperate....[107]

3. Cuba

José Martí and Antonio Maceo, the leaders of Cuba's struggle for independence from Spain, understood the danger that U.S. domination might replace Spanish domination. Arguing against depending on U.S. help in the fight against Spain, Martí asked, "Once the United States is in Cuba, who will get it out?"[1] Similarly, Maceo asked, "Why do we need and of what advantage to us is foreign intervention and foreign meddling?"[2] But, alas, what Martí and Maceo feared came to pass. In 1898, the United States intervened militarily in Cuba's revolutionary war against Spain, ended the revolution with a series of counterrevolutionary measures, and frustrated Cuba's attainment of true independence.

Among the first counterrevolutionary measures was to disarm the Cuban army. Since this army constituted the only conceivable military threat to U.S. control of Cuba, the United States wanted to get rid of it as soon as possible. This was not just a theoretical consideration—in the Philippines, the rebel forces that had fought against Spain were mounting an uprising against U.S. occupation and the authorities in Washington were nervous about the possibility of a similar uprising in Cuba. The United States offered $3 million to help get the Cuban army demobilized; each soldier would get $75 on turning in his rifle. In his book, *The United States in Cuba, 1898-1902,* David F. Healy calls the demobilization of the Cuban army "a major victory" for the U.S. military government.[3]

Another counterrevolutionary measure was to force Cuba to accept the Platt Amendment both in its constitution and in a treaty with the United States. This amendment made a sham of Cuban independence. Here are two key clauses:

> That the government of Cuba consents that the United States may exercise the right to intervene for the preservation of Cuban independence, [and] the maintenance of a government adequate for the protection of life, property, and individual liberty....
>
> That to enable the United States to maintain the independence of Cuba, and to protect the people thereof, as well as for its own defense, the government of Cuba will sell or lease to the United States land necessary for coaling or naval stations at certain specified points....[4]

Senator Platt had attached these and other similar provisions as an amendment to an appropriations bill. The amendment was a means of coercing Cuba: It authorized the President to end the military occupation only when a Cuban government had been established under a constitution that included its provisions.

When the people of Cuba learned about the amendment, a storm broke out. In Havana, a torchlight procession delivered a petition of protest to the U.S. Military Governor, Leonard Wood, while in other cities and towns throughout the island, public meetings poured out protest messages. But the United States insisted. Secretary of War Elihu Root wrote Wood that the delegates to the constitutional convention should understand that "they cannot escape their responsibility by a refusal to act" because then the United States would simply convene another convention.[5]

The United States also began early to lay the basis for dominating Cuba economically. It used its power to get Cuba to agree in 1902 to a Reciprocal Trade Agreement, by which each side granted imports from the other favorable tariff treatment. On the surface, this agreement sounds innocent, a measure designed to promote increased trade and closer relations.

But even if the concessions granted by the United States had been equal to those granted by Cuba, which they were not, the agreement involved more than increased trade. It was the entering wedge for the mechanism which produced a structural deformation of the Cuban economy. With Cuban sugar given easy access to the United States, U.S. companies began to take over a large proportion of Cuba's best land, converting it to the production of sugar cane. At the same time the unimpeded flow of manufactured goods from the advanced, efficient industries of the United States choked off the growth of manufacturing in underdeveloped Cuba. By concentrating Cuban production and exports on sugar and preventing Cuba from developing its own range of diversified manufacturing industries, the U.S. corporations turned the whole Cuban economy into little more than a sugar plantation for the United States.

Companies like the Cuban-American Sugar Co. and the United Fruit Co. made big investments in sugar lands and mills. Bethlehem Steel invested in mining. Speyer and Co. of New York made large loans. Between 1896 and 1911, U.S. investments in Cuba leaped from $50 million to $205 million.[6]

CONSCIOUS OF ITS LARGE and growing interests in Cuba, the United States kept the nominally independent country on a short tether. In the 15 years following the end in 1902 of the original U.S. occupation, the United States intervened militarily three times.

The first time was in 1906. The government of President Tomás Estrada Palma had secured his reelection by engaging in widespread fraud and violence, and the opposition, in answer, had mounted an insurrection. The American consul in Havana appealed to Washington for intervention. Estrada Palma, he cabled, wanted him to ask President Theodore Roosevelt to send two vessels. "They must come at once.... The government is unable to protect life and property."[7] Roosevelt was reluctant to intervene militarily; his Secretary of State, Elihu Root, was just completing a tour of South America in an attempt to allay suspicions of U.S. policy. So he sent Secretary of War William Taft and Assistant Secretary of State Robert Bacon to try to get the Cubans to compose their differences. Taft gives his view of the insurrection in one of his reports. The idea that

> the present insurrectionary force...be treated as a government *de facto* makes me shiver at the consequences. It is not a government with any of its characteristics, but only an undisciplined horde of men under partisan leaders. The movement is large and formidable and commands the sympathy of the majority of the people of Cuba, but they are the poorer classes and the uneducated.[8]

Roosevelt soon found that he did have to send troops. The United States stationed two thousand Marines near Havana and later 5,600 more men in various other parts of Cuba. Taft and Bacon took over from Estrada Palma, setting up a provisional government under themselves. Their most pressing task was to disarm and disband the insurrectionaries.

Washington soon replaced Taft with Charles E. Magoon, a former governor of the Panama Canal Zone. Magoon's regime distinguished itself by setting a new high in corruption: the Cuban historian, Julio Le Riverend, states that the cost of a kilometer of road was seven times greater under him than under Estrada Palma.[9] The U.S. military occupation lasted from 1906 to 1909.

The next military intervention came in 1912 on the occasion of an uprising by a political party of black Cubans, the *Partido Independiente de Color*. Miserable as was the condition of most Cubans, black Cubans suffered even more than average. The *Partido Independiente de Color* had a broad program calling not only for the elimination of racial discrimination, but also for the 8-hour day, free obligatory education, and the abolition of the death penalty. But neither the misery of the black Cubans nor the progressive nature of their program was what U.S. officials saw when the uprising erupted. The State Department's minister in Havana, A.M. Beaupré, reported that "the negroes now in revolt are of a very ignorant class, and, although it may or may not be the intention of their leaders to attack foreigners and destroy their property, it would at any time require only a well-conceived appeal to their prejudices or cupidity to precipitate serious disorders."[10] Over the repeated protests of the Cuban government, the United States sent warships to the Guantánamo naval base it had established on the basis of the Platt Amendment as well as to Santiago, Nipe Bay, and Havana. U.S. Marines took charge of the city of Guantánamo, the copper mines at El Cobre, and a number of sugar mills in Oriente. When, in a few weeks, the Cuban government got the upper hand over the rebels and the uprising collapsed, the United States withdrew its forces.

The third military intervention came in 1917, again as in 1906 on the occasion of an insurrection precipitated by an election dispute. In 1916, Cuban president Mario Menocal was running for reelection. Menocal had formerly been the principal Cuban agent for the Cuban-American Sugar Co. He was popular with the U.S. Government, but in Cuba striking workers—smarting under his virtually dictatorial rule—called him "the Kaiser." When his government announced his reelection, the opposition Liberals appealed to the Cuban Supreme Court, claiming that election boxes had been opened, returns falsified, and Liberals sometimes barred from voting by armed force. The Court sustained the claims. Unconvinced that new elections after the Court's decision would be more honest, the Liberals took to arms. Shortly after the insurrection broke out, the United States declared publicly:

> The armed revolt against the Constitutional Government of Cuba is considered by the Government of the United States as a lawless and unconstitutional act and will not be countenanced.
>
> The leaders of the revolt will be held responsible for injury to foreign nationals and for destruction of foreign property.[11]

U.S. warships blockaded various Cuban ports. Marines landed at Santiago, taking over the city from Liberal forces. Other troops occupied Guantánamo, Manzanillo, and Nuevitas. Within a few months, the insurrection ended and Menocal began his second term. The Marines, with Menocal's agreement, stayed on, serving as guards for U.S. business property and strike preventers. It was not till January 1922 that they finally left.[12]

IN THE EARLY 1920S, a new revolutionary tide began to flow, much deeper and stronger than those of 1906, 1912, and 1917. U.S. economic penetration had accelerated after 1910 and by the end of the decade, Cuba's economy was dominated by U.S. finance capital and dependent on one crop—sugar. National City Bank had moved in in 1915, its business revolving mainly around sugar. The sugar business had done fantastically well during the war and for a while afterward. The price of sugar reached 22 cents a pound in May 1920. But in June it began to plummet and by the end of the year stood at 3 cents a pound. A bank panic followed—a run by depositors trying to withdraw money which the banks were unable to provide. Despite the government's declaration of a debt moratorium, most Cuban banks failed, leaving the field to U.S. and other foreign banks. Many other businesses failed, while those that remained slashed wages. Cuba had already seen one wave of strikes, set off by the soaring cost of living, in 1918-1919. Now a new wave got under way.

The weakness of Cuba's dependent, one-crop economy made itself felt. The rest of the world recovered from the 1920-1921 downturn and went on to reach new economic highs. Cuba's recuperation was only partial. Years before the Great

Depression, while other countries were enjoying postwar prosperity, the Cuban economy was already bogged down.

The graphic demonstration of what it means to have a dependent economy awakened a new round of anti-imperialist sentiment. The horrible conditions faced by workers and the successive waves of strikes raised the militancy of the working class and helped spread revolutionary sentiments among the students. The Russian Revolution inspired many Cubans. In 1925, a group headed by Julio Antonio Mella founded the Cuban Communist Party.

The unrest led to talk in U.S. and Cuban business circles of the need for a "firm hand" to govern Cuba. Gerardo Machado, who became president in 1925, filled the need. He ran demagogically on a program of "water, roads, and schools," and spoke out against the Platt Amendment. But he was a creature of the U.S. corporations. He had been a director of the Compañía Cubana de Electricidad, a subsidiary of Electric Bond and Share. A month before he assumed office, he took a trip to the United States to explain to bankers and businessmen what he stood for. In a speech at the Bankers Club in New York, he "assured" the audience that his administration would "absolutely guarantee" their interests.[13] To a group gathered at the Hotel Astor, he declared that while he was president no strike would last 24 hours.[14]

Machado soon began to repress opposition and Mella dubbed him a "tropical Mussolini." Thugs beat up those expressing ideas that Machado didn't like. The police arrested Mella, who went on a hunger strike in protest and then, after popular pressure had forced Machado to free him, left for exile in Mexico. Newspaper editors found they needed long "vacations" abroad. Labor leaders and Communists disappeared mysteriously.

In 1928, Mella published in Mexico a *Manifesto* of his party naming some of the people assassinated by the "Butcher Machado." Following are three examples:

Enrique Varona, Organizing Secretary of the Cuban Sugar Industry, assassinated in the city of Morón, September 19, 1925.

Alfredo López, Secretary General of the Workers Federation of Havana, assassinated after mysteriously disappearing July 20, 1926.

Tomás Grant, leader of the railroad workers of Camaguey, assassinated August 4, 1926.[15]

A year later, Machado agents shot and killed Mella himself in Mexico City.

Machado had promised that he would not seek reelection, but later decided that he did want to extend his time in office. He planned to do so through a revision of the constitution, for which he knew he needed U.S. approval. On a trip to the United States in 1927, he presented his plan to President Coolidge, explaining that he needed more time "to complete his work" and that it was "absolutely essential that the next election in Cuba should be postponed...." Coolidge told him that the question of revising the constitution was for Cuba to decide.[16] Franklin D. Roosevelt's Secretary of State, Cordell Hull, later stated in an official document that Machado "obtained the tacit approval of the American government" for the legislative act "providing for the proroguing" of his term.[17]

U.S. businessmen also approved. National City, Chase, J.P. Morgan, Electric Bond and Share, and other companies gave luncheons for Machado. Thomas Lamont of J.P. Morgan said he hoped the Cubans would find a way of keeping Machado in power indefinitely.[18]

In 1928, Machado ran an election for delegates to a constitutional convention. Restrictions on who could participate kept the vote down to less than ten percent of the population and the ballots used contained no candidates other than those who favored extending Machado's presidency. The rigged convention set up a six-year presidential term to run until 1935. Then Machado had himself chosen for the new term in an election in which he ran unopposed.

The *prórroga* — as Cubans called it — of the Machado dictatorship plus the onset of the Depression gave new force to the revolutionary tide in Cuba. The Depression hit the fragile Cuban economy like an explosion. The sugar harvest plummeted from 5.2 million (Spanish) tons in 1929 to less than 2 million in 1933. Unemployment, high in the best of times, soared still higher. Wages fell below the levels of 1910. People starved.

Student protest boiled up after Machado's farcical election. Strikes spread as the Depression worsened. In March 1930, Rubén Martínez Villena, a Communist, led a general strike involving 200,000 workers. The government suppressed the strike, forcing Martínez Villena into exile. The students held a gigantic funeral demonstration for one of their leaders killed by the police, and the government shut the University. The press was troublesome, so the government established censorship and shut down newspapers. In five provinces, the regime designated military supervisors to take over government from the civil authorities.

What was the U.S. reaction to the turmoil? Ambassador Harry Guggenheim told in his dispatches how he held "numerous conversations with President Machado, Colonel [Carlos] Mendieta and other members of both the Government and the *Unión Nacionalista*," a grouping of opposition politicians from different establishment parties. His aim was "to encourage cooperation." But the *Unión Nacionalista* was unwilling to consider any compromise that didn't call for a new presidential election within three years and Guggenheim "consistently refused to have anything to do with this proposal."[19]

Guggenheim completely disregarded the people of Cuba and their massive demonstrations and strikes demanding Machado's ouster. He maneuvered with Machado and opposition politicians acceptable to the United States to try to calm things down by some mild changes such as including a few of the opposition politicians in Machado's cabinet. But he was against getting rid of Machado. He notes that Machado "made every reasonable concession to his opponents....[but] refused pointblank...to admit any discussion of the constitutionality of his election." Guggenheim used his "personal good offices" to try to obtain agreement, "but the continued obstinacy of Colonel Mendieta and his associates in demanding Machado's resignation made it impossible to reach an accord."[20]

Guggenheim also disregarded the terror and bloodshed with which Machado maintained himself in power. He noted approvingly "the firmness with which the Government has refused to tolerate any seditious movement...."[21]

The State Department was as strong as Guggenheim in supporting Machado. When Guggenheim, a few months after the failure of his first mediation efforts, talked again of using his good offices, Secretary of State Henry Stimson admonished him: "I am somewhat troubled at the implications involved in your taking any initiative in extending good offices..., particularly in your saying anything to the Opposition which they might take as encouragement at this critical time."[22]

Despite what he and the State Department were doing, Guggenheim complained about "the distortion of news in the press, tending to give the impression that the United States Govern-

ment is upholding the Machado Administration." He cited a
Scripps-Howard story which asserted that "there is dissatisfaction in Congressional circles over the apparent conflict between
first-hand reports from Cuba picturing grave unrest bordering on
revolution and State Department information, which is, in effect,
that everything is about normal."[23]

In 1933, the turmoil surged to a new high. Shootings of students, workers, and others opposed to the regime occurred almost daily. Giant demonstrations took place. Strike followed
strike. Revolutionary bands derailed trains in different parts of
Cuba. One band in Oriente province attacked a Rural Guard
post. In February, Guggenheim reported:

> With the exception of eight bomb explosions on the night of the
> 23rd, the seizure of supplies of arms and ammunition in the build-
> ing formerly occupied by the local Y.M.C.A. and numerous arrests
> of alleged conspirators, the day passed off quietly in Habana.[24]

The only things holding up Machado now were U.S. backing
and the Cuban army, and in the army there were signs of ferment. Franklin D. Roosevelt, as incoming President, named
Sumner Welles ambassador to Cuba to deal with the situation.
Welles' actions constitute a classic example of U.S. maneuvering when a dictator Washington has supported begins to lose
his grip.

Secretary of State Hull's instructions to Welles illuminate the
maneuvering. Hull was concerned about the

> situation developing in the Republic of Cuba which would appear,
> perhaps, to result at some time either in the remote or in the near
> future in open rebellion against a Cuban Government....[25]

What was the essence of his instructions?

> You will...regard as your chief objective the negotiation of a defi-
> nite, detailed, and binding understanding between the present
> Cuban Government and the responsible leaders of the factions
> opposed to it, which will lead to a truce in the present dangerous
> political agitation to continue until such time as national elections
> can be held in Cuba....[26]

The strategy was to prop up Machado until elections could be
held and a new regime satisfactory to the United States installed. The method was to ignore the people and those who were
actually leading them in their revolt and deal with the "responsible" leaders of the "factions" opposed to the regime, in other

words, individuals who though opposed to Machado were satisfactory to the United States.

This strategy depended on whether Machado could be maintained. By mid-May, after a few days in Cuba, Welles knew that
this would be difficult. So he began to modify the strategy, but
carefully. In a cable to Hull, he stated that

> If the present acute bitterness of feeling against the President and
> the members of his Government persists or becomes intensified
> during the coming year it would in all probability be highly de-
> sirable that the present chief executive be replaced at least during
> the electoral period.... I do not feel, however, as a practical ques-
> tion that any attempt should be made to anticipate such a
> change.[27]

Welles had expressed the "hope" that elections would be
held in the fall of 1934, so not "anticipating" the replacement of
Machado meant at least another year of the hated regime. Welles threw his weight against any "premature" replacement of
Machado. A "Revolutionary Junta" in New York proposed the
creation of a new provisional government. Even though the
Junta consisted of "responsible" politicians, Welles rejected the
proposal, because "a solution must be based upon the preservation of the structure of constitutional government...."

On July 17, Welles informed Roosevelt of a plan worked out
through his "good offices" that he said was "strictly within the
limits of constitutional procedure." Since no opposition party
would participate in elections with Machado in office, he would
resign in May 1934. A vice president, still to be selected, would
take control. Elections could then take place in November.

But the revolutionary tide was surging ever higher, threatening to wreck Welles' plan. The working class, the students, the
whole people of Cuba rose up against the dictator. On August 5,
a general strike erupted. Welles describes it in a cable to Hull:

> The general strike has now spread throughout the Republic. Every
> form of transportation is tied up. The Government employees of
> the Departments of Sanitation, Communications, and of the Trea-
> sury, have declared themselves on a strike and consequently no
> telegraphs are functioning and the ordinary sanitary requirements
> of the city will no longer be complied with. All of the provision
> merchants, restaurants, and even the hotels, are closed and there
> will be a state of near starvation within the next 24 hours.[28]

A few hours later, Welles cabled:

The streets are filled this afternoon with almost unmanageable crowds and the police have been firing upon them to prevent them from congregating around the capitol and around the President's palace.[29]

Welles now faced the danger that unless something were done quickly, the situation would get completely out of control. So he again modified his plan: Machado would have to go immediately, to be replaced by General Alberto Herrera, former chief of the army, who would occupy the Presidency until a vice-presidency could be created and a newly named vice president could take over in 1934. Welles described Herrera to Hull:

He is exceedingly amenable to suggestions which represent the interest of the United States Government.[30]

Machado, however, didn't want to resign, so Welles maneuvered to get him out. He got Roosevelt to tell the Cuban ambassador in Washington that Welles was acting with "his fullest authorization and approval" and that Machado should "prove to the world his high purpose" and "step out."[31] Then Welles passed around in Cuba the cable from Washington telling what Roosevelt had said. Cubans informed of the cable understood it as an ultimatum and a few high military officers, fearful that if they didn't get rid of Machado the United States would intervene militarily, began to conspire to get him out.[32] On August 11, Welles reported that Machado had agreed to resign because all the ranking officers of the army had informed him that they would no longer support him.

But the officers would not accept Herrera because he had been too intimately connected with Machado.[33] In discussions with the officers, Welles angrily insisted on Herrera, but they remained adamant. So Welles proposed Carlos Manuel de Céspedes, whom he described to Hull as "a most sincere friend of the United States," and the officers accepted.[34] On August 12, Machado fled Cuba.

But the revolutionary upsurge was too strong to be stopped by Welles' maneuver. The student organization—*Directorio Estudiantil Universitario*—issued a manifesto rejecting the government "manufactured in the diplomatic retorts of the North American Embassy."[35] Welles reported that "public opinion was rolling up tremendously" against continuing in office anyone from the old regime. The students were "constantly issuing

inflammatory proclamations...." The labor situation was "disquieting," conditions on the large sugar plantations "very grave."
Where demands for an 8-hour day and union recognition were
not agreed to, "unruly mobs" formed. The government could
only cope with this problem "when [military] detachments
[were] sufficiently large to inspire respect." Discipline within
the army was not "sufficiently good to give the Government
assurance that its orders [would] be complied with...." In sum,
"a general process of disintegration [was] going on."[36]

The Céspedes government lasted 23 days. On September 4, a
group of sergeants headed by Fulgencio Batista took control of
the army by deposing the officers and then, together with a
group of students from the *Directorio,* named a new government. Batista became chief of staff of the Army.

The overthrow of Céspedes disconcerted Welles: he was
losing control; the wrong people were getting power—people
he considered "the extreme radical elements." His reaction
was immediate. He recommended that the United States send
"at least two warships to Habana and one to Santiago de Cuba
at the earliest moment," asserting that military intervention
might become necessary.[37] He called a meeting of Cuban political leaders to discuss the possibility of a counterrevolutionary
coup that would get rid of the new government. As he put it in a
cable to Hull:

> I explained to them my own view of the situation and suggested
> that through consultation among themselves they determine whe-
> ther they can devise any plan to prevent the utter break-down of
> government which in my judgment is inevitable under the present
> regime.[39]

The meeting concluded that the only way in which a government resulting from a new coup could be kept in power was
with the help of the Marines who would maintain "order in
Habana and Santiago de Cuba and perhaps one or two other
points...," while Cuban officers organized a new Cuban army.[39]
The next few days were feverish for Welles as he conspired, not
just with this group but others as well, in a frantic search for a
way to carry out the action he wanted. But he was unsuccessful
in his attempt to promote an immediate coup. Roosevelt and
Hull, fearful about Latin American reaction and anxious about
their newly proclaimed good neighbor policy, vetoed proposals
by Welles for armed intervention. Welles had to accept the

continuance for a while of the new regime.   Meanwhile, U.S. officials had arrived at an important conclusion, expressed by Hull in a telephone conversation with Welles: "It seems to us that the whole thing down there revolves around the army...."[40]

The new government was headed by Ramón Grau San Martín—the son of a wealthy family, a physician with a large clientele among the well-to-do, a professor at the University—and was far from being composed of "extreme radical elements." But it did contain one true anti-imperialist and revolutionary, Antonio Guiteras, the Secretary of the Interior.   Cuba was boiling,   with workers striking, occupying sugar mills, establishing "soviets."   Carried along by the turmoil and led by Guiteras, the Grau government put through a series of progressive measures: an 8-hour day; a minimum wage; a reduction in electric power rates; the "intervention"—government takeover—of the U.S.-owned Cuban Electric Company.   To Welles, this government was anathema—"completely incapable of maintaining even a semblance of public order."[41]

Forced to accept the new government temporarily, Welles followed a policy of "watchful expectancy"—of less frantic, more sustained maneuvering.   A key element of this policy was to withhold diplomatic recognition.   Welles told Hull that "we ought not even to consider recognizing any government of this character...."   The United States not only never recognized the Grau government but worked to keep other governments from doing so.   Nonrecognition was, for Welles, a weapon of war.   It could serve both to exert pressure on the government and to encourage those who were thinking about overthrowing it.   In Welles' view, "no government here can survive for a protracted period without recognition by the United States...."[42]

Welles talked to the Student Directorate, to Grau, and to Batista, probing for anything that could be used to weaken and overthrow the government, or get it to change its ways.   He did find some openings in his talks with the students and Grau. Three or four student leaders, he reported, "were weakening materially in the uncompromising attitude they had heretofore taken" and Grau was "extremely conciliatory."[43]   Nevertheless, Welles didn't place much hope on the students or Grau, concluding that

> The Department will easily gather from this summary of my conversation how utterly impractical and visionary Grau San Martín is

and how little hope of success there can be from a government controlled by him and by the students.[44]

Welles soon realized that Batista was the key to his problem. Batista controlled the army. Practically the first thing he had done after the fall of Céspedes was to call on Welles to determine whether a government headed by the new revolutionary group would be "favorably regarded" by the United States.[45] Within two weeks, Welles reported a view held by opposition political leaders he was working with: "Those of them who have personal contacts with Batista appear to be very confident that a direct understanding with him is possible...."[46] A few days later, Welles reported on an interview of his own with Batista:

> His attitude throughout the conversation was extremely reasonable and he repeatedly emphasized the fact that neither the stubbornness of the Student Council nor that of Grau San Martín should be permitted to stand in the way of a solution of the immediate political problem.[47]

The plotting against the government revolved ever more around Batista. Welles cultivated Batista, steered him. "I told him," Welles reported,

> that in my judgment he himself was the only individual in Cuba today who represented authority. I added that this was due in part to the fact that he appeared to have the loyal support of a large part of his troops and in part to the very determined and effective action taken by the troops in Habana as well as in a lesser degree in other cities against the Communistic and extreme radical elements. This I told him had rallied to his own support the very great majority of the commercial and financial interests who are looking for protection.... It must be evident to him, I said, that the present government of Cuba did not fill any of the conditions which the United States Government had announced as making possible recognition by us....[48]

A few days later, Welles had another talk with Batista who told him that "he realized now fully that the present regime was a complete failure.... [and] that he would not cease his pressure until a new government supported by public opinion was installed through peaceful methods." He also "assured" Welles

> of his intention to proceed immediately with a firm hand in all of the American sugar plantations where labor troubles still existed, by arresting and removing all Communist leaders and by using the troops to restore order wherever it was necessary.[49]

The plotters negotiated the composition of the new government. On October 27 Welles cabled Hull: "Batista has just sent word that he is in full accord [with] Mendieta as Provisional President...."[50]

Welles didn't stay for the actual coup, leaving Havana in December to be replaced by Jefferson Caffery. Having completed the basic arrangements, he was no longer needed. As he had pointed out in an earlier dispatch, there were disadvantages to his staying on—he was by now too much in the public eye. Caffery could finish the job less visibly.

In January, Batista overthrew the Grau government, installing Mendieta as president, while retaining real power himself. Five days after Mendieta took office, Hull sent Caffery a telegram instructing him to "extend immediately to the Government of Cuba on behalf of the United States a formal and cordial recognition."[51]

Batista began immediately to deal with the problem of "public order" that had so troubled Welles. Confronted with revolutionary strikes and takeovers in a number of sugar centrals, he declared: "Habrá zafra o habrá sangre [There will be a sugar harvest or there will be bloodshed]," and used the army against the strikers. The army also provided protection to strike breakers loading cigars on ships. When truck and bus drivers, telephone employees, and nurses struck in sympathy with the striking stevedores, the government dissolved their unions and imprisoned their leaders. Mendieta promulgated a series of fascist "decree-laws" to help in the repression. Decree-Law No. 3 prohibited general strikes and declared that all strikes then under way were to "remain in suspense." Decree-Law No. 51 declared those who engaged in sympathetic strikes or issued subversive propaganda to be "common criminals." Offenders were to be tried summarily by a special Tribunal of National Defense, empowered to impose penalties of two years imprisonment and a $5,000 fine.[52]

A report published in the United States describes what Batista did:

> Batista...administered a terrible blood purge. Army trucks plunged into every town, and the soldiery fired right and left to terrorize the inhabitants. Every night in the streets of Havana, men were dragged from their homes by soldiers and Batista's police and shot down without trial, without mercy, and left dying in the public highway.[53]

The U.S. bankers were pleased with the Batista coup. In its Monthly Bank Letter for February 1934, the National City Bank wrote:

> The Cuban situation has taken a sudden and most gratifying turn for the better, by the accession of Dr. Carlos Mendieta to the presidency of the provisional government, with the support of representative groups apparently strong enough to accomplish the restoration of order and constitutional government.[54]

BATISTA'S FIRST REGIME lasted eleven years. In the presidential elections of 1944, he ran a hand-picked candidate, confidently expecting victory. But his candidate lost. With the United States and Cuba engaged in a war against the fascist powers and the word "democracy" on everybody's lips, it was not a good time to set aside the results of an election. Batista went into exile in Florida. But by 1952, times had changed, the cold war was at its height, and he was back with another coup, overthrowing the elected president, Carlos Prío Socarrás.

Philip Bonsal, ambassador to Cuba in 1959-1960, writes that "the coup was on the whole not unwelcome to Americans with interests in Cuba and to their advisors and associates in Havana."[55] It was also not unwelcome to the U.S. Government. Two weeks after the coup, the State Department sent a memorandum to President Truman requesting authorization to recognize the Batista government. The new regime, it said, "has made satisfactory public and private statements with regard to Cuban intention to fulfill its international obligations; its attitude towards private capital; and its intention to take steps to curtail international communist activities in Cuba."[56]

The coup set off a new revolutionary cycle in Cuba. It widened the opposition to the existing order. It shocked a number of young people into the idea of overthrowing the regime by armed force. A group led by Fidel Castro attacked the Moncada barracks in 1953 in the hope of setting off a mass uprising. The attempt failed and Fidel and other survivors were imprisoned. But the pressure of public opinion forced his release in 1955 and in 1956 he landed with another group in Oriente to begin a guerrilla war against the regime. As the revolutionary struggle deepened, Batista stepped up his repression. Hatred of the Batista regime unified the overwhelming mass of the Cuban people behind the Revolution.

But there was much more behind the Cuban Revolution than just the brutal Batista dictatorship. The whole system in Cuba was a mass of irrationality and injustice.

Turning the Cuban economy into a one-crop appendage of the U.S. economy condemned it to stagnation. For decades the sugar industry had not been growing; the harvest in 1955 was less than that in 1925. The whole Cuban economy suffered. According to a *Report on Cuba* published in 1951 by the International Bank for Reconstruction and Development (World Bank), the per capita income of $300 was only slightly above that of the early 1920s.

The sugar industry also imparted a pernicious seasonal rhythm to the Cuban economy. It employed up to 500,000 workers—a quarter of the labor force—during the 3-month cane harvesting season, and then left them to starve during the rest of the year.

The growth of other industries couldn't take up the slack because of the flood of imports from the United States. Only a minute portion of the manufactured goods consumed in Cuba was produced there. The foreign corporations did put in some plants turning out paint, tires, cans, and detergents. But these plants performed only the final operations in the manufacturing process. They were mechanized or automated, used few workers, and provided jobs for only three percent of the Cuban labor force.

How did Cubans live? How well could they live with an average per capita income of $300 per year? Since the top layer of the population enjoyed incomes far above the average, the income of the majority of the people was well below $300.

A survey taken in 1956 showed that average per capita income in the countryside, including homegrown food, was less than $100 per year. The basic diet of agricultural workers consisted of rice and beans. Only 4 percent ate meat regularly, 2 percent ate eggs, 11 percent drank milk.[57]

A population census in 1953 found that of 463,000 rural dwellings, 63 percent were thatched-roof huts with earthen floors. Ninety percent had no electricity or bath, 85 percent no inside running water, 54 percent no toilets of any kind.[58]

Illiteracy was 24 percent in 1953, 42 percent in the countryside. Large stretches lacked doctors or medical facilities. In Oriente, there was only one doctor for every 2,550 people compared to one in 420 in Havana province.[59]

HOW DID THE UNITED STATES react to the new revolutionary upsurge? So long as Batista's hold on power seemed secure, it supported him without wavering. In 1955, Vice President Nixon visited Cuba. Philip Bonsal writes:

> While in Havana, Mr. Nixon reinforced the impression that the United States was as pleased with Batista as it had ever been—an impression Batista valued. I was a member of the Vice President's party in Havana and witnessed the atmosphere of intimate cordiality generated by Ambassador Arthur Gardner in his relations with [Batista].[60]

But after the rebels under Fidel established themselves in the mountains and began to gain strength, the United States faced a familiar problem: a dictator it had supported was losing his grip. The first step it took to meet the problem was to replace Gardner. The new ambassador, Earl E.T. Smith, writes that he had instructions from the State Department "to alter the prevailing notion in Cuba that the American Ambassador was intervening...to perpetuate the Batista dictatorship."[61]

The State Department began to consider how to replace Batista with a new government that would not include Fidel. Smith writes:

> By December 1957, it was becoming more and more clear that the only way to salvage the situation was eventually to have Batista relinquish the Presidency and concurrently appoint a broadly based national unity government without Castro and without representatives of the terrorists, but including representatives of the better elements of the opposition.... I had an exchange of views with this in mind with Cuban civic leaders....[62]

Ambassador Smith was not alone in thinking about somehow replacing Batista with an acceptable alternative. Wayne S. Smith, who served under him in the Embassy, writes that in March and April 1958

> there was a good deal of talk in the Department of State staff meetings about such a solution. Indeed, William Wieland, the director of Caribbean and Mexican affairs, had prepared a policy-recommendation paper in which he strongly urged just such an approach—i.e., of encouraging Batista to leave and responsible moderates to step in before it was too late.[63]

But big difficulties stood in the way of transferring power to a successor government satisfactory to the United States. Upon whose authority would a new government be named? Batista's? Who would recognize that authority? If not Batista's authority, whose? People were now increasingly following the lead of Fidel's July 26th Movement which repeatedly stated its refusal to have anything to do with a government produced by palace maneuvering. If the United States brought about the kind of government it wanted, what would prevent its being repudiated by the people—as Céspedes was in 1933?

The U.S. answer to the repudiation of Céspedes had been to use the army to make a coup. But the army was no longer the trump card it had been in 1933. It not only no longer enjoyed a monopoly of armed power, but was actually being defeated by the Rebel Army.

The State Department floundered for a while, probing for ways to keep Fidel and his movement from coming to power, but without making its mind up on what action to take. Ambassador Smith and officials in Washington disagreed continually. Then, as the downfall of Batista drew close, the Department decided to act. In a memorandum to President Eisenhower, Acting Secretary of State Christian Herter stated the policy: The State Department

> does not want to see Castro succeed to the leadership of the Government.... Therefore, we have been attempting in every appropriate way, through all means available, without openly violating our non-intervention commitments, to help create a situation in which a third force could move into the vacuum between Batista and Castro....[64]

Put in English, the United States was maneuvering secretly to promote a coup that would block Fidel. An official memorandum of the Board of Inquiry into the Bay of Pigs invasion, now declassified in a "sanitized" version, reveals:

> In late 1958 CIA made two attempts (each approved by the Department of State) to block Castro's ascension to power. The first attempt was made in November 1958 when contact was established with Justo Carillo and the Montecristi Group. The second attempt was made on or about the 9th of December 1958 when former Ambassador William D. Pawley, supported by the CIA Chief of Station in Havana, (Blank), and (Blank), approached Batista and

proposed the establishment of a Junta to whom Batista would turn over the reins of government.[65]

Carillo was a former president of the Cuban Agricultural and Industrial Development Bank who had developed ties to anti-Batista military officers and had been trying for several years to promote a coup against Batista. Pawley was a wealthy U.S. businessman with longstanding connections in Cuba. He later testified about "the men we had selected" for the junta. It was to be a military junta.

Both the Carillo and Pawley maneuvers failed, but the United States kept trying. The State Department sent Smith to ask Batista to resign. Smith writes that he told Batista that "the State Department still believed that there were Cuban elements which could salvage the rapidly deteriorating situation." As the regime staggered through its final days, Smith flailed around, talking to Batista's Prime Minister and his generals, communicating indirectly with Batista himself, in an effort to set up a new cabinet, a junta, something. "I was still making a last effort to keep out Castro...."[66]

General Eulogio Cantillo, whom Batista left as army chief of staff when he fled, did try to form a junta, but Fidel immediately blocked the maneuver by demanding the unconditional surrender of Batista's forces and calling for a general strike to help enforce the demand. After many historical reverses, a revolution had finally triumphed in Cuba. In a speech in Santiago the day after Batista's flight, Fidel said:

> This time the Revolution will not be frustrated.... It will not be like '95 when the Americans came and made themselves the masters here.... It will not be like '33 when the people began to believe that a revolution was being made and Batista came and betrayed it, took power, and installed a dictatorship that lasted 11 years.... This time it really is Revolution....[67]

Two weeks later the State Department issued a statement denying all that it had been doing in Cuba:

> Recent statements in the Cuban and American press critical of United States policy in Cuba and of Ambassador [Earl E. T.] Smith reflect a widespread lack of understanding of what United States policy toward Cuba has been.
>   The policy of the United States with respect to the Cuban revolution has been strictly one of nonintervention in Cuban

domestic affairs, and the Ambassador's role has conformed always to this policy.[68]

THE VERY NEED TO DEFEND Smith showed that, like Batista, he had outlived his usefulness. The United States replaced him with Philip Bonsal. Whereas Smith was a right-wing businessman who knew no Spanish, lacked diplomatic experience, and flatly rejected anything that by his loose standards smacked of communism, Bonsal spoke Spanish, was a professional diplomat, and as ambassador to Bolivia had dealt with the government of the National Revolutionary Movement there. In Bolivia, U.S. policy had been to solve the problem of revolution not by meeting it head on, but by the more subtle method of apparently accepting and then taming it.

Bonsal defines the U.S. position at the time he took over as "one of benevolent, if nervous, watchfulness." He describes how he saw the problem posed by the Revolution. "There were, of course, disquieting elements in Castro's past.... But it seemed reasonable to hope that the responsibilities of power and the checks inherent in the community Castro was called upon to lead would keep him within bounds...." Bonsal felt that Cuba's economic dependence on the United States would help keep her in line. "I shared a belief based on the Cuban American experience of sixty years that the reciprocal economic interests of Cuba and the United States would exercise a stabilizing and a moderating influence on developments in Cuba."[69]

Bonsal's view was the dominant one in the State Department. The United States quickly extended recognition to the new government. The strategy was one of appearing friendly, while waiting for the economic and other "realities" to sink in and bring the young revolutionary leaders "to their senses." This strategy did not involve the disadvantages of the only apparent alternative—eliminating the Revolution by force.

But a troubling problem appeared immediately—the Cuban leaders showed no signs of "coming to their senses" and submitting to control. Within days after the Revolution came to power, the U.S. media and various Congressmen created a furor over the trial and execution of Batista soldiers accused of war crimes. They seemed to expect normal, peacetime Anglo-Saxon legal procedures to be applied in revolutionary Cuba. Fidel didn't buckle. He answered, repeatedly stressing Cuba's sovereign right to decide for itself what to do.

> I believe that this people has the same right to govern itself as other peoples, to determine its own destiny freely....
>   I don't have to give an accounting to any Congressman of the United States.[70]

Within the U.S. Government, doubts about the strategy of waiting for the revolutionaries to change began to mount. Journalist Tad Szulc writes that on March 10, 1959, only two and one half months after Batista's defeat, the secret agenda of the National Security Council "included as a principal topic the modalities of bringing 'another government to power in Cuba.'"[71]

Richard Nixon quickly made up his mind against the State Department-Bonsal strategy. He writes that after a three-hour conference with Fidel during the latter's visit to Washington in April 1959,

> I wrote a confidential memorandum for distribution to the CIA, State Department, and White House. In it I stated flatly that I was convinced Castro was "either incredibly naive about Communism or under Communist discipline" and that we would have to treat him and deal with him accordingly—under no further illusions about "fiery rebels" in the "tradition of Bolivar."[72]

The promulgation in June of a land reform law—the first major economic measure of the Revolution—brought a new surge of hostility in Washington. Even the overt reaction to the reform reveals how hard it was for U.S. officials to accept a Cuban government that did not listen obediently to them. Soon after the law was published, Bonsal, at the State Department's instructions, sent a note to the Cuban Foreign Minister which contained the following:

> In view of the many occasions in the past in which consultation on problems affecting both countries has proved mutually beneficial I regret that to date the Government of Cuba has found no opportunity to hear the views of those United States investors in Cuba whose interests would appear to be adversely affected.[73]

The reaction behind the scenes was far stronger. The United States began to press other countries not to sell arms to Cuba. Belgium and Italy were doing so and stopped. Cuba tried to obtain arms from West Germany, Switzerland, and Israel, but was unsuccessful. Under U.S. pressure Britain, which had ag-

reed to sell Hawker Hunter jet fighters to Cuba, refused to carry
out the deal.[74]

Why was the U.S. Government working to prevent Cuba from
obtaining arms? Because it was planning to get rid of the Revolution. One possibility was to choke it to death with an economic embargo. The lopsided Cuban economy was highly vulnerable. But an embargo might not be enough. So the Government wanted to keep open the option of using armed force, and
for this it was desirable to keep Cuba disarmed.

What conclusions could the leaders of the Revolution draw
when they learned — as they quickly did — of the effort to keep
them from obtaining arms? From the time the Revolution came
to power, they had feared a forceful U.S. reaction. Fidel had
early alluded to the danger of U.S. military intervention. What
could the action on arms do except confirm the fear? Years
later, Fidel told Tad Szulc: "Since we proclaimed the Agrarian
Reform Law in May 1959, the United States had taken the decision of liquidating the revolution, one way or another."[75]

The United States took other action besides that on arms.
Small planes piloted by Cuban exiles began to make raids into
Cuba from Florida, dropping leaflets, dropping incendiary
bombs, strafing. The CIA began to arm counterrevolutionary
guerrilla bands which appeared in the Escambray mountains.
In December 1959, the CIA began to interview Cuban exiles as
possible recruits for a force to invade Cuba.

At a news conference during this same month, Secretary of
State Christian Herter foreshadowed later U.S. economic action
against Cuba.

> I think... [Ambassador Bonsal] has made very little progress [in
> negotiating for compensation of American property expropriated
> under the Cuban agrarian reform law]. I think that the standard
> answer he receives is that they do not have money and hence
> must make compensation in terms of long-term bonds....
>
> I would not discuss "punitive action" *at the present time*
> [against the Government of Cuba through the pending revision of
> sugar import quotas]. The whole question of the drawing of the
> new sugar agreement, which lapses this year, is going to pose a
> great many problems. (Words in brackets added by State Depart-
> ment; italics ours.)[76]

In January 1960, a bill was introduced in Congress giving President Eisenhower the power to eliminate the Cuban sugar quo-

ta in the United States. Preparations for an economic attack on Cuba were now clearly under way.

In February, capping a highly publicized visit by Soviet trade minister Anastas Mikoyan, Cuba signed a series of commercial agreements with the Soviet Union. The Soviets committed themselves to buy a million tons of sugar from Cuba in each of the years 1960-1965. These agreements were equivalent to a declaration of real, not just formal, independence by Cuba. They responded to a philosophy that had come down from José Martí—Cuba must keep the door open for trade with everybody. But in the situation that was then developing, they were more than that. They were a measure of self-defense, of protection against the economic warfare the United States was preparing as part of a program to kill the Revolution.

Bonsal describes Washington's reaction to Mikoyan's visit and the sugar agreement:

> The pleasantries exchanged by Mikoyan and Castro in February had been given the most alarming significance in some Washington quarters. The economic arrangements between Cuba and the Soviet Union seemed intolerable to people long accustomed to a dominant American position in Cuba.[77]

In March, Eisenhower approved a program of covert action to overthrow the Revolutionary Government. The program, according to a report by the Senate Intelligence Committee headed by Frank Church, "covered four areas: sabotage, economic sanctions, propaganda, and training of a Cuban exile force for a possible invasion."[78]

U.S. officials were also at this time discussing another type of action—assassination. J.C. King of the CIA had written a memorandum to its Director, Allen Dulles, recommending that

> thorough consideration be given to the elimination of Fidel Castro. None of those close to Fidel, such as his brother Raul or his companion Che Guevara, have the same mesmeric appeal to the masses. Many informed people believe that the disappearance of Fidel would greatly accelerate the fall of the present Government.[79]

Dulles approved the recommendation. He and King attended a White House meeting of the Special Group, the secret interdepartmental committee charged with the supervision of covert operations. According to the minutes,

> There was a general discussion as to what would be the effect on
> the Cuban scene if *Fidel and Raul Castro and Che Guevara should
> disappear simultaneously.* (Italics in original.)[80]

Soon the CIA was plotting and carrying out attempts at assassination. In July, the CIA home office learned from a case officer in Havana of a Cuban who had offered to assist in gathering intelligence and who would be in contact with Raul Castro. It sent a cable to the officer stating that "Possible removal top three leaders is receiving serious consideration at HQS" and inquiring whether the Cuban was willing to risk "arranging an accident" involving Raul Castro. "After successful completion" of the assassination the Cuban would receive $10,000. The Cuban agreed and left on his mission. Then the case officer received another cable saying, "Do not pursue.... Would like to drop matter." But it was too late, since the Cuban was gone. When he returned, he told the case officer that he had not had an opportunity to arrange an accident.[81]

In August, the CIA took steps to enlist the help of the Mafia in assassinating Fidel, indicating this time that it was willing to pay $150,000. Ray S. Cline, a former Deputy Director of the CIA, writes:

> Once the assumption was made that it was essential to get rid of
> Castro by assassination, it was not illogical to try to do it through
> the Mafia, since its former Havana gambling empire gave them
> some contacts to work with and since a gangland killing would be
> unlikely to be attributed to the U.S. Government.[82]

Meanwhile, the rest of the U.S. Government was working toward the economic sanctions called for in the program to topple the Revolution. In April, Cuba had purchased 300,000 tons of crude oil from the Soviet Union under the trade agreement signed in February. To get oil in exchange for sugar instead of dollars would greatly benefit Cuba's dollar balance. But when in June the Cuban government asked the three oil companies (Standard Oil, Texaco, and Shell) to accept Soviet oil in their local refineries, they refused. Their action reflected U.S. Government rather than company policy. Bonsal learned from an oil company executive how it came about.

> Representatives of the two American companies with refineries in
> Cuba had been summoned to the office of the Secretary of the
> Treasury, Robert Anderson, and had been informed by the Sec-

retary that a refusal to accede to the Cuban government's request would be in accord with the policy of the United States government toward Cuba.... They were further told that the situation was being discussed in London with the Shell company along the same lines.[83]

Bonsal writes that to say he was "startled" at Anderson's decision would be "putting it mildly." He wrote Assistant Secretary of State Roy Rubottom that he "very much hoped that our government knew what it was doing in assuming the responsibility for so serious a challenge to the Cuban Revolution—one which involved the very existence of that revolution." As Bonsal feared, the Cuban government did not back down. It "intervened"— took over—the refineries.[84]

U.S. policymakers had hoped to create an oil scarcity in Cuba. The companies had deliberately allowed their stocks of crude to fall dangerously low. The policymakers counted on the Soviet Union not being able to transport oil in the required amounts from the Black Sea to Cuba. But the Soviet Union found the necessary tankers and an oil scarcity did not develop.

On July 6, a week after the intervention of the refineries, Eisenhower eliminated the Cuban sugar quota for 1960. Some writers, says Bonsal,

> have regarded this action as in the nature of a reprisal for the intervention of the refineries. I do not believe this was the case. The suspension of the sugar quota was a major element in the program for the overthrow of Castro.[85]

Just before the suspension of the quota, Fidel had announced that Cuba would retaliate by nationalizing U.S.-owned property in Cuba. The nationalizations began in August. By mid-October, all significant U.S. business property had been taken over.

For some time, the Cuban government had been expecting the United States to impose an embargo on exports to Cuba. In November, the embargo came, a prohibition on all exports except foodstuffs and medicines. One after another the ferry lines to Cuba stopped running and exports, even the theoretically exempt foodstuffs and medicines, fell to zero.

The United States also worked to get others to participate in the economic warfare. It ordered foreign subsidiaries of U.S. companies not to sell Cuba the spare parts it needed for U.S.-made machinery, pressed countries receiving U.S. aid not to buy

Cuban sugar, tried to get its European allies to cut off credit to Cuba.

THE TRUMP IN THE PROGRAM to overthrow the Revolution was military force. By his March decision approving the program, Eisenhower directed the CIA to recruit and train a Cuban exile force for military action to overthrow the Cuban government and to bring together a group of exiles who could form a new government to replace it.

Even before Eisenhower gave his formal approval, the CIA had begun to interview possible recruits for the military force, laid plans for an instructor cadre to train them, and selected a site in Guatemala for training. With the approval, the program moved forward rapidly. By midsummer, recruits began to arrive in Guatemala.

The CIA also began in early 1960 to organize the political front. It cajoled several leading exile groups into forming the *Frente Revolucionario Democrático*. Arthur Schlesinger, Jr., who dealt with this group during the Kennedy administration, writes that "the *Frente* was appropriately named: it was a front and nothing more." Its members talked among themselves, while the CIA ran things.[86]

At first, the CIA's recruits received training in guerrilla warfare. The initial plan was to form small bands designed to slip into Cuba and start guerrilla fighting. The hope was that, like Fidel's rebels, these bands could win support from the people and grow. But the CIA's bands didn't grow. Unlike Fidel's rebels, they were facing not a friendly population, but a hostile one. So the CIA switched from guerrilla warfare to a new idea—a direct assault on the Revolutionary Government by landing a force of exiles on the Cuban coast. It began to train the exiles as a small conventional army equipped with a few planes to provide the air support required for amphibious operations.

As an extension of the strategy of landing a little expeditionary force, the CIA also developed a new political idea—it would, once the landing force had established a beachhead, fly in a provisional government. If the invaders could hold out for ten days or so, the United States would recognize this government, which could then request U.S. aid. The other American republics would then also recognize the new government.

John F. Kennedy, soon after his election in November 1960, received a briefing from CIA Director Allen Dulles on the Cuban project and told him to carry the work forward. He visited the White House in January to receive a briefing on foreign policy from the outgoing administration. In a memorandum to Kennedy two weeks later giving his recollections of the meeting, Defense Secretary Robert S. McNamara recalled:

> President Eisenhower stated that in the long run the United States cannot allow the Castro Government to continue to exist in Cuba.[87]

By March, Kennedy was putting some of his own stamp on the project. He directed the CIA to form an exile organization more liberal than the *Frente*. He stipulated that the invasion plan should be based on the idea that there would be no military intervention by U.S. forces.

Through the power it held over the exile organizations, the CIA was able to form a new organization with a more "liberal" tinge than the *Frente*. The *Frente* was nothing more than a creature of the CIA, which provided it with a headquarters building, paid the salaries of its officials, and put money into its newspapers.[88] The more liberal MRP (*Movimiento Revolucionario del Pueblo*), while more inclined to independence, also depended on the CIA for what it wanted—U.S. action to overthrow the Revolutionary Government. By threatening to call off its project if they didn't go along, the CIA forced the two organizations to get together, choose a provisional president of Cuba, and confer on him authority to organize a "Cuban Revolutionary Council." José Miró Cardona, the "respected moderate" chosen as president, announced that the Council would become the provisional government of Cuba once it had gained "a piece of Cuban soil."[89] Thus the Council, from the minute of its founding, was carrying out the military and political strategy cooked up by the CIA.

Shortly after the Council was formed, Schlesinger received from Tracy Barnes of the CIA a first draft of a proposed political manifesto the Council had prepared. He describes it as "a document so overwrought in tone and sterile in thought that it made one wonder what sort of people we were planning to send back to Havana." Feeling no need to respect the ideas of the puppet Council, Schlesinger and Barnes decided to ask two Latin American specialists from Harvard "to suggest guiding principles" for a more satisfactory program.[90]

Among the final touches in the preparations for the invasion was a State Department White Paper on Cuba. The United States needed a propaganda justification for what it was about to do—invade a small neighbor with troops recruited, paid, trained, equipped, and taken to the point of action by the CIA; place on the beachhead a few members of the artificial Council that the CIA had created, and recognize them as the government of Cuba. Kennedy gave the assignment to turn out the justification to Schlesinger. The State Department issued the White Paper with well-managed fanfare on April 3, two weeks before the invasion began.

The Paper's main theme was that the Revolution had been betrayed. Whether the Cuban people thought so was apparently not relevant. The document was full of high-flown phrases about freedom, democracy, and the Cuban people being "our brothers," but what it really expressed was the U.S. Government's unwillingness to let "our brothers" determine for themselves what sort of government and society they would have.

Meanwhile, in Cuba, the CIA was carrying out what journalists Tad Szulc and Karl E. Meyer describe as "a well thought out softening-up process."[91] It supplied explosives and weapons to the MRP, and Navy planes flew cover for MRP speedboats which carried them to Cuba. Bombs exploded daily in Havana, as many as twelve in one day. Saboteurs lit big fires at the former Esso refinery, the Hershey sugar mill, a large wholesale warehouse in Santiago. El Encanto, the big Havana department store, went up in flames one night.

CIA intelligence reports about Cuba were optimistic. One report stated:

> The Castro regime is steadily losing popularity.... Travelers throughout the interior have reported that the disenchantment of the masses has spread through all the provinces.... It is generally believed that the Cuban army has been successfully penetrated by opposition groups and that it will not fight in the event of a showdown.... The morale of the militia is falling....[92]

On April 10, unmarked U.S. aircraft began to ferry the CIA's troops in Guatemala to the embarkation point at Puerto Cabezas, Nicaragua.[93] There, U.S. officials briefed the troops on the invasion plan. The chief U.S. advisor told them that they were to hold the beach for 72 hours.

> We will be there with you for the next step. But you will be so strong, you will be getting so many people to your side, that you won't want to wait for us. You will go straight ahead. You will put your hands out, turn left, and go straight into Havana.[94]

Nicaraguan dictator Luis Somoza came to the dock to see the troops off. Surrounded by gunmen, he waved and said, "Bring me a couple of hairs from Castro's beard."[95]

The Revolutionary Council, supposed to become the "Provisional Government" of Cuba within a few days, had not been informed of the invasion plan. On April 13, the CIA invited the Council to New York and put it up at the Hotel Lexington for a series of conferences. The following night the Council was told that an air strike against Cuba would take place the next morning.

During the night, nine CIA B-26s piloted by Cuban exiles took off from Puerto Cabezas. They bore fake Cuban Air Force markings. Eight were bound for Cuba, with the mission of destroying the Cuban Air Force before it could get off the ground. The ninth was headed for Miami to spread the cover story: that the planes were piloted by defecting members of the Cuban Air Force who had decided to do some damage before escaping.

The bombing failed to achieve its goal. U-2 overflights showed that it had destroyed five planes. Eight still remained—four British-made Sea Fury light attack bombers, three T-33 jet trainers, and one B-26.

The cover story was also unsuccessful. At the U.N., Ambassador Adlai Stevenson "categorically" rejected the charge that the United States was committing aggression against Cuba.

> No United States personnel participated. No United States Government airplanes of any kind participated. These two planes to the best of our knowledge were Castro's own Air Force planes, and, according to the pilots, they took off from Castro's own Air Force fields.
>
> I have here a picture of one of these planes. It has the markings of Castro's Air Force right on the tail, which everyone can see for himself.[96]

But the CIA had overlooked something. The B-26 in the picture had a solid nose, whereas the planes the Revolutionary Government had inherited from Batista had Plexiglass noses. Cuba's representatives at the U.N. pointed this out and the cover story collapsed.

On April 17, the CIA-controlled station on Swan Island in the Caribbean broadcast to Cuba a statement issued in the name of Miró Cardona, president of the Cuban Revolutionary Council: "Before dawn Cuban patriots in the cities and in the hills began the battle to liberate our homeland...." In New York, a Madison Avenue public relations firm, Lem Jones Associates, issued the statement as "Bulletin No. 1" of the Council.[97] At the time, the Council was being held by the CIA under armed guard in a deserted house at an abandoned airbase at Opa-Locka, Florida, until it could be flown to Cuba to establish the "Provisional Government." Schlesinger describes how the members of the Council, listening to the radio the next morning,

> were stunned to hear an announcement "from the Cuban Revolutionary Council" that the invasion had begun. Unknown to them, a New York public relations man..., Lem Jones, was putting out in the name of the Council press releases dictated over the phone by the CIA.[98]

The invasion failed just as miserably as the air bombing and its cover story. The fundamental assumption on which it rested—that the Cuban people would rise up and join the invaders—was wrong, and this by itself guaranteed that the invasion would fail. To boot, U.S. officials committed many blunders, while the Cubans under Fidel's leadership defended themselves vigorously and with skill. The CIA concentrated the ammunition reserve for ten days in a single ship which a Cuban Sea Fury sank the first morning. The U.S. military planners ignored the three Cuban T-33 trainers, considering them noncombat planes. But they were jets, and when the Cubans armed them with 50-calibre machine guns they became formidable weapons which shot down four of the invaders' lumbering B-26s.

Fidel, aware of the CIA strategy of landing and recognizing a provisional government, moved urgently to liquidate the enemy beachhead before this strategy could be realized. He rushed troops, artillery, and tanks to the battle zone. He ordered the Cuban Air Force into action immediately, the T-33s to take on the enemy's planes, the Sea Furies to concentrate on sinking as many invasion ships as they could as quickly as possible. In his biography of Fidel, Tad Szulc writes that "Castro made a point of personally urging his pilots to find and destroy the ships, impatient over every minute elapsing."[99]

The Sea Furies forced the invasion fleet to flee to the open sea. The T-33s deprived the invaders on the beachhead of air cover. An overwhelming force moved against them on land. The invasion lasted 72 hours. As it ended, two U.S. destroyers approached the beach to rescue survivors.[100]

THE DEFEAT LEFT THE KENNEDY administration humiliated and frustrated. "We were hysterical about Castro at the time of the Bay of Pigs and thereafter," Defense Secretary McNamara later recalled. Chester Bowles remembered a high-level White House meeting on the day the invasion was ending: "The consensus was to get tough with Castro. Some...took an attitude of 'He can't do this to us.'" President Kennedy asked Richard Nixon, "What would you do now in Cuba?" Nixon replied, "I would find a proper legal cover and I would go in." A Cuba Study Group, headed by Maxwell Taylor and including Attorney General Robert Kennedy, concluded a few weeks after the debacle: "There can be no long-term living with Castro as a neighbor."[101]

The administration began anew to think about how to eliminate the Revolutionary Government, analyzing along with other things a direct invasion by U.S. forces. Robert Kennedy, impatient to reverse what he saw as a great humiliation, wrote on June 1:

> The Cuba matter is being allowed to slide. Mostly because nobody really has the answer to Castro. Not many are really prepared to send American troops in there at the present time but maybe that is the answer.[102]

In the fall of 1961, according to the Church Committee,

> the Kennedy administration considered the consequences of Castro's removal from power and the prospects for United States military intervention if that occurred.... National Security Action Memorandum 100 (NSAM 100) directed the State Department to assess the potential courses of action open to the United States should Castro be removed from the Cuban scene, and to prepare a contingency plan with the Department of Defense for military intervention in that event.[103]

National Security Advisor McGeorge Bundy later testified that the contingency referred to in NSAM 100 was "what would we do if Castro were no longer there" and that "clearly one of the possibilities would be assassination." One of the ideas being considered was to assassinate Fidel and then use the occasion for military intervention.[104]

The Kennedy brothers' impatience about Cuba again manifested itself. According to testimony received by the Church Committee, Richard Bissell, the CIA's director of covert operations, was "chewed out in the Cabinet Room of the White

House by both the President and the Attorney General for... sitting on his ass and not doing anything about getting rid of Castro and the Castro regime."[105]

In November, President Kennedy issued a memorandum approving Operation Mongoose—to "use our available assets...to help Cuba overthrow the Communist regime." To oversee Operation Mongoose, a new control group, the Special Group Augmented (SGA), was created, with high-ranking members such as National Security Advisor McGeorge Bundy, CIA Director John McCone, and Deputy Defense Secretary Roswell Gilpatric, "augmented" by Maxwell Taylor and Robert Kennedy. Secretary of State Rusk and Defense Secretary McNamara sometimes attended meetings.[106]

The President gave General Edward Lansdale the task of coordinating the Mongoose operations. Lansdale had acquired a reputation in the Philippines and Vietnam for knowing how to deal with revolutionary insurgencies in underdeveloped countries.

At a January 1962 meeting on Mongoose in Robert Kennedy's office, a CIA participant took notes which contained the following:

> Conclusion Overthrow of Castro is Possible.
>
> "...a solution to the Cuban problem today carried top priority in U.S. Gov[ernmen]t. No time, money, effort—or manpower is to be spared."
>
> "Yesterday...the President had indicated to him that the final chapter had not been written—it's got to be done and will be done."[107]

The notetaker attributed the words "top priority in the U.S. Gov[ernmen]t. No time, money, effort—or manpower is to be spared" to Robert Kennedy.

Operation Mongoose quickly grew. Schlesinger writes in his biography of Robert Kennedy:

> Task Force W, the CIA unit for Mongoose, soon had four hundred American employees in Washington and Miami, over fifty proprietary fronts, its own navy of fast boats, a rudimentary air force and two thousand Cuban agents. The Miami headquarters became for a season the largest CIA station in the world. All this cost over $50 million a year.[108]

In February 1962, Lansdale, according to the Church Committee, "detailed a six-phase schedule for Mongoose, designed to culminate in October 1962, with an 'open revolt and overthrow of the Communist regime.'" But how could an internal revolt, without the intervention of U.S. troops, overthrow the Revolutionary Government? The Bay of Pigs invasion had shown that the overwhelming majority of the Cuban people supported that government. Lansdale himself reported that "Castro...had aroused considerable affection for himself personally with the Cuban population...." Actually, the proponents of Mongoose were thinking of more than internal revolt. According to a CIA memo, "one of the options of the project was to create internal dissension and resistance leading to eventual U.S. intervention." In August 1962, Maxwell Taylor "told the President that the SGA saw no likelihood that Castro's Government would be overturned by internal means without direct United States military intervention...."[109]

Some U.S. writers downplay the importance of the invasion threat to Cuba by stressing that there were no final plans, only contingency plans. Raymond Garthoff writes that "No doubt a military contingency 'plan' was on file (the United States in 1941 even had a 'war plan' for conflict with Great Britain)...."[110]

However, just because something is a contingency plan doesn't mean it is without significance. The plan for the Bay of Pigs invasion was a contingency plan until only two weeks before the invasion occurred. How significant a contingency plan is depends on the overall situation and the chances of the contingency occurring. The comparison with Britain is ridiculous. The United States didn't have an Operation Mongoose against Britain, was not trying to assassinate its leaders, was not working to stir up dissension and revolt—all in the hope of creating an opening for invasion. The contingency of a U.S. war with Britain was so remote that it could be discounted for practical purposes.

But by its own admission the United States undertook in 1962 a program to overthrow the Revolutionary Government, something it knew could not be done without invasion. It was engaged in a series of escalating aggressions, the logical outcome of which was an invasion.

WHAT REACTION COULD BE expected from the Cubans? Schlesinger, who saw what was happening from a high post in the administration, writes:

Certainly, Castro had the best grounds for feeling under siege. Even if double agents had not told him the CIA was trying to kill him, the Mongoose campaign left little doubt that the American government was trying to overthrow him. It would hardly have been unreasonable for him to request Soviet protection.[111]

After talking about U.S. sabotage in Cuba, Schlesinger comments again:

The secret war, not unreasonably seen by Castro as preparation for a new and better invasion, intensified the Cuban desire for Soviet protection.[112]

To meet the threat, Cuba and the Soviet Union decided to install nuclear missiles on the island. Fidel later explained:

Naturally the missiles would not have been sent...if we had not felt the need for some measure that would unquestionably protect the country. We made the decision at a moment when we thought that concrete measures were necessary to paralyze the plans of aggression of the United States....[113]

Upon discovering the presence of the missiles in Cuba, the United States precipitated the Cuban missile crisis in which, in the words of Robert McNamara, "the world was faced with...the greatest danger of a catastrophic war since the advent of the nuclear age."[114] Demanding that the missiles be removed, the United States imposed a blockade on the shipment of "offensive weapons" to Cuba, calling it a "quarantine" because a blockade has traditionally been considered an act of war. It instituted what Garthoff describes as an "open all-out build-up of the contingent air-strike and invasion forces of the U.S. Army, Navy, Air Force, and Marines."[115] It threatened military escalation if its demands were not met.

By what right did the United States demand the removal of the missiles? It had missiles in Turkey, close to the Soviet Union. How did the missiles in Cuba differ?

Did the missiles in Cuba significantly change the nuclear balance? Defense Secretary McNamara didn't think so. He later commented:

The assumption that the Soviet missiles in Cuba shifted the strategic nuclear balance is wrong.... I believe we had 5,000 nuclear warheads at that time and the Soviets had 300. What difference would it have made if they had 340? Did putting 40 launchers in

Cuba change the military balance of power? I didn't believe it then and I don't believe it today.[116]

Theodore Sorensen, who was close to Kennedy, also thought that the balance was unchanged. "These Cuban missiles alone, in view of all the other megatonnage the Soviets were capable of unleashing upon us, did not substantially alter the strategic balance *in fact*...." He adds, however, that the balance "would have been substantially altered *in appearance*; and in matters of national will and world leadership, as the President said later, such appearances contribute to reality." The missiles, Kennedy felt, could "politically change the balance of power" in the cold war.[117] Kennedy's actions, in other words, had to do with appearances and with the cold war, not with a real threat to the military security of the United States.

Even assuming that Kennedy had no choice but to get the missiles out of Cuba, why didn't he try to do so by negotiation instead of immediately manufacturing a crisis? Was there any justification for bringing the world so close to nuclear disaster?

The crisis ended with an agreement between the United States and the Soviet Union: The United States committed itself not to invade Cuba and the Soviet Union committed itself to withdrawing the missiles. The United States also committed itself to withdrawing its nuclear missiles from Turkey and Italy, although it insisted for the sake of appearances that this not be publicly mentioned as part of the deal.

SHORTLY AFTER THE END of the crisis, the administration cancelled Operation Mongoose, but in 1963 Kennedy approved a new sabotage program. The Church Committee writes that "in contrast to the MONGOOSE program, which sought to build toward an eventual internal revolt, the 1963 covert action program had a more limited objective, *i.e.*, 'to nourish a spirit of resistance and disaffection which could lead to significant defections and other byproducts of unrest.'"[118]

Despite the more limited objective, the new program was big. It aimed at "four major segments of the Cuban economy" — electric power, petroleum refining and storage facilities, railroad and highway transportation, and production and manufacturing. In October, the administration approved 13 major operations, including the sabotage of an electric power plant, an oil refinery, and a sugar mill, all to be carried out within three months.[119]

The assassination attempts also continued. The CIA tried one scheme after another. A Mafia agent set up a sniper nest at the University of Havana to pick off Fidel as he arrived for an appearance, but the Cuban security police discovered the nest. An employee of the Habana Libre Hotel, bribed by the CIA, tried to slip a cyanide capsule into a milk shake ordered by Fidel, but the employee was nervous, the capsule broke, and the attempt failed.[120]

A 1965 CIA document reveals what the United States hoped to achieve through sabotage and assassination:

> B1 ["the leader of an anti-Castro group"] is to be in Cuba one week before the elimination of Fidel....
>
> B1 is to arrange for recognition by at least five Latin American countries as soon as Fidel is neutralized and a junta is formed. This junta will be established even though Raul Castro and Che Guevara may still be alive and may still be in control of part of the country....
>
> One month to the day before the neutralization of Fidel, B1 will increase the number of commando attacks to a maximum in order to raise the spirit and morale of the people inside Cuba....[121]

Even after the hope of overthrowing the Revolutionary Government had begun to wane, attempts at sabotage and assassination went on. Here is an example of sabotage from the book, *The Fish Is Red: The Story of the Secret War Against Castro*, by Warren Hinckle and William Turner:

> In March 1970 a U.S. intelligence officer passed a vial of African swine fever virus to a terrorist group. The vial was taken by fishing trawler to Navassa Island, which had been used in the past by the CIA as an advance base, and was smuggled into Cuba. Six weeks later Cuba suffered the first outbreak of the swine fever in the Western Hemisphere; pig herds were decimated....[122]

In 1971, the CIA made several attempts to assassinate Fidel during his trip to Chile as a guest of the Popular Unity Government. In Santiago, agents set up a television camera with a hidden gun. In the north of Chile they arranged for a disabled car with 400 pounds of dynamite to block the narrow road on which Fidel was being driven to a copper mine. In Peru, where Fidel stopped on the way home, they arranged for a Beechcraft with a 20mm cannon behind the door to be positioned for blasting away at his Ilyushin when it landed. As luck would have it, all the attempts failed. One of the agents with the gun in the TV camera got an attack of appendicitis and wasn't there; the other refused to do the job alone. The dynamite in the car didn't go off. Fidel's plane unexpectedly pulled into a special security area where it was blocked from the Beechcraft. But the CIA was not discouraged. Several years later it was trying to get a detailed itinerary of a trip by Fidel to Angola.[123]

EVEN WHILE THE PROGRAMS of sabotage and assassination were in full swing, Cuba began to reach out for a possible accommodation. In the fall of 1963, the Cuban delegation at the United Nations let U.S. officials there know that they were interested in discussions that could lead to an improvement in relations. Conversations took place. President Kennedy asked Jean Daniel, a French newsman about to visit Cuba, to tell Fidel that he was prepared to explore the possibilities of an accommodation. Fidel later told Tad Szulc: "Kennedy would not have received a rebuff from us.... I was meditating and thinking very much and I was considering giving him a constructive and positive answer."[124] Then Kennedy was assassinated and the new administration broke off communications.

U.S.-Cuban relations remained frozen for almost 15 years thereafter. From time to time Cuba made overtures. But the United States had a long-standing, "not negotiable" condition for better relations, expressed in a speech in 1964 by Undersecretary of State George Ball: Cuba must end its "political, economic, and military dependence upon the Soviets."[125]

This demand involves more than appears on the surface. What would giving up Cuba's close ties to the Soviet Union mean—giving up the market the Soviet Union provided for a large part of Cuban sugar, giving up the Soviet Union as a source of oil? For Cuba to give these up would mean to place itself once again in economic dependence on the United States. Would ending close ties mean giving up the military supplies the Soviet Union provided? The history of U.S. aggression against Cuba shows that for it to give up these things would be to risk its security, to place the very existence of the Revolution in jeopardy. Actually, the United States was demanding that the Revolution surrender.

After noting the nonnegotiable condition, Ball stated that "there seems little sign of a possibility of serious negotiations with the present regime...." But, in fact, negotiations were possible. They were prevented by Washington's unwillingness to reconcile itself to the Revolution, by its insistence on a condition it knew the Cuban government could not and would not accept. As Wayne S. Smith, who was following events from inside the State Department, puts it:

> Clearly, we did not wish to talk to Castro. Our hard reply was simply a way of saying no without appearing to do so.[126]

Only years later did the United States enter into negotiations. U.S. officials had lost their feeling that "the present regime" was only temporary and there were troublesome problems that could be solved only with Cuban cooperation. Hijacking was one. Negotiations took place and in 1973 the two countries signed an anti-hijacking agreement.

The United States interrupted the improvement in relations when Cuba sent troops to Angola in 1975 to help fight invading South African army units. The South Africans, allied with CIA-backed forces, were trying at the last minute to prevent the Popular Movement for the Liberation of Angola (MPLA) from consummating its revolutionary victory. For a while, reports circulated that the Pentagon was renewing plans for a blockade, and even a military attack, against Cuba.[127]

At the outset of the Carter administration, relations began to improve again. Secretary of State Cyrus Vance wanted an improvement. He wasn't thinking of full-scale normalization; nobody of significance in the administration was. What he wanted was a measured, limited improvement that, he felt, could serve better than outright hostility to achieve U.S. goals:

> Our objective was to see whether it might be possible slowly to change Castro's perspective on relations with the United States from one of fear and hostility to one in which he might see benefits in restraining his revolutionary adventurism and in lessening his dependence on the Soviet Union. I felt we had some significant leverage—the prospect of lifting the economic blockade, [etc.]....[128]

For a while, the Vance strategy prevailed. Besides signing agreements on fishing and maritime boundaries, the two countries agreed to the establishment of interests sections in each other's capitals, interests sections being small diplomatic offices established by countries that do not have normal diplomatic relations. Thus, after 16 years of no diplomatic relations, the

United States took a limited step toward reestablishing them, while continuing to maintain its trade embargo.

Not everybody in the Carter administration agreed with Vance's strategy. Zbigniew Brzezinski, the National Security Advisor, had argued against better relations as a member of the "transition team" that prepared foreign policy positions for the incoming administration. Nothing was to be gained from trying to improve relations, he maintained. He discovered suddenly that Cuba had too many troops in Angola and that this made normalization "impossible." He used the presence of Cuban troops in Ethiopia (where they were helping to repel an invasion by Somalia) to work against even minor steps at accommodation. Brzezinski succeeded in stirring up hostility to Cuba and reversing the trend toward improvement in relations that Vance had started.[129]

THE REAGAN ADMINISTRATION added open menace to the hostility, raising tension to the highest level since the missile crisis. Starting during the election campaign, Reagan and his advisors spoke repeatedly about the possibility of a naval blockade of Cuba. White House Advisor Edwin Meese, asked if there might be a blockade, replied: "I don't think we would rule out anything." The commander of the Atlantic fleet, Admiral Train, told reporters that the United States was in a position to blockade Cuba.[130]

Secretary of State Alexander Haig, talking in February 1981 about the revolution in El Salvador, declared that the United States had to "deal with the immediate source of the problem — and that is Cuba." In October Haig escalated his threat. In a talk with the Soviet ambassador and in communications with other governments, he backed assertions by the newspaper columnists Evans and Novak that Cuba had sent 500 to 600 elite troops to El Salvador by way of Nicaragua. When Cuba denied these allegations and demanded proof, Haig accused Cuba of "interventionist activities" in Central America and hinted at retaliatory measures. The next day the U.S. Navy began maneuvers in the waters around Cuba.[131]

A few days later, the *New York Times* reported that Haig was "pressing the Pentagon to examine a series of options for possible military action in El Salvador and against Cuba and Nicaragua."

The options with respect to Cuba included

a show of airpower, large naval exercises, a quarantine on the shipment of arms to the island, a general blockade as part of an act of war, and an invasion by American and possibly Latin American forces.[132]

Cuba had to take the threats seriously. It certainly couldn't ignore a threat like invasion, especially since by taking appropriate action it could reduce the chances of its being carried out. Soon after Reagan's election, it responded by forming a Territorial Troop Militia, building it up quickly into a force that Wayne Smith, then head of the U.S. interests section, says was "500,000 strong."[133]

Immediately after the U.S. Navy began its Caribbean maneuvers, Cuba went on a full alert, mobilizing reserves and putting the economy on a war footing. *Granma*, the Communist Party newspaper, published a quote from a speech given by Fidel a few weeks earlier:

We will save peace if its enemies know that we are prepared to die for it rather than yield to blackmail and fear.[134]

Cuba was not alone in taking the invasion threat seriously. During the maneuvers, *Pravda*, the Soviet Communist Party newspaper, charged that the United States was preparing to attack Cuba and warned that "aggressive actions against Cuba are fraught with dangerous consequences."[135]

Why did the United States fail to follow through on Haig's threats, on his idea that "the way was open to solve the problem in Central America, and solve it quickly, through the unequivocal application of pressure?" Others in the administration disagreed with him. Haig relates that "the President's advisors continued to seek some solution that might bring success in Central America without subjecting the President to the risk of what they judged might become a protracted minor war or even a superpower confrontation."[136]

Several factors worked against Haig: the Vietnam syndrome (the people of the United States did not want another Vietnam war); Cuba's preparations, which ensured that an invasion would bog down the United States in a long and bloody people's war; a rapidly growing popular concern about the threat of nuclear conflict. Commenting on the Cuban mobilization, Wayne Smith writes that "at that point the steam went out of the campaign of steadily escalating threats."[137]

The easing of the military threat by no means signified that the Reagan administration was ending all hostile actions against Cuba. It continued such actions, reimposing a travel ban that had been lifted by Carter, setting up a broadcasting service—Radio Martí—to wage psychological warfare, and tightening enforcement of the trade embargo.

But again there were problems that could be solved only with Cuba's cooperation. In 1984 the administration entered into negotiations which resulted in an agreement on immigration. Fidel characterized the agreement as a "constructive and positive" sign that could lead to negotiations in other areas. But Secretary of State George Shultz dismissed Fidel's overture as "a lot of rhetoric."[138]

In May 1985, Radio Martí went on the air and within hours Cuba suspended the immigration agreement. Later in the year, Reagan charged that Cuba was part of "a confederation of terrorist states" run by "the strangest collection of misfits, Looney Tunes, and squalid criminals since the advent of the Third Reich." But by the fall of 1987, the two countries were again engaged in negotiations and in November they announced the restoration of the immigration agreement. The *New York Times* reported that relations which had been "icy" were now in a "warming trend."[139]

But in May 1989, the recently elected president, George Bush, briefed a group of anti-Castro Cubans:

> And this I pledge—unless Fidel Castro is willing to change his policies and behavior we will maintain our present policy toward Cuba—(applause)—knock off this wild speculation as just that—some suggesting that our administration is going to unilaterally shift things with Fidel Castro—I am not going to do that....[140]

THUS, THROUGH MANY ADMINISTRATIONS the U.S. Government has remained hostile to revolutionary Cuba. Thirty years after the Revolution took power, the trade embargo was still in effect. True, there have been ups and downs in relations—ups and downs which have their importance. But throughout, including the periods of declining tension, the basic attitude of the U.S. Government has been one of deep, unwavering hostility.

The Government has not been able to completely avoid dealing with Cuba and there have been negotiations and agreements. But the United States limited the negotiations and agree-

ments to specific problems for which it needs Cuban cooperation, while otherwise maintaining its deliberate hostility.

Even those who—like Cyrus Vance and Wayne Smith—have
argued for "dialogue" with Cuba have envisaged "improved relations," not normal ones. The following comment by Smith illustrates:

> We were convinced...that important American interests could be
> served by improving relations with Cuba—but the process would
> take time. Only over a period of years could we hope to bring
> about conditions under which Cuba might begin to show greater
> independence of the Soviet Union.[141]

The Cuban relationship with the Soviet Union has continued
to occupy the same central role in U.S. policy that Ball's statement gave it in 1964. In 1984, Kenneth Skoug, head of the State
Department's Office of Cuban Affairs, asserted that in considering relations with Cuba "the first and most critical" concern for
the United States is Cuba's "special relationship with the Soviet
Union."[142]

The policy of refusal to normalize relations shows that, even
after thirty years, the U.S. imperialists have still not reconciled
themselves to the Revolution. They hope to tame it. They even
dream of getting rid of it.

The persistent underlying goal of the imperialists surfaced
after the electoral defeat of the Sandinistas in Nicaragua in February 1990. Suddenly the attention of the media and key political figures focussed on Cuba, as if to say, Cuba is next. The *New
York Times* wrote that "diplomats here [in Managua] began talking about President Castro's future on Sunday afternoon as soon
as they first sensed the Sandinistas' impending defeat...."[143]
Richard Nixon intoned on the steps of the Capitol that "the cor-
relation of forces" had moved against Cuba and that without
Soviet support Fidel Castro would go down.[144] Meanwhile, the
United States was pressing the Soviet Union to end its support
and getting ready to beam TV Martí into Cuba in an effort to
undermine the Cuban government. The imperialists—their
hopes clearly higher than they had been in a long time—were
preparing for stepped up aggression against Cuba.

4. Vietnam

The Vietnamese struggle against the United States was the culmination of a long series of rebellions stretching from the time the French seized control of Indochina in the second half of the 19th century. Land and foreign domination were the central issues. The Depression of the 1930s which, as in other colonies, brought untold suffering to Vietnam, saw the founding of the Communist Party and the first big uprisings involving workers. But with more than ninety percent of the population peasants, the land question remained central, along with foreign oppression, in the liberation struggle against the Japanese during World War II.

When in 1945 Ho Chi Minh, leader of the Vietnamese Communist Party and the broad liberation movement known as Vietminh, proclaimed the formation of the independent Democratic Republic of Vietnam (DRV), the United States refused recognition. Despite its high-sounding pronouncements against colonialism, it did not want to allow colonies unfettered self-determination.

Truman ignored repeated appeals from Ho Chi Minh to get France to respect Vietnam's independence. When France set out to reconquer its old colony, the United States contented itself with declarations like that of Secretary of State Marshall who hoped that "a pacific basis for adjustment of the difficulties could be found."[1] As the Defense Department itself declared in its history of U.S. "decision making" on Vietnam (*The Pentagon Papers*), "Nonintervention by the United States on behalf of the Vietnamese was tantamount to acceptance of the French."[2]

The French stressed that they were fighting not a colonial but an anticommunist war, and soon the U.S. position began to shift even further toward them. In 1949, the United States welcomed the formation by France of "the new unified state of Vietnam."[3] It had encouraged France to install the ex-emperor, Bao Dai, as the head of this state and now pressed for policies that would give the new government greater "nationalist" appeal in its struggle with the DRV for the allegiance of the Vietnamese people.

Open U.S. intervention in the affairs of Vietnam began soon after the "loss" of China when the United States decided "to block further Communist expansion in Asia."[4] In January 1949, France requested military aid for its war in Indochina. Secretary of State Dean Acheson, recommending that the aid be granted, wrote in a memorandum to Truman:

> The choice confronting the U.S. is to support the legal govern-
> ments in Indochina or to face the extension of Communism over
> the remainder of the continental area of Southeast Asia and pos-
> sibly westward.[5]

What the memorandum called "the extension of commu-nism" was clearly not the result of foreign aggression. The only foreign aggression in Indochina was that of the French. What was happening was a rebellion of the people against their colo-nial oppressor. An NSC memorandum in 1952 stated:

> The primary threat to Southeast Asia ... arises from the possibility
> that the situation in Indochina may deteriorate as a result of the
> weakening of the resolve of, or as a result of the inability of the
> governments of France and of the Associated States [Cambodia,
> Laos, and Vietnam] to continue to oppose the Vietminh rebel-
> lion....[6]

Washington prodded France to do more and offered help in training "indigenous forces" to take over the fighting. U.S. aid soared from $10 million approved in early 1950 to over $1 billion in 1954, by which time the United States was covering 78 per-cent of the French war burden.[7]

Increasing aid meant increasing U.S. interference, and gra-dually the United States took over more and more direct respon-sibility for running the war. In the spring of 1953, the first U.S. military mission arrived in Saigon and set up the Military Assis-tance Advisory Group (MAAG). MAAG grew with the arrival of officers to train the Vietnamese Army and of Air Force mecha-nics to service the B-26s and C-47s made available to the

French. Despite French displeasure, U.S. military men increasingly bypassed the old French colonial administration and established direct control over Vietnamese officials.

As the French military position weakened, some leading U.S. officials began in 1954 to press for direct U.S. military intervention. Vice President Nixon in off-the-record remarks to newspaper editors, launched a trial balloon. As paraphrased by the *New York Times*, he said that

> The United States as a leader of the free world cannot afford further retreat in Asia. It is hoped the United States will not have to send troops there, but if this government cannot avoid it, the Administration must face up to the situation and dispatch forces.[8]

Secretary of State Dulles, in a speech at the Overseas Press Club, accused the "Chinese Communists" of having "stepped up their support of the aggression [in Indochina]" and then declared that

> The imposition on Southeast Asia of the political system of Communist Russia and its Chinese Communist ally, by whatever means, must be a grave threat to the whole free community.... [which] should not be passively accepted but should be met by united action.[9]

Admiral Arthur W. Radford, chairman of the Joint Chiefs of Staff, pressed for direct U.S. intervention. He urged using U.S. bombers from aircraft carriers to save a French garrison beleaguered at Dien Bien Phu even if this meant running the risk that the United States would be drawn deeply into the war and perhaps also into war with China.[10]

But the efforts to obtain direct U.S. intervention to stave off a Vietminh victory did not succeed. Eisenhower decided that the United States should not go into Indochina without Congressional support. The leaders of Congress refused support unless the United States acted as part of a coalition which included Britain. Britain refused to go along. Besides, the members of the Joint Chiefs other than Radford did not think it advisable for the United States to become directly involved in the Indochina war. The fall of Dien Bien Phu on May 7 marked the defeat of French colonialism in Indochina.

FOR THE NEXT two and one half months, the Geneva Conference—attended by Britain, the Soviet Union, the United States,

France, and China as well as the Indochinese—dealt with the Indochina question. The United States had not been eager to have such a conference, fearing that the French would make concessions to "the communists." Dulles, unlike the foreign ministers of the other participants, did not take part. The instructions to Undersecretary of State Walter Bedell Smith, who attended in his stead, stated that the people of the region "should not be amalgamated into the Communist bloc of imperialist dictatorship." The United States played little part in the negotiations and did not join the other participants in the Final Declaration endorsing the agreements concluded. Smith limited himself to a "unilateral declaration" stating that the United States "takes note of the Agreements...and declares...that it will refrain from the threat or the use of force to disturb them...."[11]

The agreement on Vietnam called for a cessation of hostilities and laid the basis for a political settlement. It provided for a military demarcation line, with the forces of the Vietminh regrouped in the north and those of the French Union in the south. Each party would administer the zone into which its forces had been regrouped "pending the general elections which will bring about the unification of Vietnam." The agreement prohibited "the introduction into Vietnam of any troop reinforcements and additional military personnel" as well as "arms, munitions, and other war material." It also prohibited the establishment of any "military base under the control of a foreign state." The Final Declaration provided that "general elections shall be held in July 1956."[12]

But the United States was not interested in a political settlement. The CIA determined in August, shortly after the conclusion of the agreement, that "if the scheduled national elections are held in July 1956, and if the Viet Minh does not prejudice its political prospects, the Viet Minh will almost certainly win."[13] Soon the United States, together with the government in Saigon, was violating the agreement, always claiming that neither it nor Saigon was bound by it.

In June 1954, even as the Geneva talks were going on, Colonel Edward G. Lansdale, head of the covert Saigon Military Mission (SMM), arrived in Vietnam. Its own report describes the SMM as "a 'cold war' combat team" whose mission was "to undertake paramilitary operations against the enemy and to wage political-psychological warfare."[14]

Lansdale, selected because of his success in suppressing a guerrilla uprising in the Philippines, soon had things humming.

Hundreds of Vietnamese acquaintanceships were made quickly....
A new psychological warfare campaign was devised for the Vietnamese Army and for the government in Hanoi. Shortly after, a refresher course in combat psywar was constructed and Vietnamese Army personnel were rushed through it. A similar course was initiated for the Ministry of Information.[15]

The second ranking member of the SMM, Colonel Lucien Conein, "was given responsibility for developing a paramilitary organization in the north, to be in position when the Vietminh took over...." Conein's group moved north immediately and organized a paramilitary group.[16] The SMM set up training camps overseas, one in "a hidden valley on the Clark AFB [Air Force Base]" in the Philippines.[17]

Another SMM officer organized a paramilitary group in the south. The SMM "smuggled into Vietnam about eight and one half tons of supplies" for this group. And, says the SMM report, when the Vietminh took over Haiphong in May 1955,

our...teams were in place, completely equipped. It had taken a tremendous amount of hard work to beat the Geneva deadline, to locate, select, exfiltrate, train, infiltrate, equip the men of these two teams and have them in place, ready for actions required against the enemy.[18]

Rumor campaigns constituted one key activity of the various SMM groups. "The first rumor campaign was to be a carefully planted story of a Chinese Communist regiment in Tonkin taking reprisals against a Vietminh village whose girls the Chinese had raped...."[19] Later, the SMM issued false leaflets, claiming to be signed by the Vietminh, "instructing Tonkinese on how to behave for the Vietminh takeover of the Hanoi region...."[20] The SMM report talks with pride of the results of this activity.

The day following the distribution of these leaflets refugee registration [from north to south] tripled. Two days later, Vietminh currency was worth half the value prior to the leaflets.[21]

Meanwhile, the United States was also moving to take over control from the French of the Vietnamese government in the south. It had encouraged the emperor Bao Dai to appoint Ngo Dinh Diem prime minister. Besides being anticommunist Diem was also anti-French. He had spent several years in the United

States and was adept at promoting himself to U.S. officials. They felt that his anti-French nationalism would appeal to the Vietnamese and be useful against the French. U.S. officials helped Diem run a referendum in October 1955 which enabled him to depose Bao Dai and proclaim the Republic of Vietnam with himself as head. U.S. influence was supreme.

Diem was a Catholic in a mainly Buddhist country, a scion of an old aristocratic family from Hue, a mandarin not inclined to democracy. He set up a corrupt and repressive regime around his family, the landholding elite from Hue, and a small number of ambitious Catholic refugees from the north. Only support from the United States enabled this regime to establish a separate "Republic of Vietnam" south of the 17th parallel.

U.S. aid to Diem in the first year after Geneva reached $322 million.[22] Lansdale arranged for the training of a loyal and efficient Palace Guard and also helped avert an attempt by Diem's own Army to oust him. A U.S.-French planning group had been developing a "plan for the pacification of Vietminh and dissident areas." Now Lansdale's SMM took over and changed "the concept from the old rigid police controls of all areas to some of our concepts of winning over the population...." The paper prepared by SMM, with a few changes, was issued by Diem as a "National Security Action (Pacification) Directive."[23]

Besides the SMM, the U.S. Government also used a Michigan State University (MSU) Group, which employed 54 professors. Vice President Nixon himself had called John Hannah, the president of the university, to get its support. "From 1955 to 1960," writes Robert Scheer, "the Michigan team had the major responsibility for training, equipping, and financing the police apparatus for Diem's state." It reorganized the secret police, turned the regular police force into a paramilitary unit especially trained to deal with uprisings, and organized a rural militia of 40,000 men to pacify the countryside.[24]

The MSU Group also worked on a constitution, setting up a civil service, and other problems of public administration. Such projects for a separate administration showed that neither the Diem government nor the United States had any intention of abiding by the Geneva agreement calling for elections and unification.

Despite talk within the U.S. Government of the need for Diem to win popular support, his government was inherently unable to do so. It was a government representing landholders facing a people that desperately needed and wanted land reform.

The Pentagon historians recognized the significance of the land problem on Diem's standing with the people.

> One of Diem's primary failures lay in his inability ... to capture loyalties among his 90 percent agricultural people. The core of rural discontent was the large land holdings: in 1954 one quarter of one percent of the population owned forty percent of the rice growing land.[25]

Diem began a so-called land reform in early 1955, but for a large portion of the peasantry his program meant not reform but counterrevolution. The Vietminh had already been carrying out land reform in the areas they controlled in south Vietnam and, as the historian Gabriel Kolko points out, for those who had benefitted from the Vietminh's reforms, Diem's measures brought fear of losing valuable gains. "The moment he abolished the legal standing of the Viet Minh's land reforms, he unleashed social discontent and created actual and potential enemies."[26]

The government officials who administered the land reform, beginning with the minister in charge, were themselves landholders. Diem's reform returned to the landlords land the Vietminh had distributed to the peasants. It restored rents, sometimes running as high as forty percent, on land the peasants had been working for several years without rent. Only a minor proportion of the peasants received land under Diem's program and they had to pay for it. In 1959, 75 percent of the land still belonged to 15 percent of the landholders.[27]

Another reason for Diem's failure to gain popular support was the repression he immediately imposed. Diem clearly felt that he couldn't establish his political control without repression. The Vietminh had been establishing ties with the people, especially in the countryside, for many years. It was offering an alternative, including real land reform, to the program he was proposing. His program couldn't compete, leaving repression as the only way to establish control.

The first Diem troops to take over in the countryside, writes a Pentagon historian, "behaved toward the people very much as the Vietminh had led the farmers to expect." In the summer of 1955, Diem launched an Anti-Communist Denunciation Campaign. Meetings to denounce "Communists" took place everywhere. In January 1956, the government authorized the arrest and detention of anyone deemed dangerous to the state and by the end of the year, according to a French observer, 50,000 people were in jail. Fearing that the Vietminh might win posts, Diem abolished elections for village councils and instituted a system under which his district and province chiefs appointed officials to these bodies. The officials appointed were outsiders—Diem cronies, northern Catholics, city dwellers. "They and their police," writes Kolko, "personified the...daily oppression and corruption over the peasantry...."[28]

As long as there was still hope that the Geneva agreement would be carried out and reunification elections held, Vietminh activists in the South stuck to political action, organizing meetings, handing out petitions, and holding demonstrations. But after Diem's U.S.-backed move to create a separate "Republic," after the July 1956 date passed with no move toward holding the elections, and after Diem's rule turned increasingly repressive, open political activity became impossible and pointless. Yet the peasants wanted the land which Diem's "reform" was denying them and people in general were being provoked into action by Diem's terror. A growing spontaneous popular revolt forced the Communist Party and the Vietminh to organize armed struggle.

As armed rebellion grew, so did antirebel military sweeps in the countryside, police repression in the cities, and massive incarcerations in prisons and concentration camps. By 1958, according to the French writer Philippe Desvillers,

> a certain sequence of events became almost classical: denunciation, encirclement of villages, searches and raids, arrest of suspects, plundering, interrogations enlivened sometimes by torture (even of innocent people), deportation, and "regrouping" of populations suspected of intelligence with the rebels.[29]

U.S. aid financed the large-scale relocation of peasants; the "objective," according to a Pentagon historian, "was to resettle peasants out of areas where the GVN [Government of South Vietnam] could not operate routinely, into new policed communities...." Most peasants moved "unwillingly, for it often meant abandoning a cherished ancestral home, tombs, and developed gardens and fields for a strange and desolate place." Often the peasants resisted. Instead of increasing the government's security, the relocation program increased peasant hostility and rebellion.[30]

After a while the rebellion began to develop a structure, a leadership, and a program. In March 1960, the Veterans of the Resistance Association published a statement declaring that the Diem government had "driven the people of South Vietnam to take up arms in self-defense" and that they were fighting "to put an end to the Fascist dictatorship of the Ngo family."[31]

In December 1960, the National Liberation Front for South Vietnam was formed. The first point in its program was to

> overthrow the camouflaged colonial regime of the American imperialists and the dictatorial power of Ngo Dinh Diem, servant of the Americans, and institute a government of national democratic union.[32]

Soon the Front's newly created People's Liberation Army was carrying out armed actions and the NLF was able to set up its administration in entire regions.

THE BURGEONING NLF SUCCESS confronted John F. Kennedy when he assumed the presidency in January 1961. As Arthur Schlesinger, Jr. remembered later, "there were by now perhaps 15,000 Viet Cong [the term applied by Diem's government to the NLF and its fighters] in South Vietnam, and they were overrunning half the country, and more by night."[33]

To Kennedy, the rebellion against the Diem government was confirmation of his belief that guerrilla war was being used by "world communism" to circumvent U.S. nuclear superiority, and he saw the answer in the newly developed doctrine of "counterinsurgency." He became interested in the theory of guerrilla warfare, and according to Schlesinger, read "Mao Tse Tung and Che Guevara himself on the subject [and] told the Army to do likewise."[34]

The Army expanded its Special Forces, gave them elite status as Green Berets, and set up bases to train them in unconventional warfare. Counterinsurgency became a fad. Townsend Hoopes describes how

> soldiers, diplomats, and economic aid administrators of all ranks were required to take a "counterinsurgency course" before being posted to underdeveloped countries; special warfare centers were established in several parts of the world, and a high level Counter-Insurgency Committee under General Taylor...was created to keep

close watch on situations of incipient subversion in every corner of the globe.[35]

Kennedy was aware of the political aspect of guerrilla warfare. He knew that without the support of the people guerrillas will fail. Schlesinger writes that "he insisted that the Special Forces be schooled in sanitation, teaching, bridge-building, medical care, and the need for economic progress." He often bewailed Diem's unwillingness to undertake economic, social, and political reforms.[36]

But even with all their emphasis on the political, economic, and social aspects of counterinsurgency, Kennedy and his advisors failed to comprehend the nature of the Vietnamese revolution. They did not understand the inherent inability of the Diem regime to compete with the NLF for the people's support. They urged Diem—in the words of a State Department study—"to evoke the positive support of the peasantry" by giving "more emphasis to non-military aspects of the counterinsurgency program...."[37] But they never came to grips with the reasons he found it impossible to do so. For all the liberal rhetoric of the Kennedy administration, its basic response to the Vietnamese revolution was to increase U.S. military involvement.

The escalation began modestly. In April 1961, Kennedy ordered an increase of 100 in the number of military advisers in Vietnam. The significance of the decision, writes a Pentagon historian, is that it "signalled a willingness to go beyond the 685-man limit on the size of the U.S. military mission in Saigon, which, if it were done openly, would be the first formal breach of the Geneva agreements."[38] Kennedy also ordered 400 Green Berets to be sent to Vietnam to train Vietnamese Special Forces.

Within days of these decisions, the Joint Chiefs of Staff proposed open intervention with U.S. troops, and in the months that followed a number of Kennedy advisers, some after visits to Vietnam, recommended that the number of U.S. troops there be increased. Vice President Lyndon Johnson wrote in a memo to the President:

> We must decide whether to help these countries to the best of our ability or throw in the towel in the area and pull back our defenses to San Francisco and [a] "Fortress America" concept.[39]

General Taylor cabled Kennedy:

The risks of backing into a major Asian war by way of SVN [South Vietnam] are present but are not impressive....I have reached the conclusion that the introduction of...military Task Force without delay offers definitely more advantage than it creates risks and difficulties. In fact, do not believe that our program to save SVN will succeed without it.[40]

Secretary of State Dean Rusk and Secretary of Defense Robert McNamara in a joint memo recommended that:

We now take the decision to commit ourselves to the objective of preventing the fall of South Vietnam to Communism and that, in doing so, we recognize that the introduction of United States and other SEATO forces may be necessary to achieve this objective.[41]

Kennedy faced problems in increasing the number of U.S. troops in Vietnam. As an unsigned note of a National Security Council meeting put it, "Pres receiving static from Congress; they against using U.S. troops." To help meet the problems, Rusk and McNamara had drawn a distinction between two categories of troops: (A) those "required for the direct support of South Vietnamese military effort" and (B) "larger organized units with actual or potential direct military mission." Category (A) *"should be introduced as speedily as possible.* Category (B) units pose a more serious problem in that they are much more significant from the point of view of domestic and international political factors...."[42]

Kennedy tried to send only Category (A) support troops and avoid sending Category (B) combat troops. But as *New York Times* reporter, Hedrick Smith, says in his commentary, this "careful bureaucratic distinction... was hard to maintain in the field."[43] The distinction also became harder to maintain politically as U.S. casualties rose: from 14 in 1961 to 109 in 1962 to 489 in 1963.[44] By October 1963, there were 16,700 U.S. troops in Vietnam, compared to 2,000 when Kennedy took office, and they were increasingly participating in combat.[45]

DESPITE THE KENNEDY administration's talk about the need for increased democracy in South Vietnam, for two and one half years it held to a policy that the news correspondents dubbed "sink or swim with Ngo Dinh Diem." The administration knew better than anybody that Diem was a fascist dictator, but so long as the war seemed to be going well it accepted him. In 1962, according to reports by the U.S. military and Embassy in Vietnam and statistics presented by McNamara, the war did seem to be going well. Some correspondents dissented, arguing that it was going badly and could not be won with Diem. But most key members of the administration held to an optimistic view. In the spring of 1963, McNamara authorized the Defense Department to announce that "we have turned the corner in Vietnam."[46]

Then in May a group of Buddhists demonstrated in Hue against a government order forbidding the display of their flag. Diem's troops fired into the demonstrators, killing nine. Protests erupted throughout South Vietnam. Diem's answer, as always, was repression. The protests became more frequent and the repression more severe. At one mass demonstration after another, a Buddhist monk doused in gasoline would set himself on fire. Diem's CIA-trained Special Forces, headed by his brother Nhu, carried out massive raids against Buddhist pagodas, beating and arresting people and desecrating religious property.

The Buddhist demonstrations "created a crisis for American policy," writes a Pentagon historian.

> The US policy of support for South Vietnam's struggle against the Hanoi-supported Viet Cong insurgency was founded on unequivocal support of Diem....When the Buddhist protest revealed widespread public disaffection, the US made repeated attempts to persuade Diem to redress the Buddhist grievances, to repair his public image, and to win back public support. But the Ngos [Diem and Nhu] were unwilling to bend.[47]

So the United States began to promote a coup to remove Diem. Ambassador Frederick Nolting had cultivated friendly relations with Diem. Kennedy replaced him with Henry Cabot Lodge. Less than 48 hours after his arrival in Saigon, Lodge cabled the State Department that he was receiving coup feelers. The Department cabled back:

> Diem must be given chance to rid himself of Nhu and his coterie.... If he remains obdurate, then we are prepared to accept the obvious implication that we can no longer support Diem. You may also tell appropriate military commanders we will give them direct support in any interim period of breakdown central government mechanism....

Ambassador and country team should urgently examine all possible alternative leadership and make detailed plans as to how we might bring about Diem's replacement....[48]

The mission in Saigon worked with plotting Vietnamese generals. The key U.S. contact was Lucien Conein of the CIA. At a meeting between Conein and the Vietnamese general, Duong Van Minh, Minh made clear that he did not need "specific American support," but did need assurances that the United States would "not attempt to thwart his plan." He outlined to Conein three possible plans for accomplishing "the change of government," one of which involved assassinating Diem. Conein stated that he "could not advise concerning the best of the three plans."[49]

With Lodge's authorization, the CIA provided the generals with intelligence about the arms and encampments of the pro-Diem military forces.[50] Conein gave them 3 million piasters ($42,000) to help meet emergency financial needs.[51]

The White House supervised Lodge's actions. One White House cable told him that it was "essential that this effort be totally secure and fully deniable." A cable from National Security Adviser, McGeorge Bundy, told Lodge that "we [are] concerned that our line-up of forces in Saigon ... indicates [an] approximately equal balance of forces, with substantial possibility [of] serious and prolonged fighting or even defeat." Another Bundy cable instructed Lodge that "if you should conclude that there is not clearly a high prospect of success, you should communicate this doubt to [the] generals in a way calculated to persuade them to desist at least until chances are better." But the cable continued, "once a coup under responsible leadership has begun..., it is in the interest of the U.S. Government that it should succeed."[52]

The day of the coup, the Vietnamese generals invited Conein to their General Staff Headquarters. Conein was with them practically throughout the operation, maintaining telephone contact with the Embassy.[53]

The generals offered to grant Diem safe conduct to the airport to allow him to leave Vietnam. They asked Conein to procure an aircraft and he relayed the request to the Embassy. The Embassy replied that no aircraft would be available for the next 24 hours. A few hours later, General Minh told Conein that Diem and his brother Nhu were dead, that they had committed suicide. Actually, soldiers bringing them in to the General Staff Headquarters had murdered them.[54]

After the coup, the State Department delayed recognition of the new government. "Rusk felt," writes a Pentagon historian,

> that a delay would be useful to the generals in not appearing to be U.S. agents or stooges and would assist us in our public stance of noncomplicity. He further discouraged any large delegation of the generals from calling on Lodge as if they were "reporting in."[55]

Both Schlesinger and Sorensen, in their books on the Kennedy administration, explicitly deny U.S. complicity:

Schlesinger:

> It is important to state clearly that the coup of November 1, 1963, was entirely planned and carried out by the Vietnamese. Neither the American Embassy nor the CIA were involved in instigation or execution.[56]

Sorensen:

> On November 1, 1963, as corruption, repression, and disorder increased, a new effort by the Vietnamese military to take command of the government was launched and succeeded. It received no assistance from the United States, nor did this country do anything to prevent or defeat it.[57]

The Pentagon internal history puts it differently:

> For the military coup d'état against Ngo Dinh Diem, the U.S. must accept its full share of responsibility. Beginning in August of 1963 we variously authorized, sanctioned and encouraged the coup efforts of the Vietnamese generals and offered full support for a successor government. In October we cut off aid to Diem in a direct rebuff, giving a green light to the generals. We maintained clandestine contact with them throughout the planning and execution of the coup and sought to review their operational plans and proposed new government.[58]

The overthrow of Diem didn't solve any problems: The new government was also incapable of winning popular support. After a fact-finding trip to Vietnam, McNamara reported to President Johnson on December 21, 1963:

> *Viet Cong progress* has been great during the period since the coup, with my best guess being that the situation has in fact been deteriorating in the countryside since July to a far greater extent than we realized because of our undue dependence on distorted

Vietnamese reporting. The Viet Cong now control very high proportions of the people in certain key provinces, particularly those
directly south and west of Saigon.[59]

McNamara added that "my appraisal may be overly pessimistic. Lodge, [U.S. Commander Gen. Paul D.] Harkins, and Minh
would probably agree with me on specific points, but feel that
January should see significant improvement."[60]

Instead of improving, however, the situation continued to deteriorate. Not only did the military situation get worse, but at the
end of January another coup took place, deposing Minh. The
fall of Diem had ushered in a period in which the government
would change every few months.

U.S. officials in Washington and Vietnam thrashed around for
ways to control the situation. Although the CIA held that "the
primary sources of communist strength in South Vietnam are
indigenous,"[61] the United States decided on a plan of clandestine military attacks against North Vietnam in the hope that this
would force it to call off the revolution. The plan called for
"progressively escalating pressure:" first U-2 spy flights, leaflet
drops, and "20 destructive undertakings;" then, more numerous
and intensive "destructive operations" against "targets identified
with North Vietnam's economic and industrial well-being." Besides the attacks, the United States would carry out covert destroyer patrols in the Gulf of Tonkin, both as a show of force and
to collect intelligence that could be useful to raiding parties and
bomber pilots.[62]

But the deterioration in the South continued. After another
fact-finding visit in March 1964, McNamara noted, "The situation
has unquestionably been growing worse...."[63]

In 22 of the 43 provinces, the Viet Cong control 50% or more of the
land area....
    Draft dodging is high while the Viet Cong are recruiting ener-
getically and effectively.[64]

McNamara didn't conclude that the people of South Vietnam
were behind the revolution, that they were rebelling against the
United States and its puppet government. Gone was the liberal
Kennedy administration rhetoric. What McNamara did was recommend "Graduated Overt Military Pressure by the GVN and
U.S. Forces." The United States, he said, "must continue to
make it emphatically clear that we are prepared to furnish assis-

tance and support for as long as it takes to bring the insurgency under control."[65]

President Johnson approved McNamara's recommendation and the government prepared to carry it out. Assistant Secretary of State William Bundy sent the President a 30-day scenario for graduated military pressure that would culminate in mining North Vietnam's ports and bombing attacks by U.S. aircraft against "POL (petroleum, oil, and lubricants) storage, selected airfields, barracks/training areas, bridges, railroad yards, port facilities, communications, and industries."[66] The military began to determine specific targets. By summer a list of 94 targets was ready.

The preparations were not just military, but also political. The scenario called for obtaining on D-Day minus 20 a joint Congressional resolution "authorizing whatever is necessary with respect to Vietnam." Bundy drafted the resolution on May 25.[67]

By early August, the administration was well prepared for action; what it needed was a pretext. The Tonkin Gulf "incidents" provided the pretext. On August 2, the U.S. destroyer *Maddox* exchanged fire with several North Vietnamese patrol boats in the Gulf. The United States immediately warned of "the grave consequences which would inevitably result from any further unprovoked offensive military action against United States forces."[68] Actually, the North Vietnamese had earlier been fending off attacks on their islands by South Vietnamese speedboat teams secretly organized by the United States. Within a few days, Senator Wayne Morse revealed that he had received a tip from a Pentagon officer: the *Maddox* had been involved in the covert raids on North Vietnam.[69] The Pentagon directed the *Maddox*, now accompanied by another destroyer and protective aircraft, to return to the Tonkin Gulf.

On August 4, President Johnson announced a second attack. The United States has never presented credible evidence that such an attack actually occurred. Stanley Karnow writes:

> Subsequent research by both official and unofficial investigators has indicated with almost total certainty that the second Communist attack in the Tonkin Gulf never happened. It had not been deliberately faked, but Johnson and his staff, desperately seeking a pretext to act vigorously, had seized upon a fuzzy set of circumstances to fulfill a contingency plan.[70]

The contingency plan came into effect immediately. The Joint Chiefs of Staff began selecting targets from the 94-target list and less than six hours after the first messages about the alleged attack reached the Pentagon, the order for "reprisal" air strikes went out. Within another two hours, President Johnson was meeting with leaders of Congress to ask for the Congressional resolution called for in Bundy's scenario, and two days later, on August 7, Congress passed the resolution.

THE UNITED STATES was now openly involving itself in an undeclared war in Vietnam and deployed its forces accordingly: interceptor and fighter bomber aircraft to South Vietnam, fighter-bombers to Thailand, back-up planes to advance bases in the Pacific, and a new attack carrier group to the western Pacific. Although Johnson's election-season need to show restraint temporarily slowed down the immediate escalation of U.S. military action, planning for escalation continued apace.

Part of the planning consisted of trying to devise ways to provoke North Vietnam into actions that could be used to justify escalation. A memo by Assistant Secretary of Defense John T. McNaughton says that the actions taken by the United States

> should be likely at some point to provoke a military DRV response [and] the provoked response should be likely to provide good grounds for us to escalate if we wished....[71]

McNaughton also mentioned the idea of establishing a U.S. naval base in South Vietnam, "perhaps at Danang," and a proposal

> to enlarge significantly the US military role in the pacification program inside South Vietnam—e.g., large numbers of US special forces, divisions of regular combat troops, US air, etc....[72]

After the 1964 election was over, escalation began in earnest. On February 7, 1965, when NLF guerrillas attacked a U.S. advisers' compound and helicopter base at Pleiku, Johnson immediately ordered "retaliation" and Navy jets raided a North Vietnamese army camp at Donghoi. On February 13, Johnson authorized a long-planned operation code-named Rolling Thunder, a series of air raids of mounting intensity against North Vietnam. On March 8, the first avowed combat troops—two Marine battalions totalling 3,500 men—landed in Vietnam with the announced intention of protecting the base at Danang, from which many of the air raids were being launched. On March 9, Johnson authorized the use of napalm in new, heavier raids. In early April, he approved an 18-20,000 man increase in "military support forces," the deployment of two additional Marine battalions, and a "change of mission" permitting their "more active use."[73]

As a Pentagon analyst put it, "the change in ground rules ... posed serious public-information and stage-managing problems for the President."[74] In the memo informing the Secretaries of State and Defense and the Director of the CIA of the April decisions, McGeorge Bundy advised:

> The President desires that...premature publicity be avoided by all possible precautions. The actions themselves should be taken as rapidly as practicable, but in ways that should minimize any appearance of sudden changes in policy, and official statements on these troop movements will be made only with the direct approval of the Secretary of Defense, in consultation with the Secretary of State. The President's desire is that these movements and changes should be understood as being gradual and wholly consistent with existing policy.[75]

But the bombing campaign against the North had made it suddenly clear that the United States was at war. A crescendo of protest in newspaper editorials, on college campuses, and in Congress got under way. Calls for a negotiated settlement came from Senators Frank Church, Mike Mansfield, and George McGovern. Teach-ins at universities mobilized student opposition. In April 1965, the first mass march on Washington took place.

While the escalation was provoking an explosion of domestic opposition, it was not solving the problem in Vietnam. The RVN troops kept suffering defeat at the hands of ever more powerful NLF guerrilla units. Soon the U.S. Commander in Vietnam, General William Westmoreland, was appealing for additional U.S. troops. By June, he was asking for a buildup that would bring total U.S. deployment to 200,000 men.

As the administration was nearing a decision on the increase, Under-Secretary of State George Ball warned that it would be a "catastrophic error" and argued for "cutting our losses." In one memorandum to Rusk, McNamara and other high officials and another to the President, and in various meetings, Ball made several points: "Once large numbers of U.S. troops are committed" and "once we suffer large casualties, we will have started a well-nigh irreversible process." The "Viet Cong—while supported and guided from the North—is largely an indigenous movement. Although we have emphasized its cold war aspects, the conflict in South Vietnam is essentially a civil war within that country." South Vietnam is politically "a lost cause.... The 'government' in Saigon is a travesty." The "loss of South Vietnam does not mean the loss of all of Southeast Asia...." But Ball was alone in recommending de-escalation and disengagement and the administration rejected his advice.[76]

By the end of July, the government had to admit publicly to the continuing troop buildup, though then as later, the figures published lagged behind those already secretly agreed upon. Even after admitting in a July 28 press conference that he had asked Westmoreland "what more he needs" and would "meet his needs," Johnson denied that the troop buildup implied "any change in policy whatever."[77]

In the words of Townsend Hoopes, who watched the 1965 escalation from his position as Deputy Assistant Secretary of Defense:

> By moving with secret purpose behind a screen of bland assurances designed to minimize or mislead, by admitting nothing until pressed by the facts and then no more than was absolutely necessary, by stretching to the limit (and perhaps beyond) the intent of the Tonkin Gulf Resolution, the President carried a bemused and half-aware nation far beyond the Eisenhower and Kennedy positions to a radically different involvement in the intractable Vietnam conflict. It would have to be conceded that the performance was a piece of artful, even masterful, political craftsmanship. Unfortunately for Lyndon Johnson and the American people, it could be vindicated only by a quick and decisive military victory. But when the mists of summer confusion lifted, there were 170,000 U.S. troops in Vietnam, U.S. air forces were bombing the North with mounting intensity, and the enemy showed no sign of surrender or defeat. There was the President and there was the country— waist-deep in the Big Muddy.[78]

Instead of a decisive victory, the 1965 buildup brought what Assistant Secretary of Defense John McNaughton described in a January 1966 memo as "an escalating military stalemate." McNaughton explained the reasons the United States was not withdrawing from the quagmire:

> The present U.S. objective in Vietnam is to avoid humiliation. The reasons why we *went into* Vietnam to the present depth are

varied; but they are now largely academic. Why we have *not withdrawn* from Vietnam is, by all odds, *one* reason:... to preserve our reputation as a guarantor, and thus to preserve our effectiveness in the rest of the world. (Italics in original.)[79]

So for three more years, Westmoreland made ever fresh demands and Washington granted each new request till by the end of 1968 the steadily mounting troop level reached 536,000.

Opposition to the war mushroomed during 1967 as the number of U.S. soldiers killed mounted and draft calls hit 30,000 a month. The unexpected scale of the NLF's Tet offensive in February 1968 shattered the official picture of steady U.S. progress. Television brought scenes of the offensive—rebel attacks on dozens of towns and cities, a guerrilla assault on the U.S. Embassy in Saigon—into millions of U.S. homes. Johnson's ratings in the public opinion polls plummeted. When Westmoreland requested an additional 206,000 troops, the policy consensus in Washington fell apart. Johnson, shocked by a proposal that would require mobilization of reserves and putting the economy on a war footing, named his new Defense Secretary, Clark Clifford, to head a task force to examine the implications of Westmoreland's request.

Clifford learned that many Pentagon civilians were among those most disillusioned with escalation. A memo by Assistant Secretary of Defense Alain Enthoven noted that

> despite a massive influx of 500,000 US troops, 1.2 million tons of bombs a year, 400,000 attack sorties per year, 200,000 enemy KIA [killed in action] in three years, 20,000 US KIA, etc., our control of the countryside and the defense of the urban areas is now essentially at pre-August 1965 levels. We have achieved a stalemate at a high commitment. A new strategy must be sought.[80]

Clifford, appointed to replace the doubting McNamara, became a doubter himself in the course of his task force's deliberations. At his suggestion, Johnson assembled a group of "Wise Men," the elder statesmen of his Senior Advisory Group on Vietnam, who only five months before had backed his course. Now a majority of the Wise Men—including such luminaries as Dean Acheson, George Ball, McGeorge Bundy, Douglas Dillon, Arthur Goldberg, Matthew Ridgway, and Cyrus Vance—favored a shift in policy. As Vance later put it:

> We were weighing not only what was happening in Vietnam, but the social and political effects in the United States, the impact on

the U.S. economy, the attitude of other nations. The divisiveness in the country was growing with such acuteness that it was threatening to tear the United States apart.[81]

Robert Murphy, Abe Fortas, and Generals Omar Bradley and Maxwell Taylor remained unconvinced. But the majority of the Wise Men held that it was necessary to move toward de-escalation, negotiations, and disengagement. Shaken by pressure from Clifford, the change in line of his Wise Men, incipient revolt in Congress and in the Democratic Party, and massive protest around the country, Johnson shifted course. In a speech on March 31, he presented "a peace offer." Announcing a halt in bombing north of the 20th parallel, he called on Ho Chi Minh to respond and designated Averell Harriman to represent the United States in any peace talks that might result. He also announced his withdrawal from the 1968 presidential race.

On April 5, Hanoi accepted talks and by mid-May Harriman was meeting in Paris with the North Vietnamese delegate, Xuan Thuy. Lack of progress in the war combined with growing resistance at home had forced the United States to give up its policy of escalation.

But the change in policy was limited. The United States had by no means decided to simply get out of the war. It had not given up the idea of imposing its will in Vietnam. At the talks it haggled, rejected Hanoi's demand that it unconditionally cease bombing the North, tried to impose conditions on Hanoi's delegates, refused to recognize the NLF as an independent entity. The talks soon reached an impasse and the war dragged on.

The United States was still not facing the military-political realities. Its lack of realism meant five more years of fighting before Washington signed a peace agreement, and another two years before the war finally ended. In that time, 183,000 more soldiers—including 20,000 Americans—died, hundreds of thousands of civilians became casualties, and millions were made homeless.

AFTER THE 1968 ELECTION, Nixon and his National Security Adviser-designate, Henry Kissinger, reviewed Vietnam policy. As Nixon explains in his memoirs, several options existed. The United States could try "to administer a knockout blow that would both end the war and win it." But only two knockout blows were "available": to bomb North

Vietnam's elaborate dike system, which would have caused floods and killed hundreds of thousands of civilians, or to use tactical nuclear weapons. Nixon rejected both these options. "The domestic and international uproar that would have accompanied the use of either of these knockout blows would have got my administration off to the worst possible start." There was also the option of escalating the conventional war. But this would have required "up to six months of highly intensified fighting and significantly increased casualties" and "there was no way that I could hold the country together for that period of time...."[82]

Another option was to end the war "by announcing a quick and orderly withdrawal of all American forces." But, says Nixon, he didn't want to abandon South Vietnamese President Nguyen Van Thieu.

> I was aware that many Americans considered Thieu a petty and corrupt dictator unworthy of our support.... [But] as I saw it, the alternative to Thieu was not someone more enlightened or tolerant or democratic but someone weaker.... The South Vietnamese needed a strong and stable government to carry on the fight against the efforts of the Vietcong terrorists....[83]

So Nixon developed a strategy of placating the anti-war movement while trying to coerce Hanoi into an agreement on U.S. terms. He talked peace, but in March 1969 ordered the secret bombing of "communist sanctuaries" in Cambodia, a neutral country. The purpose of the bombing, carried out by huge eight-engine B-52s, was not just to hit North Vietnamese supply lines but to "signal" Hanoi that the United States was still committed to the war. Nixon placed great hopes on the bombing. He states:

> During the first months of the administration.... I remained convinced that the combined effect of the military pressure from the secret bombing and the public pressure from my repeated invitations to negotiate would force the Communists to respond. In March I confidently told the Cabinet that I expected the war to be over in a year.[84]

But the signal did not have the desired effect: Hanoi continued to reject the U.S. demand for a "mutual withdrawal" from South Vietnam. Faced with the growing demand in the United States for disengagement, Nixon developed the policy of "Vietnamization": phased withdrawal of U.S. troops and the training and equipping of South Vietnamese to fill the gaps. The United

States would continue to try by secret bombing, by threats, by any other way that could be dreamed up, to win "peace with honor"—which meant that the Vietnamese would have to give up their revolution and the puppet Thieu regime would be preserved.

In June, Nixon finally gave in to the public demand and announced the first withdrawal—25,000 troops. He hoped that this would "calm domestic public opinion by graphically demonstrating that we were beginning to wind down the war." But he had no real intention of winding down the war except on his terms. In July, he decided "to go for broke," to attempt "to end the war one way or the other—either by negotiated agreement or by an increased use of force." He felt he had to act quickly. "Once the summer was over and Congress and the colleges returned from vacation in September, a massive new antiwar tide would sweep the country...." Together with Kissinger, he "developed an elaborate orchestration of diplomatic, military, and publicity pressures we would bring to bear on Hanoi." He decided to set November 1, 1969 "as the deadline for what would in effect be an ultimatum to North Vietnam."[85]

Nixon started with a personal letter to Ho Chi Minh, sent through a French diplomat, whom he instructed to also pass along a verbal warning that unless a "serious breakthrough" in the Paris talks was achieved by the November 1 deadline, "I would regretfully find myself obliged to have recourse to measures of great consequence and force." He reiterated the warning in private conversations with President Nicolae Ceausescu when he visited Rumania on August 2. For his part, Kissinger initiated secret negotiations with the North Vietnamese representatives in Paris with the threat of "measures of the greatest consequences" if there were no "major progress" in the deadlocked talks.[86]

To back up the ultimatum, Kissinger requested a plan for possible escalation against the north. Code-named Duck Hook, the plan, as described by Seymour Hersh,

> called for the massive bombing of Hanoi, Haiphong, and other key areas in North Vietnam...; the destruction—possibly with nuclear devices—of the main north-south passes along the Ho Chi Minh Trail; and the bombing of North Vietnam's main railroad links with China.... In all twenty-nine major targets in North Vietnam were targeted for destruction in a series of air attacks planned to last four days and be renewed, if necessary, until Hanoi capitulated.[87]

Kissinger set up a working group in the NSC to study Duck Hook. As one participant later recalled, Kissinger told them he "refuse[d] to believe that a little fourth-rate power like North Vietnam does not have a breaking point."[88] On August 25, just before he died, Ho Chi Minh answered Nixon's secret letter. His answer concluded:

> In your letter you have expressed the desire to act for a just peace. For this the United States must cease the war of aggression and withdraw their troops from South Vietnam, respect the right of the population of the South and of the Vietnamese nation to dispose of themselves, without foreign influence.[89]

Nixon saw this as a "cold rebuff," but felt that Ho's successors might not be bound by his reply, and decided to "orchestrate the maximum possible pressure on Hanoi" in the time remaining before the November 1 deadline.[90] One way of doing this was to try to get the Soviet Union to move Hanoi to yield. In conversations with Ambassador Anatoly Dobrynin, Kissinger often complained about lack of Soviet help in ending the war. During one conversation, a staged phone call from Nixon interrupted. When Kissinger hung up, he told Dobrynin, "The President just told me in that call that as far as Vietnam is concerned, the train has just left the station and is now headed down the track."[91] According to Kissinger, Dobrynin "always evaded a reply" to his demands and complaints and "in response, we procrastinated on all the negotiations in which the Soviet Union was interested...."[92]

Finally, Nixon "moved the pressure on Hanoi up a notch" when in a conversation with several Senators he planted a story he "knew would leak." A week later, a Rowland Evans and Robert Novak column reported that he was considering blockading Haiphong harbor and invading North Vietnam.[93]

But Nixon's ultimatum didn't work. He and Kissinger tried to buy time for it to work by talking of troop withdrawals, by camouflaging what they were really trying to do. But as time passed and peace didn't come, opposition to the war once again surged. The first Vietnam Moratorium Day on October 15, 1969, brought 250,000 demonstrators to Washington and hundreds of thousands more to rallies in other cities. Nixon admits:

> Although publicly I continued to ignore the raging antiwar controversy, I had to face the fact that it had probably destroyed the credibility of my ultimatum to Hanoi.[94]

Nixon and Kissinger drew back from their intended blow. In an address to the country on November 3, Nixon, as he says in his memoirs, "emphasized that our policy would not be affected by demonstrations in the streets." But the policy was, of course, affected.

> The message... was that we were going to keep our commitment in Vietnam. We were going to continue fighting until the Communists agreed to negotiate a fair and honorable peace or until the South Vietnamese were able to defend themselves on their own.... At the same time we would continue our disengagement based on the principles of the Nixon Doctrine.[95]

The Nixon Doctrine was the principle of Vietnamization applied not just to Vietnam, but to Asia as a whole and other areas. It was a strategy of trying to reduce the opposition of the people of the United States to intervention and war by having local surrogates do the fighting and take the losses.

The pressure to pull more and more troops out of Vietnam came not only from the people and Congress, but also from the Defense Department. The Vietnam War was devouring so much in military resources that Defense Secretary Laird became concerned about the U.S. capacity to project a "credible" military posture in the rest of the world. Only in the timing of withdrawal announcements did Nixon have leeway. Having failed to pacify the opposition with successive small withdrawals in June, September, and December of 1969, he decided that "the time had come to drop a bombshell on the gathering spring storm of antiwar protest," and on April 20, 1970 made a one-time announcement of "the withdrawal of 150,000 men over the next year."[96]

But ten days later, Nixon dropped a second bombshell which prevented him from reaping any political benefits from the first: he announced that he was sending troops into Cambodia. Lon Nol, a virulent anti-communist, had overthrown Cambodia's neutralist ruler, Norodom Sihanouk, in a coup. Nixon thought "we need[ed] a bold move" to help Lon Nol "survive." Without any evidence, he held that North Vietnamese forces "were closing in on Phnom Penh," the Cambodian capital. Against the judgment of Defense Secretary Laird and Secretary of State Rogers, he felt that an attack on the "communist sanctuaries" in Cambodia would be of decisive help in the war in Vietnam.[97] He announced the move on television, adding:

If, when the chips are down, the world's most powerful nation... acts like a pitiful, helpless giant, the forces of totalitarianism and anarchy will threaten free nations and free institutions throughout the world.[98]

THE NEW EXPANSION of the war brought a fresh outburst of opposition. The National Guard fired at students demonstrating at Kent State University in Ohio, killing 4 and wounding 9. A few days later, police fired at students protesting against war and racism at Jackson State University in Mississippi, leaving two dead and 12 wounded. Further demonstrations erupted at hundreds of campuses and in many cities. Kissinger writes:

> Washington took on the character of a besieged city. A pinnacle of mass public protest was reached by May 9 when a crowd estimated at between 75,000 and 100,000 demonstrated on a hot Saturday afternoon on the Ellipse, the park to the south of the White House. Police surrounded the White House; a ring of sixty buses was used to shield the grounds of the President's home.[99]

Congress also lost patience with the administration over a war that instead of winding down was spreading. It protested the usurpation by the President of its war making powers and took steps to tie his hands. In June 1970, the Senate passed the Cooper-Church Amendment which demanded that Nixon remove all U.S. troops from Cambodia by July 1—the first time that Congress had ever imposed such a requirement on a president during a war.

Just as the Vietnam Moratorium the year before had stopped the administration from acting on its November ultimatum, the vehement popular and Congressional opposition now cut short the Cambodian invasion. Repeatedly in the following months, fear of the political consequences restrained Nixon from trying to use massive bombing and blockade to end the war without a U.S. defeat.

Kissinger writes that "Nixon's mood oscillated wildly." At one point he asserted that if negotiations failed, he would throw restraint to the winds. A week later, he fretted that the war was sapping his political support. After two conservative Senators urged him to end the war quickly, Nixon "wanted to bring matters to a head by blockading the North, resuming bombing, and simultaneously withdrawing all our forces." But Kissinger warned that "in view of the trouble we had in sustaining a campaign of eight weeks' duration to a distance of twenty miles in Cambodia, we would not be able to stick to such a course unless there had been overwhelming provocation."[100]

"Bringing matters to a head" was a strategy of desperation. Vietnamization wasn't working and the U.S. position was getting weaker. Kissinger's secret negotiations with the North Vietnamese in Paris were making no progress.

Washington's position in the negotiations reflected its lack of realism. It was overestimating its strength in relation to that of the revolutionaries. It kept demanding concessions which did not correspond to its steadily declining ability to pursue the war.

The people of the United States were demanding an end to the war. A National Committee for a Political Settlement in Vietnam led by the educator Clark Kerr urged a unilateral U.S. ceasefire. In June 1971, the Senate passed the Mansfield Amendment which called for a total withdrawal from Vietnam within nine months in exchange for the release of all U.S. prisoners. But the administration persisted in its attempts to settle the war on its own unrealistic terms.[101]

With none of its strategies working, the administration shifted in frustration from one to another. In December 1971, expecting a new communist offensive and wanting, as Kissinger puts it, "to seize the initiative," Nixon ordered two days of full-scale bombing of fuel depots, airfields, and other strategic targets in southern North Vietnam. Simultaneously, the United States sent "strong notes to both Moscow and Peking... warning that an offensive would evoke the most serious retaliation."[102]

The offensive came later than expected, but when it did come, its power caught the Saigon forces unprepared. "Official U.S. analysts then and later," writes Kolko, "felt that the war would probably have ended in spring 1972 had America not employed huge amounts of air power in South Vietnam."[103]

Besides air power, the United States also employed diplomatic pressure. Kissinger met with Dobrynin three times in less than a week. He "accused the Soviet Union of complicity in Hanoi's attack." He warned that "if the offensive continued, we would be forced into measures certain to present Moscow with difficult choices...." He threatened "drastic measures to end the war once and for all."[104]

Kissinger also sent an assistant to see Huang Hua, the Chinese ambassador at the U.N. "We protested China's public backing of the North Vietnamese invasion" and "we repeated that we attached 'extreme importance' to the improvement of our relations with China—implicitly warning that Vietnam was an obstacle."[105]

At Nixon's insistence, the United States mounted a massive air offensive against North Vietnam. Nixon felt that the bombing proposals of the Pentagon were "timid" and laid down his view in a memo to Kissinger: "What all of us must have in mind is that we must *punish* the enemy in ways that he will really hurt at this time...." The United States carried out more than 700 B-52 raids over North Vietnam in April 1972.[106]

A Vietnamese historian describes the effects of the bombardment:

> Almost all North Vietnamese cities were wholly or partially destroyed, and all industrial installations were hit. Washington sought to systematically destroy the entire industrial economy of the country. Agriculture was also targeted, with all-out bombing of the most important hydraulic works. To crown the escalation, the network of river and sea dikes of North Vietnam were the target of numerous attacks, with a view to causing catastrophic floods during the heavy rains around July-August.[107]

On May 8, Nixon announced the long-threatened ultimate escalation: the mining of Haiphong and all other North Vietnamese harbors, a blockade to interdict delivery of supplies, the cutting of rail and other communications, and continued air and naval strikes throughout North Vietnam.

In January, Nixon had made public the existence of secret negotiations in Paris to shore up his political position in an election year. Now he and Kissinger hoped to use the pounding and blockade of the North to get the terms they wanted at the negotiations. They expected to benefit from Nixon's trips to Beijing in February and Moscow in May for summit meetings. They hoped, in Kissinger's words, "to complete the isolation of Hanoi by giving Moscow and Peking a stake in their ties with us."[108] And they hoped to portray themselves before the people of the United States as architects of world peace who could be trusted to end the war in Vietnam.

But even with the bombing, blockade, and high-powered diplomacy, the administration did not achieve the terms it sought. The balance of forces did not support such terms. As with Chiang's troops in China, the Saigon soldiers lacked motivation and desertions ran high. Large parts of the army disintegrated during the communist offensive. Re-escalating the use of U.S. ground troops was politically out of the question. The bombing hurt Vietnam cruelly, leaving effects that would last for many years. But Soviet and Chinese supplies continued to arrive by railroad, circumventing the blockade.

So the Paris negotiations finally, after three years, got down to serious dealing. The North Vietnamese wanted mainly to get the United States out of Vietnam. With the United States out, the revolution was bound to prevail. For its part the United States was being forced to withdraw, though the administration remained stubbornly confident that one way or another it could help an anticommunist regime to survive. Nixon tried to transmit this confidence to Thieu in secret letters designed to overcome his resistance to any agreement.

By October 12, Kissinger and his Vietnamese counterpart, Le Duc Tho, had arrived at an agreement and set dates for initialing and signing it. The agreement provided for a cease fire, the withdrawal of U.S. forces, and the release of prisoners. Kissinger would have liked it to provide for the withdrawal of North Vietnamese forces. But by now he understood that this was "an objective we could reach only by the total defeat of Hanoi, through all-out war, which in turn our public and the Congress would not support."[109]

Nixon began immediately to welch on the agreement. Thieu didn't want to see it go through and demanded numerous changes. Kissinger cabled from Saigon that "his demands verge on insanity." Nixon himself considered Thieu's conduct "infuriating."[110] But told by his advisers that he didn't need the agreement to win the 1972 election, Nixon, using Thieu as a pretext, tried to get Hanoi back to the conference table. The North Vietnamese balked at major changes in an agreement already concluded. The dates for initialing and signing the agreement passed. At a mid-December meeting in Paris, the talks collapsed.

Now, safely re-elected, Nixon decided on one more effort to use terror against North Vietnam. He ordered B-52 strikes on the Hanoi-Haiphong area and the re-mining of Haiphong Harbor. As he saw it, "the only question was how much bombing would be needed to force Hanoi to settle." He called Admiral Moorer and told him: "I don't want any more of this crap about the fact that we couldn't hit this target or that one. This is your chance to use military power effectively to win this war, and if you don't, I'll consider you responsible."[111]

The twelve days of bombing inflicted great damage but changed nothing basic. Forewarned by the usual Nixon administration threats, the Vietnamese had evacuated much of Hanoi and Haiphong, prepared the population, and stiffened their defenses. The inaccurate B-52s, a weapon of terror rather than targeted strikes, destroyed workers' quarters and the biggest hospital in Hanoi, causing numerous civilian casualties. But U.S. aircraft losses were heavy and 44 pilots were captured.

The Christmas bombing, as it was called, provoked a strong reaction in the United States, some of which Nixon describes:

> The Washington *Post* editorialized that it caused millions of Americans "to cringe in shame and to wonder at their President's very sanity." Joseph Kraft called it an action "of senseless terror which stains the good name of America." James Reston called it "war by tantrum," and Anthony Lewis charged that I was acting "like a maddened tyrant." In Congress there were similarly critical outbursts from members of both parties. Republican Senator William Saxbe of Ohio said that "President Nixon... appears to have left his senses on this issue." And Mike Mansfield said that it was a "stone-age tactic."[112]

Although it tried to act tough, the administration knew it had to come to an agreement to end the war or face the possibility of Congress simply forcing it to pull out. Nixon notes in his memoirs that on January 2, 1973, "the House Democratic Caucus voted 154 to 75 to cut off all funds for Indochina military operations as soon as arrangements were made for the safe withdrawal of U.S. troops and the return of our POWs. Two days later Teddy Kennedy proposed a similar resolution to the Senate Democratic Caucus, where it passed 36 to 12."[113]

On January 8, Kissinger and Le Duc Tho were meeting again. By January 27, they had signed the Paris Agreement, a settlement which, except for some cosmetic changes, was the same as that agreed to in October.

The United States made it clear immediately that it intended to respect the agreement only selectively. It began a gigantic buildup of Thieu's forces. As Nixon wrote later:

> We had tried to tip the balance of power toward the South Vietnamese by launching a massive resupply effort in late 1972. We undertook two operations—code-named Enhance and Enhance

Plus — to replace equipment and supplies lost or expended during the 1972 offensive and to improve South Vietnam's combat capability before the cease-fire agreement limited our aid to one-for-one replacements.[114]

Gabriel Kolko concludes:

At a cost of nearly $2 billion, Enhance left the RVN [Republic of Vietnam] with the world's fourth-largest air force and a huge quantity of tanks, artillery, and helicopters. It now had overwhelming firepower superiority over the DRV, and in early November, in the words of a U.S. official military history of the event, "the United States violated the spirit of the provisions of the Paris agreement" and transferred ownership of its bases to the RVN so that when the time came to dismantle them, as required, it could claim it had none. Everything was done to prepare Thieu for a protracted war during the post-treaty period.[115]

But like Diem ten years earlier, Thieu lacked the support of the people. His regime was, therefore, incapable of successfully waging either political or military struggle against the revolutionaries. The application of the Paris Agreement would have turned the struggle into a political one. But neither his U.S. mentors nor Thieu himself had any intention of accepting a political struggle that they knew he would lose. Ignoring the Agreement's provisions for a political settlement, Nixon publicly reiterated recognition of Thieu's regime as "the sole legitimate government" in South Vietnam. With U.S. backing, Thieu treated the agreement as a scrap of paper. Immediately after signing, he redoubled his repression and attacks on "communists."

The trouble was that Thieu's regime was equally unable to win a military struggle. Flush with weapons supplied by the United States, his now million-strong force soon undertook new military offensives. But despite early optimism among the U.S. advisors who — now camouflaged in the Defense Attaché's Office — coordinated the anti-communist war as before, the effort was doomed by the growing rot of the regime.

In Washington, Watergate gave the crowning touch to the administration's impotence. The spreading scandal, the growing rebelliousness of Congress, the threat of impeachment all meant that a renewal of direct intervention was unthinkable. Even military and economic aid had begun to dry up by 1974 because of Congressional opposition. The rapidity with which South Vietnam's forces disintegrated in early 1975 took even

Hanoi by surprise. By the end of April, with the last U.S. personnel helicoptered out of Saigon hours before the arrival of communist troops, the war was over.

THE FIGHTING HAD AT LAST ended, but for Vietnam the consequences would last a long, long time. The destruction was unprecedented: the United States had expended twice the volume of munitions it had used in World War II. In an article prepared for *World Armaments and Disarmament: SIPRI Yearbook 1982*, Dr. Arthur H. Westing summarized the effects of the war:

> All five of North Viet Nam's industrial centres were demolished. All 29 provincial capitals were bombed and 12 of them razed.... Virtually every railway and highway bridge was destroyed as were many hundreds of public buildings.... Many hundreds of water conservancy works and irrigation dikes and much farmland and livestock were damaged or destroyed. Countless unexploded munitions remained at the end of the war that continue to cause scores of casualties annually....
>
> About 9,000 of approximately 15,000 rural villages in South Viet Nam were damaged or destroyed and millions of people were driven into Saigon, Danang, Hue and other urban areas. Saigon swelled from a pre-war population of 1.4 million to 4.2 million. When the war ended, South Viet Nam was burdened with more than 600,000 war orphans, several hundred thousand war widows, about 400,000 invalided war cripples, some 3 million unemployed, of the order of 600,000 prostitutes and an estimated 500,000 drug addicts. As in North Viet Nam, there remains a legacy in South Viet Nam of unexploded munitions....
>
> [The Vietnamese conflict] was an innovative war in that a great power attempted to subdue a peasant army through the profligate use of technologically advanced weapons and techniques [a number of which] were inescapably anti-ecological, especially those employed against the land and people of South Viet Nam. The result...was the widespread, long-lasting and severe disruption of forest lands, of perennial croplands and of farmlands—that is to say, of millions of hectares of the natural resource base essential to an agrarian society.[116]

The peace agreement called for the United States to "contribute to healing the wounds of war and to postwar reconstruction." The United States not only failed to contribute, but engaged in what can only be called economic and political warfare. It imposed an economic embargo, refused to establish diplomatic relations, tried to isolate Vietnam internationally, and worked to keep other countries, international organizations, and even U.S. civilians from providing help for rebuilding the war-shattered country.

Fifteen years after the end of the war, the United States still maintained its hostility.

5. Nicaragua

Few countries have suffered as long and as much from U.S. imperialism as Nicaragua. From 1909 to 1933, the United States dominated Nicaragua through armed intervention by gunboats and Marines. From 1934 till the Sandinista Revolution triumphed in 1979, the United States dominated through the National Guard it had trained and armed to replace the Marines and the puppet dictatorship of the Somoza family which headed the Guard. After the Sandinista victory, it organized an anti-Sandinista military force, led mainly by former National Guardsmen, and inflicted a counterrevolutionary war on the Nicaraguan people.

In 1909, when U.S. intervention in Nicaragua got under way, the United States had a number of interests there. U.S. companies owned investments in coffee, bananas, lumber, and gold, and in railroads, port facilities, and river and ocean transport. U.S. banks were competing for a lucrative and growing banking business. And the U.S. Government had a great strategic interest in Nicaragua: it was an excellent site for a canal between the Atlantic and Pacific oceans. The United States was already constructing a canal through Panama, but wanted control of the Nicaraguan route to prevent any other country from building a rival canal.

The president of Nicaragua, José Santos Zelaya, was a nationalist who saw himself as trying "zealously to preserve the political and economic independence of my country."[1] Earlier in his presidency, he had defended Nicaraguan sovereignty against the British who were claiming special rights on the eastern coast. Later, as the U.S. presence began to expand rapidly, he defended Nicaraguan interests against the North Americans. When concessions to U.S. capitalists didn't bring Nicaragua the expected benefits, he cancelled them. Against the opposition of Secretary of State Philander Knox, he contracted a loan of several million dollars with London bankers. In the hope of having a canal built in Nicaragua, he turned to countries other than the United States, including Great Britain and Japan.

These actions, especially the canal negotiations, led the United States, which had been friendly when Zelaya was at odds with the British, to become hostile. On October 7, 1909, Thomas C. Moffat, the consul at Bluefields, Nicaragua, reported to the Secretary of State that he had "received secret information...that a revolution will start in Bluefields on the 8th." Moffat not only knew in advance that there would be an uprising against Zelaya; he also knew about secret troop movements and what the insurrectionaries intended to accomplish. They would "constitute an independent republic" in eastern Nicaragua, "with Bluefields the capital....The [insurrectionary] army would proceed south at once, augmented in numbers already arranged for, enter the capital, overthrow the President and consolidate into another republic the Pacific States of Nicaragua."[2]

Not only did the United States have advance knowledge of the revolt—U.S. companies operating in Nicaragua financed it. According to the *New York Times*, Juan Estrada, leader of the rebels, admitted having received $1 million from "U.S. companies on Nicaragua's Atlantic coast."[3] Adolfo Díaz, a local official of a U.S. corporation (later, under U.S. auspices, to become president of Nicaragua), advanced $600,000, although his salary was only $1,000 a year. According to Zelaya, steamers of the United Fruit Company transported men, arms, and munitions for the rebels with the knowledge and assistance of State Department representatives in Central America.[4]

The United States found a pretext for breaking with Zelaya when his government executed two U.S. citizens who had been caught trying to blow up two steamers carrying government forces. The Nicaraguan chargé in Washington pointed out that the two men had been courtmartialled according to Nicaraguan military law and had confessed their guilt, and that this was not their first offense. But the United States refused to accept the chargé's argument. It sent him a note which not only broke relations, but openly placed the United States on the side of the rebels.

The Government of the United States is convinced that the revolution represents the ideals and the will of a majority of the Nicaraguan people more faithfully than does the Government of President Zelaya....[5]

On top of everything else, a U.S. cruiser, the *Des Moines*, prevented government forces from attacking the rebels at Bluefields, turning the town into a safe refuge for the rebels and preventing their defeat.

Zelaya resigned, explaining in a statement to the Nicaraguan National Assembly:

> You ... know the hostile attitude of a powerful nation which, against all right, has intervened in our political affairs and publicly furnished the rebels the aid which they have asked for.... I am disposed to separate myself from the Government.... I desire that this determination shall contribute to the good of Nicaragua by the establishment of peace and above all, the suspension of the hostility manifested by the American Government to whom I do not desire to be a pretext, that it may continue intervening in any way in the destiny of the country.[6]

But the United States continued its intervention, now against the government of José Madriz, whom the assembly had chosen to replace Zelaya. The Minister General of the Madriz government, in a letter to the Mexican Foreign Office, explained what the United States was doing.

> Our civil war was about to be finished by the taking of Bluefields by our army. The commander of the American cruiser *Paducah* landed forces [Marines] at Bluefields and he warned us that he would oppose our occupying the place, although the center and forces of the revolutionary party are there. We captured the Bluff, which is the key to Bluefields, defeating the armed resistance, and were going to establish a blockade.... The commander of the *Paducah* threatened that he would sink our boats if our forces attacked Bluefields, and that he would enforce respect for American commerce with his guns, even in the case of munitions for the revolutionary forces. These, though now confined to Bluefields, are safely making their preparations there to attack us.[7]

Finding that he, too, was unacceptable to the United States and after his forces had suffered defeats at the hands of the reorganized insurgents, Madriz resigned on August 20, 1910. A week later, the insurgents entered the Nicaraguan capital, Managua.

WITH THE INSURGENTS' VICTORY, the United States became the dominant force behind the government of Nicaragua. It dispatched a special agent, Thomas Dawson, aboard a warship to present to the leaders of the new government U.S. demands concerning a new constitution, the collection of customs revenues in such a way as to provide security for a loan by U.S. bankers, and the punishment of those responsible for the execution of the two U.S. citizens. Dawson worked out a series of agreements which stipulated the conditions under which the United States would recognize the new government. He felt, he reported to Washington, that "a popular presidential election is at present impracticable and dangerous to peace."[8] So one of the conditions for recognition was that a constitutional assembly be chosen which would name as president Juan Estrada, the insurgent leader, and as vice president Adolfo Díaz, the former official of a U.S. corporation who had helped finance the insurgency.[9]

Evidence as to how the people of Nicaragua felt about the United States and the president it had imposed on them appears in the State Department's own dispatches. In February 1911, the U.S. minister to Nicaragua reported to the Secretary of State that "the natural sentiment of an overwhelming majority of Nicaraguans is antagonistic to the United States...."[10] Two months later he reported that "President Estrada is being sustained solely by the moral effect of our support and the belief that he would unquestionably have that support in case of trouble."[11]

Estrada lasted only a few months. The people of Nicaragua were opposed to his agreements, all of which violated Nicaraguan sovereignty. They were especially against a proposed loan agreement under which Nicaragua couldn't alter its export or import duties or name a collector of customs without the agreement of the United States.[12] Estrada had to resign in favor of Vice President Díaz. But Díaz was no less unpopular than Estrada. The United States intervened to make sure the Nicaraguan Assembly confirmed him in office. The U.S. minister worked on the Assembly, telling the State Department that "a war vessel is necessary for the moral effect."[13]

Díaz was simply a puppet of the United States. As he handed over Nicaragua to U.S. bankers, opposition to him grew even stronger. In July 1912, a revolt broke out. The United States landed 412 Marines, the advance guard of a larger force consist-

ing of 2,700 men and eight warships. The State Department
declared that "the American bankers who have made investments in relation to railroads and steamships in Nicaragua, in
connection with a plan for the relief of the financial distress of
that country, have applied for protection." It also asserted that

the United States has a moral mandate to exert its influence for the
preservation of the general peace of Central America.[14]

One leader of the revolt surrendered to the Marines, but another, Benjamín Zeledón, defiantly rejected a Marine ultimatum
and, in a note to the admiral in command of the U.S. forces,
protested the violation of Nicaraguan sovereignty. The Marines
attacked Zeledón's troops, mercilessly bombarding the city of
Masaya in the process. Many Nicaraguans died fighting this
early battle against U.S. imperialism, but Zeledón's troops were
defeated. Zeledón himself was captured and shot by government troops fighting alongside the Marines.

NOT ALL THE MARINES left Nicaragua after Zeledón's defeat. A
"legation guard" of at least 100 men remained. Except for a
nine-month period in 1925-26, the United States maintained
Marines in Nicaragua from 1912 till 1933. In Nicaragua in those
days 100 Marines was a sizable force. Its presence made clear
that ultimate power was held by the United States. The Marines
served to guard not only against revolution, but against the formation of any government unacceptable to the United States.
There were two political parties in Nicaragua in 1912: the Liberals were anti-imperialist, the Conservatives were submissive to
the United States. The introduction of the Marines laid the basis
for a succession of puppet governments run by Conservatives.

By 1912, the United States had, in effect, turned Nicaragua
into a colony. All important political decisions were made at the
State Department in Washington or the U.S. legation in
Managua. The president of Nicaragua, in the words of one U.S.
writer, "found that he could do nothing of his own volition, but
was required to take orders like a butler."[15] Economically, U.S.
bankers and other businessmen along with the U.S. Government controlled everything in Nicaragua that was worth controlling. U.S. banks owned 51 percent of the stocks of the Nicaraguan National Bank. North Americans administered the customs and railroad systems to make sure of their receipts, which
served as security for U.S. bank loans. A "Mixed Commission"

whose members were mostly North Americans named by U.S. bankers or the State Department decided economic and financial questions for Nicaragua.[16]

An early result of the U.S. takeover was the Bryan-Chamorro Treaty, signed in 1914 and ratified by the U.S. Senate in 1916. Under the treaty, Nicaragua granted the United States "in perpetuity" the "exclusive" rights for construction and operation of an interoceanic canal. "To enable ... the United States to protect the Panama Canal" and its rights under the new treaty, Nicaragua also granted it for ninety-nine years the right to establish a naval base on the Gulf of Fonseca on the Pacific and leases for the Corn Islands in the Caribbean. In exchange for these concessions and also "for the purpose of reducing the present indebtedness of Nicaragua," the United States granted $3 million.[17]

The treaty left to the United States whether and when a canal would be built. As explained by Clifford D. Ham, the U.S. customs collector in Nicaragua, it eliminated forever "the danger of a foreign power seeking and obtaining those concessions."[18] If the United States did not choose to build a canal, Nicaragua would have given up one of its most important potential assets for a small sum of money which would go not to new uses but to the bankers in payment of old debt.

State Department correspondence shows how U.S. officials interpreted the treaty. In a dispatch sent while the treaty was being negotiated, the chargé d'affaires in El Salvador refers to "the proposed protectorate of Nicaragua by the United States."[19]

Here is what Senator Elihu Root, former Secretary of both War and State, said about the treaty:

> I have been looking over the report of the commanding officer of our marines in Nicaragua and I find there the following:
> "Their present government is not in power by the will of the people; the elections of the House of Congress were mostly fraudulent."
> And a further statement that the Liberals, that is to say, the opposition, "constitute three-fourths of the country." It is apparent...that the present government...is really maintained in office by the presence of the U.S. Marines in Nicaragua....
> Can we afford to make a treaty so serious for Nicaragua, granting us perpetual rights in that country, with a president who we have every reason to believe does not represent more than a

quarter of the people of the country and who is maintained in office by our military force...?[20]

THE UNPOPULARITY OF Nicaraguas's puppet governments repeatedly provoked rebellion. From 1913 to 1924, more than ten uprisings occurred. The governments, with the backing of the Marines, declared martial law and were able to maintain themselves. But by 1927 a revolt that was incomparably stronger than the previous attempts was under way, the guerrilla war led by Augusto Sandino.

The immediate background for this revolt was a big U.S. political and armed intervention. The Marines had left Nicaragua in 1925; they were a political embarrassment to the United States which planned to have a U.S.-trained local constabulary take over. A few weeks after their departure, a defeated presidential candidate carried out a coup d'état and a civil war broke out between Conservatives and Liberals. The United States didn't want the Liberals to win. It rushed cruisers and Marines to Nicaragua, got the Nicaraguan Congress to install the U.S. puppet Díaz as president, and sent former Secretary of War Henry Stimson to settle the conflict.

Stimson told the leading Liberal general, José María Moncada, "Peace is imperative. I have instructions to attain it willingly or by force."[21] He let Moncada know that the United States would not allow the defeat of Díaz and proposed retaining him as president until 1928 when elections would be held under U.S. supervision. Left with the choice of either accepting Stimson's terms or fighting the United States, Moncada accepted, as did all his generals but one—Augusto Sandino.

Unlike Moncada, Sandino would not let himself be coerced. He was willing, if need be, to fight the United States. Reports about his activities soon began to flow into the State Department. The U.S. minister in Nicaragua reported an attack by Sandino's forces against the Marines at Ocotal and had the following to say about Sandino himself:

> Sandino is reported to be an erratic Nicaraguan about 30 years of age with wild communist ideas acquired largely in Mexico.... [He] preached Communism, Mexican brotherly love and cooperation, and death to the Americans, until the rabble of the whole north country joined him in his plan to massacre Americans there....[22]

What was Sandino really like? He was a Nicaraguan worker—a mechanic—with a *campesino* background who had strong anti-imperialist sentiments. He was born in a little village—Niquinohomo—which consisted of huts of straw and mud. Zeledón's battle with the Marines in 1912 took place not far from this village and Sandino as a youth saw the patriot's body paraded on a horse by the soldiers who had killed him. Sandino left Nicaragua as a young man and worked for such U.S. companies as the Honduras Sugar and Distilling Co. in Honduras and the United Fruit Co. in Guatemala, ending up as a mechanic with the Huasteca Petroleum Co. in Mexico.

Mexico had been having a revolution and was in the midst of a struggle with its U.S.-owned oil companies. The United States had already intervened with armed force, landing troops at Vera Cruz and sending an expedition into northern Mexico. Now the threat of intervention was again in the air. A wave of revolutionary, anti-imperialist sentiment had swept Mexico, and Sandino came under its influence.

When he heard about the Liberal uprising in Nicaragua, Sandino returned home to participate. His thinking comes through in various statements:

> Seeing that the United States of North America, lacking any right except that with which brute force endows it, would deprive us of our country and our liberty, I have accepted its unjust challenge....[23]

> If the United States wants peace in Nicaragua, it must leave in the presidency a legitimate Nicaraguan, truly elected by the people.[24]

> The only one responsible for everything that happens here in Nicaragua, now and in the future, is the President of the United States Calvin Coolidge, because he persists in maintaining in power his lackey Adolfo Díaz, who enjoys the complete contempt of all good Nicaraguans.[25]

> We have been robbed of our rights over the canal. Theoretically they paid us $3 million. Nicaragua, or rather the bandits who then controlled the government with the aid of Washington, received a few thousand pesos which, spread among Nicaraguan citizens, would not have bought each one a sardine on a cracker.[26]

> Nicaragua must not be the patrimony of oligarchs and traitors, much less do we have to accept humiliations from the expansionist dollar pirates, and therefore I will fight while my heart gives signs of life.[27]

Sandino formed a little army, mostly from the poor and oppressed of the countryside, and took on the Marines. The untrained, ragged Sandinista soldiers fought with whatever they could lay their hands on. They bought or captured rifles, somehow got hold of a little cannon, improvised grenades and bombs by filling sardine cans with dynamite and nails. They learned how to fight by fighting. The ambush quickly became their basic tactic.

Sandino's men enjoyed several advantages over the Marines. They were fighting to liberate themselves, not to oppress someone else. They were on their home ground and knew the terrain intimately. They had the support of the people who kept them informed about the movements of the enemy, supplied them with food, and participated in combat. Not only were the Marines unable to wipe out the Sandinistas, but the little army, after a rough start, began to win battles.

International support for Sandino quickly spread and opposition to the Marine intervention appeared within the United States. The *New York Times* could call Sandino a "bandit" but throughout Latin America he was a hero who was demonstrating that it was possible to fight the imperialist colossus. Sandino also aroused enthusiasm in western Europe, the Soviet Union, and Japan. Henri Barbusse, the famous French writer, sent a letter: "General, I send you this greeting in personal homage and in that of the proletariat and revolutionary intellectuals of France and Europe, who have on many occasions authorized me to express on their behalf our admiration for the heroic figure of Sandino and his splendid troops."[28] Within the United States, Senator Burton K. Wheeler remarked that if the job of the Marines was to fight bandits, they ought to go to Chicago. The Pan-American Anti-Imperialist League organized demonstrations in Washington.[29]

In 1928, the elections that Stimson had talked about to Moncada took place. Two U.S. military writers tell how General Frank R. McCoy, with the help of several thousand Marines, conducted the elections. "Only U.S.-approved candidates could run, and...only U.S.-controlled areas could vote." Naturally, "Sandino and any other 'bandits' would not be allowed to run." In both the United States and Latin America, there were protests against these elections.[30]

To avoid the disadvantage of having to use its own troops in Nicaragua, the United States pressed on with the idea of developing a local constabulary. On December 22, 1927, the United States and Nicaragua signed an agreement which obligated Nicaragua "to create without delay an efficient constabulary to be known as the Guardia Nacional de Nicaragua...."[31] Within a year, members of the National Guard were in the field against Sandino.

But even with the addition of the Guard, the United States was unable to get rid of Sandino. The number of engagements between the Sandinistas and the Marines or National Guard grew steadily: 73 from May 1927 through the end of 1929; 120 in 1930; 141 in 1931; 170 in 1932.[32] In 1932, the U.S. minister to Nicaragua wrote to the Secretary of State of "a bandit situation fully as strong as, if not stronger than at any time since its inception."[33] Complaints about Marine casualties and international pressure caused the United States, after a while, to restrict the Marines to the role of "technical advisers." In late 1932, the Marines began to evacuate Nicaragua. Sandino's forces were intact, flourishing.

The United States' intention in setting up the National Guard was to provide not just an additional force to fight Sandino, but an instrument for the long-run control of Nicaragua. The 1927 agreement provided that the Guard would be "the sole military and police force of the Republic" and would have control of all arms and ammunition.[34] Thus, the Guard was to have a monopoly of armed power in Nicaragua and whoever controlled it would control the country. For the first several years after the Guard was formed, its commander, as well as almost all its other commissioned officers, were U.S. citizens appointed by the Navy Department.

In 1932, as the time for the Marines to leave approached, the United States arranged for a Nicaraguan to take over command and President Juan B. Sacasa named Anastasio Somoza. Richard Millett, in his book on the National Guard, writes that

> for years many Nicaraguans have claimed that Somoza was hand-picked by Hanna [the U.S. Minister], a view at least partly confirmed by both Willard Beaulac, Hanna's First Secretary in Managua, and Arthur Bliss Lane, his successor as Minister to Nicaragua. As early as October 28, 1932, Hanna had informed the State Department of his preference for Somoza, declaring, 'I look on him as the best man in the country for the position....'[35]

Somoza had been educated in Philadelphia and spoke fluent English. He had translated for Stimson, who noted in his diary, "Somoza is a very frank, friendly, likable young Liberal and his attitude impresses me more favorably than almost any other."[36] From being a translator Somoza graduated to subcabinet and cabinet posts, and throughout, cultivated the North Americans — the Marines, the minister, the minister's wife.

Thus the United States did not withdraw the Marines until it had a replacement — the National Guard. And it made sure that the right person was left in command of the Guard, one in whom a number of high-ranking U.S. officials had expressed confidence.

When the Marines left, Sandino agreed to a truce and entered into a peace agreement with the Sacasa government. But the National Guard immediately began to violate the truce and sabotage the agreement. On the pretext of repairing telegraph lines, a detachment of the Guard marched out and attacked Sandinista troops. Guard units arrested and shot Sandinistas, on the ground that they were bandits.[37] The Sacasa government wanted a peace settlement, but was powerless to control the Guard.

The contradiction between the Marines and the Sandinistas had given way to a contradiction between the Guard and the Sandinistas. The Guard wasn't interested in Sacasa's coming to terms with Sandino. It wanted the Sandinistas eliminated. Sandino, on the other hand, was opposed to the existence of a National Guard that defied the President. In negotiations with the government and declarations to the press, he kept reiterating that the Guard had been foisted on Nicaragua by the United States, that it "tacitly consider[ed] itself superior to the government," that it was "outside the law."[38] He declared that "the Guard doesn't obey the President [so] we don't obey the Guard."[39] He offered President Sacasa the help of the Sandinistas to "regulate...the National Guard in accordance with the constitution..." and "to strengthen your authority."[40]

The contradiction between the Guard and the Sandinistas was basically a contradiction between the United States and the Sandinistas. The Guard and Somoza were creatures of the United States.

While Sacasa and his representatives carried on protracted negotiations with Sandino, the Guard clashed with the Sandinista army and plotted to eliminate it altogether. On February 15,

1934, Sandino complained about the aggressions of the Guard to Sofonías Salvatierra, who had been sent by Sacasa to bring him to Managua for negotiations. "I'm being surrounded," he said. "For about a month the Guard has been taking up positions around Wiwilí. What is this? The President is deceiving me." "No," replied Salvatierra, "the President is loyal."[41]

The next day Sandino arrived in Managua. The negotiations centered on the question of Sandino's troops turning over their arms to the National Guard. According to the U.S. minister, Arthur Bliss Lane, Sandino said "that he would not turn over his arms to the Guardia Nacional because of the unconstitutionality of that organization." Somoza insisted that Sandino turn over the arms. Sacasa "maintained a more conciliatory attitude."[42]

Lane and Somoza conferred with each other constantly during Sandino's stay. Somoza "has told me several times," Lane reported, "that he would like to 'lock [Sandino] up.'"[43] Lane advised caution.

On the morning of February 21, Somoza telephoned that he wished to see Lane urgently. On receiving Somoza, Lane found him "unusually excited." Somoza told him, reported Lane, that the "President had exchanged letters with Sandino implying that [the] Guardia should be reorganized within 6 months; also that General Portocarrero, former Sandinista candidate for President, had been chosen" to be in charge of the northern provinces where Sandino's forces were concentrated. This appointment, said Somoza, "would put the Guardia under the control of Sandino." Lane told Somoza to be calm and again "advised caution." They lunched together. At six, Lane and Somoza met again. Somoza told Lane "that he would not 'start anything' without prior consultation with [him]."[44]

Somoza left Lane for a meeting with the top officers of the Guard. An officer present wrote later that Somoza told the group that he had just come from a conference with Lane who "has assured me that the Washington government supports and recommends the elimination of Augusto César Sandino, considering him as it does a disturber of the country's peace."[45]

Later that evening, a Guard patrol arrested Sandino and two of his generals as they were leaving the grounds of the Presidential Palace in Salvatierra's car. They had been having dinner with President Sacasa. The patrol loaded the three prisoners onto a truck, drove them to the Managua airfield, set up a machine gun, and murdered them.

The next day the Guard attacked at Wiwilí where Sandino, in anticipation of a peace settlement, had been organizing his people into agricultural cooperatives. More than three hundred of Sandino's followers—men, women, and children—died in the slaughter. A small band, led by General Pedro Altamirano, fought on in the mountains. But eventually, Altamirano was killed and even this last resistance faded.

Four months after Sandino's assassination, Lane sent a brief dispatch to the State Department:

> General Somoza is quoted by the press and reliable witnesses as having in effect accepted responsibility for the murder of Sandino in a speech at a banquet in his honor on June 17 at Granada.[46]

WITH THE ELIMINATION of Sandino and his army, Somoza became the most powerful Nicaraguan. He enjoyed the backing of the United States and he headed Nicaragua's main armed force. Sacasa wanted to get rid of Somoza and to bring the unruly Guard under control. He made preparations for defense against a military coup by the Guard. But Lane supported Somoza and the Guard. Sacasa doesn't realize, he reported to Washington,

> that it is of vital importance for him not to continue to irritate the Guardia with preparations for defense against them.... Unfortunately the President is surrounded by influences which I fear are not for the good of the country: persons who wish to humiliate Somoza regardless of the consequences.[47]

Many people in Nicaragua understood that Somoza and the Guard were instruments of the United States. Lane reported being told by the Minister of Foreign Affairs that the Guard

> is responsible for the circulation of the rumor that I [Lane] am the intellectual author of the killing of Sandino. He said that the Guardia is convinced that I—and hence the United States Government—favors the Guardia as against the Government.[48]

In other dispatches, Lane reported that Somoza was asserting that "I am furnishing the motive power for his ambitions" and that a rumor was circulating "to the effect that I am supporting the candidacy of General Somoza for President in the elections of 1936." Somoza was, in fact, working toward taking over the presidency, using the thinly disguised support of the United

States as well as his power as head of the National Guard in his maneuvers.[49]

Somoza used Guardia funds to pay demonstrators and provide free liquor at a demonstration he organized for himself. He had the Guard arrest adherents of Sacasa and others whom he found troublesome. He held a parade of Guard troops to overawe the Chamber of Deputies when it passed a bill granting amnesty to a prisoner he didn't want to release. Lane concluded from the incident that Somoza, "through a show of force..., would probably be able to control the Congress."[50]

What was the United States doing as it watched Somoza move toward his takeover? First, it was maintaining an embargo on arms shipments to Nicaragua. Since only the Sacasa government lacked sufficient arms, while the Guard was well-stocked from earlier U.S. shipments, this embargo served only to strengthen Somoza.[51]

Second, it was using its influence to keep other countries from helping the Sacasa government with arms. Hearing rumors that El Salvador and Costa Rica might do so, Lane met with representatives of these countries, as well as Guatemala and Mexico, and laid out the U.S. position—that it was best to avoid "meddling in Nicaraguan political matters."[52]

Finally, the United States was discouraging the formation in Nicaragua of any effective movement to oust Somoza as head of the Guard. When people came to Lane with proposals to oust Somoza, he answered that "intervention is a thing of the past" and that everyone should "work for peace."[53]

Sheltered by the U.S. nonintervention policy, Somoza moved ahead. The Guard arrested the publisher of *El Imparcial*, an anti-Somoza newspaper. In one place after another, it fomented disorders which it then used as a pretext for replacing local officials. By the end of May 1936, local officials favorable to Somoza were in power in almost all Nicaragua's main towns. A fort at León still contained troops loyal to Sacasa, so Somoza sent a large force to attack it. Other Guard troops moved against Sacasa's defenders dug in around the Presidential Palace in Managua. Facing far superior forces, Sacasa surrendered. A few days later, he resigned and went into exile.[54]

Conveniently for Somoza, the United States had recently announced the abandonment of its policy of refusing recognition to Central American governments that came to power through violence. It now instructed its minister in Managua to deal with the government installed by Somoza.

Six months later, Somoza held elections in which he ran for the presidency. With the National Guard controlling the election machinery and the opposition boycotting the election, he won overwhelmingly. The United States, after ending the more than 20-year occupation of Nicaragua by the Marines, had installed the Somoza dictatorship which, counting the whole dynasty — the Somoza who murdered Sandino and the sons who succeeded him — was to hold Nicaragua in its grip for over forty years.

HAVING WIPED OUT the strongest opposition even before he took office, Somoza had little trouble instituting a regime of repression. He showed that he would use the Guard against all opposition by having it raid a Conservative party gathering and arrest a number of those present. He subjected the press to a system of informal censorship, backed by the threat of Guard action against those who violated orders. He had the Guard organize an intelligence service, directed mainly against domestic dissidents. To ensure the Guard's loyalty, he gave it a pay increase in 1938 — from thirty percent for high officers to fifty percent for privates.

At the same time, Somoza opened the way for further U.S. economic penetration. He promoted U.S. investment, helping along the process that was turning Nicaragua into an economic appendage of the United States.

Somoza didn't neglect his own financial interests. He exacted a tribute of one and a half cents per pound on exported cattle as well as contributions from various industries, using much of the money obtained to buy land. Land was a good investment: he could get it at far below its real value by coercing the owners and then greatly increase its value by having the government build a road to it. By such methods, Somoza soon became the richest person in Nicaragua's history.[55]

Following the example of their leader, the members of the Guard also used their positions to enrich themselves. The opportunities were great since the Guard served as police, customs inspectors, and immigration officers. Guardsmen engaged in wholesale cattle smuggling. "The corruption," writes Millett, extended from the Minister of War ... to the private on the street who would demand, "pay me five córdobas or be arrested." The rural population came to fear the Guardia, claiming that the local soldiers, who were also the rural police, could simply walk into their homes and take anything, leaving them no possible redress.[56]

In 1939, President Roosevelt invited Somoza to visit the United States and then gave him red carpet treatment similar to that given a little later to King George and Queen Elizabeth of England. There is an oft-repeated story that when Roosevelt was asked about Somoza, he commented, "He may be a sonofabitch, but he's *our* sonofabitch."

Soon after the visit, the United States, responding to a request by Somoza, assigned a U.S. Army officer to act as director of the Guard's Military Academy. A wartime lend-lease agreement provided $1.3 million in military supplies to the Guard which never engaged in a single action against the Axis. West Point admitted Somoza's younger son, whom he was grooming to take over leadership of the Guard. The practice began of having cadets at the Nicaraguan Academy spend their senior year in Panama to receive instruction from U.S. officers at Fort Gulick.[57]

After the war, as the United States got its various anti-communist programs under way, its military assistance to the Guard grew larger and more systematic. During the years 1952-1954, the United States set up Army and Air Force missions in Nicaragua and began a Military Assistance Program.[58]

In 1956, a young Nicaraguan poet named Rigoberto López Pérez shot and severely wounded Somoza at a banquet in León. For the U.S. Embassy, the event created what its Counselor called an "emergency." At 2:30 in the morning, the ambassador drove to León and received a medical statement which served as the basis for a request to Washington to dispatch immediately the "best available medical specialist from U.S. and Panama."[59] By 9:30 the next morning, President Eisenhower had decided to send the commander of the Walter Reed Army Hospital and several other prominent U.S. physicians. These doctors recommended the transfer of Somoza to the U.S. hospital in the Canal Zone. Despite these efforts, Somoza died. Secretary of State Dulles expressed his sentiments: "His constantly demonstrated friendship toward the United States will never be forgotten."[60]

To control the country, the Guard imposed martial law.   It began arresting what an Embassy dispatch called "listed persons," subjecting many to beatings and torture.   The next week the puppet Congress unanimously elected Somoza's older son Luis interim president.   Four months later the government staged an electoral farce; only the day before had it lifted martial law.   Luis won the presidency for the next five years.   The lifting of martial law was temporary: four of Luis's five years in office would be years of martial law.

At first, the State Department wasn't sure that Luis would be able to stay in power and tried to maintain a position that would enable it to get along with any new government that might take over.   Even then it leaned to the Somozas.   We must "be most careful," wrote Assistant Secretary of State Roy Rubottom, "not to cause the Somoza brothers to interpret our position as a reversal of what they may feel, with some reason, was a policy of support for their father...."   After a month of Luis's presidency, Ambassador Whelan was reporting that "everything points to ... continued stability of the government...."   Whelan was one of Luis Somoza's chief supporters, helping to consolidate the dynasty.   After a year, he wrote:

> I am emphatically of the opinion that it is time we gave Nicaragua some new assistance.... This country has been our staunchest friend in Latin America, and both Luis and his father have done a good job of keeping it economically sound and politically stable.[61]

The electoral farce of 1957 was not the last.   Others followed in 1963, 1967, and 1974.   Mostly, the farces put a Somoza in the presidency.   In 1963, the Somozas installed René Schick as president, but true power continued to rest with them through their control of the National Guard.   The farce of 1967 placed a Somoza—younger brother Anastasio—once again in the presidency.   With the death of Luis that same year Anastasio inherited the full powers of the dynasty.

All the while, the Somoza family continued to pile wealth on top of wealth, coming to own by itself a large share of the Nicaraguan economy.   By the time Anastasio became president, it owned the national airline, the national merchant marine, the only cement plant, and several dozen other large enterprises.   It was by far Nicaragua's leading landholder, eventually owning one third of the arable land.[62]

What was life like for the people in this Somoza fiefdom? Half the children and a large part of the adult population suffered from malnutrition. Seventy-seven percent of all houses had no electricity, 62 percent no sewage system, 61 percent no potable water, 55 percent no garbage disposal facilities. Enteritis and other diarrheal diseases were by far the leading cause of death. Less than half the population ten years and older could read.[63]

The main cause of these conditions was the imperialist-Somoza partnership. Turning the Nicaraguan economy into an appendage of the U.S. economy helped starve Nicaraguan children. Commenting on the reasons for malnutrition, a study prepared by the American University states: "The increasing proliferation of large estates producing cotton, coffee, and other export crops greatly reduced the amount of land utilized for basic subsistence foods." And the Somozas were not interested in spending money on housing, health, and education. What little they did spend was concentrated on a few hospitals and elite-oriented education for the middle and upper classes of the cities.[64]

The Somozas held up their end of the partnership not only by controlling Nicaragua and promoting U.S. economic penetration, but by helping the imperialists in some of their international dirty work. The best known example is the training and operations bases provided by the Somozas for the Bay of Pigs invasion of Cuba. But there are others: When in 1954 the United States decided to overthrow the government of Jacobo Arbenz in Guatemala, it sent arms to the Somozas who turned them over to Carlos Castillo Armas, the one designated to carry out the coup d'état. Troops of the Nicaraguan National Guard took part in the United States intervention in the Dominican Republic in 1965. Two years later, Anastasio Somoza offered to send members of the Guard to help in the war against Vietnam.

WITH THE DEATH OF SANDINO, the revolutionary movement in Nicaragua entered into a period of stagnation which lasted more than twenty years. After the shooting and death of the elder Somoza in 1956, it began to move forward again. In 1960-1961, the revolutionaries formed the Sandinista Front of National Liberation (FSLN) which helped bring coherence to the previously fragmented struggles. In the years that followed, the revolutionary movement had its ups and downs, but basically it was progressing. The revolutionaries were gaining political and military experience, testing strategy and tactics, building ties to the people, organizing them. As always, it was the support of the people that was decisive. By the end of 1974, the revolutionaries had developed sufficient mass support to be able to move to the offensive.

Throughout the struggle, the United States supported the Somozas. The Guard could torture and murder people—Ambassador Turner Shelton arranged a meeting between Anastasio, jr. and Nixon in 1971 to help bolster the dictator's prestige. Somoza could steal massively from the foreign aid money that flowed in after a big earthquake hit Managua in 1972—the United States admitted his younger son to his alma mater, West Point. Somoza could institute press censorship and martial law in 1974—the United States continued to back him.[65]

An article in *Foreign Affairs* describes the situation after the FSLN raided the National Palace in 1978:

> For the next several weeks, the world witnessed what one observer called a national mutiny.... It was literally the revolt of the Nicaraguan people against the dynasty and the National Guard: citizens at the barricades, government armored cars, artillery, and airplanes loosed on the cities, troops dragging young people from their homes and shooting them in the streets.... Yet even after it became clear that a Somoza bent on maintaining himself in power was quite capable of unspeakable crimes against his own people, Washington's response was still cautious and "evenhanded," accompanied by endless explanations to the effect that the United States did not wish to intervene.[66]

As in Cuba and elsewhere, only when it became clear that the dictator couldn't hold out much longer, did the United States turn away from him. It then engaged in its standard maneuver of trying to ease him out so it could prevent the revolutionaries from coming to power. What the United States wanted was to replace Somoza with a "moderate" while preserving the National Guard.

The United States began its moves toward the end of 1978. It led an Organization of American States (OAS) team to Managua in a "mediation effort." The idea was to hold an internationally supervised election which would exclude the Sandinistas. On December 21, Ambassador William Bowdler told Somoza: "If you win the election you remain as president.... If you lose, you step aside but the Liberal Party [controlled by the Somozas] will remain and so will the Guardia Nacional."[67] Somoza refused to go along.

In February 1979, the Carter administration began to distance the United States from Somoza. The State Department announced that because of the Nicaraguan government's refusal to accept "mediation," the United States could not "continue to maintain the same level and kind of presence in Nicaragua as we have had in the past."[68]

By June, Somoza's fall was clearly approaching and the United States went further. Secretary of State Cyrus Vance declared at an OAS meeting on the 21st that a solution of the problem in Nicaragua "must begin with the replacement of the present government with a transitional government of national reconciliation...." He proposed that the OAS set up "a peace-keeping force to help restore order and to permit the will of Nicaraguan citizens to be implemented in the establishment of a democratic and representative government."[69] But the majority of the OAS rejected Vance's proposal, which it saw as an attempt to create a cover for U.S. military intervention.

On June 26, a new U.S. ambassador, Lawrence Pezzullo, arrived in Managua. His first assignment was to get rid of Somoza and he got right to the point in his first meeting with the dictator. "We don't see a solution without your departure." Somoza's staying in power would "open the door to an extreme leftist takeover."[70] The strategy was to save the Guard by sacrificing Somoza and use the Guard as a counter-power to the FSLN. Pezzullo noted in a cable to Washington on "National Guard Survival" that with "careful orchestration we have a better than even chance of preserving enough of the GN to maintain order and hold the FSLN in check after Somoza resigns."[71]

Somoza asked for guarantees for himself and his family. He brought up his services to the United States, such as helping overthrow the Arbenz government in Guatemala and providing bases for the Bay of Pigs operation. He argued that the Guard should not be "thrown to the wolves." After all, "these people... have been fighting communism, just like you taught them at Fort Gulick and Fort Benning and Leavenworth." Pezzullo reassured him. "We are not abandoning the Guard."[72]

At first, Pezzullo worked to create a new interim government that would exclude Somoza, but change little else—a government that even he admitted "would smack somewhat of Somocismo sin [without] Somoza."[73] The effort got nowhere. The

FSLN had grown too strong and had already, together with members of the non-Sandinista oppostion to Somoza, formed a provisional government. So the United States decided to salvage what it could. It accepted FSLN participation in the new government as inevitable, but tried to minimize FSLN influence and preserve the National Guard. Pezzullo came up with an arrangement in which Somoza would resign and the Nicaraguan Congress would elect a "constitutional" successor, Francisco Urcuyo, who would announce a cease-fire and turn over power to the provisional government. The cease-fire, by freezing each side in its positions, would keep the National Guard from being destroyed on the battlefield.

Even Pezzullo's final arrangement, with its reduced goals, didn't work. Somoza fled together with the senior command of the Guard. With the departure of Somoza and his top officers, the Guard disintegrated within 24 hours. As if this were not enough, Urcuyo didn't play his assigned role. He refused to turn power over to the provisional government. But within 48 hours, Urcuyo had to flee to Guatemala and the last remnants of the Somoza government collapsed. The FSLN had won a complete victory.

WITH THE FSLN VICTORY, the United States shifted to a new strategy: to try to control the revolutionary government by acting friendly and granting economic aid. Upon analyzing the situation, U.S. officials concluded that there were many strong "non-Marxist elements" in Nicaraguan society: the church hierarchy, the important newspaper, *La Prensa*, various political parties and private sector organizations. The economy was greatly dependent on the internal private sector and on foreign trade with the capitalist world. Nicaragua had suffered $1.5 billion in material damage in the revolutionary war and was left with almost no foreign exchange reserves and an enormous debt. The United States, the officials advised, should gear its strategy to this situation. It should avoid the open hostility that had helped radicalize the Cuban Revolution. It should grant aid to promote its objectives. As Assistant Secretary of State Viron P. Vaky wrote: "It is essential to supply aid to keep the monetary/economic system viable and enmeshed in the international economy, and to support the private sector."[74]

So the United States allocated $75 million in aid to Nicaragua, sixty percent to go to the private sector. There were conditions: Nicaragua must hold elections within "a reasonable period of time," must not support "international terrorism," must not use any of the money on operations in which Cuban personnel were participating (which meant, for example, the literacy campaign).[75]

While one arm of the U.S. Government was dispensing aid to Nicaragua, another was preparing for hostile action against it. The CIA was busily collecting intelligence, probing for vulnerabilities, identifying potential helpers and allies. One key activity was to cement connections with former members of the National Guard, many of whom had fled to Costa Rica, Honduras, El Salvador, Guatemala, and Florida and there formed anti-Sandinista groups. Some of these groups soon began to carry out armed raids against Nicaragua from Honduras. The head of one major group, Enrique Bermúdez, had long-standing ties to the United States—he had served in the Nicaraguan contingent during the 1965 U.S. intervention in the Dominican Republic and afterward had been Somoza's military attaché in Washington. Later, he was to become military commander of the "contras," the exile army organized by the United States to fight the Revolution.

In 1980, Vernon Walters, former Deputy Director of the CIA, traveled with ex-National Guard Colonel Francisco Aguirre to Argentina. "There," according to former contra spokesman Edgar Chamorro, "even before Ronald Reagan had been inaugurated, they discussed plans for forming a counterrevolutionary army.... By late 1980, some fifty former National Guardsmen were receiving training in Argentina, from where they were sent to camps in Miami and elsewhere, to train others."[76]

Also in late 1980, President Carter signed a secret "finding" authorizing the CIA to provide money and backing to opponents of the Sandinistas—the newspaper La Prensa, anti-Sandinista political organizations, etc.[77]

The Carter administration was moving against the Sandinistas not just covertly but overtly. During its last week in office, it delayed the disbursement of the final $15 million of the $75 million aid program on the ground that Nicaragua was providing aid to rebels in El Salvador.

The Reagan administration switched away from the policy of trying to control the revolutionary government with apparent friendliness and aid to one of open, rigid hostility. The Republicans had harshly criticized the Carter policy. Typical was the argument of Jeane Kirkpatrick, whom Reagan named to be ambassador to the United Nations. "What did the Carter administration do in Nicaragua?" she asked. *"It brought down the Somoza regime."* (Italics in original.)[78] It "assist[ed] actively in deposing an erstwhile friend and ally and installing a government hostile to American interests and policies in the world."[79] The Republican Party platform spoke in the same vein. "We deplore the Marxist Sandinista takeover of Nicaragua.... We oppose the Carter administration aid program for the government of Nicaragua. However, we will support the efforts of the Nicaraguan people to establish a free and independent government."[80]

The Reagan administration's open hostility manifested itself immediately. Two days after taking office Reagan suspended all aid to the Nicaraguan government. Press reports appeared of Nicaraguan exiles being trained in camps in Florida for a war against the Sandinistas.

The administration accompanied its preparations for military action with a play at "seeking a diplomatic solution"—it entered into talks which were presented to the world as negotiations but were in reality an attempt to bully the Sandinistas into submission. In August 1981, Assistant Secretary of State Thomas Enders spent two days with the Sandinista leaders in Managua. He told them, "You can forget defending yourselves because we are one hundred times bigger than you are." A U.S. official said afterward that he had never seen anything "so lacking in subtlety in three decades of negotiations in Latin America."[81]

A key Enders demand was that Nicaragua drastically limit its armed forces. The United States wanted Nicaragua to recrate Soviet tanks and ship them back and to limit its army to 15,000-17,000 soldiers, eventually to 10,000. It was like asking the Sandinista government to make it easier for the United States to overthrow it by force—to cooperate in its own destruction. Even Arturo Cruz, who later went over to the contras from his job as Nicaragua's ambassador to Washington, found the U.S. demands insulting. "I was flabbergasted. If that was my reaction as a moderate, think of what the reaction would have been in Managua. I told them, this sounds like the conditions of a victorious power."[82]

Later, even Enders lost his job for being too "soft." He had negotiated from a stance that made agreement practically impossible and he favored the exertion of military pressure on Nicaragua. But he was for a "two track" approach, negotiations as well as pressure—using pressure to gain a negotiated settlement. Kirkpatrick, National Security Advisor William Clark, and others didn't think that Enders' approach could lead to a satisfactory settlement. As Kirkpatrick saw it, according to Christopher Dickey, "Enders acted as if he were pursuing a stalemate rather than a victory."[83] The removal of Enders meant a policy hostile to negotiations. Other officials who showed excessive interest in them were later also ousted. The administration was staking its hopes on military actions, terrorist attacks, and economic warfare.

The United States rapidly built up its contra army. The number of contras, the CIA reported to Congress, jumped from 500 in December 1981 to 4,000 by December 1982, and 15,000 by April 1984.[84] A 1985 Congressional report stated that "the army is organized and commanded by former National Guardsmen... 46 of the 48 positions in the ... command structure are held by the Guard."[85]

At the same time, the United States turned Nicaragua's neighbor, Honduras, into an attack platform. With U.S. military maneuvers as a pretext, the Pentagon built for the contras bases, airfields, fuel tanks, munitions depots, and hospitals that could also be used by U.S. troops if they joined in the attack.

Using mostly the contras but for special jobs the CIA's own personnel, operating mostly from Honduras but also from Nicaragua's southern neighbor, Costa Rica, as well as from the surrounding seas, the United States attacked Nicaragua from all sides. There were terrorist and sabotage attacks and contra ground offensives.

In December 1981, an explosion destroyed an Aeronica (Nicaraguan airline) jet at Mexico City's international airport, luckily before anyone had boarded; the contra organization claimed responsibility. In October 1983, CIA commandos set fire to a fuel storage tank at Nicaragua's largest commercial port, Corinto. One hundred people were injured; the entire city had to be evacuated; the fire raged out of control for two days.[86]

In early 1984, CIA teams mined Nicaragua's main ports, both Atlantic and Pacific. By mid-April, ten commercial vessels, as well as many more fishing boats, had struck mines. A number of ships turned away from Nicaraguan waters. It was the season for shipping out Nicaragua's main exports, coffee and cotton, which now began to pile up on the docks. Nicaragua suffered a loss of over $10 million due to disruption of exports, damage to ships and loss of merchandise, increasing insurance costs, and the expense of having to truck goods to and from ports in neighboring countries.[87]

On the ground, contra forces attacked villages, coffee plantations, agricultural cooperatives, electric power plants, bridges, etc. In their book *David and Goliath*, Robinson and Norsworthy tell of one attack. In July 1982, a force of one hundred contras swooped down from a base in Honduras on the town of San Francisco del Norte. "The contras indiscriminately fired on the inhabitants, killing fourteen and injuring another four. The local militia leader, Victorio Centeno, was captured by the contras, dragged down the main street, and ordered to shout 'Long Live Somoza!' When Centeno defiantly replied with revolutionary slogans, the contras beat him to death in the presence of the townspeople."[88]

Besides hit-and-run attacks, the contras also mounted ambitious general offensives. One, launched in December 1982, aimed at taking the town and valley of Jalapa, an area in northwest Nicaragua surrounded on three sides by Honduras. The idea was to declare the area a liberated zone and install a provisional government which would be recognized and supported by the United States and other countries such as Honduras and Argentina. But the offensive failed: the contras suffered heavy losses but were unable to reach the town of Jalapa. Several other attempts to take Jalapa also failed.[89]

A key element in the war against Nicaragua was the U.S. military maneuvers in Honduras and off Nicaragua's coasts. The first, in October 1981, lasted three days; the second, in July-August 1982, two weeks. The series that began in August 1983 lasted six months and involved two battleship groups and more than 14,000 U.S. troops. By 1984, the maneuvers had become almost continuous. In 1987, the United States deployed a force of 50,000 in the area.[90]

As Peter Kornbluh points out:

> The Reagan administration used the maneuvers to advance three fronts in its "total war" against the Sandinistas: 1) to provide covert support for CIA/contra operations; 2) to wage psychological warfare against the Sandinistas; and 3) to build the infrastructure for a possible overt military intervention in Central America.[91]

The United States backed its military warfare with economic warfare. After cutting off aid, the Reagan administration eliminated a variety of credits, including one for wheat purchases. The administration also passed the word to private banks not to lend to Nicaragua and was able to block most loans by the World Bank and the Inter-American Development Bank. Other private companies, besides banks, also got the word: in late 1982, the Standard Fruit Co. pulled out of a contract it had signed earlier for the purchase of Nicaraguan bananas. In 1983, the administration reduced the quota for the import of Nicaraguan sugar from 58,800 tons to 6,000 tons. In 1985, it imposed an embargo on U.S. trade with Nicaragua and cancelled docking and landing rights for Nicaraguan ships and planes.

What goal was the United States pursuing? It claimed at first that its purpose was to interdict the flow of arms from Nicaragua to the Salvadoran rebels. But it was never able to prove that Nicaragua was shipping arms or that it was interdicting them. Then in February 1985, Reagan admitted that his objective was to "remove" the "present structure" of the government in Nicaragua. When asked if this did not mean that he was advocating the overthrow of the Nicaraguan government, he replied, "Not if the present government would turn around and say...uncle...."[92]

How did the United States propose to overthrow the Sandinistas? Even when Enders was in charge, the administration envisaged the possibility of getting rid of the Sandinistas through an invasion by U.S. forces, though this was considered unlikely. A State Department briefing paper outlined policy for George Shultz as he was taking office in June 1982. "Barring serious miscalculation by the other side, there will be no opportunities for a quick decisive action to end the problem."[93] A "quick decisive action" meant a direct U.S. intervention. The statement indicates that although an opportunity for such an intervention could not be counted on, it might arise.

Then came the removal of Enders as well as the piling up of evidence that the contras alone couldn't topple the Sandinistas. The contras could cause many deaths and great damage, but they couldn't capture or hold towns and, by the CIA's own account, were failing to win significant political support within Nicaragua.[94] The administration began to think more and more about the possibility of a U.S. invasion.

On July 17, 1983, the *New York Times* published some of the contents of a secret National Security Council report obtained from an administration official "said to fear that the current policy is leading toward a major increase in United States military involvement in Central America." The report, prepared by an interagency task force, stated that "the situation in Central America is nearing a critical point." It discussed prepositioning U.S. equipment in Honduras for use in a crisis and the improvement of Honduran air and naval installations.

The report also stated that "it is still possible to accomplish U.S. objectives without the direct use of U.S. troops...." and brought out Pentagon caution about direct U.S. intervention. The Pentagon was leery of undertaking intervention without the support of Congress.

The administration was facing a dilemma. It wanted desperately to overthrow the Sandinistas and was considering direct U.S. intervention for doing so. But the "Vietnam syndrome" — the actual and potential opposition of the people — was enforcing caution.

On July 23, the *Times* reported that "President Reagan has approved a plan calling for a substantial increase in American military involvement in Central America and preparations for a possible limited military blockade of Nicaragua...." The plan "does not envisage any immediate combat role for United States forces, but does call for making preparations so that American forces can be swiftly called into action if necessary...." Senate Minority Leader Robert C. Byrd, Democrat of West Virginia, expressed concern. "I hope we would not rush pell-mell into a military adventure in this area."

Nine months later, the *Times* reported that, according to senior administration officials, "contingency plans are being drawn for the possible use of United States combat troops in Central America if the current strategy for defeating leftist forces in the region fails." Previously, such officials had been asserting that there were no plans for U.S. forces to fight in Central America, but now, "in response to inquiries, officials in private raised the possibility of intervention by United States combat forces." Such an action would require the consent of Congress under the War Powers Act of 1973. But the officials "contended that few members of Congress would be willing to abandon Central America to Communist rule." Fifteen days later the *Times* reported that, in the view of military specialists and members of Congress, "the Pentagon is now in a position to assume a combat role in Central America should President Reagan give the order."[95]

But, though prepared, the Pentagon remained cautious. Defense Secretary Caspar Weinberger explained its philosophy in a speech in November 1984. U.S. forces, he said, should be committed to combat only as "a last resort" and when there is "reasonable assurance we will have the support of the American people and their elected representatives in Congress." But "if we decide it is necessary" to commit troops, "we should do so wholeheartedly and with the clear intention of winning." Weinberger cited the U.S. intervention in Grenada as an example of how to use troops with "resolve."[96]

On June 4 and 5, 1985, the *Times* ran a pair of articles which asserted that discussion of an invasion of Nicaragua had "become commonplace in official circles." No one in government, said the articles, "is suggesting that an invasion of Nicaragua is imminent or desirable." But "interviews with numerous American and foreign government officials in Washington and in Central America indicate that the possibility of United States military involvement in Nicaragua has become a matter of open discussion." Specifically, "President Reagan, Secretary of State George P. Shultz and other senior officials have for the first time begun warning that if other policies fail, the United States may be left with little choice in the years ahead."

When asked under what circumstances the United States might attack Nicaragua, U.S. officials "say the line is most clearly drawn against the acquisition by Nicaragua of high performance warplanes." Another "circumstance would be the establishment of a Soviet-bloc military base in Nicaragua." Still another "would be the consolidation of Nicaragua's Government into what administration officials often call 'a second Cuba.'"

With "a second Cuba," said Senator Richard Lugar, Chairman of the Senate Foreign Relations Committee, "we might be invited" by Nicaragua's neighbors to invade "as we were invited in the East Caribbean." Before the invasion of Grenada in October 1983, the leaders of several Caribbean countries, in a move clearly instigated by the United States, requested U.S. military intervention. Senator Lugar also said that if diplomatic relations with Nicaragua were ended, "then we might recognize a government in exile." According to the *Times*, Lugar was "referring to an idea that has been discussed among Administration officials."

On the same page as the second invasion article, the *Times* carried a story headlined, "Most Americans in Survey Oppose Aid for Overthrow of Sandinistas." A *New York Times*/CBS News poll showed that "a majority of Americans still oppose help for efforts to overthrow the Nicaraguan government." More people were worried about a war in Central America than about a "Communist takeover."

Because the people were opposed to invasion, the administration had to consider some difficult questions. What sort of pretext would best sway public opinion? How many U.S. casualties would there be? How long would an invasion take? Would the U.S. forces be able to go in, do their job, and quickly withdraw before public opinion had a chance to make itself felt? Or would the United States become bogged down in a long guerrilla war? Would U.S. intervention quickly expand into a regional war covering all of Central America as the Sandinistas were predicting?

The administration evidently could not find satisfactory answers to these questions. Nicaragua, though small, is much larger than Grenada and posed a far more difficult military problem. It was strongly armed. Its leaders enjoyed strong support among the people and had maintained their unity. An invasion would have been costly. Despite the administration's desire to get rid of the Sandinistas, it did not invade.

EVEN WITHOUT AN INVASION by U.S. forces, the war against Nicaragua exacted a terrible toll. Nicaraguan President Daniel Ortega told the U.N. General Assembly in October 1987 that the war had inflicted 45,714 casualties.[97] (The equivalent for the United States would be 3.5 million.)

In addition, the war wrecked the Nicaraguan economy. Wrecking the economy to undermine the Sandinista government became the main aim of the war as the United States recognized that the contras could not win militarily.

The fighting zones along the Honduran border are among Nicaragua's most productive agricultural areas. Contra attacks caused reductions—in some years as much as a third—in the harvest of coffee, the main export. Other export crops such as tobacco also suffered. The attacks cut down the production of corn and beans for domestic consumption, making increased imports necessary. The reduced exports and increased import requirements, combined with the U.S. blocking of credits, created an enormous balance of payments problem. It became impossible for Nicaragua to import all that its people and economy required.[98]

To defend itself against the contras and create a disincentive to U.S. invasion, Nicaragua had to greatly expand its armed forces. With the number of people in the military comparable to those in the U.S. armed forces at the height of World War II, labor shortages became inevitable. Supplying these forces placed a heavy burden on a country as poor as Nicaragua.

The war created an impossible budgetary problem. Defense expenditures mounted to more than a quarter of the gross national product. The budget deficit soared accordingly.[99] The only way the enormous deficit could be financed was by the creation of additional money. This flooded the country with money and caused an upsurge in inflation. By early 1986, inflation was running at an annual rate of 300 percent. By year's end, it had passed 1,000 percent and was still skyrocketing.

An inflation of such proportions coming on top of the disruption of the labor force and the loss of production due to the devastation of cultivated areas, the killing of cattle, the sinking of fishing boats, the destruction of electric power plants, and the shortages of imported raw materials, was bound to throw the economy out of joint. The government's system for assuring the people a supply of goods at reasonable prices could no longer work. With so rapid an inflation, fixed prices in the regular markets quickly became ridiculously low and goods tended to disappear into mushrooming black markets, with fabulously high prices. Thousands of people left productive work for the far more remunerative black market operations, further aggravating the labor shortage.

Even as the Nicaraguan people suffered from extreme shortages of basic foodstuffs and other essential goods, U.S. officials gloated. Nicaragua's "economy is a bust," said Secretary Shultz.[100] Such gloating was not accidental. The strategy was not only to wreck the Nicaraguan economy, but to discredit the Sandinistas by laying the blame on them.

But the fault was not the Sandinistas'. What could the Sandinistas do about the budget deficit that was fueling the inflation? In the face of the threat from the United States, they couldn't cut defense expenditures which accounted for half the budget. Should they have slashed health care and education, the next largest items? Was it politically feasible for them to cut these services so essential for the classes that constituted the main support of the Revolution? No conceivable cuts in these items would have produced more than minor reductions in the deficit. What about increasing taxes? With the great bulk of the population poor, increasing taxes could not make a significant dent on the deficit.

What could the Sandinistas do when attacks on coffee and tobacco plantations devastated Nicaragua's exports, reducing the amount of foreign exchange available to pay for imports? They could reserve the foreign exchange for the most essential uses, but the economy had to make do with less.

Even if the Nicaraguan economy had been run by a team of the best economists of all time, the U.S. war and embargo would have produced much the same difficulties as arose under the Sandinistas. The Sandinistas undoubtedly made errors. Erors are inevitable in running an economy. But the effect of the errors was marginal. By far the chief cause of Nicaragua's economic difficulties was U.S. aggression.

The strategy for the attack on the Nicaraguan economy was fiendishly clever. At a trifling cost, the United States was able to inflict immense damage. It was able to do this invisibly, insidiously, without most North Americans seeing the process, without their realizing that their government was dooming a whole generation of Nicaraguan children to the lifelong effects of malnutrition.

The strategy worked. A coalition of fourteen widely diverging opposition parties—formed at the instigation of the United States—won against the Sandinistas in a national election in February 1990.

A large number of foreign observers, including former President Jimmy Carter, monitored the election to guard against cheating by the Sandinistas. These observers testified that the election was fair. Technically, it was. But basically, the election was anything but fair.

The Nicaraguan people were voting under duress. Worn down by eight years of fighting and economic torture, they desperately wanted an end to the war, the draft, the deaths, the U.S. sanctions. The United States deliberately fostered the view that a Sandinista victory would mean continued war and sanctions, that the only hope of relief lay in voting for the opposition. To maintain the threat that the war would continue, the administration, going against demands in Congress and an agreement signed by the five Central American presidents (Esquipulas II), refused to dissolve the contra army, even though it had long been clear that this army could not overthrow the Sandinistas by military force. To help keep up the pressure, it continued the economic sanctions. Faced with the prospect of an indefinite continuation of war, sanctions, and almost unbearable hardship, a majority of Nicaraguans voted for the opposition. It is testimony to the strength of revolutionary sentiment in Nicaragua and the stout-heartedness of its people that despite the cruel choice 41 percent voted for the Sandinistas.

6. Central and Southern Africa

Congo-Zaire, Angola, Namibia, South Africa

The first important U.S. intervention in Africa was in the Congo, an ex-Belgian colony that won independence in 1960, confronting U.S. officials with what they viewed as the threat of a "communist takeover." The United States was concerned about the Congo not only because of its size and its copper, uranium, and diamonds, but because of its strategic location in central Africa. If it became "another Cuba," it could infect the whole continent.

The Belgians had hoped to maintain control even after independence, but they had not reckoned with the energetic action of the Congolese prime minister, Patrice Lumumba, organizer and leader of the Mouvement National Congolais. Lumumba informed the Congolese people of what was happening by frequent radio speeches and reports to Parliament. He warned that "the political independence they have given us with their left hand they want to take away with their right hand through economic domination." He explained the maneuvers of the imperialists. "Those who covet our riches are attempting to provoke anarchy, demoralize the members of our government... turn the population against us and make our government fall. They propose to use puppets who will not hesitate to blindly sign any kind of agreement to place the Congo under foreign domination."[1]

Lumumba was an anti-imperialist, a person who wanted the Congolese to be masters of their own country. At an All-African Peoples' Conference in Ghana in 1958, he had called for an end to the domination and injustices of colonialism, for independence with full rights for Africans, and for African unity in the face of the divide-and-rule tactics of the imperialists. He ended his speech to the conference with the cry: "Down with colonialism and imperialism! Down with racialism and tribalism! Long live the Congolese nation, long live independent Africa!"

At the independence day ceremony on June 30, 1960, Lumumba upset the Western dignitaries present by referring to the fate of the Congolese people during eighty years of colonial rule, to "the wounds too painful and fresh" to be "erased from our memory."

> We have known backbreaking work, required of us in exchange for wages that did not allow us to satisfy our hunger, clothe or house ourselves decently, or raise our children as beings dear to us.
>
> We have known ironic taunts, insults, and blows morning, noon, and night because we were blacks....
>
> We have seen our lands despoiled in the name of what was supposed to be the law but was really only a recognition of the right of the strongest.
>
> We have known that the law was never the same for whites and blacks: accommodating for one, cruel and inhuman for the other....
>
> We have known that there were magnificent homes in the cities for whites and ramshackle straw huts for blacks, that a black was never admitted into the so-called European movie theaters, restaurants, or stores....
>
> Finally, who can forget the rifle bursts from which so many of our brothers perished, the dungeons into which those who would not submit to a regime of justice through exploitation and oppression were thrown?[2]

Lumumba's declarations marked him as a dangerous rabble-rouser in the eyes of the U.S. imperialists who, just as they had done in many other parts of the world, were moving in to take over as a weakened old European empire disintegrated. U.S. authorities began to watch Lumumba carefully. The U.S. consul general in the Congo, Claire Timberlake, claimed in a pre-independence report that Lumumba's campaign funds "appeared to derive in large part from Communist and radical African sources."[3]

Trouble began immediately for Lumumba's government. Five days after independence on June 30, 1960, several Congolese army units mutinied against their Belgian officers. Lumumba calmed the soldiers by arranging for Africanization of the officer corps. But in Elizabethville, capital of copper-rich Katanga province, Belgian officers did not hand over their command and additional mutinies occurred. The U.S., British, and French consuls in Elizabethville requested Belgian military intervention. Two days later, without the consent of Lumumba's government, Belgium sent in troops.[4]

Also within days after independence, the Premier of Katanga, Moise Tshombe, acting with the support of the Belgian corporation Union Minière du Haut Katanga, announced the province's secession on the ground that the central government was trying to establish a "ruinous and Communist state."[5] Lumumba denounced the move as "a coup meticulously prepared by the Belgian government for several months."[6]

Adamant about both getting rid of the Belgian troops and reintegrating Katanga, Lumumba looked around for help. Jointly with the president of the Congo, Joseph Kasavubu, he appealed to Timberlake, now ambassador, who told them to go to the United Nations. They appealed to the U.N. on July 12, and the next day in a follow-up message added: "If the assistance requested is not received without delay the Republic of the Congo will be obliged to appeal to the Bandung Treaty Powers [a group of African and Asian anti-colonialist nations]."[7] The Security Council passed a resolution calling on Belgium to withdraw its troops and sent a U.N. force to the Congo.

Meanwhile, U.S. officials were sizing up Lumumba and discussing what to do about him. Allen Dulles, head of the CIA, presented an assessment of Lumumba at a meeting of the National Security Council. According to the official minutes:

> Mr. Dulles said that in Lumumba we were faced with a person who was a Castro or worse....Mr. Dulles went on to describe Mr. Lumumba's background... as "harrowing"....It is safe to go on the assumption that Lumumba has been bought by the Communists; this also, however, fits with his own orientation.[8]

The State Department requested advice on "handling" Lumumba from the ambassador to Belgium, William Burden. Burden thought it would be

> only prudent ... to plan on basis that Lumumba government threatens our vital interests in Congo and Africa generally. A principal objective of our political and diplomatic action must therefore be to destroy Lumumba government as now constituted, but

at the same time we must find or develop another horse to back which would be acceptable in rest of Africa and defensible against Soviet political attack.[9]

Soon after the arrival of the U.N. force in the Congo, Lumumba found himself at odds with the U.N. representatives there. They were not taking action to get the Belgian troops out or to reintegrate Katanga. He explained in a radio speech what his government would do if the U.N. didn't solve these problems.

We protested to the U.N., demanding immediate withdrawal of Belgian troops, enemy troops, troops of occupation.... We have said that if there is no way to obtain satisfaction immediately we will call on Soviet troops and Afro-Asian troops.[10]

Lumumba also used the speech to respond to the charge that he was a communist:

We are not communists, contrary to the campaign of destruction and obstruction that the enemies of our independence have carried out throughout the country.... We are simply Africans. We want to make the Congo a great free nation.[11]

Lumumba did not obtain satisfaction through the U.N. force. The United States dominated the United Nations and Dr. Ralph Bunche, the chief U.N. representative in the Congo, was a U.S. national. On a trip to the United States in late July, Lumumba received a telegram from the vice-prime minister, Antoine Gizenga:

I have made demands to Dr. Bunche for United Nations troops to be sent to Katanga. He seems to find difficulties and does not promise dispatch now.... United Nations troops are disarming our soldiers and allowing Belgian forces to keep their arms, which is incomprehensible.[12]

Lumumba's denial that he was a communist didn't help him with Undersecretary of State Douglas Dillon and other U.S. officials whom he saw on his trip. The Senate (Church Committee) report, *Alleged Assassination Plots Involving Foreign Leaders,* states that "according to Dillon, Lumumba impressed American officials as an irrational, almost 'psychotic' personality." Dillon testified to the Committee that

When he was in the State Department meeting...he would never look you in the eye.... You had a feeling that he was a person that was gripped by this fervor that I can only characterize as messianic.... [T]he impression that was left was...very bad, that this was an individual whom it was impossible to deal with.[13]

Dillon also testified that shortly after Lumumba's visit, he was present at a meeting at the Pentagon attended by representatives of the State and Defense Departments, the Joint Chiefs of Staff, and the CIA. "A question regarding the possibility of an assassination attempt against Lumumba was briefly raised," said Dillon, but the subject "was turned off by the CIA." Dillon felt that the CIA's reaction might have stemmed from the feeling that the group was too large for discussion of such a sensitive subject.[14]

Besides Lumumba's other faults in the eyes of U.S. officials, he had committed an unpardonable sin by asking the Soviet Union for economic aid. In an August 2 letter to the U.N. Security Council, the Soviet government stated that in response it had already dispatched 10,000 tons of food and would soon send 100 trucks, spare parts, a repair shop accompanied by instructors, as well as a group of doctors and medical personnel.[15]

Through early August, Lumumba still hoped that the U.N. force might help end the Katanga secession. On August 9, a new Security Council resolution again called on Belgium to withdraw its troops and declared that the entry of the U.N. force into Katanga was necessary to implement this resolution. Lumumba sent a message of thanks. U.N. Secretary General Dag Hammarskjold came to the Congo to take personal charge of the efforts to settle the Katanga question. When Lumumba saw how Hammarskjold handled the entry of U.N. troops, he lost hope. Hammarskjold didn't consult with him on the operation; sent only European, not African, troops; and by requesting Tshombe's permission, implied recognition of the secessionist government.

Hammarskjold and the U.N. mission were acting in tandem with the United States. The United States was not interested in getting rid of the Tshombe government, but rather in maintaining it as a counterforce against the Lumumba government. Lumumba fired off several letters to Hammarskjold demanding the withdrawal of U.N. forces from the Congo.

Coming on top of Lumumba's acceptance of Soviet economic aid, his demand for U.N. withdrawal brought U.S. antagonism to him to a head. At a meeting of the National Security Council, Dillon maintained that the elimination of the U.N. would be a disaster which...we should do everything we [can] to prevent. If the U.N. were forced out, we might be faced by a situation where the Soviets intervened by invitation of the Congo.[16]

Eisenhower said at this meeting that

the possibility that the U.N. would be forced out was simply inconceivable. We should keep the U.N. in the Congo even if we had to ask for European troops to do it. We should do so even if such action was used by the Soviets as the basis for starting a fight.[17]

At one NSC meeting—probably the same one—Eisenhower called for action against Lumumba. Robert H. Johnson, an NSC staff member who was responsible for writing a memorandum of the discussion, testified before the Senate Committee that "Eisenhower said something... that came across to me as an order for the assassination of Lumumba...." Johnson also thought that he might have heard Eisenhower order a coup, but "explained that his allowance for the possibility that he had heard an order for a coup did not disturb his recollection of hearing an assassination order."[18]

The next day James Reston wrote in the *New York Times*:

There have been a series of urgent and private meetings here all last week leading to a very simple but hard conclusion, namely, that unless the irresponsible Congo "Government" of Patrice Lumumba is contained, the future of the U.N. and of the whole of Africa will be seriously affected.[19]

A week later, Allen Dulles signed a cable to the CIA Station Chief in Leopoldville stating:

In high quarters here it is the clear-cut conclusion that if [Lumumba] continues to hold high office, the inevitable result will at best be chaos and at worst pave the way to Communist takeover of the Congo with disastrous consequences for the prestige of the UN and for the interests of the free world generally. Consequently we conclude that his removal must be an urgent and prime objective and that under existing conditions this should be a high priority of our covert action.[20]

The coup came ten days later, on September 5. As the Church Committee report puts it, "President Kasavubu dismissed Premier Lumumba from the government despite the strong support for Lumumba in the Congolese Parliament."[21] CIA and other U.S. officials along with members of the U.N. mission helped promote the coup. According to Andrew Tully in his book, *CIA — The Inside Story*, Kasavubu "sat at the feet of the CIA men, who reminded him that it was within his realm of responsibility to depose Lumumba and form a new government." Andrew Cordier, the U.S. national then in charge of the U.N. mission, has written that Kasavubu consulted him about the coup beforehand and that he began to "plan our resources for safeguarding law and order." Cordier started by providing a guard for Kasavubu's residence. Once the coup began and after consulting with the U.S. ambassador, he used U.N. troops to shut down the airports, thereby preventing loyal soldiers from coming to Lumumba's assistance. Then, after Lumumba got on the radio to call on the army and the people for help, Cordier closed down the radio station.[22]

The United States continued to view Lumumba as a threat even after the coup. He had strong popular backing, controlled a majority of the Parliament and most units of the army, and had strong international support from the African and Asian countries. So the United States continued to work against him.

According to the Church Committee report, "the day after Kasavubu deposed Lumumba, two CIA officers met with a high-level Congolese politician" and then reported to headquarters:

> To [Station Officer] comment that Lumumba in opposition is almost as dangerous as in office, [the Congolese politician] indicated understood and implied might physically eliminate Lumumba.[23]

Lumumba quickly showed that U.S. fear of his prowess was justified. Two days after being dismissed, he appeared in the lower house of Parliament. Ambassador Timberlake reported that he "devastated the points raised by the opposition.... He made Kasavubu look ridiculous."[24] The next day the lower house voted overwhelmingly to reinstate him and a day later the Senate followed suit. U.S. officials realized that Kasavubu was no match for Lumumba. They also worried that he was not firm enough in his opposition to Lumumba and might allow him to be included in a new government.

A few days later, on September 14, another coup came, this one by Colonel Joseph Mobutu who announced that he was "neutralizing" the politicians, suspending parliament, and installing as government a College of Commissioners composed of recent Congolese university graduates and students. Soon afterward, Mobutu announced the expulsion of Soviet, Czech, and "other Socialist" personnel.

Who was Mobutu? Lawrence Devlin, a CIA officer who became Station Chief in the Congo after independence, had spotted him earlier, in Brussels, when Mobutu was there on a fellowship. The CIA began to build him up. He became a member of Lumumba's party and helped mollify the soldiers during the mutinies which followed independence. The Lumumba government named him chief of staff of the army. U.N. officials, engaged in reorganizing the army, felt he was the kind of officer they needed and, to build up his authority, allowed him to claim credit for paying the soldiers with money they were supplying. According to *Time* magazine, he "became a frequent visitor to the U.S. Embassy and held long talks with officials there." When U.S. officials became dissatisfied with Kasavubu, the CIA had the man to take over.[25]

After Mobutu's coup, Lumumba asked the U.N. force for protection. His concern about his safety was justified. The Church Committee report states:

> The day after Mobutu's coup the Station Officer [Devlin] reported that he was serving as an advisor to a Congolese effort to "eliminate" Lumumba due to his "fear" that Lumumba might, in fact, have been strengthened by placing himself in U.N. custody.... "Only solution is remove him from scene soonest."[26]

Two days later, the station reported a request from a leading Congolese Senator for a "clandestine supply [of] small arms" to equip a "core [of] armed men willing and able [to] take direct action." The CIA operative who received the request recommended to headquarters that it "have [arms] supplies ready to go...."[27]

Worry about Lumumba even after Mobutu's coup extended to the highest levels of the U.S. Government. A week after the coup, Allen Dulles, briefing the National Security Council in the presence of the President, concluded:

> Mobutu appeared to be the effective power in the Congo for the moment but Lumumba was not yet disposed of and remained a grave danger as long as he was not disposed of.[28]

Three days later, Dulles sent a personal cable to Station Chief Devlin which stated that we wish give every possible support in eliminating Lumumba from any possibility resuming governmental position....[29]

Two days after the cable, according to the Senate report,

Joseph Scheider [a pseudonym for the CIA's Chief of Technical Services Sidney Gottlieb], under assignment from CIA Headquarters, arrived in Leopoldville, provided the Station Officer with poisons, conveyed Headquarters' instruction to assassinate Lumumba, and assured him that there was Presidential authorization for this mission.[30]

For two months after Gottlieb's arrival in the Congo, "a regular stream of messages" discussing how to carry out the assassination flowed through a special high-security channel between CIA Headquarters and Leopoldville. CIA officials explored how to "penetrate" Lumumba's entourage and inject poison into his food or toothpaste. They plotted how to lure him out of U.N. custody or use a "commando type group for abduction." But no opportunity arose for carrying out any of the different plans.[31]

Then, on November 14, the Station cabled Headquarters that it had learned that Lumumba's followers in Stanleyville wanted him to "break out of his confinement" and that it was "studying several plans of action" to use if he did so.[32] On November 27, Lumumba left his U.N.-guarded house and the Station cabled Headquarters:

[Station] working with [Congolese government] to get roads blocked and troops alerted [block] possible escape route.[33]

Mobutu's troops arrested Lumumba while he was on his way to Stanleyville. Even after his arrest, the CIA station considered him a threat and kept informed of his whereabouts. Unrest in the army and pressure from the African and Asian countries to reconvene Parliament fed the Station's fear of Lumumba. On January 12, 1961, Station Chief Devlin cabled Headquarters that the army and police were threatening mutiny unless they were given big pay raises and that a mutiny "almost certainly would bring about [Lumumba] return power."[34]

A day later, Devlin advised against allowing Parliament to reopen. Lumumba's "powers as demagogue," he said, would "insure [his] victory in Parliament." He added that "refusal to take drastic steps at this time will lead to defeat of [United States] policy in Congo."[35]

The next day the Congolese government advised Devlin that it was transferring Lumumba to Bakwanga, capital of another province. But when those directing the operation learned that there were U.N. troops at the Bakwanga airport, they redirected the plane in mid-flight to Katanga. The Church Committee report says that, according to a U.N. investigation, "Lumumba was killed on January 17, almost immediately after his arrival in Katanga, probably with the knowledge of the central government and at the behest of the Katanga authorities."[36]

With the death of Lumumba, leadership of the nationalist forces in the Congo fell to Antoine Gizenga, who had set up a government in Stanleyville. The Soviet Union, the People's Republic of China, Ghana, Guinea, and the United Arab Republic promptly recognized it as the legal government of the Congo. Three rival governments were now contending with each other—that of Kasavubu-Mobutu in Leopoldville, Gizenga in Stanleyville, and Tshombe in Elizabethville, Katanga. The United States began to worry that a civil war might break out, and bring to power a radical government.

The Kennedy administration took office around the time of Lumumba's murder, bringing changes in strategy. It favored a "liberal" line in Africa—one more accommodating to the anti-colonialists and the newly independent states. The administration feared that a hard conservative line would push "moderate" nationalists into the arms of "radicals." It felt that the best way to fight the radicals was in cooperation with the moderates.

While a Task Force was working out strategy toward the Congo, a heated discussion was going on at the United Nations. The Afro-Asian countries were blaming the United States and the other Western countries that controlled the U.N. Congo operation for Lumumba's murder and for the failure to expel the Belgians and end the Katanga secession. They presented, and the Security Council adopted, a resolution calling for the immediate withdrawal of the Belgians, the use of force if necessary to prevent civil war, and the reconvening of the Congo Parliament.

In April 1961, the Task Force recommended that the United States work for reconvening Parliament and the formation of a government of national unity including Lumumbists. As Secretary of State Dean Rusk later put it:

We considered that the risks of Gizengist inclusion in the Government in a minority position and controlling no politically sensitive ministries would be less of a risk than leaving Gizenga in his Orientale [Stanleyville] redoubt where he is a standing invitation to Communist penetration....[37]

The Gizenga government worried the United States because of the support it enjoyed among the Congolese people. As Congo scholar Catherine Hoskyns noted, this government "despite its recent formation and lack of organization could certainly count on a wider support than either Leopoldville or Katanga."[38]

The United States acted on several fronts to carry out its strategy of forming a national unity government. It worked to undermine the Stanleyville government, trying though diplomatic pressure to cut down its foreign support and through bribery to win away internal adherents. It tried to build an anti-Lumumbist alliance, including Kasavubu and Tshombe and their followers, that would prevent a Lumumbist majority. It looked for a politician who could be promoted as acceptable to all parties as head of a new government. After a while, two of the three Congolese camps—Leopoldville and Stanleyville—agreed to participate in a reconvened session of Parliament. In Elizabethville, however, Tshombe refused, weakening the anti-Lumumbist front.

As a candidate for prime minister, the United States came up with Cyrille Adoula, a former labor leader associated with the anti-communist International Confederation of Free Trade Unions in Brussels. Adoula had opposed Lumumba in the tumultuous period following independence. Ambassador Timberlake described him as

an intelligent and well-balanced moderate whose chief interest has been in organizing an independent African labor movement. A forceful and articulate spokesman for the Congo, Adoula is strongly anti-Communist. He has talked openly with the American Embassy in Leopoldville, which long considered him one of the best prospects for leadership in the Congo.[39]

When the Parliament finally assembled in July 1961, it seemed for a while that, despite the U.S. plans, the old Lumumbist majority might reassert itself and elect Gizenga prime minister. Gizenga supporters won thirteen out of fourteen parliamentary offices. Only the presidency of the Senate went to a "moderate."

Kennedy, Rusk, and CIA Director Dulles all became concerned. Undersecretary of State U. Alexis Johnson sent a cable
to McMurtrie Godley, interim U.S. ambassador in the Congo:

> Secretary desires emphasize for your guidance that Gizenga as
> prime minister not only question prestige abroad and reaction at
> home but involves our most vital interests in Africa....Blocking
> Gizenga from controlling government is a specific object of policy
> for which your full attention and imaginative effort are required.[40]

The U.S. mission in the Congo mobilized its forces and let it
be known which candidate the United States wanted to win.
The CIA began to hand out bribes to the parliamentarians.
Mobutu, known to enjoy U.S. backing, warned that if a "unity
premier" were not confirmed, the army would intervene.
Weakened by bribery and afraid of another Mobutu coup, the
Lumumbists agreed to support Adoula as premier in exchange
for half the ministries in his government. On August 2, Parliament confirmed Kasavubu's selection of Adoula as prime minister.[41]

The *New York Times* later reported that

> Money and shiny American automobiles, furnished through the
> logistic wizardry of Langley [CIA Headquarters], are said to have
> been the deciding factors in the vote that brought Mr. Adoula to
> power.[42]

Having installed Adoula, the United States proceeded to
strengthen his government. A CIA memorandum in President
Kennedy's files reveals the U.S. program as of November 1961:

> The [State] Department, in conjunction with other branches of the
> Government, is endeavoring to help Adoula improve his political
> base of support and enhance his domestic power and stature.
> This activity is in the areas of political organization with connected
> trade union and youth groups, public relations and security ap-
> paratus.[43]

Also, after trying unsuccessfully to bring about a reconciliation
between the central government and the Tshombe regime, the
United States supported U.N. military action to end the Katanga
secession.   The Katanga regime was one thing when it
weakened a central government headed by Lumumba, another
when it weakened one headed by Adoula and supported by the
United States.

A third item on the U.S. agenda was to get rid of Gizenga. Ambassador Edmund Gullion held constant discussions with Adoula about ways to accomplish Gizenga's removal. When Gizenga, after briefly participating in the Adoula government, returned to Stanleyville, Gullion urged Adoula to purge him from the Cabinet and arrest him. In January 1962, Adoula had Gizenga arrested. Soon other Lumumbist ministers began to lose their posts.

Finally, the United States began to provide economic and military aid to the Congo. In the three years following Adoula's election, the United States pumped in over $175 million in economic aid. The Congo became the first country in Africa to become dependent on U.S. financial assistance.[44]

Direct military aid to the CIA strongman, Mobutu, was the centerpiece in the U.S. strategy of promoting a strong central government that it could control. In July 1962, the United States sent a military team to work out plans for the aid. The first plan called for setting up a U.N. sponsorship for the operation and for a number of other countries to participate along with the United States. But because of the objections of the Afro-Asian and socialist countries, the U.N. cover never materialized and the United States began openly to build up Mobutu's forces without it. By mid-1964, the U.S. military mission in Leopoldville had grown to eight men and the United States had provided $5 million in overt aid, including trucks, helicopters, and combat planes.[45]

But direct, overt aid was only part of the assistance the United States provided. It also helped indirectly by its support for the U.N. force in the Congo and covertly through the CIA. U.S. financial contributions, diplomatic support, and military transport planes helped the U.N. force end the Katanga secession. After the U.N. force was withdrawn from the Congo, the CIA together with Belgium carried out a covert paramilitary campaign against a rebellion by Lumumba supporters that flared through several provinces in 1964.

Finding that Adoula wasn't the man to cope with the rebellion, the United States in cahoots with Belgium worked for his removal. The main vehicle for accomplishing this was an informal group of leading Congolese figures known as the Binza Group, after the Leopoldville suburb in which they lived. The group included such people as the army chief of staff, General Mobutu, and the head of the secret police, Victor Nendaka, who were financed and dominated by the CIA. The Binza Group urged Kasavubu to replace Adoula and in mid-1964 he did so, recalling Tshombe from exile to become prime minister and end the rebellion. Pretense of moderation disappeared. Tshombe formed a rightist government.

With Tshombe installed, the United States and Belgium mounted their paramilitary operation. Belgium took the front role. The United States quietly contributed financial assistance and jeeps, trucks, communications equipment, transport planes, helicopters, and light tanks. It also helped recruit mercenaries, mostly South Africans and Rhodesians, and it created an "instant air force" piloted by counterrevolutionary Cubans.[46]

Within a few months, the interventionist forces began to push back the rebellion, inflicting enormous casualties on civilians as well as rebels. "In one town alone," writes Stephen Weissman, "the mercenaries admitted killing at least 3,000 Congolese of all ages."[47] An attack on Stanleyville was the main blow against the rebellion. U.S. C-130 transports dropped Belgian paratroopers on the city. White mercenaries spearheaded columns of Tshombe's Congolese troops. Again the interventionists butchered people.

Africa exploded in protest. Violent demonstrations took place in Algeria, Burundi, Congo-Brazzaville, the Sudan, Tanzania, and the United Arab Republic, and even "moderate" countries expressed dismay. Africans, Asians, and progressives throughout the world demanded an end to the aggression, condemned the atrocities committed by the mercenaries, and denounced the "imperialist stooge," Tshombe, who had brought the mercenaries in.

When Kasavubu in October 1965 declared Tshombe's "transitional tasks" completed and named an anti-Tshombe leader to form a new government, he gained some popularity in Africa. But his move didn't sit well with the United States. Young and Turner write in their book on Zaire (Congo): "To Washington, the Kasavubu group seemed embarked on a dangerous opening to the left." The imperialists considered what to do. "The Mobutu alternative...appeared to promise both stability and reliability."[48] The United States promoted a second Mobutu coup in which the strongman ousted Kasavubu and the prime minister-designate and named himself chief of state.

Thus the CIA's man, Mobutu, whom it had discovered years earlier in Brussels, who had already in 1960 made a coup the United States wanted, who had solved the problem of Lumumba by arresting him and turning him over to be murdered in Katanga, who throughout all the twistings and turnings in the Congo had been a favored recipient of U.S. aid, now became military dictator. For a while, Mobutu maintained parliamentary trappings. Then in 1966, he sacked even the obedient colonel he had named prime minister. In 1967, he established himself as permanent head of a presidential government fully under his control.

Through its counterrevolutionary action against the movement for a truly independent Congo, through its promotion of the Mobutu dictatorship, the United States had developed a client state in central Africa. Mobutu's Zaire would be a tool of U.S. policy in Africa, a center for CIA operations and a staging area for interventions in other countries. Mobutu's outstanding service to the United States would be Zaire's collaboration in a 1975 intervention in neighboring Angola, where both Washington and its puppet in central Africa saw a new "communist threat" in the revolutionary liberation movement that had taken root in the 1960s.

In 1990, the United States was still pumping in military and economic aid to Mobutu. But in the minds of some in the U.S. imperialist establishment he was outliving his usefulness. The *New York Times* finally discovered that "wholesale repression, corruption and megalomania have deformed Zaire." It added:

> American aid dollars have not measurably helped Zaire's people. Annual per capita income is about $150; living standards are *lower* than when Mr. Mobutu took power. His Government has not built a single hospital in its 25 years....
>
> Meanwhile Mr. Mobutu's personal fortune has, by some estimates, grown to $6 billion. His holdings include perhaps a dozen French and Belgian chateaus, a Spanish castle and a 32-bedroom Swiss villa....
>
> [But] Mr. Mobutu has supported anti-Communist iniatives of successive U.S. Administrations, especially in Angola. (Italics in original.)[49]

THE ANGOLAN WAR of independence began in 1961, a war by the people of Angola against the Portuguese colonial system. The Kennedy administration reacted at first with the same liberal, "pro-Africa" line as in the Congo. It talked of backing the African nationalists.

But soon the pro-Africa line came up against the hard facts of imperialist interests. Portugal was a NATO ally and provided the United States with an important base—the Azores. Also, Portugal was touting its colonies as outposts of Western civilization, bulwarks against the spread of communism. The Portuguese colonialists knew what they were doing when they played on the anti-communism theme. While the United States wanted to appear as champion of independence for the nations of Africa, it placed its highest priority on preventing "communist expansion."

Two organizations claimed leadership of the liberation movement in Angola in 1961. One was the Popular Movement for the Liberation of Angola (MPLA), which in February led an attack on the main jail in Luanda to free political prisoners, the action now considered to mark the beginning of Angola's war of independence. From its foundation in 1956, the MPLA had stressed the need for a broad anti-colonialist alliance. Its founding manifesto stated:

> Portuguese colonialism will not fall without a fight.... This struggle can be won only by a united front of all Angola's anti-imperialist forces, irrespective of their color, social situation, religious beliefs, or individual preferences....[50]

The other organization was the Union of the Peoples of Angola (UPA), a precursor of the National Front for the Liberation of Angola (FNLA), which consisted mainly of Bakongo, a tribe whose members inhabit northern Angola and southern Zaire. Its aims and methods were narrowly tribalist. In March 1961, the UPA instigated a Bakongo attack on Portuguese settlers and farmers in northern Angola.

Leading the UPA-FNLA was Holden Roberto. Though born in Angola, Roberto had been brought up in the Congo where, according to former CIA officer John Stockwell, he had worked for eight years as an accountant for the Belgian colonial administration. He was related by marriage to Mobutu.[51]

Roberto knew enough to emphasize his anti-communism to U.S. and Congolese officials. He presented himself as the only alternative to a takeover of the liberation movement by "Marxists" of the MPLA. U.S. officials began to cultivate him. Arthur M. Schlesinger, Jr. writes from direct personal knowledge that Robert F. Kennedy "got CIA money for Holden Roberto in Angola."[52]

Both the MPLA and the UPA established themselves in Leopoldville after Congolese independence. The Congo, after the elimination of Lumumba, was the ideal place for the United States to carry out its policy of supporting the UPA and opposing the MPLA. The U.S.-dominated Congo government became an instrument for carrying out this policy. President Adoula served as a conduit for transmitting U.S. aid to Roberto and the UPA.[53] The powerful General Mobutu became a friend and patron of the UPA and an enemy of the MPLA. Mobutu's troops and UPA forces cooperated in arresting MPLA militants trying to cross the border to Angola to fight the Portuguese. The Congolese government allowed the UPA to establish a military base in the Congo at Kinkuzu, while in 1963 it expelled the MPLA from the country.

The MPLA made repeated efforts, while in the Congo and afterward, to establish unity between the two movements. In May 1961, Roberto met with an MPLA leader and accepted "close cooperation" in principle, but then failed to cooperate. Later talks on unity brought a similar result. In November 1961, Roberto's troops murdered the twenty-one members of an MPLA column whom they had captured in northern Angola, causing his own chief of staff to speak out against the "fratricidal" strife.[54] Roberto's forces made forays into Angola, but they spent more time fighting the MPLA than the Portuguese.

The initially liberal line of the Kennedy administration showed itself in declarations by leading figures and in U.S. actions at the United Nations. Assistant Secretary of State G. Mennen Williams declared that "Africa should be for the Africans" and repeatedly called on Portugal to make preparations for self-determination in its African territories. Reversing the position of the Eisenhower administration, the United States voted in favor of a Security Council resolution which called on Portugal to institute reforms in Angola and to prepare for independence.

Some members of the administration wanted to go even further. A Task Force on Portuguese Territories organized by Williams concluded that "the situation in Angola is explosive" and rebellion might soon spread to Mozambique. It recommended setting "a timetable" for independence and mounting "a massive effort of persuasion and coercion" to get Portugal to go along. The United States should threaten to end military aid. The Defense Department should prepare contingency plans for the possible loss of the Azores bases. Undersecretary of State

Chester Bowles and U.N. Ambassador Adlai Stevenson, along with other liberals, supported the Task Force recommendations.[55]

But others in the Government quickly made known their opposition. The Pentagon considered that "any action which would jeopardize retention of the Azores...would be unacceptable." The deputy assistant for national security, Walt Rostow, argued that with a crisis in Berlin, it was not the time to upset NATO or jeopardize U.S. military capabilities. The National Security Council agreed and rejected the idea of demanding a firm timetable for Angolan independence or an end to military aid to Portugal.[56]

Even after this decision, the administration tried to maintain a liberal facade for its Angola policy. It tried to get Portugal to commit itself to self-determination, explaining that this did not mean immediate independence. Meanwhile, the Angolans, backed by various African countries, charged that Portugal was using U.S. weapons against them. Such use violated the NATO agreements under which the weapons were supplied, and the United States protested. But Defense Secretary McNamara cautioned that "any further public pressure on the Portuguese regarding the use of U.S. military materiel in Angola should be avoided" since it would jeopardize the use of the Azores. Afterward, U.S. representatives at the U.N. simply denied that U.S. weapons were being used in Africa.[57]

After a while, the administration began to back away from even the liberal facade. It cut down its liberal rhetoric, pulled away from its anti-colonialist position at the U.N., and removed liberal Undersecretary Bowles.

In a 1963 reassessment of U.S. policy, Walt Rostow, now chief of policy planning at the State Department, noted that the United States was "caught between competing interests in maintaining the good will of the new nations of Africa and our direct security interests in Southern Africa." It wanted to promote self-determination but also to avoid violent conflicts "which would open avenues of exploitation by the [communist] bloc."[58]

What gave way was the U.S. interest in self-determination. While maintaining the fiction that weapons supplied under NATO agreements were not for use in Africa, the United States supplied Portugal with weapons for precisely such use. In 1965, for example, a CIA front called Intermountain Aviation secretly flew seven B-26s to Portugal. As Marchetti and Marks explain:

"The sale directly violated the official United States policy against arms exports to Portugal for use in Angola.... [But] the U.S. government, at its highest level, had decided to sell twenty B-26s to Portugal, and the CIA proprietary was following official orders."[59]

In 1966, Jonas Savimbi, who had served as Roberto's "foreign minister," created his own organization, the National Movement for the Total Independence of Angola (UNITA). He had withdrawn from Roberto's organization two years earlier, accusing his former chief of being "flagrantly tribalist" and in "collusion with the American imperialists." However, Savimbi himself later collaborated with Portugal, South Africa, and the United States, as well as Roberto, against the MPLA.[60]

Of the three contending liberation organizations, only the MPLA developed into what Davidson, a long-time British observer of Western Africa, calls a "mass movement of multiethnic composition." The MPLA had the support of the people, the prime requisite for the success of a revolutionary guerrilla movement.[61]

Roberto's organization (now called the FNLA) made little headway inside Angola despite its protected status in the Congo, CIA assistance, and early recognition by several foreign countries. Davidson writes:

> Discounting the propaganda, one may conclude that [Roberto]'s movement between 1961 and 1971 achieved two military objectives. First, they built a small fighting force in the western Congo, based on the camp at Kinkuzu, and used this to seal off the frontier against any use of it by the MPLA. They also sent members of this force on infrequent short-range raids across the frontier.... Secondly, they retained a small guerrilla presence in northern Angola.... Given their logistic and other advantages, these objectives can only be described as minimal.[62]

On UNITA, Davidson writes:

> In October 1969 a UN survey noted "...there has been no mention of UNITA in the Portuguese military bulletins since 1968," while reports by Finnish, Italian, West German, and OAU observers in eastern districts, as well as those of the present writer, were unanimous in contending that UNITA had become, by 1970, little more than another distracting side show.[63]

When the Nixon administration came to power in 1969, it faced the same dilemma on southern Africa that had been noted by Rostow six years earlier. A National Security Council study on the region ordered by Kissinger concluded:

> The aim of present policy is to try to balance our economic, scientific, and strategic interests in the white states with the political interests of dissociating the US from the white minority regimes and their repressive racial policies.[64]

On the Portuguese colonies, the study stated:

> Our approach to Angola and Mozambique is influenced by countervailing factors. On the one hand Portugal is a NATO ally which we equip with arms and whose islands, the Azores, we find important for use as an air base. On the other hand we sympathize with the aspirations of the Angolans and Mozambicans for self-determination.[65]

If even the liberal Kennedy administration had placed a higher priority on preserving the U.S. position in the Azores than on promoting self-determination, what could be expected of the Nixon administration? Under Nixon, policy tilted even more toward support of Portugal.

Of the several policy options presented in the study, the one the administration followed was Option 2, whose "premise" was:

> The whites are here to stay and the only way that constructive change can come about is through them.[66]

Under this option, the United States

> would maintain public opposition to racial repression but relax political isolation and economic restrictions on the white states.[67]

The new tilt showed in many ways. The administration decided to grant Portugal full access to Export-Import Bank credit. It relaxed the already weak arms embargo, in particular on "dual purpose" equipment having both civilian and military uses. At the United Nations, the United States began to vote against resolutions condemning Portugal.

In return for an extension of the lease on the Azores, Portugal received an aid "package" of $436 million, including $400 million in Ex-Im loans and guarantees. It needed a means of rapidly transporting its troops to the faraway scene of the fighting in its colonies. Ex-Im credit financed the purchase of Boeing 707s, 727s, and 747s, whose sale the administration authorized knowing that Portugal used them as military transports in Africa. Ex-

Im credit also financed the purchase of helicopters and photo-reconnaissance aircraft.[68]

Meanwhile, the U.S. Commerce Department encouraged investment in the Portuguese colonies, describing favorably in its annual reports the "stability and security" maintained by Lisbon. Large U.S. oil and mining companies speeded up their investment in exploration and development of natural resources in Angola and Mozambique.

When revolution came to Portugal in April 1974 and the new government arranged for the rapid movement of the colonies to independence, the United States (along with other Western powers, South Africa, and various groups in Portugal) wanted to preserve imperialist control of Angola by having the right groups come to power. It was adamantly opposed to the MPLA winning power and increased its support of the FNLA.

The CIA's station in Kinshasa, Zaire began funding Roberto with small amounts in July 1974. Even the small amounts, writes Stockwell, were "enough for word to get around that the CIA was dealing itself into the race." Then in January 1975, the 40 Committee (the NSC subcommittee in charge of covert operations) authorized the CIA to pass $300,000 to the FNLA.[69]

During the same month, the MPLA, FNLA, and UNITA, under pressure from the Organization for African Unity (OAU) to get together, signed a joint agreement with Portugal setting November 11 as the day of independence and providing that a transitional government representing all three movements and the Portuguese would rule until that date. But almost immediately, the FNLA broke the agreement. Stockwell writes that in February 1975,

> encouraged by Mobutu and the United States Roberto moved his well-armed forces into Angola and began attacking the MPLA in Luanda and northern Angola. In one instance in early March they gunned down fifty unarmed MPLA activists. The fate of Angola was then sealed in blood.[70]

The fighting spread to different parts of Angola. The invading FNLA forces were able to take over many towns in the north. Soon UNITA joined forces with the FNLA, occupying towns in the south.

Besides attacking militarily, the FNLA, conscious of its political weakness, especially in Luanda, the capital, hurriedly tried to develop political support. With CIA and Zaire money, it bought

Luanda's largest newspaper and a television station. It sent armed activists into the city and it tried to set up a political apparatus.

But the main popular support went to the MPLA. Organizing the people and recruiting new fighters, it was able to prevent the FNLA from taking over Luanda and to clear out UNITA from a string of towns it had occupied in the south. Savimbi's reaction to his setbacks was to turn to South Africa for help.

By midyear, both the United States and South Africa were feverishly planning how to prevent a "Marxist takeover" in Angola. South Africa's Bureau of State Security (BOSS) held meetings with Roberto in Zaire, Savimbi in South Africa, and MPLA defector, Daniel Chipenda, in Namibia.[71]

In the United States, the NSC and the 40 Committee discussed Angola in June and early July. After a meeting of the 40 Committee on July 14, Kissinger gave the CIA 48 hours to come up with a covert action plan. On July 17, the 40 Committee met again to consider the plan and on July 18, President Gerald Ford approved it. On July 29, the first planeload of arms left South Carolina for the transfer point in Zaire.[72]

Eventually, the operation cost $32 million: $2.75 million for Mobutu for sending arms to the FNLA and UNITA; $2 million to Roberto and Savimbi for running their movements; the remainder for arms, aircraft to transport the arms to Angola, and mercenaries.[73] A Congressional investigating committee later asserted that it had "reason to believe that the actual U.S. investment is much higher." [74]

Thus, the United States had two allies in its Angola operation: Mobutu's Zaire and South Africa. Both to cover its tracks and to strengthen relations with Mobutu with whom frictions had arisen, the United States channeled much of its aid through Zaire. Mobutu, besides allowing Zaire to be used as a transfer point for arms, also committed Zairean troops to the operation. His troops had long cooperated with Roberto and in March had helped the FNLA occupy parts of northern Angola. Now in July, Mobutu committed a commando company and an armored squadron to Angola, and in August two paratroop companies.

In the south, meanwhile, the South Africans were helping UNITA with arms, training, and advisers. In August, South Africa, announcing that it had to protect the Cunene dam in which it had an interest, sent a contingent of its regular troops into Angola. Stockwell writes about the U.S.-South African collaboration:

> To the CIA, the South Africans were the ideal solution for central Angola. [Chief of the Africa Division James] Potts, [Chief of the Kinshasa Station Stuart E. Methven], and the [Chiefs of Station] of Pretoria and Lusaka welcomed their arrival in the war.... Quietly South African planes and trucks turned up throughout Angola with just the gasoline or ammunition needed for an impending operation. On October 20 ... two South African C-130 airplanes... feathered into Ndjili Airport [outside Kinshasa] at night to meet a CIA C-141 flight and whisk its load of arms down to Silva Porto [Savimbi's base in central Angola]. CIA officers and BOSS representatives met the planes at Ndjili and jointly supervised the transloading. At the same time [Methven] requested and received headquarters' permission to meet BOSS representatives on a regular basis in Kinshasa.... On two occasions the BOSS director visited Washington and held secret meetings with Jim Potts.... The [Chief of Station], Pretoria, was ordered to brief BOSS about [the Angola operation], and nearly all CIA intelligence reports on the subject were relayed to Pretoria so his briefings would be accurate and up to date....
>
> Thus, without any memos being written at CIA headquarters saying "let's coordinate with the South Africans," coordination was effected at all CIA levels and the South Africans escalated their involvement in step with our own.[75]

Together with South Africa, the United States, through the CIA, ran the secret undeclared war against the MPLA, supplying money and weapons and using Zaireans, South Africans, anti-independence Portuguese Angolans, and miscellaneous mercenaries to beef up the FNLA and UNITA. But despite the foreign help, the FNLA and UNITA were unequal to their task. In September, the MPLA routed a joint FNLA-Zairean force advancing on Luanda from the north. In the south, it inflicted defeats on UNITA. The CIA threw itself into saving the situation. Mobutu flew down two elite commando battalions which helped the FNLA turn the tide. In October, South Africa dispatched a column of its own soldiers with tanks, artillery, and logistical support to join UNITA and Portuguese Angolan mercenaries in a drive on Luanda from the south. Within days the column had penetrated hundreds of miles inside Angola and by November 3 was within 250 miles of Luanda.

Journalist Wilfred Burchett explains the objective of the attacking forces: "the north-south columns would link up in Luanda before November 11 so that the Portuguese would hand over independence to an UNITA-FNLA coalition." At a minimum, the attackers hoped to occupy Luanda's water and electric power stations and paralyze the city by shutting off supplies if it remained in MPLA hands.[76]

In addition to the columns advancing on Luanda, an invasion force from Zaire launched an attempt to capture oil-rich Cabinda, an enclave separated from the rest of Angola by a strip of Zairean territory. Mobutu had long coveted Cabinda and his greed grew when oil was discovered there in the late sixties. In October 1975, Mobutu saw his chance and, says Stockwell, "approached the CIA." The CIA responded. "We promptly flew in a one-thousand-man arms package for use in the invasion ...." The invasion began on November 2.[77]

Then Cuba entered the fray. It had sent instructors in October to train troops for an MPLA threatened by Zairean and South African invaders. Now it received an urgent appeal from the MPLA, which was facing fresh foreign intervention on three fronts. As Fidel later explained, Cuba decided to immediately send a battalion of regular troops with antitank weapons "to help the Angolan patriots resist the invasion of the South African racists." More Cuban troops followed, while armaments and supplies arrived by sea and air from the Soviet Union. Again the tide turned, this time in favor of the MPLA.[78]

On November 11, the MPLA proclaimed Angolan independence and the formation of the People's Republic of Angola. Thirty countries immediately recognized it. The same day, Roberto proclaimed the independence of the People's Democratic Republic of Angola and a day later he and Savimbi announced the formation of its provisional governing body—the "Joint National Council for the Revolution." Not a single country, then or later, recognized the government formed by Roberto and Savimbi.[79]

Within a few weeks of independence, the MPLA controlled twelve of Angola's sixteen provincial capitals. In the north, the MPLA carried out a counteroffensive almost entirely by itself, routing the Zairean invaders who by mid-January were fleeing across the border. "Cuban armor and artillery were used almost exclusively against the South Africans...," says Burchett. MPLA-Cuban forces mounted a counteroffensive the third week in January and by February 3, South African Defense Minister P. W. Botha was announcing that his troops, whose presence in Angola he had repeatedly denied, had withdrawn to the border zone.[80]

The U.S. Government flailed around in reaction to the Cuban intervention. As Stockwell puts it:

> Competitive juices stirred in Washington....The National Security Council ordered the CIA to outline a program which could *win* the war. Sophisticated weapons were now discussed freely: Redeye ground-to-air missiles, antitank missiles, heavy artillery, tactical air support, C-47 gun platforms. The working group considered major escalations: the formal introduction of American advisers, the use of American army units, a show of the fleet off Luanda, and the feasibility of making an overt military feint at Cuba itself to force Castro to recall his troops and defend the home island.[81]

But, as Stockwell points out, "there was a thread of unreality, of wishful thinking in these discussions." The CIA's secret Contingency Reserve Fund, with which the Angola operation had been financed, was exhausted. Further action depended on Congress providing the money and Congress had become fearful of this new foreign adventure that might turn into another Vietnam-type quagmire.[82]

Dick Clark, chairman of the Senate Subcommittee on African Affairs, was "skeptical," writes Stockwell, "of his CIA briefings and of the Angola program," after making a fact-finding trip to Africa. He was "concerned that we were secretly dragging the United States into a broad conflict with dangerous, global implications" and "that the CIA was illegally collaborating with South Africa...." With Senators John Tunney and Alan Cranston he introduced an amendment to a defense appropriations bill to forbid the use of any funds for covert activity in Angola. The Senate approved the amendment by 54 to 22 and the House by 323 to 99. The lopsided vote forced President Ford to sign the bill.[83]

The Clark Amendment was the first important manifestation of the Vietnam Syndrome. It not only hobbled the Ford administration on Angola but would continue to dampen the adventurism of future administrations in other areas as well.

The last minute anti-MPLA intervention caused damage estimated by Angola at $6.7 billion.[84] But with the South Africans forced by the Cuban-Angolan offensive to withdraw and the CIA winding down its operation for lack of funds, Angola had won its "Second War of Liberation." By the end of February, the majority of the world's countries, including almost all of Western Europe, had recognized the new government.

But U.S. official hostility did not waver. Washington not only refused to recognize the People's Republic, but vetoed Angola's admission to the United Nations on June 23. Only in November, faced with overwhelming support for Angola among U.N. members, did Washington allow admission by abstaining in the voting. Continued non-recognition remained U.S. policy through the Ford, Carter, and Reagan administrations.

BY THE TIME OF ANGOLAN independence, South Africa had become a junior partner of the United States in promoting counterrevolution in central and southern Africa. The United States had found, over the years, that South Africa could be useful. It could provide mercenaries for the Congo when the United States needed them to put down rebellion in 1964. It could train and support UNITA to fight the MPLA in Angola. It could send its own troops into Angola.

In some respects, the United States and South Africa had different interests, so there were difficulties in the partnership. The United States could not openly seem too close to the universally condemned apartheid regime and often it had to join in the condemnation. But underneath the differences, the U.S. imperialists and South Africa had deep common interests—in particular, an interest in fighting the spread of revolution.

The collapse of the Portuguese empire created problems for South African and U.S. strategists. Previously, a white-ruled buffer zone—South African-occupied Namibia, white-ruled Southern Rhodesia, and the Portuguese colonies, Angola and Mozambique—had sheltered South Africa from the revolutionary storms in the rest of the continent. Now with Angola and Mozambique independent and Rhodesia moving toward independence, South Africa felt threatened and moved to build up its military machinery and adjust its strategy.

South Africa's military budget exploded (from 650 million rands in 1975 to over 2 billion in 1979 and 4 billion in 1984).[85] Its Defense Department developed a strategy of trying to dominate and control nearby states through a variety of means—influencing "moderates" by pointing to the "Marxist threat;" creating dependence on South Africa by increasing economic ties and granting economic aid; destabilizing and even carrying out military attacks on countries that could not be controlled.

The United States no more wanted to see radical regimes spread in the region than did South Africa. It developed a two-fold strategy to meet the threat. It moved a little toward the policy of talking reform even while quietly supporting the South African strategy of trying to dominate the region. In a speech in Lusaka, Zambia in April 1976, Kissinger "urge[d] the South African Government to announce a definite timetable acceptable to the world community for the achievement of self-determination" by Namibia.[86]

The Carter administration moved even farther toward a policy of talking reform. To play an effective role in Africa, thought Secretary of State Cyrus Vance, "we would have to overcome [the] negative legacy of African suspicion," the feeling that the United States didn't care about African problems "except as they affected East-West rivalry," that what it wanted was "to protect American and Western strategic interests through a strong Republic of South Africa shielded by a barrier of black client states dependent upon Pretoria's political, economic, and military support."[87]

Vance believed that "American participation in resolving the conflicts in Rhodesia and Namibia and in seeking an end to apartheid in South Africa was vital." But even while propounding a policy of having the United States show interest in African problems for their own sake, he still tied the problems to the East-West rivalry. "Like the previous administration...we recognized that identifying the United States with the cause of majority rule was the best way to prevent Soviet and Cuban exploitation of the racial conflicts of southern Africa."[88]

As Vance explains, the United States involved itself in the Namibian negotiations not so much out of interest in Namibian independence as to avoid unpleasant alternatives for itself.

> Without a strategy for achieving Namibian independence, the Western nations would soon be faced with the dilemma of how to respond to African demands for mandatory sanctions against South Africa. If there were no credible negotiating initiative, the Africans would be able to force a Security Council vote. We would then either damage our relations with black Africa by vetoing the resolution, which would be at odds with the Carter administration's Africa policy, or by approving it, destroy the negotiating process and harm important Western economic interests in South Africa....[89]

SOUTH AFRICA HAD RULED Namibia—an ex-German colony—
since World War I, originally under a League of Nations mandate granted in the days when colonialist Britain and France
dominated the world's international body. From 1966, when the
U.N. General Assembly terminated the mandate, South Africa
lacked legal cover, but continued its rule anyway. Five thousand white farmers held the bulk of the best land, producing
mainly cattle and karakul pelts for export. Multinational corporations, based in the United States, Britain, West Germany,
France, and South Africa, controlled the rich mineral resources—diamonds, copper, lead, zinc, and uranium. To better exploit Namibia, the racist regime implanted the same apartheid
system as at home. It divided the Africans into tribal groups
assigned to ten "homelands," restricted their movement, and
instituted a system of "contract labor" that kept most workers
separated from their families.

The Namibian liberation movement, the South West African
People's Organization (SWAPO), had its origin in the struggles
against the contract labor system. After broadening its goal to
include national independence, SWAPO took up armed struggle
in 1966, when South Africa rejected U.N. termination of the
mandate. Its support among the people grew despite repression that forced much of its activity underground. It was accepted as the legitimate representative of the Namibian people
by the OAU in 1965 and by the U.N. in 1973.

The victory of the revolutionaries in the Portuguese colonies
helped increase revolutionary fervor in Namibia. South Africa's
fear of SWAPO's growing strength led it in 1976 to promote its
own "internal solution" based on "self-government" by a coalition of whites and compliant African representatives called the
Democratic Turnhalle Alliance (DTA). South Africa's maneuvers
ran counter to the principles for an internationally acceptable
settlement laid down in U.N. Security Council Resolution 385 of
January 1976, which demanded the withdrawal of South Africa's
illegal administration and the holding of free elections under
U.N. control. Growing African anger and impatience over Pretoria's intransigence worried the United States.

At U.S. urging, the five Western members of the Security
Council in January 1977—the United States, Britain, Canada,
France, and West Germany—formed a so-called Contact Group
to act as intermediary between South Africa and SWAPO. Afri-

can countries hoped that members of the Contact Group, whose trade and investment ties to South Africa gave them leverage, would be able to convince Pretoria that it must settle. But the Contact Group countries proved unwilling to use their power, unwilling to apply or even credibly threaten economic sanctions.

The independence plan presented by the Contact Group in 1978, moving backward from Resolution 385, made concessions to South Africa. In particular, it allowed South Africa to continue to administer Namibia during the transition. In September, the U.N. Security Council adopted the Contact Group plan (Resolution 435).

But despite the concessions, South Africa showed no inclination to allow Namibia to become independent. After formally accepting the plan, it began to stall—endlessly raising new objections and demanding new concessions. It raised objections over the election date, the size of the U.N. military presence during the transition, the location of SWAPO bases after a ceasefire, etc. Vance writes about one of these occasions: "Once again, the South Africans appeared to agree to the main elements of the UN role, but raised new issues that prevented implementation."[90]

In December, South Africa organized illegal elections, used its military to intimidate people, and installed a puppet DTA government. The Security Council declared the elections null and void, but with the United States and other Western powers unwilling to apply sanctions, South Africa blithely ignored the U.N. decision. The attempt of the Contact Group to bring about independence came to nought.

Nevertheless, the Contact Group operation was not a failure for the United States which, as Vance explains, obtained benefits for its larger African strategy:

> I believe that the establishment of a negotiating framework for the Namibian question was important for U.S. and Western interests.... Without the Namibia negotiating process...the United States would have no workable strategy for improving its relations with black Africa and blocking the spread of Soviet and Cuban influence in southern Africa.[91]

EVEN WHILE THE UNITED STATES was making a show of urging South Africa to agree to Namibian independence, it was aiding its partner. The Contact Group operation provided the "credible negotiating initiative" Vance had wanted to help stave off African pressure for sanctions. When sanctions resolutions did come up at the United Nations, the United States vetoed all but one. And for years, United States insistence that it would veto helped keep them from even being presented.

Under the Reagan administration, the U.S.-South Africa partnership became more overt. Undersecretary of State for African Affairs Chester Crocker introduced what he called a policy of "constructive engagement." Crocker dismissed the possibility of exerting "effective coercive influence" on South Africa and warned that "comprehensive sanctions" could "wreak major damage on its economy (and on U.S. and allied economic interests there)." The United States, he held, should work to create "a regional climate conducive to compromise and accommodation"—meaning accommodation to white-led "evolutionary change." Finally, the United States should be ready "to bring our policies out into the open and to meet publicly with South Africa's top leadership when circumstances warrant it."[92]

In April 1981, Crocker held discussions in Pretoria with South African Foreign Minister Roelof (Pik) Botha and Defense Minister Magnus Malan. A leaked secret State Department "Memorandum of Conversation" reveals what was said. "Botha presented vision of southern Africa's future, in context of 'Constellation of States' concept. He appealed for USG[overnment] support for South Africa's view of region's future...." The Foreign Minister was referring to Pretoria's strategy of trying to make neighboring states depend on South Africa and to create a South African sphere of influence. Crocker, with his similar idea about getting the right "regional climate," tacitly went along. "The top U.S. priority," he said, "is to stop Soviet encroachment in Africa."[93]

Malan, talking of Namibia, stated that the South African Government "could not live with a SWAPO victory that left SWAPO unchecked power." Further, the "SAG[overnment] sees Savimbi in Angola as buffer for Namibia." Malan felt that "Angola is one place where U.S. can roll back Soviet/Cuban presence in Africa." Crocker "agreed on relation of Angola to Namibia.... Our view is that South Africa is under no early military pressure to leave Namibia. The decision belongs to SAG, and ways must be found to address its concerns." He promised to push for "add-ons" to the U.N. Namibia plan to meet South African concerns.[94]

Washington immediately made good on Crocker's promise. On the eve of a NATO meeting in Rome, it convinced the other members of the Contact Group to propose changes in the Namibia independence plan that would make it acceptable to South Africa. The front-line and nonaligned states denounced the further concessions to South Africa and the Namibian independence process remained stalled.

The discussions between Crocker and the South Africans went so well that the United States invited Botha to visit Washington the next month. To prepare Secretary of State Alexander Haig for his meeting with Botha, Crocker wrote a "Scope Paper" whose introductory summary stated the basic premise of the talks:

> *The possibility may exist for a more positive and reciprocal relationship between the two countries based upon shared strategic concerns* in southern Africa. (Italics in original.)[95]

Crocker also advised Haig

> to make it clear to Pik that *we share the South African hope that,* despite political differences among the states of southern Africa, *the economic interdependence of the area and constructive internal change within South Africa can be the foundations for a new era of cooperation, stability, and security in the region.* (Italics in original.)[96]

Finally, Crocker suggested to Haig that he remind Botha of the recent U.S. veto at the U.N. (of four Security Council resolutions calling for sanctions on South Africa because of its intransigence on Namibian independence) and that he indicate a U.S. willingness to *"work to end South Africa's polecat status."* (Italics in original.)[97]

At an official dinner for Botha, Haig gave a toast, reassuring South Africa that it could "rely on our determination and backbone as leader of the free world" and drinking to "friendship and cooperation between the United States and South Africa." The strengthening of the U.S.-South African alliance not only fortified South Africa in its intransigence on Namibian independence, but encouraged it to carry out a series of aggressive actions throughout southern Africa.[98]

PART OF SOUTH AFRICA'S strategy was what it called "forward defense," in reality aggressive cross-border strikes against neighboring states. Under the pretext of "hot pursuit" of "terrorists" or the need to wipe out "terrorist bases" of SWAPO or South Africa's own internal liberation organization, the African National Congress (ANC), the South African army and mercenaries it controlled carried out air strikes, commando attacks, sabotage, and destabilization in Angola, Mozambique, Zimbabwe, Zambia, Botswana, and Lesotho.

The aim was both military and strategic. Military: to discourage the neighboring countries' support of liberation forces and to prevent the development of any threat from these forces to Namibia or South Africa itself. Strategic: to derail the neighboring countries' efforts at independent development and so enforce South Africa's domination, thus furthering the creation of the "constellation of states" that was the long-term objective.

"Forward defense" had been South Africa's strategy for some time. Now, under the shelter of the Reagan administration's policy of "constructive engagement," the aggressive actions escalated.

The most frequent, violent, and destructive attacks were directed at Angola. Angola had known no real peace since independence. As it reported in a 1983 White Paper to the United Nations:

> Since 27 March 1976, the date when the first big South African invasion...ended, Pretoria's armed forces have never ceased to keep [the southern and southeastern provinces of Angola] under constant pressure, through air space violations and bombing raids, incursions of heliborne troops, acts of provocation, infantry attacks supported by armoured units, artillery shelling, mine laying in fields and on bridges and highways, and the looting and destruction of varied material and means of production.

> Added to these military operations are combined attacks on settlements and villages, in close co-ordination with the UNITA puppets, who are trained and equipped in military camps in Namibia, while South African forces ensure the transport of UNITA's men and war material into Angolan territory and also provide the air cover needed for such penetration.[99]

In August 1981, South Africa launched a large-scale invasion of Angola from Namibia. A massive air bombardment by six Mirages and two Buccaneers prepared the way for the entry of a force consisting of 11,000 men, 36 Centurion M-41 tanks, 70 armored cars, 200 armored troop carriers, 90 planes and helicopters, as well as 155mm guns and 127mm ground-to-ground mis-

siles. Six days after the invasion started, the South Africans occupied 40,000 square kilometers. In September, having been
stopped by the Angolan army from advancing further north, they
started a partial withdrawal, taking with them their tanks and
heavy artillery along with looted Angolan vehicles, tractors and
trailers, cattle, and food supplies. However, they left a force for
the long-term occupation of a strip of southern Angola.[100]

When the U.N. Security Council took up Angola's complaint
about invasion, one speaker after another condemned South
Africa's attacks. Thirteen of the 15 Council members voted for a
resolution that demanded immediate and unconditional withdrawal, compensation, and sanctions. Britain abstained. A U.S.
veto prevented adoption. Pretoria saw that it had U.S. protection and could act with impunity.

In December 1983 South Africa launched another large-scale
invasion into Angola. Again a U.S. veto prevented the Security
Council from taking action in response.

The U.N.'s Anti-Apartheid Committee summed up the effects
of the aggressions in its 1985 report to the General Assembly:

> South African aggression and UNITA attacks have cost Angola over
> $15 billion, devastated the country's economy and resulted in the
> death of tens of thousands of people and the displacement of
> hundreds of thousands of others.[101]

For its part, the United States used the South African military
pressure, along with that exerted by their joint protégé Savimbi
and his UNITA guerrillas, to support coercive diplomacy against
Angola. It made a series of demands on the Luanda government—that it send home the Cuban troops, negotiate power-
sharing with UNITA, make concessions on the Namibian question, and press SWAPO to accept such concessions. The United
States made the sending home of Cuban troops a precondition
for recognition of Angola and for a settlement on Namibia.

Thus, the U.S.-South African partnership provided a *quid pro
quo* for both sides. The United States protected South Africa
and collaborated with it on the Namibian problem. South Africa
did the United States' dirty work in Angola. Not only did it make
military incursions, but it supported Savimbi when the Congressional restrictions of the Clark amendment limited the U.S. ability to do so.

UNDER THE SAME U.S. protection, South Africa also carried out a campaign of aggression against Mozambique in an attempt to subject it to its will. The Portuguese had developed Mozambique in a way that made it dependent on South Africa: its workers hired out to South African mines, its Cabora Bassa dam produced electricity for South African industries and cities, and its railroads and ports handled South African goods. Besides depending on the sale of labor power, electricity, and services to South Africa for most of its foreign exchange, Mozambique had to import many necessities, including foodstuffs, from its powerful neighbor. Thus economic warfare was an easy weapon to use against Mozambique. Between 1975 and 1982, South Africa slashed the number of Mozambicans working in its mines from 120,000 to 45,000 and cut its transit trade through the port of Maputo from 600 to 100 million tons.[102]

At first, South Africa left outright military force to the like-minded white minority regime that still ruled Rhodesia (Zimbabwe) when Mozambique gained its independence. The Rhodesian intelligence service created a terror organization named Mozambican National Resistance (Renamo) to attack Mozambique. Renamo destroyed farms and crops, schools and clinics, often forcing the population to abandon agricultural production and flee. When Zimbabwe won its independence in 1980 and Renamo seemed near defeat without its foreign bases and support, South Africa took over the remnants and transferred them to its northeast province of Transvaal, adjacent to Mozambique.

Like those against Angola, the attacks against Mozambique escalated with the coming of "constructive engagement" in 1981. On January 31, South African commandos brazenly raided Matola, a suburb of the capital, Maputo, and attacked ANC houses there, killing a dozen ANC refugees. A few weeks later, Mozambique expelled four U.S. Embassy officials, accusing them of being CIA spies who had pinpointed the targets for the raid. The United States, which had been giving Mozambique economic aid to encourage "moderation," retaliated by cutting off shipments of desperately needed wheat, rice, and corn.[103]

The U.S. aid cutoff went hand in hand with South Africa's unleashing both Renamo and its own forces in a campaign of sabotage. Mozambique had joined nearby states in organizing the Southern Africa Development Coordinating Conference (SADCC), dedicated to reducing the dependence on South Africa that colonialism had imposed on the region. A key objective was to develop Mozambique's harbors and connecting railroads so that the landlocked countries would no longer depend on South African ports. Now South Africa's creature, Renamo, concentrated its attacks on the very facilities—ports, railroads, and bridges—needed to make SADCC's plans a success.[104] Pretoria also at times used its own commandos to sabotage such targets.

In a 1984 report, the Mozambican Council of Ministers estimated the total cost of the damage inflicted by South Africa, through both economic warfare and attacks by Renamo and its own commandos, at $4 billion.[105]

South Africa also engaged in aggression against other neighboring countries it wanted to control. It conducted raids with its own forces against Lesotho (December 1982, December 1985), Botswana (June 1985), and simultaneously against Botswana, Zimbabwe, and Zambia (May 1986). It financed and supplied armed rebels inside Zimbabwe and Lesotho. And on several occasions, it tried to coerce its neighbors by threatening or carrying out border closings, restrictions on the use of its railways and harbors, and reductions in its import of labor. The knowledge that the United States would shield it against international sanctions emboldened Pretoria to persist in such actions despite universal condemnation.

The U.S.-South African counterrevolutionary campaign against Angola and Mozambique left these countries economically prostrate, just as the U.S.-created contra assault on Nicaragua wreaked economic havoc there. A 1987 UNICEF report estimates that "8.5 million Angolans and Mozambicans—roughly half the rural population of the two countries—have been displaced or are internal refugees in their own countries."[106] With economies torn apart, forced into enormous military expenditures by the need to defend themselves, these countries were unable to start the process of independent development that liberation from the Portuguese yoke made possible.

But the United States and South Africa did not come even close to achieving their full goals in southern Africa. The planned constellation of states dominated by South Africa did not take shape.

IN 1988, SOUTH AFRICAN forces found themselves bogged down in southern Angola after being defeated by Cuban-Angolan troops at Cuito Cuanavale. South Africa's Foreign Minister Roelof Botha commented: "I am personally of the opinion that if the enemy is dug in over a broad front and is equipped with a deadly arsenal, you must think twice before you simply allow hundreds of your sons to be killed."[107]   South Africa finally became ready to talk and Crocker set up negotiations among Angola, Cuba, South Africa, and the United States.

The negotiations resulted in two agreements. One provided for the implementation of the U.N. independence plan for Namibia and the withdrawal of South African troops from that country. Another between Angola and Cuba set a schedule for the phased withdrawal of Cuban troops from Angola.[108] The agreements cleared the way for Namibian independence and reduced South Africa's ability to commit aggression against Angola. In April 1989, the plan for Namibian independence got under way.

But peace in Namibia, Mozambique, and Angola were by no means assured. How South Africa and the United States would treat an independent Namibia remained to be seen. In Mozambique fighting between the South Africa-supported Renamo and the government continued. And in Angola, the United States continued to withhold recognition and support UNITA. In 1989, Herman J. Cohen, assistant secretary of state for African affairs in the Bush administration, stated: "Sure, the MPLA is the government, it's in the UN, it's been recognized by the OAU.... But we really see Angola as two governments at the present time."[109] His deputy, Warren Clark, Jr., put it even more clearly:

> The United States will continue appropriate and effective assistance to UNITA...until national reconciliation is achieved. Second, until national reconciliation is achieved, the United States will not recognize any government in Angola.[110]

WITH THE LAST COLONY in southern Africa gone, the center of the liberation struggle shifted to South Africa itself. How has the United States reacted to the long struggle in South Africa? In its declarations it has abhorred apartheid and called for reform. But in its actions, the United States has gone along with South Africa's policies.

What is the apartheid (separateness) system against which the overwhelming majority of South Africa's people have been struggling? It is a system based on race under which whites, who make up 17 percent of the population, control 87 percent of the land and every aspect of life for the overwhelming majority of the people—mainly Africans, but also "Coloreds" (of mixed parentage) and Asians. Millions of Africans have to live in "tribal homelands" to which they have been assigned by the government—remote, barren terrain, largely unfit for farming. Millions have remained in "white areas" and cities only at the sufferance of the authorities, to serve as cheap labor, unable to have their families join them. The government has swept up several million people from the "white" areas and cities in "forced removals" to the separate so-called homelands in an effort to divide the majority population into different ethnic groups and deny it South African nationality. In their own country, most people have virtually no citizenship rights.

The African population resisted colonization and white domination from the beginning, but the modern organized liberation struggle dates from the founding of the African National Congress in 1912. The ANC's declared aim was to promote full rights for Africans. Black resistance reached new heights in the 1950s after the government imposed pass laws to enforce apartheid. The requirement that blacks carry a passbook at all times brought forth mass protests and civil disobedience campaigns which the government met with police violence and massive arrests and detentions. The struggles led to the rapid growth of the ANC and to the formation of a unified Congress Alliance comprising African, Colored, Indian, and white organizations. In 1955, the Alliance held a "Congress of the People" which adopted a Freedom Charter that is still the basic document of the liberation struggle. The Charter calls for a multiracial democracy in which "all national groups shall have equal rights" and "the people shall share in the country's wealth."[111]

On March 21, 1960, the anti-apartheid struggle burst into the world news when South African police fired on peaceful anti-pass demonstrators in Sharpeville, killing 69 and wounding nearly 200. Further militant actions—nonviolent mass marches, workers' stayaways, pass burnings—followed the massacre and the government met them with more police violence. A worldwide protest erupted, and the United States, afraid that apartheid would provoke revolution, joined in a U.N. vote calling on South Africa to abandon it.

The Kennedy administration, with its policy of trying to gain favor with the new African nations, backed the idea of international pressure to end apartheid. When Pretoria ignored a U.S. aide-mémoire calling for the abandonment of apartheid, the

United States in 1962 announced a selective arms embargo against South Africa. In 1963, the United States voted with the majority of the Security Council to urge all nations to impose an arms embargo.

South Africa, not allowing itself to be swayed by worldwide condemnation, took fascist-type measures to meet the danger of revolution. It declared a state of emergency and arrested and detained thousands. It used open police terror to suppress demonstrations and resistance and ordered a massive military mobilization. It outlawed the ANC, arrested its entire national leadership, and sentenced Nelson Mandela and other top leaders to life imprisonment.

Even while the United States was promoting reform to prevent revolution, it was collaborating with the apartheid regime in fascist measures to suppress it. The CIA fingered Mandela, providing the South African security forces with the information that enabled them to arrest him. On July 10, 1990, the *New York Times* reported on a Cox News Service story which confirmed what many had suspected for years. The *Times* report quotes a "senior C.I.A. officer" who said shortly after Mandela's arrest: "We have turned Mandela over to the South African Security branch. We gave them every detail, what he would be wearing, the time of day, just where he would be." The *Times* explains that

> the American intelligence agency was willing to assist in the apprehension of Mr. Mandela because it was concerned that a successful nationalist movement threatened a friendly South African Government. Expansion of such movements outside South Africa's borders, the agency feared, would jeopardize the stability of other African states....

As with the Congo and Angola, the U.S. "liberal" stance toward South Africa proved short-lived. The U.S. interest in South African reform depended on the danger of revolution. After a while, the danger of revolution receded and with it the U.S. interest in reform.

The Nixon administration followed a policy of relaxing economic restrictions on South Africa. The National Security Council regional study ordered by Kissinger described the policy as follows:

Remove constraints on EXIM Bank facilities for South Africa; actively encourage US exports and facilitate US investment consistent with the Foreign Direct Investment Program.[112]

U.S. economic ties with South Africa began to expand rapidly. Between 1968 and 1975, U.S. direct investment jumped from $700 million to $1.6 billion and U.S. exports tripled from $450 million to $1.3 billion. Export-Import Bank credits and guarantees rose from $34 million in 1971 to $109 million in 1974.[113]

Among the 400 U.S. corporations with investments in South Africa were some of the largest corporate giants, including First National City (later Citibank) and Chase Manhattan, Mobil, Caltex, General Motors, Ford, Chrysler, GE, Goodyear, Firestone, IBM, and ITT. The U.S. corporations helped South Africa finance its economy, withstand sanctions, and build up a formidable military-industrial complex.

Citibank and Chase, along with other U.S. and non-U.S. banks rescued South Africa from a balance of payments crisis in the mid-1970s. Chase chairman David Rockefeller had asserted at a Pretoria press conference in 1974: "People I have talked to are of the opinion that foreign investment here is advantageous to all concerned."[114]

To reduce its vulnerability to an oil embargo, South Africa was eager to develop its own petroleum sources as well as alternative forms of energy. Mobil and Caltex helped with petroleum exploration. Mobil boasted of its help in an advertisement in the South African *Financial Mail* in 1971. "Everyone is conscious of South Africa's need for its own supply of crude oil—and Mobil is doing something about it." Other U.S. corporations helped South Africa build a plant for the production of oil from coal. South Africa also wanted nuclear power plants, and here again U.S. corporations helped, providing enriched uranium, computers, and technology.[115]

U.S. investments in the motor vehicle, electrical equipment, and communications industries helped South Africa move toward another of its goals—self-sufficiency in weapons and military equipment. A 1972 report of the Institute for Strategic Studies pointed out that "in a relatively short time South Africa would be able to produce all her own counter-insurgency equipment, apart from helicopters and large transport aircraft."[116] U.S.-made or licensed versions of equipment that South Africa did not produce—Augusta Bell 205A armored helicopters, Lockheed L-100 Hercules transports—found their way to South Africa.[117]

BY THE MID-1970S, the successes of the revolution in the Portuguese colonies were leading to a new upsurge of militancy in South Africa. The growing unwillingness of the people, especially the youth, to tolerate the apartheid system produced a smoldering rebellion. In June 1976, an uprising by youths against the apartheid school system flared up in Soweto, a huge black township near Johannesburg. The police had orders to shoot to kill and killed and wounded hundreds. Soweto became another milestone like Sharpeville. It set off a chain of disturbances that quickly spread throughout the country and would last—on and off—for years.

Once again the world expressed shock and revulsion. The United States felt compelled to go along as the U.N. Security Council "strongly condemn[ed] the South African Government for its resort to massive violence against and killings of the African people including schoolchildren and students...."[118]

When the Carter administration took office, Washington began to lecture South Africa on human rights. Vice President Walter Mondale met with South Africa's Prime Minister John B. Vorster in May 1977 and, according to Vance, "underscored the fact that our policy was rooted in our view of human rights, and was not solely based on anti-Communism." Mondale "told Vorster that our future relations would depend on Pretoria's actions and attitude toward political and racial change in southern Africa, including the beginning of a progressive transformation of South African society away from apartheid."[119]

But when it came to backing its rhetoric with effective action, the United States refused. In October 1977, when the U.N. Security Council took up proposed resolutions calling for sanctions—a ban on investments in South Africa, an end to nuclear cooperation with it—the United States, together with Britain and France, vetoed them.

Its one apparent acceptance of sanctions illuminates U.S. motives and tactics. After successfully working to water down the arms embargo resolution the African countries wanted, the United States joined in a unanimous Security Council vote to approve the resulting text. A Rockefeller-sponsored study later commented:

If the purpose of the embargo was to defuse African diplomatic pressure (and some domestic pressure in the West) for more extensive mandatory sanctions on trade or investment, the embargo has worked....[120]

Again the liberal policy toward Africa didn't last. A new problem had arisen: the "danger" that the Soviet Union and Cuba would gain influence in the Horn of Africa through their support of revolutionary Ethiopia against a Somali invasion. Vance, chief promoter of the liberal policy, lost influence to National Security Advisor Zbigniew Brzezinski, who was stressing the need for combatting "Soviet assertiveness." Washington's concern with black African opinion faded. In the last two years of the Carter administration even rhetorical attacks on apartheid subsided.

The Reagan administration, with Crocker's "constructive engagement," carried the swing away from the liberal policy to its logical conclusion. Besides dismissing the possibility of exerting "effective coercive influence" on South Africa, Crocker argued that since "whites continue to hold effective power and cannot be *forced* to share or transfer it," the United States should support "white-led change."[121]

"Constructive engagement" meant supporting the apartheid regime. Part of the revolutionary force beating against South Africa consisted of the international movement to force it to mend its ways. The South African government was managing through drastic repression to retain some control of the internal situation, but it was vulnerable to international action. For the United States to work against using "coercive influence" — sanctions — meant to buttress the regime at its weakest point.

In 1983, the United States commended as "a step in the right direction" a "new constitution" announced by South Africa. The constitution created Indian and "Colored" chambers of parliament, but excluded Africans — 70 percent of the population — from any political rights. Even the Indian and Colored minorities to whom it gave limited voting rights overwhelmingly rejected the new constitution: four fifths boycotted the elections held under it in 1984. The U.N. Security Council voted to declare the constitution and the elections "null and void," with only the United States and Britain abstaining. The resolution called for "the establishment of a non-racial democratic society based on majority rule, through the full and free exercise of universal adult suffrage" as the only solution to the "explosive situation" in South Africa.[122]

The outlawed ANC, the very group Washington saw as the "communist" enemy, played a key part in the United Democratic Front (UDF) that organized the resistance to the new constitution and the boycott of the 1984 elections. In its 1985 New Year's message, the ANC called on the people "to make South Africa ungovernable" and apartheid "unworkable." School boycotts, rent and bus-fare strikes, workers' stayaways, protests against puppet township councils, mass demonstrations, the funerals of victims of police violence, all built into a crescendo of resistance that created a new wave of international solidarity.

To check the revolutionary outburst, the regime stepped up its repression, imposing a state of emergency in the most affected areas in July 1985 and an even harsher version extending to the whole country in June 1986. According to the U.N. Committee Against Apartheid,

> During the first emergency [from July 1985 to March 1986], over 500 people were killed in police violence and nearly 7,800 were detained, including more than 2,000 children under 16 years of age. Many were assaulted and others tortured during interrogation. The security forces were given sweeping powers to act as they wished, without any criminal or civil responsibility.[123]

The police violence and arrests continued during the second emergency, but this time the regime instituted a blackout on news of the struggle. The blackout was useful not only to Pretoria but also to the Reagan administration which was coming under increasing pressure to act against the apartheid regime.

With the TV news bringing daily scenes of the surging, inspiring rebellion in the black townships and the violent repression by the security forces, the anti-apartheid movement was gaining strength in the United States. Actions in favor of disinvestment, boycott, and sanctions erupted across the country—on campuses, in churches and union halls, and on the streets. Legislators, labor leaders, artists, and others were engaging in civil disobedience and getting arrested at the South African Embassy in Washington.

Congress got ready to act but Reagan, in a preemptive move, ordered limited sanctions of his own in September 1985. The move didn't work. Congress, overriding Reagan's veto, passed an anti-apartheid act which imposed a ban on new investments and bank loans and on the import of coal, iron, steel, textiles, uranium, and agricultural products.

But the administration stuck to its position. It stalled on enforcement of the new law and continued to sabotage international efforts to act against Pretoria by repeatedly using its veto in the Security Council.

Here is a partial list of vetoes:

Resolutions proposing sanctions against South Africa over its Failure to implement

Namibian independence plan	November 15, 1985
Aggression against Angola	June 18, 1986
Policy of apartheid	February 20, 1987
Continued noncompliance on Namibia	April 9, 1987
Continued racist apartheid repression	March 3, 1988

These vetoes, not Washington's declarations about its dedication to freedom and justice, expressed the true policy of the United States on South Africa.

Flashes of the true policy also showed in the comments of President Bush and other U.S. officials after Pretoria released ANC leader, Nelson Mandela, from a twenty-seven-year imprisonment in February 1990. Asked about Mandela's support of the ANC policy that mines, banks, and monopoly industry should be nationalized, Bush responded:

We are not for nationalizing; we're for privatization across the — and we're for free markets. And so if we have a difference there that's fine; we'll discuss it with him. But I am not about to embrace the idea that what we want to do is go down to more socialism....[124]

Meanwhile, Herman J. Cohen, Assistant Secretary of State for African Affairs, was already eager to start removing sanctions, as though the release of Mandela meant that the struggle to end apartheid was over. He stated on a TV program, according to the *Times*, that "'we're rapidly reaching that point' where it would be appropriate to relax some of the sanctions on South Africa."[125]

7. Soviet Union:

1946-Early 1990

As it shifted during 1945 from alliance with the Soviet Union to cold war, the United States began on a variety of fronts to take action appropriate to the new policy. It began to develop the required military and diplomatic strategy, the doctrine that the Soviet Union sought world domination, and security programs for controlling the American people.

On September 19, 1945, a month after Japan's surrender, the Joint Chiefs of Staff approved a memorandum entitled "Basis for the Formulation of a U.S. Military Policy," which redirected U.S. military strategy to point against the Soviet Union. The memorandum spoke of the "possibility of a breakdown between [the] major powers," meaning a split between the United States and the Soviet Union. It asserted that "any nation, which in the future may attempt to dominate the world, may be expected to make her major effort against the United States...." And it laid out the preparations required: "To maintain mobile striking forces... [in] readiness for prompt and adequate action.... To develop and maintain a system of outlying bases.... To develop and maintain an intelligence system.... To promote research, development and provision of new weapons...."[1]

The memorandum, basing its proposed program on the U.S. monopoly of the atomic bomb, promoted a first-strike strategy:

> When it becomes evident that forces of aggression are being arrayed against us by a potential enemy, we cannot afford, through any misguided and perilous idea of avoiding an aggressive attitude to permit the first blow to be struck against us. Our government, under such conditions, should press the issue to a prompt political

decision, while making all preparations to strike the first blow if necessary.[2]

Shortly thereafter, the JCS commissioned a study of an atomic attack on the Soviet Union. The study, completed a few weeks later, analyzed the impact of a first strike using twenty to thirty atomic bombs and earmarking twenty Soviet cities, including Moscow and Leningrad, for obliteration. It envisaged the use of the bomb either in response to Soviet "aggression" or in a "preventive war" in which the United States launched a surprise attack. The study stated that "the Soviet Union cannot attack the continental United States within the near future. With no navy of importance and with a second-rate merchant marine, Soviet overseas operations generally would be out of the question."[3]

While the Joint Chiefs were preparing their military plans, the State Department was constructing an anti-Soviet political doctrine. In February 1946, George F. Kennan sent from Moscow to Washington an 8,000-word message on the Soviet Union that became known as the Long Telegram. The reception, according to Kennan, was "sensational."

> To say the least, [the telegram] went "the rounds." The President, I believe, read it. The Secretary of the Navy, Mr. James Forrestal, had it reproduced and evidently made it required reading for hundreds, if not thousands, of higher officers in the armed services. The Department of State... responded with a message of commendation.[4]

The telegram was an exercise in the creation of a demon. Its main point lay in the image of the Soviet Union it presented: psychologically abnormal and potentially dangerous. Although it professed to recommend that we "study [the Soviet Union] with the same courage, detachment, [etc.]... with which a doctor studies unruly and unreasonable individuals,"[5] the bulk of its argument was designed to create revulsion and fear.

The telegram dismissed talk of "capitalist encirclement" of the Soviet Union. It argued that "to speak of possibilities of intervention against USSR today, after elimination of Germany and Japan and after example of recent war, is sheerest nonsense."[6] It offered its own explanation of Soviet concern about a threat from the capitalist countries:

> At the bottom of the Kremlin's neurotic view of world affairs is [the] traditional and instinctive Russian sense of insecurity.[7]

Kennan completely ignored the history of the Soviet Union from the intervention, through the attempt to get Hitler to attack it, to the growing U.S. hostility after Roosevelt died.

Russian rulers, says Kennan, "have learned to seek security only in patient but deadly struggle for [the] total destruction [of] rival power, never in compacts or compromises with it."[8] This is scary—the neurotic Soviet Union working patiently, implacably for the total destruction of the United States. But Kennan was unable to back his broad, profound-sounding generalization with concrete facts. He didn't say that the Soviet Union was planning to conquer the United States by military force. He couldn't. The best he could do was refer to Soviet policies on a "subterranean plane," to "an inner central core of Communist parties... working closely together as an underground operating directorate of world communism," to an international "conspiracy." Kennan was developing a basic anti-Soviet argument, one that would be useful not only against the Soviet Union but also in fighting progressive movements and revolutions throughout the world.[9]

Kennan himself later disowned the Long Telegram. "I read it over today with a horrified amusement. Much of it reads exactly like one of those primers put out by alarmed congressional committees or by the Daughters of the American Revolution, designed to arouse the citizenry to the dangers of the Communist conspiracy." He also explained why Washington received it so enthusiastically. "More important than the observable nature of external reality, when it comes to the determination of Washington's view of the world, is the subjective state of readiness on the part of Washington officialdom to recognize this or that feature of it."[10] Put more simply: Washington needed a myth about the Soviet Union and when Kennan provided one, grabbed it.

A few weeks after the Long Telegram, the State Department provided the JCS with a memorandum entitled "Political Estimate of Soviet Policy for Use in Connection with Military Studies." The memorandum tried to dispel two "misconceptions:" 1) that Soviet actions are motivated by a legitimate desire for security "against the threat of hostile action on the part of 'capitalist encirclement;'" and 2) that they can be explained by Soviet suspicions of other countries' motives. The memo asserts, without explaining why, that "the very use of the words 'capitalist encirclement'...prompts the logical conclusion that

Soviet expansionist aims are unlimited...." It claims further that "Soviet suspicion of the motives of other countries is a deliberately artificial thesis spread by the Soviet Government...."[11]

Only in the context of what had been happening can we properly judge Soviet suspicion and concern about security. Truman had begun to show his hostility to the Soviet Union in his encounter with Molotov, a year earlier. The United States had shown in many ways, including its abrupt ending of Lend-Lease and its policy on reparations from Germany, that it was shifting away from the wartime policy of cooperation with the Soviet Union. At Hiroshima and Nagasaki, it had demonstrated its willingness to use the atomic bomb. Instead of withdrawing from bases acquired during the war, it was beginning to form them into a permanent system from which it could threaten the Soviet Union. Churchill, invited by Truman, had given his war-mongering Fulton speech and many leading U.S. newspapers had hailed it. The Soviets had grounds for suspicion and concern.

Like the JCS document cited above, which had stated that "the Soviet Union cannot attack the United States within the near future," the State Department memo made a revealing admission:

> There is no evidence that the Soviet Union desires a major war at this time. On the contrary, there are many indications that it needs and wishes a period of reconstruction and development.[12]

Thus "the Soviet threat" which the United States was conjuring up was a myth. According to the Pentagon, the Soviet Union couldn't attack the United States. According to the State Department, it didn't want war, but rather peace for reconstruction and development. It was the United States that was planning a possible preventive war, when by its own estimates there was no threat of military aggression from the Soviet Union.

At bottom, the memo's argument carried the same implications as Kennan's: The Soviet Union had unlimited hostile goals. According to Kennan, it was aiming at the "total destruction" of the United States. According to the memo, it was pursuing "unlimited expansion." This was a more subtle idea than "total destruction," one with broader application. A revolution in Greece or Communist advances in Italy or France were simply manifestations of Soviet expansionism, to be treated accordingly.

In September 1946, at Truman's request, his Special Counsel, Clark Clifford, submitted a report in which he formulated a comprehensive policy toward the Soviet Union. To prepare it, Clifford consulted with the Secretaries of State, War, and the Navy, the JCS, the head of the CIA, the Attorney General, and others.

Clifford used the Long Telegram, but went far beyond it. He didn't beat around the bush about Soviet aims: The Soviet leaders were on "a course of aggrandizement designed to lead to eventual world domination by the U.S.S.R."[13] He talked glibly about a Soviet military attack on the United States.

The main deterrent to Soviet attack on the United States, or to attack on areas of the world which are vital to our security, will be the military power of this country.[14]

He argued that

to maintain our strength at a level which will be effective in restraining the Soviet Union, the United States must be prepared to wage atomic and biological warfare.[15]

He further argued that

the United States, with a military potential composed primarily of highly effective technical weapons, should entertain no proposal for disarmament or limitation of armament as long as the possibility of Soviet aggression exists.[16]

He recommended that

within the United States, communist penetration should be exposed and eliminated whenever the national security is endangered.[17]

Finally, came a key recommendation: that the United States be prepared "to confine Soviet influence to its present area."[18]

THE CLIFFORD REPORT reflected already existing policies and foreshadowed others that evolved from them. Within six months, its recommendation "to confine Soviet influence" was official policy, embodied in the Truman Doctrine, proclaimed in connection with a new program of aid to Greece and Turkey.

To obtain Congressional approval for the aid, the administration manufactured a "crisis," a technique that was to be used repeatedly from then on. On February 21, 1947, Britain informed the United States that by the end of March it would have to stop providing military and economic aid to Greece and reduce its aid to Turkey. Greece was in the midst of a civil war and there was a danger that the reactionary, corrupt, and unpopular government would collapse. The administration decided, Dean Acheson writes, "that it was vital to the security of the United States for Greece and Turkey to be strengthened to preserve their national independence...."[19] At a meeting of Truman and his advisers with the leaders of Congress, Secretary of State Marshall, says Acheson, "flubbed his opening statement"—he was not dramatic enough. Acheson requested permission to speak:

> These congressmen had no conception of what challenged them; it was my task to bring it home.... No time was left for measured appraisal. In the past eighteen months, I said, Soviet pressure on the Straits, on Iran, and on northern Greece had brought the Balkans to the point where a highly possible Soviet breakthrough might open three continents to Soviet penetration. Like apples in a barrel infected by one rotten one, the corruption of Greece would infect Iran and all to the east. It would also carry infection to Africa through Asia Minor and Egypt, and to Europe through Italy and France, already threatened by the strongest domestic Communist parties in Western Europe. The Soviet Union was playing one of the greatest gambles in history at minimal cost.[20]

Actually, as one authority quoted by the historian Daniel Yergin says, "The Greek crisis was basically a domestic affair...." which the Soviet Union had neither "cause[d] nor aggravate[d]."[21] It was not the Soviet Union that had been interfering in the Greek civil war, preventing the Greek people from determining their own destiny. It was Britain, which was now asking the United States to do the same.

As for Turkey, Kennan—then teaching at the War College—pointed out to the students "that [its] situation...differed quite fundamentally from that of Greece. There was no serious Communist penetration in Turkey—no comparable guerrilla movement. The Turks had nothing to fear but fear."[22] Kennan offers an explanation for the inclusion of Turkey in the aid program:

> I suspected...that what had really happened was that the Pentagon had exploited a favorable set of circumstances in order to infiltrate a military aid program for Turkey into what was supposed to be primarily a political and economic program for Greece.[23]

So the basic fact that Acheson had to go on was that the rotten government of Greece was under threat from domestic forces in a civil war. From this one fact he built a far-reaching, exciting tale: a "Soviet breakthrough," the infection of "Iran and all to the east," the infection of "Africa through Asia Minor and Egypt" and "Europe through Italy and France," and "one of the greatest gambles in history."

On March 12, 1947, Truman addressed a joint session of Congress. He referred to "the gravity of the situation which confronts the world" and claimed that the "national security of this country" was involved. "The very existence of the Greek state is today threatened by the terrorist activities of several thousand armed men, led by Communists...." Turkey's "integrity is essential to the preservation of order in the Middle East." Then, before asking for approval of aid to these countries, he laid down his doctrine:

> I believe that it must be the policy of the United States to support peoples who are resisting attempted subjugation by armed minorities or by outside pressures....[24]

With this doctrine, the United States appointed itself policeman of the world, authorized itself to decide for other countries which changes were permissible and which not. The United States was arrogating to itself the right to freeze the world into the mold that suited its imperialist interests.

The doctrine established a pattern for future U.S. foreign policy. No matter how small a country was or how far away, the U.S. Government could declare that "the national security of the United States is involved." No matter how dictatorial, corrupt, and hated by its own people a government was, the United States could support it and claim to be defending freedom. No matter how terrible the domestic conditions fueling a particular revolution and how clear the evidence that the Soviet Union had nothing to do with it, the United States could charge "Soviet expansionism" to justify its intervention. Couched in the language of freedom, the Truman Doctrine provided the rationale for the exact opposite—intervention and domination.

At the same time that the Truman Doctrine carried implications for the whole world, the program for Greece and Turkey was a direct thrust against the Soviet Union. When Kennan asserts that the Pentagon was infiltrating a military aid program for Turkey into a political and economic program for Greece, he is telling only half the story. The Pentagon and others in the administration were aware of the potential military usefulness of both Greece and Turkey. These countries could provide bases in the eastern Mediterranean, the gateway both to the Middle East and to the Black Sea and the Soviet Union. The program of aid to Greece and Turkey was part of a plan to ring the Soviet Union with U.S. military bases. A Congressional study later reported that "America's defense literature is replete with assertions that Greece and Turkey in concert comprise the keystone of U.S. strategy in the eastern Mediterranean."[25]

An intellectual rationale for the Truman Doctrine soon appeared in an article entitled "The Sources of Soviet Conduct" in the magazine *Foreign Affairs*. The article was signed "X," but newspapermen quickly identified Kennan as the author. He was then director of the State Department's Policy Planning Staff, and people took the article to be authoritative.

The article contained the same type of pseudo-scientific analysis of Soviet conduct as the Long Telegram. The leaders of the Soviet Union suffered from "a fanaticism unmodified by any of the Anglo-Saxon traditions of compromise." They came from "the Russian-Asiatic world" and therefore were skeptical about the possibilities for "peaceful coexistence of rival forces." They "insisted on the submission or destruction of all competing power."[26]

But the main subject of the article was *containment*. In vague metaphors, whose concrete meaning is impossible to establish, Kennan explained that Soviet power is expansive and recommended a policy for dealing with it. Soviet

> political action is a fluid stream which moves constantly, wherever it is permitted to move, toward a given goal. Its main concern is to make sure that it has filled every nook and cranny available to it in the basin of world power....
>
> The main element of any United States policy toward the Soviet Union must be that of a long-term, patient but firm and vigilant containment of Russian expansive tendencies....
>
> Soviet pressure against the free institutions of the Western world is something that can be contained by the adroit and vigilant application of counter-force at a series of constantly shifting geographical and political points, corresponding to the shifts and maneuvers of Soviet policy....[27]

As with the Long Telegram, Kennan later disowned his article, saying that it had been misunderstood. He had not, he claimed, been talking about military containment; in fact, the article was a plea that war was not inevitable, nor "a suitable answer."[28] If so, Kennan had a peculiar way of making his plea.

How could one tell from his murky metaphors that by containment he didn't mean ringing the Soviet Union with U.S. bases and hostile military alliances and that the phrase "the vigilant application of counter-force" didn't refer to military force? Everybody took Kennan's article to be the theoretical underpinning for the Truman Doctrine, and "containment" as applied in Greece and Turkey, which included, even stressed, military containment, became official U.S. policy.

But even apart from confusion over whether it refers to military action, the term "containment" is misleading. It purports to be a policy of defensive action to counter Soviet aggression. In reality, it is an offensive, aggressive policy. It has meant continuous efforts, using every conceivable means, to weaken and isolate the Soviet Union. It has meant U.S. intervention throughout the world.

AT THE TIME THE ADMINISTRATION was working on the Truman Doctrine, it was also preparing to open another front against the Soviet Union—covert action. Actually, the Office of Strategic Services (OSS), the forerunner of the CIA, had begun systematic intelligence operations against the Soviet Union much earlier. Thomas Powers writes in his book on the CIA:

> The Cold War began long before it was named. In April 1945, [Allen] Dulles [then OSS's Chief of Mission in Berne, later head of the CIA,] asked an OSS officer named Frank Wisner to begin talks with Reinhard Gehlen, the former commander of Fremde Heere Ost (Foreign Armies East),[a German] intelligence unit targeted on the Russians. Gehlen had hidden his files and escaped to the West in the firm conviction that the Americans would want his services. He was right.[29]

The OSS was organized for covert operations as well as to gather intelligence, but in October 1945, Truman disbanded it, leaving the United States for a while without an agency specifically organized to carry out covert operations. But U.S. officials felt that they needed covert action against the Soviet Union. As the report of a Congressional committee that investigated intelligence activities put it:

> For U.S. officials, the perception of the Soviet Union as a global threat demanded new modes of conduct in foreign policy to supplement the traditional alternatives of diplomacy and war.... Covert

action was... something more than diplomacy but still short of war.[30]

In December 1946, the Government adopted guidelines for the conduct of psychological warfare and soon began preparations for other forms of covert action. The establishment of the CIA followed.

What were the aims of the covert action? One aim was preparation for war, to be achieved through projects like setting up a network of agents in eastern Europe who would sabotage Soviet airfields in case of war. Another aim was subversion which might possibly, even without war, lead to the overthrow of the Soviet government. According to a 1948 National Security document entitled *U.S. Objectives with Respect to Russia*:

> It is not our peacetime aim to overthrow the Soviet Government. Admittedly, we are aiming at the creation of circumstances and situations which would be difficult for the present Soviet leaders to stomach, and which they would not like. It is possible that they might not be able, in the face of these circumstances and situations, to retain their power in Russia. But it must be reiterated: that is their business, not ours.[31]

Some of the CIA's subversive activities during these years have become known. William Colby, former head of the CIA, writes in his memoirs:

> The CIA clandestinely supported the development of an anti-Communist resistance movement in the Ukraine and occasionally by parachute or PT boat delivered agents to the Baltic countries. A major effort to break Albania out of the curtain by stirring up a revolt against the Communist regime there was underway.[32]

As part of its program of organizing "resistance movements," the CIA supported East European emigré groups in the West. Colby writes:

> In Stockholm at the time was a large colony of refugees and exiles from Communist Europe, mainly from the Baltic states, Poland, Hungary, Rumania, and the Ukraine.... I spent hours discussing with them the situations in their homelands and their hopes and dreams of freedom from Soviet rule, and whether this could come about without war.... I was able to steer some of them to the correct channels in Europe through which they could get support for anti-Communist activities such as the publication of their newsletters and the maintenance of their exile organizations.[33]

The CIA quickly began to launch propaganda into eastern Europe. By 1948, it had established a secret printing plant in Germany and was assembling a fleet of balloons for dropping propaganda materials.[34]   In the early 1950s, it established a radio station to broadcast to the Soviet Union with the significant name Radio Liberation (later changed to Radio Liberty). It named a similar station aimed at the rest of Eastern Europe Radio Free Europe.[35]

COVERT ACTION WAS NOT the only method the United States was considering for overthrowing the Soviet Union—open war was another. In 1948, the United States began to turn out one plan after another for atomic war against the Soviet Union. It had earlier plans, but they were limited in scope by the small number and primitiveness of the bombs available. Now, with a substantial and growing number of bombs and with the bombs more powerful yet smaller and more easily deliverable, plans proliferated and became more ambitious. A plan of May 1948, code-named HARROW, called for dropping 50 bombs—apparently all that were then available—on 20 Soviet cities. A plan of December 1948—SIZZLE—called for 133 bombs on 70 cities.[36]

Some in the United States were urging preventive war. The well-known military writer, Major George Fielding Eliot, wrote: "We cannot allow the present Soviet government to come into possession of the atomic bomb plus the means to deliver atomic bombs in North America."[37] Anthony Cave Brown writes in his "editor's prologue" to one of the major war plans:

> There is some evidence that Louis Johnson, secretary of defense, 1949-1950, backed preventive war—what Hanson Baldwin of *The New York Times* called "instituting a war to compel cooperation for peace".... [And] the Joint Chiefs of Staff would have thought there was reason and excuse for preventive war in 1948-1949.[38]

But there was a hitch—it was far from clear that a preventive war would be successful. Many Air Force planners believed that an atomic air offensive would be enough to achieve victory, but others in the Pentagon had doubts. The JCS appointed a committee, headed by General Hubert Harmon, to study the problem. The committee came back in May 1949 with its conclusions:

The atomic offensive would not, per se, bring about capitulation [or] destroy the roots of Communism....The capability of Soviet armed forces to advance rapidly into selected areas of Western Europe, the Middle East and Far East, would not be seriously impaired....[39]

In September 1949 came news which cast further doubt on U.S. ability to fight a war against the Soviet Union successfully and with impunity: the Soviets had tested an atomic device. Now the United States, too, had to fear what the bomb could do. U.S. military leaders had to reappraise their strategy—to figure out how to counter Soviet possession of the bomb, as well as Soviet ability, in answer to atomic attack, to advance into Western Europe and the Middle East.

The Soviet atomic explosion caused many scientists and public officials, among them the physicist Edward Teller and Atomic Energy Commission member Lewis Strauss, to argue that the United States should develop a hydrogen bomb. The new bomb, they hoped, would provide this country with continued nuclear superiority. The Pentagon pushed for a crash program. Some of the bomb's promoters were undoubtedly thinking about its usefulness in a preventive war.

But many scientists and officials opposed development of the hydrogen bomb. Robert Oppenheimer, the physicist who had directed the Los Alamos project that developed the atomic bomb, argued against the hydrogen bomb. James Conant, a chemist and president of Harvard, warned: "The extreme dangers to mankind inherent in the proposal wholly outweigh any military advantage."[40]

Among those opposed was Kennan, who not much earlier had been hurling anathema against the Soviet Union. Now Kennan not only argued against development until the United States made "sure that there was really no possibility of arriving at international agreements that would obviate the need to embark upon this fateful course." He called into question the whole U.S. atomic policy. We were, he said,

> basing our defense posture on [atomic] weapons, and were intending to make first use of them, regardless of whether they had been or might be used against us....

"My voice would be cast most decisively," he said, to abandon the "first use" principle.[41]

But Kennan got nowhere. The National Security Council had already decided that the United States had "nothing presently to gain, commensurable with the risk" of discussing the possibility of not using atomic weapons. The major risk was that such discussion would discourage the countries of Western Europe whose "feeling of security" comes from the "atomic bomb, under American trusteeship...." A formal alliance between the United States and Western Europe did not yet exist, but U.S. policymakers had already worked out the basic principle on which it would rest — U.S. possession of nuclear weapons and willingness to use them. Henceforth, a key argument against renouncing the use of such weapons or even undertaking limited nuclear disarmament would be that such actions would weaken the alliance.[42]

Truman appointed a committee to advise him on the hydrogen bomb. The committee decided to recommend development, although one of its members, David Lilienthal, had reservations. As the committee was presenting its recommendation to the President, Lilienthal tried to make a plea that a peace initiative be undertaken before going ahead. But Truman cut him off, saying that delay was unwise.[43]

1948 saw not only a proliferation of Pentagon war plans, but also a campaign to organize an anti-Soviet military alliance which culminated in 1949 in the formation of NATO (North Atlantic Treaty Organization). The NATO treaty presented its main purpose as the provision of "mutual aid" to meet "armed attack." The publicity justifying the formation of NATO harped on "the Soviet military threat." But this threat was a myth. Nobody in authority believed that the Soviet Union intended to attack Western Europe.

Even the belligerently anti-Soviet John Foster Dulles wrote in 1950 that "most qualified persons are inclined to feel that there is no imminent danger of the Red Army's being marched out of Russia against Western Europe or Asia in a war of aggression."[44] Kennan thought that "the Russians had no idea of using regular military strength against us."[45] The National Security Council stated in a secret document of November 1948 that "a careful weighing of the various factors points to the probability that the Soviet Government is not now planning any deliberate armed action calculated to involve the United States...."[46]

What, then, did the United States have in mind in promoting NATO? Several things. NATO could have important political as well as military uses.

The United States was worried that France, Italy, or some other country might elect a leftist, even communist government or that a revolution or civil war might break out somewhere. The existence of NATO could help create an atmosphere in which such contingencies were less likely. It would also mean having at hand political instruments and military forces to deal in the name of the Alliance with any contingencies that did occur.

Militarily, NATO could help strengthen the forces arrayed against the Soviet Union. It could provide the United States with bases not only in Western Europe, but also in Greenland, Iceland, and the Azores. It could, especially once West Germany was in it, provide large ground forces, thus countering what the Harmon report had held to be a crucial weakness in the U.S. military posture—the ability of the Soviet Union, if attacked, to advance into Western Europe.

In late 1949, the United States produced a new war plan— DROPSHOT—based on the reappraisal occasioned by the Harmon report and the news about a Soviet bomb. The planners recognized that the United States needed more time to prepare. DROPSHOT assumed that the war would start on 1 January 1957. But this was an arbitrary date assumed for planning purposes; hostilities could start earlier if the United States felt it was ready.[47]

The main condition for readiness was to be able to deliver a decisive atomic blow. The plan assumed that the United States would have a ten to one superiority in nuclear bombs. It emphasized that a strategic air offensive "utilizing the A-bomb supplemented with conventional bombs should be instituted immediately after the outbreak of hostilities." It called for dropping 300 atomic bombs and twenty thousand tons of high explosive conventional bombs on 200 targets in 100 urban areas, including Moscow and Leningrad. Aiming at obtaining the maximum psychological effect, it required that the atomic phase of the bombing be completed within thirty days.[48]

The planners hoped that the bombing would bring about an early Soviet surrender.

The use of atomic weapons in reasonable quantity will permit the achievement of great physical destruction with relatively small effort within a short time. In addition to this physical destruction, it seems reasonable to anticipate that the use of the weapon would create a condition of chaos and extreme confusion.... It seems logical...to anticipate that the psychological effect, properly exploited, could become an important factor in the timing of and the effort necessary to cause the cessation of hostilities....[49]

But the planners felt that it would be imprudent to assume that the air offensive alone would bring "complete victory." Complete victory might require "a major land campaign" as well. The European NATO countries would provide the majority of the troops.[50]

Thus, the essence of the arms race at the time was as follows: The United States was racing to get the means for a decisive blow before the Soviet Union could develop a deterrent retaliatory capacity, while the Soviet Union was racing to get a deterrent retaliatory capacity before the United States acquired the means for a decisive blow.

BY 1950, SO MUCH had happened in U.S.-Soviet relations that earlier formulations of policy were no longer adequate. A group of State and Defense Department officials prepared a new formulation, known as NSC 68. This document, approved by Truman, laid down policies which the United States followed for years.

NSC 68 starts with what by then was the standard axiom used to justify U.S. policy: The Kremlin is striving for "world domination." It "seeks to impose its absolute authority over the rest of the world." This is its "fundamental design." These assertions, the document seems to say, are self-evident and hardly require proof or even discussion.[51]

NSC 68 does not argue that the Soviets intend to gain world domination by military conquest. The Soviet Union "seeks to bring the free world under its dominion by the methods of the cold war. The preferred technique is to subvert by infiltration and intimidation...."[52]

But the threat to the United States stems not just from "design," but from the Soviet system. "We can expect no lasting abatement of the crisis unless and until a change occurs in the nature of the Soviet system."[53]

To meet the threat, the United States must follow a policy of "containment," which means to

> block further expansion of Soviet power..., induce a retraction of the Kremlin's control and influence and in general, so foster the seeds of destruction within the Soviet system that the Kremlin is brought at least to the point of modifying its behavior....[54]

This is once again the Truman Doctrine with its aim of holding back the tide of social change plus an explicit policy of trying to push back socialism and even, if possible, destroy it within the Soviet Union. The document explains that to implement containment requires military superiority over the Soviet Union.

> It was and continues to be cardinal in this policy that we possess superior overall power in ourselves or in dependable combination with other like-minded nations. One of the most important ingredients of power is military strength.... Without superior aggregate military strength, in being and readily mobilizable, a policy of "containment" —which is in effect a policy of *calculated and gradual coercion* —is no more than a policy of bluff. (Italics added.)[55]

To put the United States in a position to carry out containment, NSC 68 recommended "a rapid buildup" of U.S. and allied military strength to the point where it is superior "both initially and throughout a war to the forces that can be brought to bear by the Soviet Union and its satellites." Also, "it is mandatory that...we enlarge upon our technical superiority by an accelerated exploitation of the scientific potential of the United States and our allies."[56]

NSC 68 also recommends the

> intensification of...operations by covert means in the fields of economic warfare and political and psychological warfare with a view to fomenting and supporting unrest and revolt in selected strategic satellite countries.[57]

The document explains the basic logic of U.S. policy. "The problem" is to create sufficient force to make "the Kremlin...accommodate itself." Until sufficient force exists, there can be no true negotiations. "For some time after a decision to build up strength, any offer of, or attempt at, negotiation of a general settlement...could only be a tactic."[58]

In essence, the policy laid down by NSC 68 was to build up enough strength to dictate a settlement to the Soviet Union or defeat it in a nuclear war if that became necessary.

Dean Acheson writes that the State Department's Russian experts challenged the basic premise of NSC 68: that the Soviet Union sought world domination. He took sides against the experts. "Throughout 1950...I went about the country preaching this premise of NSC 68." He explains. "The task of a public officer seeking to explain and gain support for a major policy is not that of the writer of a doctoral thesis. Qualification must give way to simplicity of statement....If we made our points clearer than truth, we did not differ from most other educators...."[59] To promote his policy, Acheson was spreading a lie.

Acheson also followed NSC 68 on negotiation. Trygve Lie, Secretary General of the United Nations, prepared a program for negotiation, insisting, according to Acheson, that he was proposing "not appeasement but 'negotiation,' which requires 'honest give-and-take by both sides.'" But to Acheson, Lie's program "sounded very much like appeasement." It proposed seating the Communists as the representatives of China in the U.N. instead of maintaining the fiction that Chiang's government on Taiwan represented them. Acheson gives his view of negotiation: "We must carry forward in our own determination to create situations of strength in the free world, because this is the only basis on which lasting agreement with the Soviet Government is possible."[60]

For all the aggressiveness of the containment policy, many Republicans found it unsatisfactory. They felt it had the United States merely reacting to emergencies, created a danger of getting bogged down repeatedly in costly land wars like the one in Korea, and didn't make enough use of the United States' strong suit—the atomic bomb. Under the Eisenhower administration, Secretary of State Dulles added a new doctrine—"massive retaliation." As he explained it, henceforth, the United States would "depend primarily upon a great capacity to retaliate, instantly, by means and at places of our choosing." Dulles also talked about "liberation," a "rollback" of socialism.[61]

The situation of strength that Acheson and Dulles wanted never came. The attempt to build up decisive nuclear superiority failed. With each passing year, the Soviet Union built more atomic bombs and developed an increasing capacity to reach the United States with them. In 1953, it announced that it had tested a hydrogen bomb.

A nuclear stalemate had developed. In early 1954, Premier Georgi Malenkov of the Soviet Union declared that a new world war would mean "the death of world civilization." Later in the year, Eisenhower spoke out: "We have arrived at that point, my friends, when war does not present the possibility of victory or defeat. War would present to us only the alternative in degrees of destruction."[62]

The stalemate rendered bankrupt both the Acheson policy of waiting for a "situation of strength" before negotiating and the Dulles policy of "massive retaliation." The way the arms race was developing, the United States would not be able to achieve a "situation of strength" that it could use to bully the Soviet Union. And with a nuclear stalemate, massive retaliation could only mean bluff or suicide.

People throughout the world pressed for peace. In January 1955, the Soviets proposed a summit conference among the United States, Britain, France, and the Soviet Union. Many Western leaders, including Churchill, argued for acceptance of the Soviet proposal. But Dulles opposed a summit. According to his biographer Townsend Hoopes, he wanted to "wait until greater strength had been gathered through West Germany's consolidation in NATO and the raising of twelve German divisions."[63] Pressure from Churchill and from Anthony Eden, who succeeded him, helped Eisenhower decide to overrule Dulles. He writes in his memoirs that "not wishing to appear senselessly stubborn in my attitude toward a Summit meeting—so hopefully desired by so many—I instructed Secretary Dulles to let it be known through diplomatic channels, that if other powers were genuinely interested in such a meeting we were ready to listen to their reasoning."[64]

Before the conference, Eisenhower and Dulles conferred on strategy. Dulles thought, writes Eisenhower, that the Soviets would "propose a specious effort to relax armament burdens, such as by 'banning the bomb'...."[65] Dulles held that "undoubtedly, one of the major Soviet desires is to relieve itself of the economic burden of the present arms race."[66] The Soviets did make disarmament proposals. They called for an absolute prohibition on the manufacture and use of nuclear weapons and a ceiling of 1.5 million men each in the armed forces of the Soviet Union, China, and the United States, with lower ceilings for Britain and France. The United States and its allies rejected these proposals. They didn't want to give up nuclear weapons and they were moving ahead with plans to strengthen NATO by incorporating West German forces into it. In place of disarmament, Eisenhower proposed a scheme for aerial inspection by the two sides of each other's territories. Khrushchev told Eisenhower that he considered this to be nothing more than an espionage plan.

The 1955 summit did not reach any agreements on the key issues dividing the two sides. Nevertheless, it did help spread the idea that resort to nuclear war would be suicidal. And it relaxed tension for a while.

THE HISTORY OF U.S. military doctrine since the development of a nuclear stalemate in the mid-1950s is one of continuing efforts to find some way around the stalemate: some way nuclear weapons can be used without committing suicide, some way to avoid having to give up these weapons. U.S. strategists felt that without nuclear weapons they could not attain military superiority, the situation of strength they wanted, the ability to coerce the Soviet Union.

Among the first to grapple with the problem created by the stalemate was Henry Kissinger in his 1957 book, *Nuclear Weapons and Foreign Policy*. Kissinger recognized that the world was in a state of revolutionary "ferment." "Never have so many different revolutions occurred simultaneously." The United States must "manage" the process of revolutionary transformation. "As a *status quo* power," it must be prepared to resist those changes which are not in its interest, in particular those that would change the world balance of power in its disfavor. Such resistance requires force. "The renunciation of force will create a vacuum into with the Soviet leadership can move with impunity." But there is a dilemma: "the enormity of modern weapons makes the thought of war repugnant, but the refusal to run any risks would amount to giving the Soviet rulers a blank check."[67]

The way out of the dilemma lies in developing "weapons systems which do not paralyze our will." We must "gain the possibility of fighting wars that will not amount to national catastrophe"—limited wars, including limited nuclear wars.[68]

Kissinger admitted that arguments against the possibility of limited nuclear war are "persuasive," but he rejected them. "There need not be an inevitable progression from limited nuclear war to all-out thermonuclear conflict." The limitation of a war requires cooperation by both sides, based on an understanding arrived at in advance, to keep it limited. "Battles," said

Kissinger, "will approach the stylized contests of the feudal period, which served as much as a test of will as a trial of strength."[69]

Finally, although Kissinger held that in an all-out nuclear war "*both* contenders must lose," he was not only willing to subject the world to the risk of such a war, but made a virtue of the risk:

> The side which is more willing to risk an all-out war or can convince its opponent of its greater readiness to run that risk is in the stronger position.[70]

Another who grappled with the problem of adjusting strategy to the nuclear stalemate was General Maxwell Taylor, whose book, *The Uncertain Trumpet*, appeared in 1959. Taylor made the Soviet Union responsible for whatever went on all over the world that did not suit the United States and spoke of "the deterrence of Communist expansion in whatever form it may take."[71] For example, there were

> Communist successes in the Middle East, where they had leap-frogged our mutual security shield of the Baghdad Pact; in Indonesia, where they appeared about to do the same behind the SEATO shield; and in North Africa, where they had a similar possibility for success around the NATO south flank.[72]

The United States was planning where necessary to use military means against such "local aggression" and for this, said Taylor, it needed "a capability to react across the entire spectrum of challenge." So Taylor promulgated a doctrine of "Flexible Response," which required a capacity to wage not only all-out nuclear war, but also limited war, both conventional and nuclear. The United States needed

> ready forces of the Army, Navy, and Air Force capable of intervening rapidly in areas where local aggression may occur. These ready forces should have the capability of employing atomic weapons when and to the extent authorized by proper authority.[73]

Taylor spoke of using tactical atomic weapons and of the "great promise of the very low-yield atomic weapons."[74]

The arguments used to support the possibility of a *limited* nuclear war were weak. Kissinger's notion that battles in such a war would "approach the stylized contests of the feudal period" is ludicrous. We are talking about war—nuclear war—not some Public School Athletic League tournament. Kissinger says that to obtain agreement on the rules "is the task of diplomacy."

Some task! If the two sides could maintain such rules in the heat and stress and chaos of war, why couldn't they in time of peace arrive at an agreement not to use nuclear weapons at all and, better yet, not to have war? By weakening the idea that nuclear weapons cannot be used, by blurring the thought that there can be no winner in a nuclear war, by lowering the threshold for starting a nuclear war, the doctrine of limited nuclear war increased the risk of all-out nuclear war.

The United States, unwilling to give up nuclear weapons and the possibility of military superiority over the Soviet Union, moved to develop the strategy, tactics, and weapons for fighting a limited nuclear war. During the early 1960s, it adopted the doctrine of Flexible Response. More than this: it continued to search for methods by which it could somehow achieve overall nuclear superiority over the Soviet Union and fight and win an all-out nuclear war.

THE U.S. PURSUIT of its aggressive military doctrine gave continuous impetus to the nuclear arms race. The United States, which had started the race with the atom and hydrogen bombs, was now pushing it forward with ever new weaponry. Robert McNamara, Secretary of Defense from 1960 to 1968, says repeatedly in his 1986 book *Blundering Into Disaster* that it was the United States that propelled the arms race forward.

> * The history of the arms race has been, in large part, the search by the West for a technological "fix" that will confer a lasting military advantage on it....
>
> * Virtually every technical initiative in the nuclear arms race has come from the United States....
>
> * From the dawn of the nuclear age to the present, the United States has sought to maintain "superior" strategic and tactical nuclear forces — or at least forces that could give us an advantage if we, rather than the Soviets, struck the first blow.[75]

The United States has been the first to develop virtually all the major nuclear weapons systems. Here are some of the examples McNamara mentions: Sub-launched Missile (1960), Solid-fueled Intercontinental Ballistic Missile (1962), Antisatellite Weapons (1963), Multiple Independently Targetable Reentry Vehicle — MIRV (1970).[76]

In a 1982 interview with Robert Scheer, McNamara emphasized repeatedly that the Soviets had to react to the U.S. arms buildup. Talking about 1961-62, he says:

> If I had been the Soviet secretary of defense, I'd have been worried as hell about the imbalance of force.[77]

He spoke of the supposed "missile gap" in favor of the Soviets in 1960 when "forces within the Defense Department" were trying to push their program for expanding missile production "by overstating the Soviet force." But soon it was clear that the missile gap was a "total misreading of the information." Within two years, "the advantage in the U.S. warhead inventory was so great vis-a-vis the Soviets that the Air Force was saying that they felt we had a first-strike capability and could, and should, continue to have one."[78] McNamara quoted from a 1962 Air Force document:

> The Air Force has rather supported the development of forces which provide the United States a first strike capability credible to the Soviet Union by virtue of our ability to limit damage to the United States and our allies to levels acceptable in light of the circumstances and the alternatives available.[79]

"My God," exclaimed McNamara, "if the Soviets thought that was our objective, how would you expect them to react?"[80]

When Scheer told McNamara that people in the Reagan administration were asking "How do you explain their continuous buildup of —," McNamara broke in:

> The way you explain it is by putting yourself in their shoes. When I've done that on several occasions, I must say I would do some things that were very similar to what they did. I'm talking about the action they took to build up their force.[81]

Despite its military doctrine, the billions it poured into the arms buildup, and the endless flow of astounding new weapons, the United States was unable to break the nuclear stalemate established in the mid-1950s. It continued, for years, to enjoy superiority in the number and quality of nuclear weapons. But it never attained a meaningful military superiority—one that would enable it to carry out a first strike on the Soviet Union without receiving a retaliatory blow that would inflict "unacceptable damage."

THIS CONTINUING STALEMATE pro-
duced a mixed reaction among the rulers of the United States.
On the one hand, they felt a constant urge to break the stalemate. On the other, some of them began to develop an interest
in easing tensions. Tense relations had their uses: they helped
get big military appropriations; they made it easier to keep
NATO allies in line. But they also had their dangers and costs.
They brought confrontations that might get out of control and
lead to a war that would bring unacceptable damage. They
prevented U.S. business from enjoying the potential benefits of
economic relations with the Soviet Union. The attempt to ease
tensions in 1955 was only the first; others followed periodically.

In 1959, high-ranking Soviet and American leaders exchanged
visits. Soviet Deputy Prime Minister Anastas Mikoyan came to
the United States to talk about trade and the problems of Berlin
and Germany. Vice President Nixon went to the Soviet Union to
open an American exhibition in Moscow. Khrushchev, whose
article urging detente had just been published in *Foreign Affairs*,
visited the United States. What he had to say encouraged Eisenhower, according to Townsend Hoopes, "to seek agreement
from his allies for a summit conference..., to be followed...by his
own visit to Russia. In effect he and Khrushchev tacitly agreed
to work toward general detente." But the plans went awry after
the Soviets downed a U-2 spy plane over their territory. Instead
of accepting a virtual invitation from Khrushchev that he dis-
avow responsibility for the flight, Eisenhower asserted that it
was "a distasteful but vital necessity."[82]   The conference collapsed and the Eisenhower visit never took place. Khrushchev
charged that some in the U.S. Government who opposed
detente had deliberately timed the U-2 flight to scuttle the summit meeting.[83]

In 1961, Kennedy and Khrushchev met in Vienna. They agreed on the need to avoid a collision between their countries,
but a fundamental difference emerged in their approach to
world developments. Kennedy berated Khrushchev on Soviet
support for national liberation and revolution. "As he saw the
problem...," writes his special assistant, Arthur Schlesinger, Jr.,
"the communists were trying to eliminate free systems in areas
associated with the west." This threatened the existing balance
of power and was dangerous.[84]

Khrushchev rejected Kennedy's argument. He thought that
"communism would triumph," but as a result of social develop-

ment, not because the Soviet Union "implanted" its policy in other states. "Changes in social systems were bound to come, but they would be brought about only by the will of the people themselves." Ideas, said Khrushchev, cannot be confined. He wanted to know whether Kennedy meant that if communism developed anywhere, the United States would be in conflict with the Soviet Union. "How could we work anything out when the United States regarded revolution anywhere as the result of communist machinations?" Khrushchev proposed that "we should both agree not to interfere" in other countries and "leave it to the people" of these countries to determine their own destiny.[85]

In 1963, soon after the Cuban missile crisis came a more successful attempt to ease tensions. Khrushchev took the initiative. A month after the crisis, he suggested to Kennedy a point by point negotiation of all outstanding issues. Kennedy, according to his special counsel, Theodore Sorensen, was "ready to negotiate."[86] Schlesinger explains that Kennedy's

> feelings underwent a qualitative change after Cuba: a world in which nations threatened each other with nuclear weapons now seemed to him not just an irrational but an intolerable and impossible world.[87]

The next month, Khrushchev wrote Kennedy that the "time has come now to put an end once and for all to nuclear tests...." Unofficial talks got under way, followed later by formal negotiations.[88]

During the domestic debate on the test ban, Kennedy made a commencement address at American University which, according to Sorensen, who drafted it, was "the first Presidential speech in eighteen years to succeed in reaching beyond the cold war."[89] Here are some excerpts:

> I have...chosen this time and this place to discuss a topic on which ignorance too often abounds and the truth is too rarely perceived — yet it is the most important topic on earth: world peace.... Total war makes no sense in an age when great powers can maintain large and relatively invulnerable nuclear forces.... Let us reexamine our attitude toward the Soviet Union.... We are both devoting massive sums of money to weapons that could be better devoted to combatting ignorance, poverty, and disease.... If we cannot end now our differences, at least we can help make the world safe for diversity.... Our most basic common link is that we

all inhabit this planet. We all breathe the same air. We all cherish our children's future. And we are all mortal.... Let us reexamine our attitude toward the cold war....[90]

Despite the opposition of Edward Teller, former AEC Chairman Lewis Strauss, former Chiefs of Staff Arleigh Burke, Arthur Radford, and Nathan Twining, the Air Force Association (composed of military officers and defense contractors), and Senators Goldwater, Stennis, and Russell, the United States entered into a partial test ban treaty with the Soviet Union. It also participated in establishing a direct communications link—"hot line"—between Moscow and Washington to facilitate dealing with crises.

Still, Kennedy had by no means given up the idea of U.S. nuclear superiority. Sorensen writes that Kennedy "had often argued that fruitful disarmament negotiations could never take place...as long as the Communists thought they could overtake us in the arms race...."[91] Schlesinger explains that "Kennedy saw the main point of the treaty as a means of moving toward his Vienna goal of stabilizing the international equilibrium of power.... The test ban now indicated a mutual willingness to halt the weapons race more or less where it was. In the Soviet case this meant acquiescence in American nuclear superiority."[92] Kennedy was still following a policy which Sorensen describes as "peace through strength."[93]

Nevertheless, Kennedy's actions were of great potential significance. He saw the test ban treaty as "an important first step—a step toward peace—a step toward reason—a step away from war."[94] He began to prepare the way for other moves toward detente. A few weeks later he was assassinated.

Under Johnson, U.S.-Soviet relations got worse instead of better. Johnson began by also talking about wanting to see the Cold War end, but then he escalated the war in Vietnam and it became the overriding foreign policy preoccupation of his administration. With the United States committing aggression against a Soviet ally and the Soviet Union providing weapons to Vietnam to fight this aggression, the war created a barrier to the improvement of relations.

Even while relations were worsening, however, the conditions that would later help create a favorable setting for detente were developing. First, the Soviet Union was progressing toward rough nuclear parity with the United States. In one key sense, parity had already existed for years: Each side had enough nuclear weapons to inflict unacceptable damage on the other so that a nuclear war was not a rational choice for either. Still, the United States had great numerical superiority and this had important consequences: U.S. military theorists tried to work out strategies through which the superiority could somehow be made to pay off; some U.S. experts held that the superiority was significant, especially during a crisis. But now the Soviet Union was closing the gap. Kissinger writes that "The decisive American superiority, which had characterized the entire postwar period, had ended by 1967.... By 1969 it was clear that the number of Soviet missiles capable of reaching the United States would soon equal that of all American missiles available for retaliation against the Soviet Union...."[95]

The growth in Soviet nuclear strength began to produce effects well before parity was actually achieved. It narrowed the margin for aggressive U.S. strategies, making it necessary to modify or even give up some of them. For example, in 1964 McNamara put forth a so-called damage limiting strategy. Such a strategy, he declared, "appears to be the most practical and effective course for us to follow.... There is general agreement that [the force needed for such a strategy] should be large enough to ensure the destruction, singly or in combination, of the Soviet Union, Communist China, and the Communist satellites as national societies,... and, in addition, to destroy their warmaking capability so as to limit, to the extent practicable, damage to this country and to our allies."[96] This strategy depended on the overwhelming nuclear superiority of the United States. As the Soviet Union acquired more missiles and put many of them into hardened silos and hard-to-reach submarines, such strategies became unworkable.

Besides forcing changes in U.S. strategy, the growth in Soviet nuclear strength also pushed the United States toward arms control negotiations. "SALT has it origins in the mid-1960s," says John Newhouse in his book on the first arms limitation talks.[97] Arms control offered no attraction to U.S. strategists when the United States enjoyed great nuclear superiority, but it became interesting as the superiority declined. Even from a narrow military point of view, the best answer to the growing number of improved Soviet weapons was not to not to pile up counter-weapons but to reach arms agreements. Newhouse again: "It was when the Defense Department was able to show that various goals could be better achieved by limiting some systems and cancelling others that restricting strategic arms became respectable, even important."[98]   In 1967, Johnson instructed Llewellyn Thompson, his ambassador to Moscow, to explore with Soviet leaders the possibility of arms control talks.[99]

A second condition favorable to detente was the development in the latter half of the 1960s of a movement toward detente in Western Europe.   Like Kennedy and Khrushchev, Western European leaders had also been pondering the meaning of the Cuban missile crisis and the developing U.S.-Soviet nuclear parity.   And they were tempted by the large potential markets in the Soviet Union and the rest of Eastern Europe.

French President Charles de Gaulle was the first to move.   At a press conference a few months after the missile crisis, he presented conclusions he drew from it.   His biographer, Alexander Werth, paraphrases: "The [NATO] Alliance by itself was all very well so long as the U.S.A. had her atomic monopoly: but now, with Russia capable of destroying America, the defence of Europe was no longer America's primary problem.   The Cuban crisis had amply demonstrated this."[100]   France must rethink its policy, must look to its own security.

In 1964, France and the Soviet Union signed a commercial agreement.   Then in 1966, de Gaulle made a milestone visit to the Soviet Union and Soviet Premier Alexei Kosygin paid a return visit to France.   The joint statements issued after the visits spoke of the need for the "easing of tensions" and "the normalization of relations."[101]   France withdrew from the NATO military organization and forced NATO to move its headquarters elsewhere.

The missile crisis also had its effects in West Germany.   Konrad Adenauer, West Germany's first Chancellor, had in 1949 laid down a hard-line policy of refusing to recognize the German Democratic Republic and the territorial changes resulting from World War II.   As William E. Griffith points out in his book on West   Germany's   Ostpolitik   (policy   toward   the   East), "Adenauer's policy was based on unquestioned American thermonuclear superiority and invulnerability."   As "Soviet strength grew, Adenauer's policy was... doomed."[102]   Signs of its weakening appeared at the beginning of the 1960s.   Then came the missile crisis, influencing the thinking of a key West German leader, Willy Brandt, then Mayor of West Berlin.   Brandt writes in his memoirs: "Addressing a German-U.S. conference in Berlin on 19 November 1962, with the Cuba crisis and my own experiences in mind, I declared that there was no all-or-nothing policy...."[103] By 1969, when Brandt became Chancellor of West Germany, U.S.-Soviet nuclear parity had rendered the hard-line policy of relying on "strength" rather than accommodation even less practicable than in 1962. Brandt carried through a new Ostpolitik. West Germany signed a treaty with the Soviet Union recognizing the postwar boundaries as "inviolable" and another with the GDR providing for mutual recognition. The tone of West German-Soviet relations changed.

Italy also improved its relations and increased its trade with the Soviet Union during this period.

The detente in Europe put pressure on the United States to follow suit. A continued difference in policy on such a basic issue could divide it from its allies.

Finally, a key part of the developing setting for U.S.-Soviet detente was the desire of the American people for an easing of tensions. Kissinger provides a revealing indication of the political importance of this sentiment. He writes that Nixon "shrewdly saw in East-West relations a long-term opportunity to build his new majority." Nixon worried that the 1967 Johnson-Kosygin summit at Glassboro might "restore Johnson's fortunes," but saw "how the inconclusive outcome had caused Johnson's popularity to dissipate as rapidly as it had spurted...."[104]

NIXON BEGAN TO WORK on East-West relations in his inaugural address:

> After a period of confrontation, we are entering an era of negotiation. Let all nations know that during this Administration our lines of communication will be open.[105]

Actually, by the time of the address, the first mutual probings of the possibility of negotiation were already under way.

Why were Nixon and Kissinger interested in detente? What principles governed their approach to it? To what extent did their approach represent a break with past policy, to what extent a continuation of it?

In a 1973 interview, Kissinger explained the reasons for detente: "We are in favor of detente because we want to limit the risks of major nuclear conflict."[106] Nixon put it similarly: Detente "is an understanding between nations that have opposite purposes, but which share certain common interests, including the avoidance of nuclear war."[107]

The main principle governing the Nixon-Kissinger approach to detente is what they call "linkage." Nixon explains that in the period between his election in 1968 and his inauguration in 1969, he and Kissinger developed the concept of linkage.

> We determined that those things the Soviets wanted—the good public relations that summits provided, economic cooperation, and strategic arms limitation agreements—would not be gained by them without a quid pro quo. At that time the principal quid pro quos we wanted were some assistance in getting a settlement in Vietnam, restraint by them in the Middle East, and a resolution of the recurring problems in Berlin.[108]

Kissinger writes that the concept of linkage was "widely challenged in 1969...[and] thought to be...a gratuitous device to delay arms control negotiations." He cites the *Washington Post*: "Arms control has a value and urgency entirely apart from the status of political issues."[109] Nevertheless,

> We insisted that progress in superpower relations, to be real, had to be made on a broad front. Events in different parts of the world, in our view, were related to each other; even more so, Soviet conduct in different parts of the world.... Displays of American impotence in one part of the world, such as Asia or Africa, would inevitably erode our credibility in other parts of the world, such as the Middle East.[110]

Thus, the new policy contained strong elements of the old. It recognized that the former nuclear superiority was gone, that a nuclear war would be suicidal for both sides, that it was vital to limit the risk of such a war breaking out. But it continued the old "containment" policy. It still aimed at getting the Soviet Union to behave. Only now it would not rely solely on its nuclear arsenal to exert pressure on the Soviet Union, but would also use "linkage"—the possibility of good relations, arms limitation agreements, economic cooperation, etc. In the words of Kissinger,

> we would pursue a carrot-and-stick approach, ready to impose penalties for adventurism, willing to expand relations in the context of responsible behavior.[111]

What about arms control? Nixon's own words about using arms control as a quid pro quo for Soviet good conduct tell us that he did not agree with the *Washington Post* that "arms control has a value and urgency" of its own. Morton Halperin, who worked under Kissinger, later remembered

> Kissinger's basic apprehension about those who advocated arms control: "Arms controllers were interested in an agreement for its own sake. They'd get an agreement on SALT to get an agreement."... Kissinger viewed the negotiations as a means to an end, a vehicle for extracting far-reaching concessions from the Soviets in other areas, such as Vietnam.[112]

Nixon's and Kissinger's lack of interest in arms control was inherent in their approach to U.S.-Soviet relations. They were continuing the policy of "containment," and so opposed true disarmament. They hoped with the carrot of good relations, economic cooperation, and trade to bribe the Soviet Union into conduct that suited the United States; but, as they themselves made clear, they needed the nuclear arsenal to coerce it if the bribe didn't work. They recognized the development of nuclear parity and realized that it worked against any exercise of coercion. But they were by no means reconciled to full, permanent parity or the renunciation of all attempts at coercion.

Nixon and Kissinger were consummately tricky operators. When they were defending arms negotiations or agreements, they stressed the arrival of parity and the horrors of nuclear war. When they presented themselves as holding the line against Soviet "expansionism," they expressed discontent with parity which, in the words of Kissinger, could turn into a "strategic nightmare" and destroy the "credibility" of the U.S. nuclear threat. At one press conference, Kissinger exclaimed, "What in the name of God is strategic superiority? What is the significance of it, politically, militarily, operationally, at these levels of numbers? What do you do with it?" Then in his memoirs he explained that his remarks "lent themselves to the oversimplification that strategic superiority had lost all significance, which was not really my view."[113]

Nixon and Kissinger recognized parity to the extent of realizing that the old overwhelming superiority was gone. But within the new equality, they wanted the United States to be more equal than the Soviet Union and they did not want to give up efforts to widen the margin of such inequality.

Why then did Nixon and Kissinger want an arms agreement? Raymond Garthoff, Executive Officer of the U.S. SALT delegation, offers an answer in his book, *Détente and Confrontation*. Nixon and Kissinger

> both saw SALT as a political enterprise, with potential domestic and international gains if it were carefully controlled. Moreover, the clear Soviet interest, even eagerness, to enter negotiations was interpreted as a sign that the Soviet Union wanted SALT—at least negotiations, and probably an agreement—more than the United States did. That meant potential leverage in getting Soviet concessions in other areas....[114]

Further, the White House

> attitude... led to the pursuit of agreements that were politically the most easy to reach in internal negotiations in Washington, rather than to the agreements that would be most effective in curbing the arms competition between the two powers.[115]

Detente came with a Nixon-Brezhnev Moscow summit in May 1972. The two sides signed a series of agreements, among them one on Basic Principles of U.S.-Soviet Relations and two on Strategic Arms Limitation (SALT). In the Basic Principles, they agreed that "there is no alternative to conducting their relations on the basis of peaceful coexistence." One SALT agreement prohibited, with a few insignificant exceptions, the deployment of anti-ballistic missile (ABM) systems. The other—an interim agreement on offensive arms—froze land and submarine-launched ballistic missiles at existing levels for five years.[116] Upon arrival in Washington from the summit, Nixon addressed a joint session of Congress:

> Last Friday in Moscow we witnessed the beginning of the end of that era which began in 1945. We took the first step toward a new era of mutually agreed restraint and arms limitation between the two principal nuclear nations. With this step we have enhanced the security of both nations. We have begun to check the wasteful and dangerous spiral of nuclear arms which has dominated relations between our two countries for a generation.[117]

But Defense Secretary Melvin Laird's emphasis was different. The day the SALT agreements were signed he described them as "major first steps in limiting strategic arms competition" but stressed that they were "made possible only by the United States' determination to negotiate from a position of strength...." He then announced a new program for the "modernization and improvement" of U.S. strategic forces.[118]

Nixon and Kissinger themselves pushed the strategic arms buildup. Kissinger later boasted that SALT "stopped no American program," that he "consistently spurred the strengthening of our own defenses," that "after the signature of SALT I, our defense budget increased and the Nixon and Ford administrations put through the strategic weapons (the MX missile, B-1 bomber, cruise missiles, Trident submarines, and more advanced warheads)...that had been stymied in the Congress *prior* to the easing of our relations with Moscow."[119]

Yet for all their limitations, detente and SALT were a big step forward. Periodically, from the October Revolution until into the 1950s, a key theme of U.S. policy, to which it reverted even after temporary deviations, was the destruction of the Soviet government by force. There was the intervention, the tacit acquiescence when England and France tried to direct Hitler eastward, the resurgence of hostility after World War II. Now the United States was signing a document that proclaimed the principle of peaceful coexistence. With the development of nuclear parity, there was no alternative to peaceful coexistence.

That the arms race continued after SALT I by no means proves that the arms agreements were useless. The ABM treaty closed off the defensive arms race that was getting under way, a race that could have introduced great instability into the nuclear relationship—an extensive anti-missile defense, by enhancing the ability to ward off a retaliatory blow, might create, or seem to create, the ability to mount a first strike and get away with it. The interim freeze on launchers was a far more modest accomplishment. It didn't limit MIRVs (multiple independently targetable reentry vehicles), qualitative improvements in missiles, or cruise or aircraft missile systems—and therefore did not prevent an acceleration of the race in offensive arms. But the launcher freeze was intended as a first step: the agreement called for "active follow-on negotiations" to conclude an agreement on "more complete measures."[120]

The political detente, which the SALT agreements helped make possible, had enormous significance. Regardless of Nixon's sincerity about arms control, talk by a president of the United States about "the end of the era that began in 1945" and reducing "the level of fear" has a great impact.

The atmosphere changed. Contacts expanded. Heads of Soviet ministries visited the United States and members of Congress, cabinet secretaries, and businessmen visited the Soviet

Union.   Major corporations—Chase Manhattan, Pepsi Cola, Oc-
cidental Petroleum—worked on deals with the Soviets.   Soviet
buyers placed large wheat orders in the United States.   The administration promised to work on granting Export-Import Bank
credits to finance Soviet purchases here and to seek from Congress the extension to imports from the Soviet Union of "most
favored nation" status (the status most other countries enjoy).

The Moscow summit set off a chain of further activity.   In late
1972, SALT II talks began.   In May 1973, Nixon and Brezhnev
held a second summit, this time in Washington.   In 1974, there
were two more summits, the first in Moscow between Nixon
and Brezhnev, the second in Vladivostok, between Gerald Ford
and Brezhnev.   At Vladivostok, Ford and Brezhnev signed an
agreement on the framework of a new arms accord.   Ford's
comment in his memoirs shows how close to final this agreement was:

> I was euphoric.   As soon as technicians had ironed out the few
> remaining problems, we would sign a SALT II accord.[121]

It looked as though a pattern of frequent summits and additional arms agreements was emerging.   Detente is a process.
For a while, it gave promise of further progress in arms control,
expansion of ties, and general improvement in relations.

But the Vladivostok agreement ran into a strong attack led by
Senator Henry Jackson.   Jackson had earlier attacked SALT I on
the grounds that it "conceded" numerical inequality to the
Soviets; Kissinger, noting the different nature of the U.S. and
Soviet strategic forces, writes in his memoirs that this argument
"was due either to a misunderstanding or to demagoguery."[122]
Now, faced with an agreement that provided for equality, Jackson blandly changed his argument—he wanted not just a "cap"
on Soviet missiles, but a one-third cut.

Then during lower level technical discussions, the Pentagon
began to resurrect issues that Ford and Kissinger had considered settled at Vladivostok.   The negotiations with the Soviets
"to iron out the few remaining problems" went on and on.   The
problems were still there as 1976—an election year—approached.

Jackson worked not only against arms agreements, but
against detente in general, "erecting," in the words of Kissinger,
"a series of legislative hurdles that gradually paralyzed the [ad-
ministration's] East-West policy."   One "hurdle" was the Jack-

son-Vanik amendment providing that unless the Soviet Union eased emigration restraints, it would not receive most favored nation status. Later, Jackson added a sharp restriction on the amount of credit the Export-Import Bank could grant to the Soviet Union.[123]

Kissinger writes that at first he hoped that at some point Jackson would compromise. But Jackson was uninterested in compromise. He "wanted an issue, not a solution. That issue was detente."[124] William G. Hyland, who then worked on U.S.-Soviet relations for the National Security Council, writes that Jackson's action on emigration "was simply another effort to break the momentum of detente. And indeed, this was the effect."[125]

Another strong opponent of detente and SALT was Defense Secretary James Schlesinger. Even while detente was in full swing, Schlesinger was working on a "new" nuclear strategy that ran directly counter to it. The Schlesinger Doctrine called for the development of so-called counterforce weapons which would permit the United States to wipe out Soviet strategic weapons. Schlesinger explained that the new strategy would give the President other options than ordering the mass destruction of Soviet civilians to be followed by the mass destruction of American civilians.[126]

But the ability to wipe out the Soviet Union's strategic weapons is the ability to destroy its retaliatory capacity, therefore the ability to mount a first strike. The new doctrine was really not so new. It was rather another expression of the longstanding United States unwillingness to reconcile itself to the fact that nuclear war means mutual annihilation.

Schlesinger not only developed the new strategy but deliberately made it public, knowing that to do so would damage detente. He worked against detente and SALT in many other ways. Nixon writes that

> The U.S. military opposition to the new SALT agreement came to a head at the meeting of the National Security Council on the afternoon of June 20 [1974] when Secretary of Defense Schlesinger presented the Pentagon's proposal. It amounted to an unyielding hard line against any SALT agreement that did not ensure an overwhelming American advantage.[127]

The Jackson-Schlesinger combination illustrates the workings of the military-industrial complex. Jackson represented the state of Washington but his nickname was "the Senator from Boeing;" the Washington-based company is a leading defense contractor, producer of the major strategic bomber, the B-52, and the major ICBM, the Minuteman. Schlesinger had worked at Rand, the California think tank financed by the Air Force to elaborate nuclear strategy. According to Arthur Macy Cox in his book on detente, Jackson and Schlesinger "had been close to each other for years" and Jackson was one of the "patrons" who enabled Schlesinger to get the job of Secretary of Defense. "So Jackson had his own man running the Pentagon."[128]

On top of detente's other difficulties, Kissinger himself helped weaken it by his reaction to developments in Angola. The introduction of Cuban troops, operating with Soviet materiel, to help the MPLA against the South African regular army units and CIA-backed mercenaries who were trying at the last minute to prevent it from consummating the victory of the revolution, struck a nerve. Ignoring the United States' own intervention in Angola and its connivance with South Africa, Kissinger repeatedly warned that the Soviet-Cuban action ran counter to detente.

"Angola...is a pattern of behavior that the United States will not accept...," Kissinger declared. "If continued it will have serious consequences for any possibility of easing of relations with the Soviet Union...." Arguing that "if adventurism is allowed to succeed in local crises, an ominous precedent of wider consequence is set," he asserted that detente cannot "survive any more Angolas."[129]

Kissinger's reaction to Angola helped the enemies of detente to exploit the affair—to cast doubt on whether detente was worthwhile, to build up anti-Soviet sentiment. The Ford administration, feeling the growing attack on detente and on itself, moved to the defensive. It decided not to try for a SALT II agreement in 1976 and to abandon the use of the term detente for the election campaign that year.

WITH THE ELECTION CAMPAIGN, the enemies of detente increased their efforts. Ronald Reagan, trying for the Republican nomination, talked about the ominous consequences of detente:

Under Kissinger and Ford, this nation has become Number Two in a world where it is dangerous—if not fatal—to be second best. All

I can see is what other nations the world over see: collapse of the American will and the retreat of American power.[130]

The opponents of SALT and detente mounted a well-orchestrated campaign to demonstrate that the CIA's estimates of Soviet strategic capabilities and intentions were too optimistic. CIA Director George Bush took the unprecedented step of convening a group of outsiders, known as Team B, to check the CIA's estimates. To get the right results, Bush loaded Team B with the right people. The *New York Times* wrote: "The conditions were that the outsiders...hold more pessimistic views of Soviet plans than those entertained by the advocates of the rough parity thesis"—the view that rough parity exists between the Soviet Union and the United States.[131]

Former Deputy Secretary of Defense Paul Nitze, a key analyst on Team B, joined with former Undersecretary of State Eugene Rostow to form the Committee on the Present Danger, an elite organization, numbering among its less than two hundred members many former high-ranking government officials and military officers. They included ex-Secretary of State Dean Rusk, ex-Treasury Secretaries John Connally and Douglas Dillon, and ex-Chairmen of the Joint Chiefs, Matthew Ridgway and Maxwell Taylor, as well as Richard Pipes, chairman of Team B.

The Committee's founding statement began by declaring: "Our country is in a period of danger, and the danger is increasing." It argued that "for the United States to be free, secure, and influential, higher levels of [defense] spending are now required." Rostow put things even more menacingly: "We are living in a prewar and not a postwar world."[132]

Soon Team B added its conclusions to the public debate. It found—not surprisingly, given its composition—that the Soviet arms program was much larger than the CIA had previously assumed. Members of Team B leaked this and other ominous conclusions to the media just as the Carter administration took office.

THE FOREIGN POLICY establishment was now divided. One wing favored detente. Another opposed it and favored a big increase in military expenditures. The second wing was growing and organizing. Two main factors spurred its development—the wave of revolution beginning to make itself felt in southern Africa and elsewhere, and the increasing consolidation of U.S.-Soviet military parity. This wing could not swallow either revolution or parity.

The Carter administration sprang from the wing of the foreign policy establishment that supported detente. But this wing was not immune to the considerations that moved the other one. In the face of spreading revolution, its enthusiasm for detente lessened. Moreover, within this wing there were differences among various groupings and individuals. Two of Carter's key appointments reflected such differences: as Secretary of State, Cyrus Vance, for whom the central theme of detente was "the mutual interest in avoiding nuclear war," and as National Security Adviser, Zbigniew Brzezinski, who held that "detente...is incompatible with irresponsible [Soviet] behavior in Angola, the Middle East, and the UN...."[133]

The conclusion of an arms agreement was the first big task in U.S.-Soviet relations facing the Carter administration. Vance favored doing this by quickly concluding the agreement outlined at Vladivostok and then proceeding to the more protracted negotiations that would be required for deeper arms cuts. Brzezinski favored disregarding Vladivostok and proceeding immediately to try to negotiate "comprehensive and deeper" cuts.

Along with Vance, Paul Warnke, whom Carter appointed chief arms negotiator, favored proceeding on the basis of Vladivostok. In addition to Brzezinski, Senator Jackson, his hard-line assistant Richard Perle, and Paul Nitze favored the comprehensive, deep cuts approach.

When Carter wrote Brezhnev about this approach, Brezhnev made clear that the SALT agreement had to be based on Vladivostok, charging that the new ideas were "deliberately unacceptable."[134] Nevertheless, Carter sent Vance to Moscow in March 1977 with a set of proposals based on the new approach. "Most of the American decisionmakers," writes Garthoff, "...anticipated a negative Soviet reaction—not only Vance and Warnke, but [Defense Secretary] Brown and Brzezinski as well."[135] Why was the proposal Vance carried foredoomed? Garthoff explains:

> The Americans were unilaterally reopening [the Vladivostok] agreement in ways that pocketed the earlier Soviet concessions.... The substantial reductions were *all* to come on the *Soviet* side.... The fact that the proposal was loaded in favor of the United States might have been more understandable...if the negotiations were starting from a clean slate, but they were not. (Italics in original.)[136]

The Soviet Union rejected the proposal. Carter called a news conference in which he referred to the proposal as "fair" and "balanced" and made the following statement:

> Obviously, if we feel at the conclusion of next month's discussions that the Soviets are not acting in good faith with us and that an agreement is unlikely, then I would be forced to consider a much more deep commitment to the development and deployment of additional weapons.[137]

The disagreement between Vance and Brzezinski over whether to disregard the Vladivostok accord was only the prelude to a broad struggle between them, and between the forces they symbolized, over the direction to be taken by U.S. foreign policy. As this struggle unfolded, policy zigged and zagged, and detente drifted. Then, as Brzezinski increasingly won out, the policy began to move clearly away from detente.

The key difference between Vance and Brzezinski was over the U.S.-Soviet relationship. For Vance, the overriding point was that the common interest in survival required that the two countries cooperate in regulating this relationship.

> Neither the United States nor the Soviet Union can provide for its own security against nuclear holocaust unless it also helps to provide that security for the other. Neither can seek a decisive nuclear advantage without the risk of provoking an attack in which both would be destroyed....
>
> It would be unconscionable to lose the chance to negotiate firm limits on strategic arms and progressively to reduce them, either because we undervalue these efforts or because we link them to other developments in East-West relations....
>
> The world is too small...to permit a drift back to cold war or worse.[138]

For Brzezinski, the common interest in survival was not the central point and he didn't view the arms negotiations as a joint effort to increase mutual security. He supported SALT not to restrain the arms race, but because he "saw in it an opportunity to halt or reduce the momentum of the Soviet military buildup." Although he didn't like to admit it clearly, Brzezinski believed in the linkage of SALT and detente to other developments. Finally, he held that "it is false to argue...that the only alternative to [detente] is a war" — meaning that cold war is also an alternative which under certain circumstances may be better than detente.[139]

Soon after Vance's trip to Moscow, the United States took other action on arms that boded ill for detente. In May 1977, it persuaded the NATO countries to adopt in principle the goal of increasing their military expenditures by at least three percent annually in real terms.   Garthoff writes that the American boosters of the 3 percent goal intended it as a tool to be used in pressing for an increase in the U.S. defense budget.[140]

In March 1978, Carter gave a speech at Wake Forest University, drafted by Brzezinski and his staff. Here are some key lines:

> Over the past twenty years the military forces of the Soviets have grown substantially....There also has been an ominous inclination on the part of the Soviet Union to use its military power to intervene in local conflicts.... We will match, together with our allies and friends, any threatening power....[141]

According to Brzezinski's memoirs, a Vance associate, Marshall Shulman, "reassured the Soviet Embassy...that the President's speech should be viewed primarily as designed for domestic consumption...." Brzezinski "felt that State was excessively deferential to the Soviets" and he "resented" Shulman's action, which he thought "weakened the speech's intent."[142]

Vance and Brzezinski also differed over policy toward Africa. Vance "did not believe Soviet actions in Africa were part of a grand Soviet plan...." He "felt realism required us to deal with those problems in the local context in which they had their roots."[143]   Brzezinski, on the other hand, wanted to make detente dependent on Soviet behavior in Africa. He obtained Carter's approval to begin "briefing the press on the growing Soviet-Cuban military presence [in Africa] and by mid-November 1977 articles started appearing, registering the growing escalation of the Communist military efforts."[144]   In March 1978, after the Soviets sent help to Ethiopia when it was invaded by Somalia, he told reporters that Soviet involvement in the Ethiopian-Somalian war would complicate efforts to reach a new agreement on strategic arms.[145]

Early in the Carter administration Brzezinski, with the support of Defense Secretary Brown, began to talk of playing off China against the Soviet Union. Brzezinski and Brown thought that "an American-Chinese accommodation" would improve the United States' strategic position and might—as Vance later described their views—"persuade Moscow to be more careful in their dealings with us and our interests for fear of pushing us into substantial security cooperation with China." Vance opposed such cooperation, believing it would have "serious repercussions" on U.S.-Soviet relations.[146]

Brzezinski badgered Carter into sending him to China in May 1978. He himself drafted Carter's letter of instructions for the trip. The letter directed him to tell the Chinese that "we have parallel, long-term strategic concerns...." and "to stress...how determined we were to respond assertively to the Soviet military buildup and to Soviet proxy expansionism around the world."[147] In his opening statement to the Chinese Foreign Minister, Brzezinski asserted that

> We should cooperate...in the face of a common threat. For one of the central features of our era—a feature which causes us to draw together—is the emergence of the Soviet Union as a global power.[148]

In June 1978, Carter gave a speech at Annapolis. Vance relates that he and Brzezinski contributed drafts, both of which Carter used, making the result "a stitched-together speech."[149] Actually, the main line of argument was Brzezinski's:

> To the Soviet Union, détente seems to mean a continuing aggressive struggle for political advantage.... To other nations throughout the world, the Soviets' military buildup appears to be excessive far beyond any legitimate requirements to defend themselves.... The Soviet Union can choose either confrontation or cooperation. The United States is adequately prepared to meet either choice.[150]

A *Pravda* article reacted to the speech by noting concern in the United States and Europe that "the basically aggressive 'hard line' of Zbigniew Brzezinski...is getting the upper hand in the White House."[151]

Finally, Vance and Brzezinski differed on the question of trade with the Soviet Union. Vance, along with Treasury Secretary Michael Blumenthal and Commerce Secretary Juanita Krebs, supported measures to expand trade. He wanted to get rid of the Jackson-Vanik amendment, grant most-favored-nation status, and increase the limit on Ex-Im Bank credit. Brzezinski wanted to hold back on increased trade as punishment for Soviet action the United States did not like.[152]

Here again Brzezinski gained the upper hand. He learned with "relief" that Carter had decided to deny the export license for a Sperry Univac computer, to reestablish export controls on oil production technology, and to defer decision on a Dresser Industries application to sell the Soviets a drill-bit factory and an electron-beam welder. He writes:

> Cumulatively, these steps meant that our highly permissive attitude toward technology transfer to the Soviet Union was now being reversed.[153]

In Congress, also, the hard liners were speaking up. In August 1978, a new Congressional grouping, the Coalition for Peace through Strength, emerged. The Coalition criticized the administration for shilly-shallying and came out flatly for the United States to achieve military superiority over the Soviet Union. It was, of course, leery of arms control. Among the co-chairmen of the grouping were such prominent Senators as Robert Dole and Paul Laxalt. With such co-chairmen and 148 members, the grouping was a strong force.[154]

Thus, a year and a half after Carter took office, the administration's actions, though marked by vacillation, were falling into a pattern. The United States was beginning a new arms buildup directed against the Soviet Union and had prevailed upon its NATO allies to adopt a program to increase their military budgets. By playing the China card, the United States was working toward a political and military encirclement of the Soviet Union. Increasingly "tough" speeches and statements by Carter and Brzezinski were stirring up anti-Soviet sentiment. Instead of easing restrictions on trade with the Soviet Union, the United States was tightening them. The United States was moving rapidly away from detente.

Vance writes that "at the beginning of 1979, there seemed a chance that the downward slide in U.S.-Soviet relations might be slowed...by the conclusion of a SALT II agreement."[155] He hoped to use the Vienna summit at which SALT II was to be signed to reaffirm detente, to discuss the expansion of trade and economic relations. But Brzezinski thwarted a plan to have Blumenthal and Krebs present at the summit for trade discussions. He wanted Carter to concentrate on the need for "regional restraint"—in effect, to stress the linkage between Soviet actions in the third world and detente.[156]

Carter raised the question of "regional restraint" with Brezhnev. A sharp exchange followed. Brezhnev objected to portraying national struggles for independence or social progress as "Moscow intrigues and plots." Why, he asked, "pin on the Soviet Union the responsibility for the objective course of history and, what is more, use this as a pretext for worsening our relations?"[157]

So the summit and the signing of SALT II didn't halt the U.S. movement away from detente. In fact, even as Carter was signing SALT II, the United States was working on a big military buildup against the Soviet Union. Besides increasing its military budget and pressing for an increase by the other NATO countries, it was working out arrangements for the deployment of Pershing II and cruise missiles in Europe. Both weapons were destabilizing: the Pershing IIs required only six to ten minutes to reach the Soviet Union and the cruise missiles combined great accuracy with being difficult to detect by radar.

The United States was also proceeding with the development of a Rapid Deployment Force. Brzezinski had proposed such a force and Carter had approved it in August 1977. Thereafter, Brzezinski kept pressing the Defense Department for progress. By 1979, he writes, he was "discouraged by the slow reaction" and began to send Secretary Brown requests in the President's name for progress reports.[158]

Senator Byrd, who was managing the campaign for ratification of SALT II by the Senate, felt at first that approval was almost assured. Then a pseudo-crisis abruptly changed the prospects. On August 30, Senator Frank Church, under fire from the right for being "soft" on defense and relations to the Soviet Union, called a press conference to announce that U.S. intelligence had reported the existence of a Soviet combat brigade in Cuba. He called on the President "to draw the line on Russian penetration of this hemisphere."[159] The *New York Times* headline read: "Church Says Soviet Tests U.S. Resolve on Troops in Cuba—Asks Immediate Withdrawal."[160] The news stories swept across the country—in Carter's phrase—"like a fireball."[161]

According to his memoirs, Carter knew that the Church story was phony, noting in his diary: "Chances are they'd had approximately this level of troops for the last 15 or 20 years.... The Soviet troop presence...is obviously not a threat to our country, not a violation of any Soviet commitment...." Nevertheless, he didn't unmask the story, but rather issued a statement saying "we consider the presence of a Soviet combat brigade in Cuba to be a very serious matter and that this status quo is not acceptable."[162]

The hand of Brzezinski appears throughout the episode. It was he who first asked the intelligence agencies to reanalyze the existing information about Soviet military activities in Cuba and to undertake new surveillance. When the crisis broke he sought "to obtain a policy decision which would put primary emphasis on the worldwide thrust of Soviet assertiveness...." He wanted the President to "use the crisis to establish his credentials as a tough-minded, Truman-type leader...."[163]

The intelligence agencies also contributed to the crisis by giving the impression that the Soviet unit had been introduced into Cuba recently. Not only did Carter suspect otherwise, but also Vance who "pressed" for further information. He writes that

> Closer examination of records revealed that earlier American administrations had known of Soviet ground units in Cuba and had not regarded them as worth concentrated intelligence surveillance.... The more resources the intelligence community devoted to the brigade matter, the farther back in time information about it went—eventually all the way to 1962.[164]

After a month, Carter ended the crisis with a television address. He declared that the Soviet unit posed no direct threat. However, he also announced a number of new measures—increased surveillance of Cuba, a promise to help any Western Hemisphere country against any threat from Cuba or Soviet forces there, and the establishment of a permanent Caribbean Task Force. Thus the administration used the crisis to stir up anti-Cuban and anti-Soviet sentiment and as a pretext for increasing the U.S. military presence in the Caribbean.[165]

The crisis not only sidetracked the SALT ratification process for over a month, but changed the political atmosphere, leaving it far more unfavorable to SALT and detente. According to Garthoff, many senior figures in the Carter administration think that this crisis was responsible for the failure to ratify SALT II in 1979.[166]

Two months after the pseudo-crisis, the administration was mounting a full-scale anti-Soviet campaign in the wake of the Soviet military intervention in Afghanistan. Carter asked the Senate to postpone indefinitely consideration of the SALT II treaty. The administration announced a series of sanctions, including a grain embargo, a ban on the sale of advanced technology, a suspension of cultural and scientific exchanges, and a boycott of the 1980 Moscow Olympics. Carter's budget message presented a program for further whopping increases in military expenditures—a five percent increase (in real terms) in 1981, an increase of $90 billion during 1981-1985.

The *New York Times* carried an op-ed piece entitled "George F. Kennan, on Washington's Reaction to the Afghan Crisis: 'Was This Really Mature Statesmanship?'" Kennan wrote:

> A war atmosphere has been created. Discussion in Washington has been dominated by talk of American military responses—of the acquisition of bases and facilities, of the creation of a rapid-deployment force, of the cultivation of military ties with other countries all along Russia's sensitive southern border.... Never since World War II has there been so farreaching a militarization of thought and discourse in the capital.[167]

Was Afghanistan the turning point at which the United States began to move away from detente? Actually, the turning point was much earlier—in 1977 when the United States began to lay plans for a big arms buildup and the encirclement of the Soviet Union, when Brzezinski and then Carter himself began to make their hostile speeches and declarations. By the time of Afghanistan, the movement away from detente had been gathering momentum for more than two years.

The United States didn't scrap detente because of Afghanistan. It reacted the way it did to Afghanistan because it wanted to scrap detente. The leaders of the United States were frustrated by the spreading revolutions—in Angola, Ethiopia, Iran, Nicaragua. They were unhappy with the ever firmer U.S.-Soviet nuclear parity—Kissinger's "strategic nightmare"—which limited their ability to control what took place in the world. They had mulled over the situation and decided on remedial measures: to build a Rapid Deployment Force, create a Caribbean Task Force, start a general arms buildup, move toward a military relationship with China. Detente, they felt, did not provide the right setting for putting through such a program. Putting it through would require an atmosphere of hostility and confrontation. So they used Afghanistan as a pretext to scrap detente.

Along with the military buildup and the scrapping of detente came yet another elaboration of strategic doctrine, presented in the secret Presidential Directive 59. According to Brzezinski, "Till PD-59 was issued, American war planning postulated a brief, spasmic, and apocalyptic conflict.... The new directives were concerned with mobilization, defense, command, and control for a long conflict, and with flexible use of our forces, strategic and general-purpose, on behalf of war aims that we would select as we engaged in conflict." PD 59 thus outlined a strategy for fighting and achieving U.S. war aims in a long nuclear war. The strategy was supposed to strengthen deterrence, not for the purpose of preventing war, but rather to enable the U.S. to impose its will. "The new strategic doctrine would provide the necessary deterrence umbrella for the needed application of American conventional force if some regional interests vital to the United States were threatened."[168]

PD 59 capped the Carter administration's switch from detente to hostility. It reflected what was already clear from the moves to hike the military budget, emplace first-strike weapons in Europe, and close the circle around the Soviet Union in China: The United States was working not to improve its ability to deter a nuclear attack. It already had this ability many times over. It was pressing for nuclear superiority, for the ability to fight and win a prolonged nuclear war.

FOR THE REAGAN administration, Carter's actions against the Soviets were weak and ineffectual — wimpy. It moved immediately to raise hostility to a new plane. Reagan set the tone in his first press conference with a statement that the Soviets "reserve unto themselves the right to commit any crime: to lie, to cheat...."[169] Later, he called for "a crusade for freedom" and asserted that the Soviet Union was "the focus of evil in the modern world...an evil empire."[170] Reagan was not just giving vent to his personal feelings with this inflammatory rhetoric. He was working to create a favorable atmosphere for the military buildup he was pushing through.

The buildup was, for peacetime, unprecedented. The 1980 Republican party platform had called for a strategy that would "achieve overall military and technological superiority over the Soviet Union." Now, on top of the enormous increase in military spending proposed by Carter, Reagan added a further big increase, to form a program that called for the expenditure of $1.6 trillion over five years.

To justify his program, Reagan talked at first of U.S. military inferiority, of a "window of vulnerability" to nuclear attack. But such talk, like talk in past years about missile gaps that never existed, soon ended. Several months after Reagan took office,

Defense Secretary Caspar Weinberger presented him with a plan to expand U.S. strategic nuclear forces. The *New York Times* reported that according to senior administration officials, the proposed plan "was intended to enable the United States to regain nuclear superiority over the Soviet Union within this decade."[171]

Then, as though MX missiles, Trident missiles, cruise missiles, B-1 bombers, and Stealth bombers would not be enough, Reagan in 1983 proposed an all-out project to develop a comprehensive, space-based ABM system. Asserting that his purpose was to create a shield that would free Americans from the threat of nuclear destruction and that, moreover, the United States would share the technology with the Soviets, Reagan called the new project the "Strategic Defense Initiative (SDI)." Almost everyone outside the administration labelled it "Star Wars."

Many scientists immediately questioned the feasibility of a leak-proof defense system. Even scientists working on SDI admitted after a while that an adequate defense against a full-scale nuclear attack was not possible. Why, then, did the administration persist in pursuing the project? The only possible answer is that it felt that Star Wars might be useful in attaining a first-strike capability and thus nuclear superiority. By itself the shield would not work; but if a first strike eliminated a high percentage of the Soviet strategic weapons, the new system might be able to hold the damage from a retaliatory strike with the remaining weapons to an "acceptable level."

Again a modification in strategy accompanied the arms buildup. On May 30, 1982, the *New York Times* ran a story describing a new Defense Guidance Plan signed by Weinberger. This document not only presented a strategy for fighting a "protracted" nuclear war, but asserted that U.S. nuclear forces "must prevail and be able to force the Soviet Union to seek earliest termination of hostilities on terms favorable to the United States." A main point in the document, said the *Times*, was that "nuclear war strategy would be based on what is known as decapitation, meaning strikes at Soviet political and military leadership and communications lines."

Also accompanying the buildup was a refusal to negotiate. In his first visit to Secretary of State Haig, Soviet Ambassador Anatoly Dobrynin brought a letter from Foreign Minister Andrei Gromyko expressing a desire for a wide-ranging exchange of views. A few days later, Dobrynin again pressed for talks, in particular on arms control. Haig gives his position in his memoirs: "At this early stage, there was nothing substantive to talk about, nothing to negotiate, until the U.S.S.R. began to demonstrate its willingness to behave like a responsible power."[172]

The effect of the Reagan policies was to push U.S.-Soviet relations to a low not seen since the Cuban missile crisis. How could the Soviets view these policies other than with deep suspicion and concern? What could they possibly think about the almost openly declared drive to regain nuclear superiority? Clearly, the United States wanted to gain a position from which it could coerce the Soviet Union—the strategy outlined in NSC 68 (1950) during the heyday of U.S. nuclear superiority. But could the Reagan administration be harboring an even more far-reaching objective—the destruction of socialism?

The Reagan policy succeeded in raising tension and whipping up the arms race, but it could not achieve its goals. It could only lead to a suicidal nuclear war or a dead end. Even thirty years earlier, when the United States enjoyed overwhelming nuclear superiority, it did not obtain what it hoped for from its nuclear policy. Now the realities were far more loaded against a policy based on nuclear weapons. Nuclear parity, a strong peace movement both in Europe and in the United States, allies who were more independent and favored detente, and the destructive effects of the military budget on the economy—these were the realities that were bound sooner or later to bring the policy down.

NUCLEAR PARITY IS STABLE. In 1980 Paul Warnke, former Director of the Arms Control and Disarmament Agency, commented on candidate Reagan's policy of striving for superiority:

> Neither the United States nor the Soviet Union can achieve military superiority unless the other side is willing to default in the competition.... The illusion that more money can buy us military superiority is simply that—an illusion.[173]

To pursue Star Wars in the hope of attaining a first-strike capability and superiority was to chase a will-o'-the-wisp. Former Defense Secretary Harold Brown, a physicist, wrote about the prospects for Star Wars:

> For defense of populations against a responsive threat, they look poor through the year 2010 and beyond.... The prognosis for the longer term...still looks questionable.[174]

A growing peace movement already existed before Reagan. Reagan administration talk of a "limited" nuclear war, a "protracted" nuclear war, and "prevailing" in a nuclear war caused the movement to mushroom. With the impending introduction of Pershing IIs and cruise missiles in Europe, massive demonstrations took place in West Germany, Britain, Holland, Belgium, and Italy. A peace rally in New York's Central Park in 1982 drew nearly a million people. A movement for a nuclear freeze began to spread. The administration became worried. The *Washington Post* reported on a memorandum by Eugene Rostow, head of the Arms Control and Disarmament Agency, to National Security Advisor William Clark in which he warned that "the nuclear war issue was infecting the public." Said the memo:

> While this movement includes such perennial elements as the old-line pacifists, the environmentalists, the disaffected left and various communist elements, there is participation on an increasing scale...of three groups whose potential impact should be cause for concern. They are the churches, the "loyal opposition," and, perhaps most important, the unpoliticized public.[175]

Having their own distinct interests and under pressure from their people, the governments of Western Europe showed no inclination to follow the Reagan administration in an anti-Soviet crusade. They refused to go along when, in response to martial law in Poland, the United States banned the sale of equipment for a Siberia-Western Europe gas pipeline. They pressured the United States to get on with arms control negotiations. Even if the United States had abandoned detente, its European allies were continuing it, and by so doing creating problems for the Reagan administration.

By fiscal year 1983, the federal budget deficit was running at the astronomical level of over $200 billion a year, in good part because of the soaring military budget. Reagan might gamble with the economy, but others—the chairman of the Federal Reserve Board, members of Congress, the allies—began to press him to bring the budget under control, and he had to recognize that his military program had its limits.

Different people within the ruling class began to express disagreement with Reagan's Soviet policy. The magazine *Foreign Affairs*, organ of the foreign policy establishment, carried, along with a few articles by exponents of the Reagan policy, article after article voicing criticism.

Seweryn Bialer wrote that "those American politicians and analysts who promote regained military superiority over the Soviet Union cannot hope to see their goal realized."[176]

Strobe Talbott wrote of "the need for a certain degree of civility in the overall relationship between the two superpowers if their diplomats were to have any chance of engaging each other usefully."[177]

John Gaddis wrote that "the Reagan administration has allowed support for containment to erode both at home and abroad by taking too casual an attitude toward the dangers of nuclear war."[178]

The pressure from all sides forced the administration to enter into arms control negotiations. Several key members wanted to resist the pressure. Weinberger, on a trip to Europe in April 1981, stressed the administration view—rearmament now, disarmament later, if ever. Richard Perle, travelling with him, said repeatedly that the United States should not enter into negotiations until it was "ready," regardless of the demands of the West Europeans. But Chancellor Helmut Schmidt of West Germany sent word to Washington that he needed a starting date for negotiations or he could not keep his government to the deployment schedule for Pershing IIs. Italy also made clear that it needed a signal of U.S. willingness to enter into talks with the Soviets. In November 1981, talks began on intermediate-range nuclear missile forces (INF).[179]

Similarly with the strategic arms negotiations. The administration had told the Senate that it would be ready for such negotiations in March 1982, but when March came it wasn't ready. Strobe Talbott describes the situation:

> Congress was getting impatient.... A wide variety of religious and academic leaders were questioning the wisdom of the Administration's policies.... There was rising sentiment in favor of a negotiated agreement with the Soviet Union to stop all further testing, production, and deployment of nuclear weapons. The White House's contacts in Congress warned that a number of liberal senators were considering resolutions in favor of such a freeze.[180]

At midyear, strategic arms reduction talks (START) began.

But the talks made little progress and relations continued to deteriorate through 1983. As Reagan's first term neared its final year, however, the realities again began to make themselves felt. The administration was discovering that, no matter how much money it spent, it could not achieve nuclear superiority as quickly as it had hoped. European criticism of the administration was growing sharper, with many in the European establishment charging that Reagan's rhetoric and arms policies were pushing NATO toward a crisis. In the United States, sentiment for arms control and an improvement in U.S.-Soviet relations was strong and growing, and a presidential election was approaching.

David Watt, Director of the Royal Institute of International Affairs in London, expressed some of the European criticism in an article in *Foreign Affairs*:

> It is in my experience almost impossible to convey even to the most experienced Americans just how deeply rooted and widely spread the critical view has become.... A devastating but entirely reputable opinion poll taken in January [1983]...showed that no less than 70 percent of the British people lacked any confidence in the judgment of the American Administration.... Leadership...entails carrying your followers with you or ultimately losing their cooperation.[181]

In another *Foreign Affairs* article, Daniel Yankelovich and John Doble presented findings from a national study of public attitudes toward nuclear arms, based on surveys conducted over several years by leading polling organizations. Among the findings:

> By an overwhelming 96 percent to 3 percent, Americans assert that "picking a fight with the Soviet Union is too dangerous in a nuclear world...." By 89 to 9 percent, Americans subscribe to the view that "there can be no winner in an all-out nuclear war...." There can be no such thing as a limited nuclear war (83 percent).... The United States no longer has nuclear superiority (84 percent), and... we can never hope to regain it....
>
> Americans are convinced that it is time for negotiations, not confrontations, with the Soviets.... The American electorate wants to reverse the present trend toward relying ever more heavily on nuclear weapons.... The public finds the long-term risks of continuing the way we are going to be simply unacceptable.[182]

Reagan's own pollsters told him that the only issue on which he was vulnerable was "peace."[183] By late 1983, according to *Time* reporter Strobe Talbott, he decided he wanted a summit

with the Soviets, but "almost solely because his political ins-
tincts and his political advisers told him that he needed one in
order to command the high ground in the presidential election
campaign."[184]

On January 16, 1984, Reagan gave a speech in which he
changed his rhetoric:

> Nuclear arsenals are far too high, and our working relationship
> with the Soviet Union is not what it must be.... We must and will
> engage the Soviets in a dialogue as serious and constructive as
> possible.... Neither we nor the Soviet Union can wish away the
> differences between our two societies and our philosophies, but
> we should always remember that we do have common interests.
> And the foremost among them is to avoid war and reduce the level
> of arms.[185]

In the following months, Reagan devoted several other
speeches to the theme of strength and dialogue. Many commentators noted that the President was trying, in an election
year, to present himself as a man of peace. The administration's
actions were contradictory and confusing: a week after the January 16 speech, Reagan sent a report to Congress accusing the
Soviet Union of seven violations of arms control agreements.

Yet dialogue with the Soviets did resume in 1984. Early in the
year, George Shultz, who had replaced Haig as Secretary of
State, had a talk with Gromyko at an international conference in
Stockholm. In September, Gromyko visited Washington and
met with the President, Reagan's first meeting with a ranking
Soviet official. Two weeks after the election, the United States
and the Soviet Union announced a new round of arms negotiations, from which the Soviet Union had withdrawn in 1983 on
the ground that the United States was not negotiating seriously.

Henry Grunwald, editor of *Time*, wrote in an article in the
Winter 1984/85 issue of *Foreign Affairs*:

> The fact is that the Reagan Administration is being pushed toward
> something that, by any other name, is still detente.[186]

Grunwald approved the shift toward detente which, he wrote,
"remains the inescapable intellectual framework for American
policy." He laid out a strategy for Reagan's second term.

> Politically, Britain, Holland and West Germany harbor strong, more
> or less neutralist-pacifist forces which want to opt out of the East-
> West conflict.... A top priority must be to undercut and contain

[these] potentially disastrous left-wing neutralist movements. This is best done through a stable, realistic policy toward the Soviets, including arms control.[187]

As he entered his second term, Reagan was already shifting strategy in the direction Grunwald indicated. He was no longer speaking of an "evil empire" and an anti-Soviet "crusade," but instead echoing the peace themes of his election campaign. The arms negotiation process had gotten under way with a Shultz-Gromyko meeting in Geneva. Reagan and Shultz were hoping that the arms negotiations would lead to a summit. In July, the United States announced that Reagan and Mikhail Gorbachev would meet in Geneva in November.

Reagan's policy toward the Soviet Union had unquestionably changed, but what were the changes? Aside from the switch in rhetoric, the sharpest change was in the attitude toward negotiations. The administration was learning that a policy of no negotiations is just not feasible in the nuclear age. Shultz, who was gaining influence, favored negotiations. He expressed himself in an article in *Foreign Affairs*, just as the arms talks were getting under way in the spring of 1985:

> In the thermonuclear age both sides have a common interest in survival; therefore both sides have an incentive to moderate the rivalry and to seek ways to control nuclear weapons and reduce the risks of war.... We must learn to pursue a strategy...based on both negotiation and strength simultaneously....[188]

How far had the administration changed its policy on achieving nuclear superiority? Grunwald wrote that "Reagan seems to have disavowed the possibility that America can permanently restore any significant nuclear superiority...."[189] Actually, what the administration had done was conclude that achieving superiority over the short run and by the older strategy of simply developing better offensive weapons like the MX and Trident II was not feasible. So it changed timing and strategy. Obtaining superiority became a longer run goal. The key to obtaining it became not just offensive weapons, but Star Wars.

Thus, in the months leading up to the Geneva summit in November, the administration was wavering, groping for a new policy while stubbornly clinging to elements of the old. Within the administration, a struggle over policy was taking place. In these circumstances, the Soviet Union in August 1985 took the first of several steps that would help increase the worldwide pressure on the administration to move toward arms control. It announced a unilateral moratorium on nuclear testing and called on the United States to follow its example.

At Geneva, Reagan and Gorbachev declared jointly that a nuclear war could not be won and must never be fought. They agreed that there would be further summits and they discussed a Soviet proposal for a 50 percent reduction in strategic nuclear weapons.

The summit made clear that the key obstacle to progress in the reduction of strategic nuclear arms was Star Wars. Put in another way, the obstacle was the administration's clinging to the goal of regaining nuclear superiority via Star Wars. The Soviet proposal for a 50 percent reduction was conditioned on banning the testing and deployment of space-based weapons. But Reagan adamantly refused to give up his SDI program. Several leading U.S. experts in arms control criticized the administration for its stubbornness.

A few weeks after Geneva, Gorbachev proposed a program for the elimination of all nuclear weapons by the year 2000, thereby helping to increase the pressure on the Reagan administration to act on arms control. Reagan said he welcomed the proposal and would study it carefully. Nevertheless, three months later, he announced that the United States would no longer abide by the SALT II treaty.

It was pressure on Reagan that brought him to a second summit at Reykjavik. Michael Mandelbaum and Strobe Talbott write:

> By June 1986, Administration national-security policies in general and SDI in particular were in trouble on the home front.... Many in Congress sought to hold funding for SDI hostage to the restoration of a promising arms-control process. It was increasingly apparent that Reagan would pay a political price if there were no return engagement with Gorbachev.[190]

Reykjavik broke up without any completed arms agreement and many U.S. commentators concluded that it was simply a failure. But this judgment ignores the progress made in the discussions — the narrowing of differences on two key proposals: to reduce long-range nuclear missiles by 50 percent and to remove medium-range nuclear missiles from Europe. Again the obstacle to agreement was Star Wars.

Meanwhile, the United States was following through on its announcement about no longer being bound by SALT II. It began to equip strategic bombers with cruise missiles in excess of treaty limits. And to get rid of an obstacle to SDI, it moved toward a "broad" interpretation of the ABM treaty, one that would, in effect, nullify it.

But, as before, there was pressure on Reagan to change his policies. No sooner had he announced his decision to abandon SALT II than the NATO foreign ministers, meeting in Canada, were criticizing his action. Soon after the Government exceeded the treaty limits, 57 Senators, including 10 Republicans, sent him a letter urging a return to compliance. Criticism of SDI and the attempt to reinterpret the ABM treaty came from many sides. The Iran-Contra scandal added to the pressure. Many Reagan advisors, including his wife Nancy, felt an arms agreement would recoup his lost political standing—and enhance his place in history.

Despite the pressure on Reagan, the arms negotiations were bogged down till the Soviets acted. In February 1987, they announced that they were willing to sign a separate agreement to eliminate Soviet and U.S. medium-range nuclear missiles from Europe, removing the Reykjavik condition that the agreement must be part of a package that included an accord on Star Wars. A *New York Times* editorial explained:

> It was the Reagan Administration that, in 1981, first formally proposed zero-zero, the idea of scrapping both sides' medium-range missiles in Europe, perhaps in the belief the Russians would never accept. The plan required the Soviet Union to give up 1,300 warheads, the United States only 300.
>
> Six years later Mr. Gorbachev has accepted not only that, but has agreed to give up 130 shorter-range missiles in Europe....[191]

From all sides came voices urging an improvement in U.S.-Soviet relations. A *New York Times* editorial said:

> After 40 years of cold war, the United States now has a basis for thinking anew about policy toward the Soviet Union....
>
> President Reagan can leave no greater legacy than to take account of the new realities in East-West relations....
>
> American resources are stretched, and beyond doubt, the Pentagon budget will be cut. The nation's educational system, the needs of the young and the old, cry out for funds. Economic deficits must be closed....
>
> It will take strong leadership to disenthrall both sides of the fear and mistrust that have grown up over the years. Yet the chances of

succeeding, and freeing hopes and energies toward more promising goals, are better now than ever.[192]

New York Governor Mario Cuomo, in a speech at a conference of Soviet and U.S. citizens in Chautauqua, N.Y., called for a "new realism" in U.S. foreign policy and said that it was time to end the cold war.[193]

The Reagan administration found itself with little choice except to enter into an arms agreement. To have rejected an agreement based on the zero option it had itself proposed would have left the United States in an impossible propaganda position. Reagan needed an agreement and a summit: they offered the only hope of lifting his presidency from the drift and despondency into which the Iran-Contra scandal had thrown it.

At the Washington summit in December, Reagan and Gorbachev signed the INF (intermediate-range nuclear forces) treaty, which didn't just set ceilings on weapons or provide for percentage reductions, but for the first time abolished two whole classes of missiles—intermediate- and short-range. The two leaders made "considerable progress"—said the U.S.-Soviet Joint Statement—toward a treaty on 50 percent cuts in long-range nuclear missiles, "expressed their commitment" to the negotiation of an agreement to abolish chemical weapons, and discussed the problem of reducing conventional weapons.[194]

Aside from progress in arms control, the Washington summit had great political significance. That this was the third summit in three years, with another scheduled for 1988, showed that the United States and the Soviet Union were engaged in a running dialogue. Along with the all-important arms question, the two sides were discussing other issues such as regional conflicts and human rights. Gorbachev said after the meeting that the discussions were "more constructive than earlier."[195] Reagan said that "we have put Soviet-American relations on a far more candid and far more realistic footing."[196] He also talked about a "new" Soviet Union whose leaders no longer feel "an obligation... to expand in the whole world."[197] He was setting a new tone, adapted to dialogue rather than confrontation.

As was to be expected, the Right exploded in fury. Howard Phillips, chairman of the Conservative Caucus, called Reagan "a useful idiot for Soviet propaganda." Eugene Rostow referred to the treaty as "a new Munich."[198] Reagan lashed back:

I think that some of the people who are objecting the most and just refusing even to accede to the idea of ever getting any understanding, whether they realize it or not, those people—basically down in their deepest thoughts—have accepted that war is inevitable and that there must come to be a war between the two superpowers.[199]

AS THE BUSH ADMINISTRATION was taking over, the U.S. foreign policy establishment was weighing the policy to be followed toward the Soviet Union. Nixon contributed his view through an article in *Foreign Affairs*. There was nothing in the article about getting rid of the nuclear menace. Instead, it devoted itself to analyzing how to use the Soviet Union's "economic failure" and other difficulties to make it conform to U.S. wishes.

Nixon's position on arms control was the one he had always held.

Arms control should be treated as only one part of Western defense policy and not vice versa. Arms negotiations are a political imperative, indispensable in holding the NATO alliance together and for winning support in Congress for adequate defense budgets.[200]

Gorbachev, says Nixon, "must be made to understand that Nicaragua is a neuralgic issue for us."[201]

Subsequent issues of *Foreign Affairs* carried articles by others taking basically the same line as Nixon. One by Kissinger, Valéry Giscard d'Estaing, former president of France, and Yasuhiro Nakasone, former prime minister of Japan, argues that with a "crisis" in the Soviet Union "our countries have a rare opportunity to change the nature of East-West relations in ways beneficial to the West...."[202]

In May, after his administration had completed its own review of U.S.-Soviet relations, President Bush stated that "our policy is to seize every, and I mean every, opportunity to build a better, more stable relationship with the Soviet Union....We have a precious opportunity to move beyond containment."

But he continued the old line on nuclear strategy.

In today's world, nuclear forces are essential to deterrence. Our challenge is to protect those deterrent systems from attack. And that's why we'll move Peacekeeper ICBM's out of fixed and vulnerable silos—making them mobile and thus harder to target.

Looking to the longer-term, we will also develop and deploy a new highly mobile single-warhead missile, the Midgetman.... We are also researching—and we are committed to deploy when ready—a more comprehensive defensive system, known as SDI.[203]

Six months later, in a Thanksgiving message, Bush stated that "America wants the Soviets to join us in moving beyond containment to a new partnership." But he also referred to Nicaragua and Cuba "holding out against their people only because of the massive support of weapons and supplies from their communist allies."[204]

Then came the Malta summit in early December. The *New York Times* reported what Bush and Gorbachev said after the conference. Bush said that "We stand at the threshold of a brand-new era in U.S.-Soviet relations." Gorbachev said that he and Bush agreed that "the characteristics of the cold war should be abandoned."[205]

But in a press conference, Bush answered a question about whether he had talked to Gorbachev about the "Soviet role in Cuba and Central America [being] the primary obstacle to a more beneficial fullscale relationship between the two countries." Bush answered that he had, "so there is no doubt in their minds that their assistance to Cuba and their lip service for the Sandinistas give us a considerable amount of difference with them."[206]

A few weeks later, Secretary of State James A. Baker testified before the International Affairs Committee of the Soviet Parliament. The Soviet deputies questioned him about the United States intervention in Panama. Baker "responded," according to the *New York Times*, "with a point-by-point defense of the Panama invasion." One deputy asked: "Is the United States ready to undertake a public promise not to use force in Latin America, provided, of course, that events there do not threaten you?" In response, Baker talked about a Soviet commitment "to cease your support for Nicaragua and Cuba."

Soviet Marshal Sergei F. Akhromeyev said to Baker:

Mr. Secretary, the Soviet Union has been reducing its armed forces for the last two years by 500,000 men and its military budget by 14 percent. The United States has barely reduced its armed forces and is only slightly reducing its military budget. I have the impression that while improving relations with us in the military sphere you continue to insist on acting in respect to the Soviet Union from a position of strength.

Baker, says the *Times*, "nodded, unabashed."

I think that relations between the Soviet Union and the United States are improving because the peace has been maintained through strength, Marshal. I think it is important in maintaining the peace that people know you will maintain your resolve.[207]

Although the world was entering a new era, the United States was still clinging to the "position of strength" policy it had followed throughout the cold war.

Conclusion

The story we have told shows the strength of the U.S. drive toward counterrevolutionary intervention. This drive cannot be ascribed to a particular president or policy. It has manifested itself under many different presidents, through many different policies, in many different times, and toward many different countries.

The United States intervened militarily, along with other countries, against the Russian Revolution and afterward maintained hostility for years. Only during the Roosevelt administration did the hostility soften, and then only partially. Even during World War II, it remained latent, not far below the surface. No sooner had the need for the Soviet ally passed than the hostility emerged again, to continue in a virulent and dangerous form for decades.

To block the progress of the 1911 revolution in China, the United States helped install the "strong man" Yuan Shikai as prime minister. After World War II, it did all it could to prevent the Chinese Communist Revolution from succeeding, and was kept from doing more only by the costs and dangers of trying to do too much in such a huge country. Here, too, U.S. hostility to the revolutionary regime was extreme and lasted for decades.

The United States has played a counterrevolutionary role throughout modern Cuban history, beginning with its actions during the war against Spain. In 1933, it arranged for the overthrow of the revolutionary government of Grau San Martín and the installation in power of the dictator Batista. When revolution finally triumphed in 1959, Washington almost immediately began preparations to destroy it. Soon the United States mounted an economic embargo, a campaign to isolate Cuba internationally, attempts to assassinate the revolution's leaders, a mercenary invasion, and a CIA campaign of harassment and sabotage in preparation for a possible invasion with U.S. forces. Although the United States has from time to time gone along with limited improvements in relations, the economic embargo and the implacable underlying hostility it expresses have come down to the present day.

At great cost and anguish to its own people and infinitely greater cost and anguish to the Vietnamese, the United States carried out its long war against the revolution in Vietnam. For years after the war was clearly lost, Nixon and Kissinger refused to accept reality and kept adding to the agony. U.S. hostility continued for years after the end of the war.

In Nicaragua, as in Cuba, U.S. counterrevolution has been an overwhelming presence throughout this century. From 1909 till 1933, with minor interruptions, the United States kept Marines in Nicaragua, where they helped puppet governments maintain themselves in power against one uprising after another. For seven years beginning in 1927, the Marines fought to put down a guerrilla war led by Sandino. From 1933 to 1979, the Somoza family ruled Nicaragua, backed by a National Guard conceived, financed, trained, and equipped by the United States. After the Sandinista revolution overthrew the Somozas, the Reagan administration mounted a contra war and a trade embargo which, in the name of democracy and freedom, inflicted death and hunger on the Nicaraguan people.

In Africa, the United States has been promoting counterrevolution on an international scale. It began in the early 1960s by getting rid of Lumumba and his anti-imperialist government in the Congo, eventually replacing him with the pro-U.S. dictator, Mobutu. Then, using the Congo, now Zaire, as a base, and in partnership with South Africa, it worked against the revolution in Angola both before and after it came to power. It went along with Pretoria's stalling on independence for Namibia and has helped preserve the apartheid regime in South Africa itself by shielding it against the imposition of effective international sanctions.

Such a powerful drive toward counterrevolutionary intervention is not the result of accidental circumstances. Its origins lie in the nature of the imperialist system. The imperialists won't suddenly develop a sense of justice that will make it disappear.

SINCE WORLD WAR II, the ultimate backing for the counterrevolutionary actions of the United States has been its nuclear arsenal. U.S. postwar history shows the strong attachment of the imperialists to nuclear weapons.

The United States was not only the first to build the atomic and hydrogen bombs, but also the first to develop almost every leading nuclear weapons system since then. Granted that the nuclear arms race developed a dynamic of its own in which the Soviet Union, too, played a role, the leading force both in starting and keeping up the race has been the United States.

From the beginning, the United States has been unwilling to renounce the use of nuclear weapons. Before the first such weapon was used, a panel of leading scientists urged that rather than drop an atomic bomb on Japan, the United States should first demonstrate it in a desert or on a barren island. But as one of the scientists put it, "We were surrounded by a kind of sound-proof wall...."[1] Truman later wrote: "I regarded the bomb as a military weapon and never had any doubt that it should be used."[2]

Truman's philosophy about possible international control of the bomb was simple: "I am of the opinion we'll never obtain international control. Since we can't obtain international control we must be strongest in atomic weapons."[3] In 1950, he made the decision to go ahead with the development of the hydrogen bomb with as little hesitation as he had shown in the earlier decision to drop the bomb on Japan.

Eisenhower relied greatly on nuclear weapons in his diplomacy and stated at one press conference:

> Now, in any combat where these things can be used on strictly military targets and for strictly military purposes, I see no reason why they shouldn't be used just exactly as you would use a bullet or anything else.[4]

Even after the threat of nuclear war to the very existence of civilization became clear, the United States did not move toward renouncing the use of nuclear weapons and trying to rid the world of them. Instead, it began to develop military doctrines (like that of "limited" nuclear war) and weapons (like small, tactical nuclear bombs and "clean" bombs) through which it could continue to rely on nuclear weapons despite the threat they posed. It relied on nuclear weapons because they provided what it saw as military superiority over the Soviets.

Nixon and Kissinger did not enter into the arms control agreements of the early 1970s because they wanted disarmament. They entered because they saw political and budgetary gains as well as military advantages — eliminating or reducing Soviet systems that were especially threatening. They were not trying to end the arms race, just control it to their advantage. They hoped, by continuing the arms race, to regain the nuclear superiority the United States had lost.

Even at the end of the 1980s, when the arms control process had progressed much further and the Soviets had proposed eliminating nuclear weapons by the year 2000, the United States was unwilling to renounce the first use of these weapons and to join with the Soviet Union in getting rid of them. Leading U.S. figures such as Kissinger asserted that the Soviet proposal is utopian: nuclear weapons cannot be eliminated. That there are problems in the elimination of nuclear weapons is only a pretext for this attitude. The real reason is that the United States has not given up the idea of somehow regaining nuclear superiority.

The United States does not need nuclear superiority to defend itself militarily. It wants nuclear superiority to back up its political strategies and actions — strategies and actions directed mainly toward counterrevolution.

OUR STUDY ALSO SHOWS that while the U.S. drive to counterrevolution and attachment to nuclear weapons are both strong, counterforces exist which restrict and weaken them.

Counterforces immediately developed when the United States and other imperialist countries intervened against the Russian Revolution. The United States and its partners wanted to strangle the revolution. Had they been free to introduce armed forces as large as they wished, they might have succeeded. But they were not free. They were afraid of the spread of revolutionary sentiment and mutiny among their soldiers and they were under pressure from their peoples to bring the troops home. The revolution survived because of its own strength, but also because of the limitations on the freedom of action of the imperialist invaders.

The counterforces were especially significant in the Vietnam War. In a narrow military sense, Vietnam could not have defeated the United States. Had the war been a just one supported by the people of the United States, had the U.S. government been free to bring in the forces necessary, Vietnam could not have won. But with casualties mounting in an unjust war and stormy opposition developing among the people, the U.S. government was not free. Once more an intervention failed because of the strength of the revolution it was opposing, but also because of popular opposition at home.

The significance of the opposition to the Vietnam War extends far beyond the war itself. The war left as heritage the Vietnam Syndrome—a widespread opposition among the people of the United States to other such adventures in the future. This syndrome was part of a broader decline in the authority of government that stemmed not only from the war, but also from Watergate and from revelations about the government's international dirty work—CIA attempts to assassinate foreign leaders and the U.S. role in overthrowing the Allende government in Chile.

The Vietnam Syndrome has exercised an important restraining influence on the government. Kissinger fumed when Cuban troops turned back the South Africans in Angola and the MPLA came to power. But he was powerless to reverse the course of events: not only couldn't he consider using U.S. troops, but Congress through the Clark Amendment cut short even his covert intervention in Angola. Reagan wanted dearly to overthrow the Sandinista government, but even he was cautious about sending in U.S. troops.

BUT THE U.S. GOVERNMENT has pushed to recover its freedom to intervene directly, while at the same time developing alternative methods for achieving its goals.

It applied its rapid deployment techniques in invasions of Grenada in 1983 and Panama in 1989. It worked out methods for manipulating the media during an intervention to keep from the people whatever it doesn't want them to know. The government satisfied itself that direct intervention is feasible, at least when certain conditions are met—proper political preparation and an operation that involves minimal U.S. casualties and can be gotten over with quickly enough to prevent a significant domestic political opposition from forming. It used the "success" of the operations to evoke chauvinistic sentiments and whittle away at the Vietnam Syndrome.

Even with the Vietnam Syndrome, there can be no certainty that the United States will not invade larger countries with conditions less favorable than in little Panama and tiny Grenada. Situations can arise in which other factors outweigh the government's fear of the syndrome. We have no guarantee that the United States would not intervene with U.S. troops to block a revolution in a country it considers of great importance — for example, the Philippines. Moreover, no one knows how long the Vietnam Syndrome will last.

The U.S. government maintains large forces designed for intervention in the third world and makes no bones about why it needs these forces. In mid-March 1990, Army Chief of Staff Carl E. Vuono and Marine Corps Commandant Alfred M. Gray each claimed before a Congressional committee that his service was the primary force for U.S. military operations in the third world. General Vuono, according to the *New York Times*, read from a "statement that advertised the fighting capabilities of the Army's 82d Airborne Division and the need for the service's 'civil affairs' units that can help third world countries rebuild after an American military intervention." General Gray defended a maritime strategy: "'Migration patterns will continue to shift populations away from the heartlands to the coasts,' adding to the demand in those areas for food and housing and making them 'breeding grounds for discontent.'" Thus most of the potential battlefields in the third world would be within reach of the ocean-borne Marine Corps.[5]

As an alternative to direct intervention, the United States has developed a doctrine of "low intensity conflict" designed to avoid or minimize reliance on U.S. troops by the use of surrogate forces and economic and political warfare. It has carried out "low intensity" warfare against several countries, relying on the contras in Nicaragua and Savimbi's UNITA in Angola. Under U.S. shelter, South Africa has used Renamo for low intensity warfare against Mozambique.

Nicaragua shows how devastating so-called low intensity warfare can be to the people of the targeted country, and how effective. Less well known in the United States is the misery it has sown in Angola and Mozambique and how it has worked to prevent the revolutions in these countries from consolidating themselves and showing what they can really do.

From the imperialist point of view, the devilishly well-thought-out technique of low intensity warfare has many advantages. It is cheap, practically supportable from the government's petty cash. Since it does not involve U.S. casualties, it does not bring forth the public opposition that a direct intervention would. And its effects can be blamed on the victims, the revolutionary governments, by accusing them of running their countries into the ground through incompetence.

The United States has been using low intensity warfare not only to weaken and destabilize the targeted countries but to try to create a general world climate which discourages third world countries from making revolutions and moving in a leftward direction.

THE COUNTERFORCES that restrict what the United States can do with its nuclear arsenal developed at their own tempo. Initially, there were almost none and the Truman administration's freedom of action was virtually complete.

But the acquisition of a significant number of atomic weapons by the Soviet Union caused Truman to talk differently about the bomb at the end of his administration than he had at the outset. In his last state of the union message in 1952, he declared:

> The war of the future would be one in which man could extinguish millions of lives at one blow, demolish the great cities of the world, wipe out the cultural achievements of the past....
> Such a war is not a possible policy for rational men.[6]

Although the change was largely one of rhetoric, it was significant. It marked the early stages of a process by which the U.S. government would be forced to recognize some of the realities about nuclear weapons.

As Eisenhower saw the Soviet Union increase its stock of atomic bombs, explode a hydrogen bomb, and develop an intercontinental bomber, he became far more troubled by the thought of nuclear war than Truman had been. More than once, not just in formal speeches prepared by speechwriters, but in his own personal comments, he expressed the view that "global war is getting well nigh unthinkable." James Reston of the *New York Times* wrote in late 1954 that "perhaps the most important single fact in world politics today is that Mr. Eisenhower has thrown the immense authority of the American Presidency against risking a military solution of the cold war."[7]

The government had advanced further in its recognition of nuclear realities. It would still be practicing nuclear diplomacy, still be getting into crises which involved a threat of nuclear war. But the new vulnerability of the United States made its policy-makers exercise increased caution and restraint. Those who were clamoring for preventive war against the Soviet Union lost their influence and their clamor died down. The original Eisenhower-Dulles strategy of massive retaliation lost credibility.

World public opinion also became an ever stronger factor in the situation. The peoples of the world were becoming increasingly worried about the danger of nuclear war. In May 1953, Churchill had issued a call for a summit meeting between the Soviet Union and the Western powers. U.S. resistance to this call was provoking increasing protests. The reason Eisenhower gives for finally agreeing to a meeting is significant: he did not wish to appear "senselessly stubborn."[8]

Besides helping to bring about a summit, world public opinion also began to press for a ban on nuclear testing. In 1954, a large U.S. nuclear explosion at Bikini showered 23 Japanese fishermen with radioactive fallout. Prime Minister Jawaharlal Nehru of India called for an end to testing. The initial reaction of the U.S. government was that the danger from fallout was minimal. But a big public debate developed. Eisenhower at first stood strongly against the suspension of tests, but as the public pressure grew, his position shifted. In 1958, the United States and the Soviet Union entered into negotiations for a test ban treaty—the first real negotiations between the two countries on the nuclear threat.[9]

Thus Eisenhower's position on nuclear weapons was contradictory. He arrived at the view that nuclear war was unthinkable, yet he did not consider—even remotely—giving these weapons up. They seemed to offer too many advantages both militarily and in diplomacy.

Kennedy's position similarly had its contradictions, as illustrated in the Cuban missile crisis. He was willing to provoke the most dangerous crisis of the nuclear age. Yet having provoked it, he was careful to avoid the outbreak of nuclear war. Of the options his advisers presented, he chose a blockade as the one least likely to escalate into nuclear conflict.

The missile crisis brought a crucial shift in Kennedy's thinking about nuclear war. His assistant Sorensen relates that

After the first Cuban crisis [the Bay of Pigs] he had stressed to the nation's editors that "our restraint is not inexhaustible." After the second Cuban crisis, questioned by the same audience about that statement, he replied: "I hope our restraint—or sense of responsibility—will not ever come to an end."[10]

Kennedy felt that "You can't have too many of those [crises]. One major mistake either by Mr. Khrushchev or by us...can make this whole thing blow up."[11] He began to talk about ending the cold war and he approved a test ban treaty.

But like Eisenhower before him, Kennedy didn't carry his thoughts on the nuclear danger to their logical conclusion: he didn't propose to give up reliance on nuclear weapons, to renounce their possible use. He was thinking about arms control, but only in a way that would preserve U.S. nuclear superiority.

Johnson was belligerent in escalating conventional war in Vietnam, but he was cautious about nuclear weapons. His opponent in the 1964 presidential race, Barry Goldwater, spoke of delegating nuclear responsibility to military men and of the possibility of using low-yield atomic weapons in Vietnam. Johnson answered:

Make no mistake. There is no such thing as a conventional nuclear weapon.

For 19 peril-filled years no nation has loosed the atom against another. To do so now...would lead us down an uncertain path of blows and counterblows whose outcome none may know.[12]

We can be sure that other U.S. politicians drew lessons from Johnson's overwhelming defeat of Goldwater.

Nixon was an admirer of Eisenhower's atomic diplomacy and tried to imitate it. Making an explicit atomic threat the way Eisenhower had was now politically impossible, so Nixon made implicit threats. He wanted the Vietnamese to believe that "I might do *anything* to stop the war."[13] But eager though they were to stave off defeat, Nixon and Kissinger never decided to use nuclear weapons in Vietnam.

Nixon faced a new nuclear situation. He had to recognize that the United States no longer enjoyed nuclear superiority. Kennedy had still claimed that the United States stood "first." Johnson also claimed superiority. But soon after taking office, Nixon announced that he preferred the word *sufficiency* to *supe-*

riority. With arms control more attractive once U.S. superiority was gone, the way was clear for the SALT I agreements of 1972.

But despite the arms agreements, the United States was still not facing the reality created by the nature of nuclear weapons and the development of parity: nuclear weapons cannot really be used and are worse than worthless. Instead, it was trying to hang on to as much as possible of its original nuclear policy, trying to continue squeezing advantage from its possession of nuclear weapons, shifting position only belatedly, when it was forced to.

The strength of the counterforces restricting U.S. nuclear policy shows under Reagan. Here was an administration that began with vitriolic anti-Soviet rhetoric, a refusal to negotiate, and the launching of a gigantic arms buildup. Yet an upsurge in the peace movement, the discovery that reestablishing nuclear superiority was not a feasible short term goal, and the development of enormous budget deficits forced a change in policy. In his second term, Reagan changed his rhetoric, entered into negotiations, and signed an agreement abolishing two classes of nuclear missiles.

Thus the nuclear realities have slowly forced the U.S. government to recognize limitations on its nuclear policy. Through the inevitable zigs and zags, a trend toward greater sobriety emerges. A process of arms control — limited thus far but significant — has gotten under way.

WHAT CAUSED THE UNITED STATES, after decades of hostility, to enter into detente with the Soviet Union? Why does it, even while easing hostility toward the Soviet Union, remain hostile toward Cuba, Vietnam, and Angola? Why did it shift policy toward the People's Republic of China?

The forces that have from time to time produced an easing of hostility to the Soviet Union stand out clearly. U.S. diplomatic recognition in 1933 had clear motives — the possible usefulness of the Soviet Union as an ally against Hitler Germany and an aggressive Japan plus the opportunities it offered to U.S. business. The alliance during World War II was based on Soviet military usefulness.

After the war, the first U.S. participation in an attempt to relax tensions came with the summit meeting in Geneva, in 1955, shortly after the Soviet Union had exploded a hydrogen bomb and developed an intercontinental bomber. Another attempt at detente came in 1963 just after the Cuban missile crisis. Yet another attempt came in the early 1970s when the Soviet Union had achieved an acknowledged nuclear parity with the United States. The timing was not accidental. Each of these moves toward easing tension came after a Soviet increase in nuclear strength which increased the vulnerability of the United States or a crisis which dramatized the nuclear danger.

Of course, other factors also played a part—the yearning of the people of the United States for an easing of tensions, the interest of U.S. corporations in the business opportunities that would arise with detente. In the detente of the early 1970s, the movement of France and West Germany to ease tensions helped move the United States. But the missile crisis and the development of nuclear parity had also helped move France and West Germany.

The stability of nuclear parity was crucial in the switch of the Reagan administration to detente. Would Reagan have moved to detente if the nuclear superiority he was looking for had proved to be achievable quickly? If the experts had told him that his Star Wars goals would soon be achieved?

Detente with the Soviet Union resulted from the stability of nuclear parity plus the political and economic advantages to the United States of easing tensions. But what will lead the United States to establish normal relations with Cuba, Vietnam, and Angola? The balance of strength—military, political, and economic—between each of them and the United States differs vastly from the Soviet-U.S. balance.

The United States calculates coldly what it stands to gain and lose by easing hostility and calibrates its relations with these countries accordingly. When one of them can do something the United States wants done, it is willing to enter into negotiations and make small concessions. But what can these countries do except surrender that will cause the United States to give up its basic hostility?

The United States suffers an economic loss from its policy of hostility. Cuba, for instance, is a natural trading partner of the United States. Were it not for the blockade, the United States could enjoy substantial trade with even a socialist Cuba. But the imperialists feel that the political advantages of maintaining hostility and blockade outweigh the economic losses from cutting off trade.

The shift in China policy under Nixon and Kissinger provides yet another variant of U.S. action. This shift did not occur because the underlying U.S. hostility to the Chinese Revolution had ceased to exist. It came about because the United States felt that China might be useful against the Soviet Union and this, for the time being, outweighed the hostility. Kissinger's statement that the new relationship was "a marriage of convenience" about whose permanence "we had no illusions" tells the story.

WHAT DOES THE NEW U.S. policy toward the Soviet Union mean? To what extent does Bush's rhetoric about "a new era" reflect something real? To what extent is the United States, behind the screen of rhetoric, still attached to the concepts and strategy of the cold war?

Here is how it looks as of this writing in early 1990:

The rhetoric about "a new era" does reflect something real: the United States has followed the lead of the Soviet Union in creating a new climate in their relations far more favorable to peace than the preceding one. It has moved away from the previous official image of the Soviet Union as the evil enemy.

Already signed (under Reagan) or in prospect are arms agreements of greater scope and significance than the earlier ones. The two countries have been moving toward substantial cuts in nuclear arms, significant decreases in conventional forces, and the elimination of chemical weapons.

The new U.S.-Soviet relationship (combined with the changes in Eastern Europe) has produced crucial shifts in public attitudes in both the United States and other countries. Most people see the cold war as over. Media people, discussing the U.S. military budget or the NATO alliance, ask the question, who is the enemy?

What has thus far happened is part of a process which is far from played out. The new situation is increasing the pressure for sharp reductions in the U.S. military budget and weakening the justification for NATO and other anti-Soviet alliances. No one can tell for sure where the process will end. The longer it goes on, the more it creates barriers to a reversal—a return to all-out cold war.

Yet, despite the opportunities created by the new climate for eliminating the nuclear threat, moving forward on a program of true general disarmament, and consolidating peace, the United States is still in certain key respects proceeding from the old cold war strategy. Baker's statement to the Soviet parliamentarians about "maintaining peace through strength" gives the gist of the matter. The United States is still guided by the "position of strength" doctrine laid down by Acheson in the Truman administration.

U.S. arms policy still does not have true disarmament as a goal. The United States has been negotiating and entering into arms agreements with several aims in mind—eliminating or reducing the number of especially troublesome Soviet weapons, reducing strains on the U.S. budget, reaping domestic political benefits, giving the Soviets a quid pro quo for concessions. But despite the more substantial cuts recently effected or in prospect, the Bush-Baker arms negotiations and agreements are no more aimed at promoting a process of true disarmament than were those of Nixon and Kissinger.

The United States has been pressing for reductions in land-based missiles where the Soviet Union is strong, but is unwilling to accept them in the area of its own strength—sea-based forces. It has been unwilling to give up research and development of Star Wars technology. It has been working not to truly end the arms race, but rather to shift the race further into the area of high technology where it considers itself to have an unbeatable advantage. It is still pursuing the goal of some day regaining nuclear superiority over the Soviet Union.

The "position of strength" doctrine also shows in U.S. policy on NATO. At a press conference in February 1990, a reporter asked President Bush: "With the breakup of the Soviet empire, and you want Germany to remain in NATO, who's the enemy?" Bush didn't answer who the enemy was, just that NATO and the U.S. troops in Europe are "a stabilizing factor."

Another reporter asked: "Mr. President, on Germany, would you be willing to consider a situation where a united Germany was not necessarily a full member of NATO?" Bush answered: "No. I think that Chancellor Kohl [of West Germany] is absolutely correct and we ought to support him [on] NATO membership."[14]

But despite Bush's smokescreen talk about NATO being simply "a stabilizing factor," it has been first and foremost a military alliance directed against the Soviet Union. Bush's insistence on not just maintaining but even strengthening it by having a united Germany join reflects the old cold war "position of strength" policy.

Why does the United States want a "position of strength?" Because despite the move away from open cold war, it still wants to have the power to coerce the Soviet Union into behaving. It has not at all given up telling the Soviet Union how to behave. Bush and Baker keep emphasizing, for example, that in every conference with Gorbachev they bring up the subject of Soviet aid to Cuba. True, the mix used to try to make the Soviet Union behave has changed sonewhat—the possibility of increased trade, credits, and access to technology play a bigger role than formerly, the use in one way or another of military strength a smaller one. But in the eyes of U.S. policymakers military strength remains part of the mix—ultimately the key part.

The new situation in Europe creates a rare opportunity to construct new arrangements that would turn the troubled, formerly divided continent into a region of firm and stable peace. The alternative is to follow, even if in veiled and attenuated form, the ideas and methods of the cold war. The administration, as well as the foreign policy establishment as a whole, seem to want to do precisely that. We have won the cold war, they feel. Let us act prudently in the present unclear situation, but let's be prepared if the opportunity arises to advance further.

The world remains one of conflict. At some time or other U.S.-Soviet relations will be subject to strain. Further insurance against a return to cold war, further progress toward peace require that the United States add certain specific actions to the rhetoric in its Soviet policy. It must act to to end rather than just re-channel the arms race, to eliminate NATO or change its nature, to dismantle the ring of bases around the Soviet Union.

TO SUM UP, our story shows both constancy and change in the reaction of U.S. imperialism to revolution. We see a powerful, practically innate drive to intervene and try to snuff out or push back revolution that imperialism sees as threatening its interests. We also see counterforces which can curb the drive.

What about the future? The process of revolution that has been coursing through the world is far from played out. With the great majority of the world's people living in misery, more revolutions are bound to occur. The insurrections under way in El Salvador, Peru or the Philippines could succeed. A revolution could erupt in Brazil or South Korea or Egypt or Zaire.

At the moment it may seem far-fetched to raise the possibility of revolution in Western Europe, but capitalism is inherently unstable and Western Europe, for all its riches, is far from having solved its problems. A leftist government might result from an election just as it threatened to do in Italy and France in the early postwar period.

What will the United States do in the face of further revolutions? No one can predict in detail how it will react in any given case. But we have every ground for assuming that U.S. intervention—including covert action, so-called low intensity warfare, and when necessary the direct use of U.S. forces—is not a thing of the past.

WE HAVE TRIED in this book to let the facts do the talking, to let readers judge for themselves. Now at the end we feel that we can offer a judgment: it is an ugly, shameful story.

From Russia in 1918 through Nicaragua and Angola in 1990, the United States imperialists have inflicted untold misery on peoples who were doing no more than trying to solve their problems—not just the peoples of the countries we have discussed, but many others as well. The imperialists have subjected peoples to U.S. armed intervention, armed attack by surrogate forces, economic warfare, the destabilization and overthrow of governments, the assassination of leaders.

To the people of Nicaragua they sent a simple message: "Vote the way we want you to or starve." To the people of Angola, they said, "Do what we tell you to or the killing and maiming by UNITA will go on." For thirty years, they have tried to coerce the people of Cuba with economic blockade and psychological warfare.

The imperialists have brought war to many countries. They brought a war of intervention to Russia. They prolonged for years the civil war in China. They mounted the Bay of Pigs attack on Cuba. They unleashed a full-scale U.S. war on Vietnam, letting loose their firepower, killing wholesale, and spreading havoc whose effects would last for generations. They brought the contra war to Nicaragua and another so-called low intensity war to Angola.

At the beginning of the nuclear era, the imperialists flirted a number of times with nuclear war. With the development of Soviet nuclear strength and the slow realization of what nuclear war would mean, they have become more sober. But they still constitute the biggest obstacle to ridding the world of the nuclear menace.

The United States has moved away from the cold war against the Soviet Union. But as Richard Nixon, according to a *New York Times* paraphrase, put it to a group of Republicans in Congress: "while the cold war was 'probably' over in Europe, it was continuing in the developing nations."[15]

The shameful story includes not just the barbaric actions of the imperialists, but also the endless procession of lies with which they have tried to disguise the true nature of these actions. The pattern was the same 70 years ago as today. Even while he was promoting counterrevolution by Cossack generals and conspiring with U.S. allies to intervene with foreign troops, President Wilson talked sanctimoniously in his Fourteen Points about giving Russia "an unembarrassed opportunity" to determine "her own political development...."

When in 1950 the State Department's Russian experts challenged the doctrine that the Soviet Union sought world domination, Acheson disregarded them. It wasn't that he thought the experts wrong, just that he needed the doctrine — needed, in his own phrase, to be "clearer than truth" — to promote his policy. The lying doctrine helped create the climate for enormous military budgets, anti-Soviet alliances, and repeated interventions.

To support their attempts to do away with the Cuban Revolution, the imperialists have handed out lies by the dozen. During the Bay of Pigs invasion, the CIA issued communiqués in the name of a phony Cuban opposition organization that was nothing but its own creature. With unabashed lies, the United States tried to convince the United Nations and the world that the air attacks on Cuba carried out by the CIA's hired pilots were the work of defectors from the Cuban Air Force.

Among the most subtle lies of the U.S. imperialists are those relating to South Africa. The U.S. government piously "abhors" apartheid in public, but behind the scenes cooperates with the racist regime to hold back revolution in southern Africa, and works at the United Nations to prevent sanctions.

We are now witnessing the birth of a new generation of lies. With the end of the cold war, the U.S. foreign policy establishment began to consider how to replace the obsolete old lies about Soviet expansionism. In the spring of 1990, the journals *Foreign Policy* and *Foreign Affairs* both carried articles by their editors discussing a new foreign policy rationale.

Charles William Maynes writes in *Foreign Policy*: "Some analysts argue that the export of democracy should replace anticommunism as the guiding principle of American foreign policy." *Export*, which Maynes himself calls the "operative word," means intervention. Maynes goes on to attribute to one influential analyst, Ben Wattenberg, the idea that "embarking on a crusade for democracy can help persuade the American people to keep defense budgets high...."[16]

William Hyland, in *Foreign Affairs*, talks about "leavening the older concerns over national security and geopolitics with greater concern for moral values, namely democracy and human rights." After recognizing that the "promotion of democracy"—like anticommunism before it—is tied to "interventionism," he concludes that "the idealism of human rights" may turn out to be "the new thrust of American policy." In short, the policy of interventionism remains the same, while the verbiage used to justify it is brought in line with the times.[17]

We have already seen the new rationale for interventionism applied in practice. The imperialists justified their invasion of Panama by talking about replacing the evil, drug-dealing General Manuel Antonio Noriega with democracy.

The interest of the peoples of the world, the interest of the people of the United States, and elementary justice all cry for a radical change in United States behavior. In essence, the change required comes down to two simple things:

* *That the United States give up its vicious practice of trying to determine for other countries what sort of social, economic, and political system they will have.* True world democracy requires that each country, large or small, be able to decide for itself.

* *That the United States cooperate honestly with other countries in a program of true disarmament and restructure its armed forces and its military strategy away from their present offensive, interventionist posture to a truly defensive one.* This means working to really stop the arms race, drastically reduce nuclear stockpiles, and eventually eliminate nuclear weapons altogether. It means sharply reducing U.S. conventional forces, and dismantling the overseas bases the United States maintains around the Soviet Union and throughout the world. And it means dismantling the military forces whose mission is to police the third world.

To those who argue that we cannot get rid of all nuclear weapons, that a few will be required to guard against blackmail

by outlaw nations, there is a simple answer: Okay, let's drastically reduce the stocks of nuclear weapons and then argue the
fine points of what to do about those that remain.

Such a change in U.S. behavior would create benefits that
would emanate in all directions. It would strengthen peace,
allow the countries of the world to develop the way their people
want them to, and free an enormous amount of resources for
use against the many problems the United States and the world
are facing.

We in the United States have more than enough problems—
unemployment, the plight of the minorities, drugs, homeless-
ness, a crisis in health care, the worst social security among the
leading developed countries, a deficient educational system, a
decrepit infrastructure, decayed inner cities and inadequate
housing, a polluted environment. Without money—huge
amounts of it—the government can only play at attacking these
problems, not truly do so.

There is also the hellish poverty of the three quarters of
humankind living in the third world. Even a fraction of the the
funds now going to the military could make a big difference.

Finally, there are the ecological problems which are closing
in on the human race. Unlike the mythical threats on which the
cold war rested, the threats to the environment—the poisoning
of the air, water, and soil, the release of gases which can bring
about ozone depletion or global warming—are real threats to
our "national interest," to our broader interest as human beings.
Our country could show true leadership by using its resources
and its prestige to promote a vigorous international attack on
these problems.

History teaches us not to have illusions about achieving the
required changes in imperialist behavior. It is not the light of
justice and reason that causes the imperialists to change their
ways. They change when they are forced to change, or when it
is in their interest to change. To achieve even part of the changes required will take long, hard struggle, in which the people of
the United States can play a crucial part. But history also shows
that with struggle, great advances can be won.

NOTES

Introduction

1. *Allende's Chile: An Inside View* (New York: International Publishers, 1977). See also by Edward Boorstein, *The Economic Transformation of Cuba* (New York: Monthly Review Press, 1968).

Russia/Soviet Union: 1917-1946

1. Bernard Pares, *A History of Russia,* cited in D.F. Fleming, *The Cold War and Its Origins* (New York: Doubleday, 1961), Vol. I, p. 11.
2. *Ibid.*
3. Frederick Lewis Schuman, *American Policy Toward Russia Since 1917* (New York: International Publishers, 1928), p. 32; and *History of the Communist Party of the Soviet Union (Bolsheviks)* (Moscow: Foreign Languages Publishing House, 1939), p. 174.
4. *Collected Works* (Moscow: Progress Publishers, 1965), Vol. 28, p. 358.
5. *Dokumenty Vneshnei Politiki SSSR,* hereafter cited as *Dokumenty...* (Moskva: Gosudarstvennoye Izdateltsvo Politicheskoi Literatury, 1957), Vol. 1, pp. 11-14. Also, Lenin, Vol. 26, pp. 249-252.
6. *Dokumenty...*, p. 17.
7. *Dokumenty...*, p. 20; and Lenin, Vol. 26, pp. 311-312.
8. *Istoriya Vneshnei Politiki SSSR, 1917-1945* (Moscow: "Nauka", 1986), p. 30.
9. David R. Francis, *Russia From the American Embassy, April, 1916-November, 1918* (New York: Charles Scribner's Sons, 1921), pp. 186-187.
10. *Papers Relating to the Foreign Relations of the United States, The Lansing Papers 1914-1920,* hereafter cited as *Lansing Papers* (Washington, D.C.: US Government Printing Office, 1940), Vol. II, pp. 343-345.
11. *Ibid.*, pp. 345-346.
12. *Ibid.*, p. 348.
13. *Ibid.*, pp. 350-351.
14. Quoted in Schuman, pp. 70-71.
15. Richard B. Morris, *Great Presidential Decisions: State Papers That Changed The Course Of History* (New York: Harper & Row, Perennial Library, 1973), p. 394.
16. *Papers Relating to the Foreign Relations of the United States,* hereafter cited as *FRUS,* 1918 (Washington, D.C.: US Government Printing Office, 1932), Russia, Vol. II, p. 42.
17. *Ibid.*, p. 16.
18. *Ibid.*, Vol. I, p. 527.
19. George F. Kennan, *Russia and the West Under Lenin and Stalin* (Boston: Little, Brown and Co., 1960), pp. 70-71.
20. See *FRUS,* 1918, *Russia,* Vol. II, pp. 150-250, *passim,* and *Lansing Papers,* Vol. II, pp. 350-370, *passim.*
21. *Lansing Papers,* Vol. II, p. 364.
22. *Dokumenty...*, pp. 286-294 and 299-300; also A. V. Berezkin, *Oktyabrskaya Revolutsiya i SShA, 1917-1922* (Moscow: "Nauka," 1967), pp. 121-123.
23. *FRUS,* 1918, *Russia,* Vol. III, p. 104.
24. *Ibid.*
25. *Ibid.*, p. 108.
26. Quoted in Schuman, p. 163.
27. Quoted in George F. Kennan, *Soviet-American Relations, 1917-1920: The Decision to Intervene* (Princeton, New Jersey: Princeton University Press, 1958), p. 395.
28. *FRUS,* 1918, *Russia,* Vol. II, p. 263.
29. Text given as an Appendix in Schuman, pp. 340-341.
30. Schuman, pp. 87-89, 104-105.
31. *Ibid.*, pp. 108, 114; and *Istoriya Vneshnei Politiki SSSR 1917-1945,* p. 73.
32. *Dokumenty...*, pp. 531-533.
33. *The World Crisis* (New York: Charles Scribner's Sons, 1929), Vol. V, pp. 164, 169.
34. *Russia and the West under Lenin and Stalin,* p. 87.
35. *Ibid.*, p. 88.
36. *Op. cit.*, pp. 136-137.
37. Schuman, pp. 151-154; and Philip S. Foner, *The Bolshevik Revolution: Its Impact on American Radicals, Liberals, and Labor* (New York: International Publishers, 1967), p. 132.
38. Foner, pp. 20 ff.
39. *Op. cit.*, pp. 157-158.
40. Foner, pp. 160-162, 167, 204-205.

41. *Ibid.*, p. 199.
42. *Ibid.*, p. 148.
43. *Ibid.*, p. 221.
44. *Collected Works*, Vol. 33, p. 150.
45. Foner, p. 202.
46. Schuman, p. 134.
47. *Ibid.*, p. 137.
48. Schuman, p. 169.
49. *FRUS*, 1920, Vol. III, p. 468.
50. Quoted in Frederick L. Schuman, *Soviet Politics At Home and Abroad* (New York: Alfred A. Knopf, 1946), p. 228.
51. *FRUS*, 1923, Vol. II, p. 787.
52. *Ibid.*, p. 788.
53. *American Policy Toward Russia Since 1917*, p. 325.
54. *Memoirs 1925-1950* (New York: Pantheon Books, 1967), pp. 29-30.
55. Charles E. Bohlen, *Witness to History 1929-1969* (New York: W.W. Norton & Company, 1973), p. 11.
56. Kennan, *Memoirs 1925-1950*, p. 33.
57. Quoted in Daniel Yergin, *Shattered Peace: The Origins of the Cold War and the National Security State* (Boston: Houghton Mifflin Company, 1977), p. 20.
58. *Memoirs 1925-1950*, p. 57.
59. Quoted in Schuman, *American Policy Toward Russia Since 1917*, p. 196.
60. Robert Paul Browder, *The Origins of Soviet-American Diplomacy* (Princeton, N.J.: Princeton University Press, 1953), pp. 28-29, 224.
61. *Ibid.*, p. 38.
62. *Ibid.*, pp. 39-40, 85.
63. *The Memoirs of Cordell Hull* (New York: The Macmilllan Co., 1948), p. 297.
64. Browder, p. 228.
65. James MacGregor Burns, *Roosevelt: The Lion and the Fox* (New York: Harcourt Brace and Company, 1956), p. 247.
66. *FRUS, Soviet Union 1933-1939*, p. 529.
67. *Memoirs 1925-1950*, pp. 56-57.
68. *The Time For Decision* (New York and London: Harper & Brothers Publishers, 1944), p. 318.
69. *Ibid.*, p. 321.
70. Quoted in Keith Middlemas and John Barnes, *Baldwin: A Biography* (London: The Macmillan Company, First American Edition 1970), p. 947.
71. Winston S. Churchill, *The Second World War: Vol. I, The Gathering Storm* (Boston: Houghton Mifflin Company, 1948), pp. 242, 275.
72. See John W. Wheeler-Bennett, *Munich: Prologue to Tragedy* (New York: Duell, Sloan, and Pearce, 1948), p. 235.
73. Quoted in Churchill, *The Gathering Storm*, p. 304.
74. *Prelude to World War II* (London: Victor Gollancz Ltd., 1953), p. 509.
75. *Against Aggression: Speeches by Maxim Litvinov* (New York: International Publishers, 1939), pp. 45, 110-111.
76. *Ibid.*, p. 116.
77. *Op. cit.*, p. 31.
78. "Quarantine the Aggressors Speech" in *Great Issues in American History*, ed. Richard Hofstadter (New York: Vintage Books, 1969), Vol. 2, pp. 389-391.
79. Burns, pp. 318-319.
80. Joseph E. Davies, *Mission to Moscow* (New York: Simon and Schuster, 1941), pp. xvi, xvii.
81. *Ibid.*, p. 6.
82. *Ibid.*, p. 141.
83. *Ibid.*, p. 417.
84. *Op. cit.*, p. 319.
85. *Memoirs 1925-1950*, p. 82.
86. David E. Koskoff, *Joseph P. Kennedy: A Life and Times* (Englewood Cliffs, N.J.: Prentice Hall, 1974), p. 136.
87. *Ibid.*, p. 158.
88. *FRUS*, 1938, Vol. I, p. 510.
89. *Ibid.*, p. 688.
90. Koskoff, p. 165.
91. Burns, pp. 387-388.
92. Quoted in William L. Shirer, *The Rise and Fall of the Third Reich* (New York: Ballantine Books, 1985), pp. 123, 124.
93. *Op. cit.*, Vol. 1, p. 655.
94. Davies, p. 434.
95. *FRUS, Soviet Union 1933-1939*, p. 749.
96. *The Gathering Storm*, pp. 373, 376.
97. *Ibid.*, p. 389.
98. *Ibid.*, p. 393.
99. Quoted in Schuman, *Soviet Politics at Home and Abroad*, p. 423.
100. (New York: Harper & Brothers, 1948), p. 303.
101. Schuman, *Soviet Politics At Home and Abroad*, p. 424.
102. James MacGregor Burns, *Roosevelt: The Soldier of Freedom* (New York: Harcourt, Brace and Co., 1970), pp. 151-152.
103. *Ibid.*, pp. 111-112.
104. *Ibid.*, p. 112.
105. Henry L. Stimson and McGeorge Bundy, *On Active Service in Peace and War* (New York: Harper & Brothers, 1948), p. 383.
106. Sherwood, p. 304

107. Schuman, *Soviet Politics at Home and Abroad*, p. 424.
108. Sherwood, p. 345.
109. *Ibid.*, p. 343.
110. *Ibid.*, p. 395.
111. *Ibid.*, p. 400.
112. *Ibid.*, pp. 393-394.
113. Stimson and Bundy, p. 525.
114. *Ibid.*, pp. 416, 418.
115. Quoted in Sherwood, pp. 519, 520.
116. *Ibid.*, p. 563.
117. *FRUS*, 1942, Vol. III, p. 594.
118. *Correspondence Between the Chairman of the Council of Ministers of the USSR and the Presidents of the USA and the Prime Ministers of Great Britain During the Great Patriotic War of 1941-1945* (Moscow: Progress Publishers, 1957), v. 1, pp. 92, 94.
119. *Ibid.*, p. 98.
120. *Ibid.*, v. 2, pp. 64-65.
121. Stimson and Bundy, p. 527.
122. *The Strange Alliance* (New York: The Viking Press, 1947), p. 16.
123. *Roosevelt: The Soldier of Freedom*, p. 374.
124. *Op. cit.*, pp. 48, 102-103, 126 ff.
125. Stimson and Bundy, p. 527.
126. *Roosevelt and the Russians: The Yalta Conference* (Garden City, New York: Doubleday & Co., 1949), p. 295.
127. *I Was There* (New York: Whittlesey House, McGraw-Hill Book Co., 1950), p. 291.
128. Sherwood, p. 870.
129. *The Second World War: Vol. VI, Triumph and Tragedy* (Boston: Houghton Mifflin Company, 1953), p. 456.
130. *Ibid.*
131. *Ibid.*, p. 402.
132. *Op. cit.*, Vol. I, p. 186.
133. *Roosevelt and Churchill: Their Secret Wartime Correspondence*, eds. Francis L. Loewenheim, Harold D. Langley, and Manfred Jonas (New York: Saturday Review Press/E. P. Dutton & Co., 1975), pp. 662, 704.
134. Elliott Roosevelt, *As He Saw It* (New York: Duell, Sloan and Pearce, 1946), p. 109.
135. Quoted in James F. Byrnes, *Speaking Frankly* (New York: Harper & Brothers, 1947), p. 91.
136. Quoted in Burns, *Roosevelt: The Soldier of Freedom*, p. 563.
137. Walter Millis, ed. (New York: Viking Press, 1951), p. 36.
138. *Roosevelt and Churchill: Their Secret Wartime Correspondence*, p. 709.

139. Quoted in Burns, *Roosevelt: The Soldier of Freedom*, p. 597.
140. *The Private Papers of Senator Vandenberg*, ed. by Arthur H. Vandenberg, Jr. (Boston: Houghton Mifflin Company, 1952), pp. 132-133, 152.
141. W. Averell Harriman and Elie Abel, *Special Envoy to Churchill and Stalin, 1941-1946* (New York: Random House, 1975), p. 344.
142. Churchill, *Triumph and Tragedy*, p. 488.
143. *Ibid.*
144. Truman, *Memoirs*, Vol. I, p. 70.
145. *Op. cit.*, p. 348.
146. *Memoirs*, Vol. I, pp. 70-71.
147. *Ibid.*, p. 77.
148. Stimson and Bundy, p. 609.
149. *The Forrestal Diaries*, p. 50.
150. *Ibid.*, p. 51.
151. *Ibid.*, p. 50.
152. Leahy, p. 351.
153. *Ibid.*, p. 352.
154. Truman, *Memoirs*, Vol. I, pp. 78-82.
155. *Ibid.*, and Leahy, p. 352.
156. Truman, *Memoirs*, Vol. I, p. 82.
157. Harriman and Abel, pp. 453-454.
158. Truman, *Memoirs*, Vol. I, p. 76.
159. Harriman and Abel, p. 291.
160. Stanislaus Mikolajczyk, *The Rape of Poland* (New York: Whittlesey House, McGraw-Hill Book Co., 1948), p. 97.
161. *Ibid.*, p. 98.
162. Byrnes, p. 31.
163. Declaration on Poland, quoted in Stettinius, p. 346.
164. Leahy, pp. 315-316.
165. Truman, *Memoirs*, Vol. I, p. 228.
166. *Atomic Diplomacy* (New York: Penguin Books, 1985), p. 86.
167. Stettinius, p. 318.
168. Sherwood, p. 894.
169. Byrnes, pp. 28-29 and Stettinius, pp. 345-346.
170. Byrnes, pp. 82-83.
171. *Op. cit.*, Vol. I, p. 292.
172. *Memoirs*, Vol. I, p. 412.
173. *Triumph and Tragedy*, p. 639.
174. *Memoirs*, Vol. I, p. 419.
175. *Mandate for Change* (New York: Signet Books, 1963), p. 380.
176. *Op. cit.*, p. 441.
177. *Memoirs*, Vol. I, p. 87.
178. *Ibid.*
179. Alperovitz, p. 251, fn.
180. Quoted in Charles Mee, *Meeting at Potsdam* (New York: M. Evans & Co., 1975), p. 164.
181. Quoted in Yergin, p. 120.
182. Quoted in Fleming, Vol. I, p. 310; and Alperovitz, p. 246, fn.
183. *Memoirs*, Vol. I, p. 412.

184. Quoted in Alperovitz, p. 273.
185. Byrnes, p. 98.
186. Stimson and Bundy, pp. 642-646.
187. Quoted in *Bulletin of the Atomic Scientists, 1945-1985, 40th Anniversary Issue*, August 1985, p. 1.
188. Quoted in P.M.S. Blackett, *Fear, War, and the Bomb* (New York: McGraw-Hill Book Company, 1949), p. 114.
189. *Present at the Creation* (New York: W.W. Norton & Co., 1969),p.123.
190. *The Forrestal Diaries*, pp. 95-96.
191. *FRUS*, 1945, Vol. II, p. 71.
192. *Speaking Frankly*, p. 275.
193. Fleming, Vol. I, p. 322.
194. Quoted in Fraser J. Harbutt, *The Iron Curtain, Churchill, America, and the Origins of the Cold War* (New York: Oxford University Press, 1986), p. 159.
195. From text of speech as given in J.P. Morray, *From Yalta to Disarmament* (New York: Monthly Review Press, 1961), p. 43.
196. This and all subsequent quotations of the speech are from Morray, pp. 43-50.
197. Harbutt, pp. 198, 229; and Fleming, Vol. I, p. 353.
198. Harbutt, p. 200 and Fleming, Vol. I, p. 351.
199. Harbutt, pp. 197-199, 321; and Yergin, p. 176.
200. Fleming, Vol. I, pp. 352-353.

China

1. Quoted in Hu Sheng, *Imperialism and Chinese Politics* (Beijing: Foreign Languages Press, 1981), pp. 10-11.
2. S.L. Tikhvinsky, ed., *Modern History of China* (Moscow: Progress Publishers, 1983), p. 185.
3. Quoted in Hu Sheng, p. 24.
4. *FRUS*, 1863, Part II, p. 828.
5. Quoted in Hu Sheng, p. 48.
6. *United States Relations With China: With Special Reference to the Period 1944-1949*, Department of State Publication 3573, Far Eastern Series 30, Division of Publications, Office of Public Affairs, 1949, p. 2.
7. Excerpt from Robert McClellan, *The Heathen Chinee: A Study of American Attitudes Toward China, 1890-1905*, given in Molly Joel Coye, John Livingston, and Jean Highland (eds.), *China Yesterday and Today*

8. (New York: Bantam Books, 1984), pp. 167, 170.
8. *Ibid.*, pp. 169-170.
9. Tikhvinsky, p. 262 and *China Yesterday and Today*, pp. 148-153.
10. *FRUS*, 1900, pp. 120-121.
11. *Ibid.*
12. *Ibid.*, p. 123.
13. *The Siege at Peking* (New York: Oxford University Press, 1983), p. 242.
14. *FRUS*, 1912, p. 47.
15. Tikhvinsky, p. 566.
16. *FRUS*, 1912, p. 55.
17. *Ibid.*, p. 64.
18. *Ibid.*, p. 71.
19. *FRUS*, 1913, pp. 84-85.
20. *United States Relations With China*, pp. 437-438.
21. Jian Bozan, Shao Xunzheng, and Hu Hua, *A Concise History of China* (Beijing: Foreign Languages Press, 1981), p. 141.
22. *United States Relations With China*, p. 441.
23. Hu Sheng, pp. 309-310.
24. Jian Bozan, Shao Xunzheng, and Hu Hua, pp. 158-159.
25. Quoted in Hu Sheng, p. 315.
26. Quoted in Dorothy Borg, *American Policy and the Chinese Revolution 1925-1928* (New York: American Institute of Pacific Relations and The Macmillan Co., 1947), p. 343.
27. *Ibid.*, p. 276.
28. *The Birth of Communist China* (New York: Frederick A. Praeger, 1966), p. 66.
29. *The Unfinished Revolution in China* (Boston: Little, Brown and Co., 1947), p. 62.
30. *FRUS*, 1927, Vol. II, p. 10.
31. *United States Relations With China*, pp. 43-44.
32. Quoted in Su Kaiming, *Modern China: A Topical History* (Beijing: New World Press, 1986), p. 149.
33. *United States Relations With China*, p. 68.
34. *China Shakes the World* (New York: Monthly Review Press, 1970), p. 149.
35. Lucien Bianco, *Origins of the Chinese Revolution, 1915-1949* (Stanford, California: Stanford University Press, 1971), p. 95.
36. *Op. cit.*, p. 152.
37. *Ibid.*, pp. 155-156.
38. *Two Kinds of Time* (Boston: Houghton Mifflin Co., 1950), p. 165.
39. *Thunder Out of China* (New York: William Sloane Associates, 1946), p. 247.
40. Graham Peck, p. 684.

41. Quoted in Felix Greene, *A Curtain of Ignorance: How the American Public Has Been Misinformed About China* (Garden City, N.Y.: Doubleday & Company, 1964), p. 40.
42. *Op. cit.*, p. 106.
43. *Op. cit.*, p. 113.
44. *Ibid.*, pp. 130, 133, 139.
45. *Op. cit.*, pp. 337-338.
46. Immanuel C.Y. Hsu, *The Rise of Modern China* (New York: Oxford University Press, 1970), p. 710.
47. *Op. cit.*, p. 189.
48. *United States Relations With China*, pp. 311-312.
49. White and Jacoby, p. 289.
50. *Memoirs by Harry S. Truman*, Vol. II (Garden City, N.Y.: Doubleday & Co., 1956), p. 62.
51. *United States Relations With China*, pp. xv, 312.
52. *Ibid.*, pp. 569, 567, 571.
53. *Ibid.*, p. 574.
54. *Op. cit.*, p. 63.
55. *Ibid.*
56. *United States Relations With China*, pp. 759-762, 780.
57. *Ibid.*, pp. 606-607.
58. *Present at the Creation: My Years in the State Department* (New York: W.W. Norton & Co., 1969), p. 143.
59. *FRUS*, 1946, Vol. X, p. 675.
60. *United States Relations With China*, p. 181.
61. *Ibid.*, pp. xiii and 218.
62. *Ibid.*, pp. 687, 688.
63. *Op. cit.*, p. 147.
64. *Op. cit.*, pp. 74-75.
65. *United States Relations With China*, p. 652.
66. *Ibid.*, p. 217.
67. Quoted in Edwin B. Hoyt, *The Rise of the Chinese Republic: From the Last Emperor to Deng Xiaoping* (New York: McGraw Hill Publishing Company, 1989), p. 214.
68. *20th Century China* (New York: Columbia University Press, 1966), pp. 277-278.
69. *United States Relations With China*, p. 694.
70. *Ibid.*, p. 357.
71. *Op. cit.*, p. 415.
72. *FRUS*, 1947, Vol. VII, pp. 2-3.
73. *United States Relations With China*, pp. 238, 729, 844.
74. *FRUS*, 1948, Vol. VII, pp. 505 and 545.
75. *Ibid.*, p. 613.
76. *Ibid.*, p. 612.
77. *Ibid.*, p. 613.
78. *Ibid.*, p. 623.
79. *United States Relations With China*, pp. 926, 927, 931, 932, 938.
80. *Op. cit.*, p. 337.
81. Truman, *Memoirs*, Vol. II, p. 339.
82. *Op. cit.*, p.338.
83. *Op. cit.*, p. 433.
84. *Mandate for Change 1953-1956* (New York: Signet Books, 1965), pp. 228-229.
85. *Ibid.*, p. 230.
86. *Op. cit.*, pp. 552-553.
87. *Ibid.*, p. 555.
88. *Ibid.*, pp. 557-559.
89. *Ibid.*, pp. 563-565.
90. *Ibid.*, pp. 568-570.
91. *Ibid.*, pp. 574-575.
92. Quoted in Townsend Hoopes, *The Devil and John Foster Dulles* (Boston: Little, Brown & Co., 1973), p. 310.
93. See Clubb, pp. 369-370 and "Zhou En-Lai's Statement on the Taiwan Strait Situation, September 6, 1958" in Roderick MacFarquhar, *Sino-American Relations, 1949-71* (New York: Praeger Publishers, 1972), p. 163.
94. Dwight D. Eisenhower, *Waging Peace 1956-1961* (Garden City, New York: Doubleday & Co., 1965), pp. 295, 692.
95. *Ibid.*, p. 693.
96. *Ibid.*, p. 300.
97. D. W. Fleming, *The Cold War and its Origins* (Garden City, New York: Doubleday & Co., 1961), Vol. II, p. 937.
98. Quoted in Hoopes, p. 450.
99. Roderick MacFarquhar, pp. 165-167, 172.
100. *Deadly Deceits: My 25 Years in the CIA* (New York: Sheridan Square Publications, 1983), pp. 25-26.
101. *The CIA and the Cult of Intelligence* (New York: Dell Publishing Co., 1980), p. 102.
102. *Ibid.*, pp. 100, 175.
103. *Ibid.*, pp. 138-139.
104. *White House Years* (Boston: Little, Brown & Co., 1979), p. 164, and *The Necessity for Choice* (New York: Anchor Books, 1962), p. 209.
105. *White House Years*, p. 194.
106. *Ibid.*, p. 1069.
107. *Ibid.*, pp. 1090-1091.

Cuba

1. Quoted in Emilio Roig de Leuchsenring, *Marti Anti-Imperialist* (Havana: Book Institute, 1967), p. 9.
2. Quoted in Philip S. Foner, *Antonio Maceo: The "Bronze Titan" of*

Cuba's Struggle for Independence (New York: Monthly Review Press, 1977), p. 240.

3. (Madison, Wisconsin: University of Wisconsin Press, 1963), p. 80.

4. From text as given in Robert F. Smith, *What Happened in Cuba? A Documentary History* (New York: Twayne Publishers, 1963), pp. 125-126.

5. Healy, pp. 159, 163, 168, 169.

6. U.S. Department of Commerce, Investment in Cuba (Washington, D.C.: U.S. Printing Office, 1956), p. 9 and Julio Le Riverend, La República: Dependencia y Revolución (Havana: Editora Universitaria, 1966), p. 73.

7. *FRUS*, 1906, Part I, p. 473.

8. Quoted in Charles P. Howland, *American Relations In the Caribbean: A Preliminary Issue of Section I of the Annual Survey of American Foreign Relations 1929*, Reprint Edition (New York: Arno Press and The New York Times, 1970), p. 29.

9. *Op. cit.*, p. 94.

10. *FRUS*, 1912, p. 247.

11. *FRUS*, 1917, p. 363.

12. Robert F. Smith, p. 155.

13. From extract of speech in Hortensia Pichardo, *Documentos Para la Historia de Cuba* (Havana: Instituto Cubano del Libro, 1973), p. 266.

14. Le Riverend, p. 234.

15. Pichardo, p. 403.

16. *FRUS*, 1927, Vol. II, p. 527.

17. *FRUS*, 1933, Vol. V, p. 280.

18. Hugh Thomas, *Cuba or the Pursuit of Freedom* (London: Eyre & Spottiswoode, 1971), p. 586.

19. *FRUS*, 1930, Vol. II, p. 649.

20. *Ibid.*, p. 650.

21. *Ibid.*, p. 649.

22. *Ibid.*, p. 671.

23. *Ibid.*, pp. 681-682.

24. *FRUS*, 1933, Vol. V, p. 273.

25. *Ibid.*, p. 283.

26. *Ibid.*, p. 285.

27. *Ibid.*, p. 290.

28. *Ibid.*, p. 336

29. *Ibid.*, p. 338.

30. *Ibid.*, p. 356.

31. *Ibid.*, p. 348.

32. From the personal account of a leader of the conspiracy, given in Pichardo, pp. 573 ff.

33. *Ibid.*

34. *Ibid.*, and *FRUS*, 1933, p. 359.

35. Pichardo, p. 601.

36. *FRUS*, 1933, Vol. V., pp. 365, 366, 371, 372, 377.

37. *Ibid.*, pp. 379, 382-383.

38. *Ibid.*, p. 384.

39. *Ibid.*, p. 388.

40. *Ibid.*, p. 389.

41. Sumner Welles, *The Time For Decision* (New York: Harper & Brothers, 1944), p. 198.

42. *FRUS*, 1933, Vol. V, pp. 390, 417.

43. *Ibid.*, pp. 441, 444.

44. *Ibid.*, p. 445.

45. *Ibid.*, p. 383.

46. *Ibid.*, p. 447.

47. *Ibid.*, p. 451.

48. *Ibid.*, p. 470.

49. *Ibid.*, p. 477-478.

50. *Ibid.*, p. 501.

51. *FRUS*, 1934, Vol. V, p. 107.

52. Commission on Cuban Affairs, *Problems of the New Cuba* (New York: Foreign Policy Association, 1935), pp. 16-17, 183-186, 202-203.

53. Quoted in Robert Taber, *M-26: The Biography of a Revolution* (New York: Lyle Stuart, 1961), p. 25.

54. Robert F. Smith, p. 206.

55. *Cuba, Castro, and the United States* (Pittsburgh: University of Pittsburgh Press, 1971), p. 11.

56. *FRUS*, 1952-1954, Vol. IV, p. 871.

57. *Selección de Lecturas de Historia de Cuba*, Tomo II (Havana: Editora Política, 1984), p. 124; and Maurice Zeitlin and Robert Scheer, *Cuba: Tragedy In Our Hemisphere* (New York: Grove Press, 1963), p. 17.

58. Zeitlin and Scheer, p. 17.

59. US Department of Commerce, *Investment in Cuba*, pp. 180-181.

60. *Op. cit.*, p. 13.

61. *The Fourth Floor: An Account of the Castro Communist Revolution* (New York: Random House, 1962), p.20.

62. *Ibid.*, p. 66.

63. *The Closest of Enemies* (New York: W.W. Norton & Co., 1987), p. 20.

64. Quoted in Richard E. Welch, Jr., *Response To Revolution: The United States and the Cuban Revolution, 1959-1961* (Chapel Hill: University of North Carolina Press, 1985), p. 197.

65. Memorandum for the Record, 23 April 1961, Subject: First Meeting of General Maxwell Taylor's Board of Inquiry on Cuban Operations Conducted by CIA, Declassified Document (Sanitized) 1978/436B.

66. Earl E.T. Smith, pp. 172, 183.

67. *Discursos del Dr. Fidel Castro Ruz*, Oficina del Historiador de la Ciudad de la Habana, 1959, p. 76.

68. Issued on January 15, 1959: "United States Policy With Respect to the Cuban Revolution and the Role of United States Military Missions in

Cuba," U.S. Department of State, *American Foreign Policy, Current Documents, 1959* (Washington, D.C.: US Government Printing Office, 1963), p. 328.

69. Bonsal, pp. 28-29.

70. *Discursos*, pp. 121, 151.

71. *Fidel: A Critical Portrait* (New York: Avon Books, 1986), p. 528.

72. *Six Crises* (New York: Pocket Books Inc., 1962), p. 379.

73. *American Foreign Policy, Current Documents, 1959*, p. 343.

74. Szulc, pp. 548-549; Welch, Jr., p. 47; and Martin Kenner and James Petras, eds., *Fidel Castro Speaks* (New York: Grove Press, 1969), p. 50.

75. Szulc, p. 619.

76. Extract of conference on December 10, given in *American Foreign Policy, Current Documents, 1959*, pp. 391-392.

77. *Op. cit.*, p. 134.

78. *Alleged Assassination Plots Involving Foreign Leaders*, An Interim Report of the Select Committee to Study Governmental Operations With Respect to Intelligence Activities (Church Committee), U.S. Senate, hereafter cited as *Alleged Assassination Plots...* (Washington, D.C.: US Government Printing Office, 1975), p. 114.

79. *Ibid.*, p. 92.

80. *Ibid.*, p. 93.

81. *Ibid.*, pp. 72-73.

82. *Secrets, Spies, and Scholars: Blueprint of the Essential CIA* (Washington, D.C.: Acropolis Books Ltd., 1976), pp. 186-187.

83. *Op. cit.*, p. 149.

84. *Ibid.*, p. 150.

85. *Ibid.*, p. 151.

86. *A Thousand Days: John Kennedy in the White House* (Boston: Houghton Mifflin Co., 1965), p. 228.

87. Memorandum of January 24, 1961, Declassified Documents, 1978/355A.

88. Tad Szulc and Karl E. Meyer, *The Cuban Invasion: The Chronicle of a Disaster* (New York: Ballantine Books, 1962), p. 81.

89. *Ibid.*, p. 107.

90. Schlesinger, pp. 259-260.

91. *Op. cit.*, p. 118.

92. Quoted in Peter Wyden, *Bay of Pigs: The Untold Story* (New York: A Touchstone Book, Simon & Schuster, 1979), p. 169.

93. Szulc and Meyer, pp. 119-120.

94. Haynes Johnson, *The Bay of Pigs: The Leaders' Story of Brigade 2506*

(New York: Dell Publishing Co., 1964), p. 83.

95. *Ibid.*, p. 85.

96. U.S. Department of State, *American Foreign Policy, Current Documents, 1961*, (Washington, D.C.: US Government Printing Office, 1965), p. 291.

97. Szulc and Meyer, p. 126.

98. *Op. cit.*, pp. 274-275.

99. *Op. cit.*, p. 609.

100. *Ibid.*, p. 613.

101. Quoted in Arthur M. Schlesinger, Jr., *Robert Kennedy and his Times* (New York: Ballantine Books, 1979), pp. 507, 509.

102. Quoted *Ibid.*, pp. 508-509.

103. *Alleged Assassination Plots...*, p. 136.

104. *Ibid.*, p. 137.

105. *Ibid.*, p. 141.

106. *Ibid.*, pp. 139-140.

107. *Ibid.*, p. 141.

108. *Op. cit.*, p. 514.

109. *Alleged Assassination Plots...*, pp. 140, 143, 146, 147.

110. *Reflections on the Cuban Missile Crisis* (Washington, D.C.: The Brookings Institution, 1987), p. 5.

111. *Robert Kennedy and his Times*, p. 541.

112. *Ibid.*, p. 534.

113. Quoted in Lee Lockwood, *Castro's Cuba, Cuba's Fidel* (New York: The Macmillan Company, 1967), p. 200.

114. In McNamara's introduction to Robert F. Kennedy, *Thirteen Days: A Memoir of the Cuban Missile Crisis* (New York: W. W. Norton & Co., 1969), p. 13.

115. *Op. cit.*, p. 37.

116. "Class Reunion: Kennedy's Men Relive the Cuban Missile Crisis," by J. Anthony Lukas, *New York Times Magazine*, August 30, 1987.

117. *Op. cit.*, p. 678.

118. *Alleged Assassination Plots...*, p. 173.

119. *Ibid.*

120. Warren Hinckle and William Turner, *The Fish Is Red: The Story of the Secret War Against Castro* (New York: Harper & Row, 1981), p. 174; and Szulc, p. 667.

121. *Alleged Assassination Plots...*, p. 90.

122. *Op. cit.*, p. 293.

123. *Ibid.*, pp. 293-294, 323. See also Szulc, p. 696.

124. Szulc, p. 652.

125. *US Policy Toward Cuba*, Department of State Publication 7690, Inter-American Series 88 (Washington, D.C.: US Government Printing Office, 1964), p. 6.

126. *Op. cit.*, p. 88.

127. Philip Brenner, *From Confrontation to Negotiation: U.S. Relations With Cuba* (Boulder, Colorado: Westview Press, 1988), p. 19.

128. Cyrus Vance, *Hard Choices: Critical Years in America's Foreign Policy* (New York: Simon & Schuster, 1983), p. 131.

129. Wayne S. Smith, pp. 122-123, 137.

130. Jane Franklin, *Cuban Foreign Relations: A Chronology 1959-1982* (New York: Center for Cuban Studies, 1984), pp. 31, 32, 37, 38.

131. *Ibid.*, pp. 36-37, 43, 44, 46; and Wayne S. Smith, pp. 249-250.

132. Jane Franklin, p. 45.

133. Wayne S. Smith, p. 246.

134. Jane Franklin, p. 44.

135. *Ibid.*, p. 45.

136. Alexander M. Haig, Jr., *Caveat: Realism, Reagan, and Foreign Policy* (New York: Macmillan Publishing Co., 1984), p. 131.

137. *Op. cit.*, p. 250.

138. Brenner, p. 38.

139. *Ibid.*, pp. 38-39 and *New York Times*, May 2, 1987 and October 4, 1987.

140. Remarks by the President at the Cuban Independence Day Briefing, White House Press Release, May 22, 1989.

141. *Op. cit.*, p. 117.

142. Brenner, p. 46.

143. February 27, 1990.

144. *MacNeil/Lehrer Newshour*, March 8, 1990.

Vietnam

1. Quoted in *The Pentagon Papers: The Defense Department History of Decision Making in Vietnam*, The Senator Gravel Edition (Boston: Beacon Press, 1971), Vol. I, p. 51.

2. Quoted in *The Pentagon Papers* as published by the *New York Times* (New York: Bantam Books, 1971), p. 8.

3. Quoted in Marvin E. Gettleman (ed.), *Vietnam: History, Documents, and Opinions on a Major World Crisis* (Greenwich, Conn.: Fawcett Publications, 1965), p. 79.

4. Quoted in *The Pentagon Papers* (NYT), p. 9.

5. *Ibid.*

6. *Ibid.*, p. 28.

7. *Ibid.*, pp. 9-10.

8. Gettleman, p. 91.

9. *Ibid.*, p. 90.

10. D. F. Fleming, *The Cold War and Its Origins* (Garden City, N.Y.: Doubleday & Co., 1961), Vol. II, p. 690 and Townsend Hoopes, *The Devil and John Foster Dulles* (Boston: Little, Brown and Co., 1973), p. 211.

11. Gettleman, p. 156.

12. *Ibid.*, pp. 140-144, 153.

13. Gabriel Kolko, *Anatomy of a War* (New York: Pantheon Books, 1985), p. 84.

14. The Pentagon Papers (NYT), pp. 53-54.

15. *Ibid.*, p. 55.

16. *Ibid.*, p. 57.

17. *Ibid.*, p. 62.

18. *Ibid.*, p. 65.

19. *Ibid.*, p. 55.

20. *Ibid.*, p. 59.

21. *Ibid.*, pp. 59-60.

22. Kolko, p. 85.

23. *The Pentagon Papers* (NYT), pp. 61-64.

24. "The Genesis of United States Support for Ngo Dinh Diem," in Gettleman, pp. 249-251.

25. *The Pentagon Papers* (Gravel), Vol. I, pp. 308-309.

26. *Op. cit.*, p. 93.

27. *The Pentagon Papers* (Gravel), Vol. I, pp. 308-310; and Kolko, pp. 93-94.

28. *Op. cit.*, p. 95.

29. Gettleman, p. 223.

30. *The Pentagon Papers* (Gravel), Vol. I, pp. 312-313.

31. Gettleman, p. 226.

32. *Ibid.*, p. 253.

33. Arthur M. Schlesinger, Jr., *A Thousand Days* (Boston: Houghton Mifflin Co., 1965), p. 540.

34. *Ibid.*, p. 341.

35. *The Limits of Intervention* (New York: David McKay Co., 1969), pp. 14-15.

36. *Op. cit.*, p. 342.

37. *The Pentagon Papers* (NYT), p. 156.

38. *The Pentagon Papers* (Gravel), Vol. II, p. 39.

39. *Ibid.*, p. 58.

40. *The Pentagon Papers* (NYT), p. 143.

41. *Ibid.*, p. 152.

42. *Ibid.*, pp. 108, 151.

43. *Ibid.*, p. 109.

44. *Ibid.*, p. 110.

45. *Ibid.*, p. 113 and Schlesinger, p. 998.

46. Quoted in Schlesinger, p. 982.

47. *The Pentagon Papers* (Gravel), Vol. II, p. 202.

48. *Ibid.*, p. 734.

49. *Ibid.*, pp. 767-768.

50. *The Pentagon Papers* (NYT), p. 159.

51. *Alleged Assassination Plots...*, p. 222.

52. *The Pentagon Papers* (Gravel), Vol. II, pp. 766, 782, 792-793.
53. *Ibid.*, p. 220.
54. *Alleged Assassination Plots...*, p. 223 and *The Pentagon Papers* (Gravel), Vol. II, p. 207.
55. *The Pentagon Papers* (Gravel), Vol. II, pp. 269-270.
56. *A Thousand Days*, p. 997.
57. Theodore C. Sorensen, Kennedy (New York: Harper & Row, 1965), p. 660.
58. *The Pentagon Papers* (Gravel), Vol. II, p. 207.
59. *Ibid.*, Vol. III, p. 494. Italics in original.
60. *Ibid.*, p. 496.
61. *Ibid.*, p. 169.
62. *The Pentagon Papers* (NYT), pp. 235, 238-240 and *The Pentagon Papers* (Gravel), Vol. III, p. 150.
63. *The Pentagon Papers* (Gravel), Vol. III, p. 501.
64. *Ibid.*
65. *Ibid.*, pp. 503, 504.
66. *The Pentagon Papers* (NYT), pp. 248-249.
67. *Ibid.*
68. Lyndon Baines Johnson, *The Vantage Point* (New York: Holt, Rhinehart and Winston, 1971), p. 113.
69. Stanley Karnow, *Vietnam: A History* (New York: The Viking Press, 1983), p. 375.
70. *Ibid.*, p. 373.
71. *The Pentagon Papers* (Gravel), Vol. III, p. 558.
72. *Ibid.*, p. 557.
73. *Ibid.*, p. 703.
74. *The Pentagon Papers* (NYT), p.389.
75. *The Pentagon Papers* (Gravel), Vol. III, p. 703.
76. *Ibid.*, Vol. IV, pp. 22-23, 609-610, 615-616.
77. *Ibid.*, Vol. III, p. 477.
78. *Op. cit.*, pp. 31-32.
79. *The Pentagon Papers* (NYT), pp. 491-492.
80. Quoted in Herbert Y. Schandler, *The Unmaking of a President: Lyndon Johnson and Vietnam* (Princeton, N.J.: Princeton University Press, 1977), p. 145.
81. Quoted in Hoopes, pp. 215-216.
82. *The Memoirs of Richard Nixon* (New York: Warner Books, 1978), Vol. 1, p. 430.
83. *Ibid.*, pp. 430-432.
84. *Memoirs*, Vol. 1, p. 482.
85. *Ibid.*, pp. 484, 486.
86. *Ibid.*, pp. 486-487, 489-490.
87. *The Price of Power: Kissinger in the Nixon White House* (New York: Summit Books, 1983), p. 120.
88. *Ibid.*, p. 126.
89. Nixon, *Memoirs*, Vol. 1, p. 491
90. *Ibid.*, p. 491-492.
91. *Ibid.*, pp. 491, 492, 494.
92. *White House Years*, p. 266.
93. Nixon, *Memoirs*, Vol.1, p. 495.
94. *Ibid.*, p. 496.
95. *Ibid.*, p. 506.
96. *Ibid.*, pp. 554-555.
97. *Ibid.*, pp. 555-557.
98. Quoted in Hersh, p. 192.
99. Kissinger, *White House Years*, pp. 511-512.
100. *Ibid.*, p. 969.
101. *Ibid.*, pp. 983, 1020.
102. *Ibid.*, p. 1043.
103. *Op. cit.*, p. 425.
104. Kissinger, *White House Years*, pp. 1114, 1117.
105. *Ibid.*, pp. 1114-1115.
106. Nixon, *Memoirs*, Vol. 2, p. 85 and Hersh, p. 507.
107. Nguyen Khac Vien, *Le Vietnam Contemporain* (Hanoi: Fleuve Rouge, 1981), p. 228. Our translation.
108. Kissinger, *White House Years*, p. 1253.
109. *Ibid.*, p. 1347.
110. Nixon, *Memoirs*, Vol. 2, pp. 202, 203.
111. *Ibid.*, pp. 241, 242.
112. *Ibid.*, p. 247.
113. *Ibid.*, pp. 252-253.
114. *No More Vietnams* (New York: Arbor House, 1985), pp. 170-171.
115. *Op. cit.*, p. 438.
116. (London: Taylor & Francis Ltd, 1982), p. 367.

Nicaragua

1. Quoted in Jaime Wheelock Román, *Imperialismo y dictadura: crisis de una formación social* (Mexico, D.F.: Siglo Veintiuno editores, 1979), pp. 107-108.
2. *FRUS*, 1909, p. 452.
3. Cited in Gregorio Selser, *Sandino: General of the Free* (New York: Monthly Review Press, 1981), p. 29.
4. Scott Nearing and Joseph Freeman, *Dollar Diplomacy: A Study in American Imperialism* (New York: Monthly Review Press, 1966), pp. 152-153.
5. *FRUS*, 1909, p. 456.
6. *Ibid.*, p. 459.
7. *FRUS*, 1910, p.752.
8. *Ibid.*, p. 765.
9. *Ibid.*
10. *FRUS*, 1911, p. 655.
11. *Ibid*, p. 656.

12. *FRUS*, 1912, pp. 1074-5.
13. *FRUS*, 1911, p. 661.
14. *FRUS*, 1912, p. 1043.
15. John Kenneth Turner, quoted in Selser, p. 213.
16. Wheelock Román, p. 109.
17. From text of the treaty, given in Nearing and Freeman, pp. 321-23.
18. Nearing and Freeman, p. 168.
19. *FRUS*, 1913, p. 1027.
20. Quoted in Selser, p. 28.
21. Quoted in Neill Macaulay, *The Sandino Affair* (Chicago: Quadrangle Books, 1967), p. 38.
22. *FRUS*, 1927, Vol. III, p. 441.
23. Quoted in Selser, p. 77.
24. Sergio Ramírez (ed.), *Augusto C. Sandino: El pensamiento vivo* (Managua: Editorial Nueva Nicaragua, 1984), Tomo 1, p. 129.
25. *Ibid.*, p. 132.
26. Selser, p. 77.
27. Ramírez, p. 151.
28. Selser, p. 109.
29. *Ibid.*, p. 139.
30. K. Bruce Galloway and Robert Bowie Johnson, Jr., *West Point: America's Power Fraternity* (New York: Simon and Schuster, 1973), pp. 196 and 271.
31. *FRUS*, 1927, Vol. III, pp. 434-439.
32. Carlos Fonseca, pamphlet entitled *Sandino Guerrillero Proletario* (Managua: Departamento de Propaganda y Educación Política del FSLN, 1984), p. 27.
33. *FRUS*, 1932, Vol. V, p. 876.
34. *FRUS*, 1927, Vol. III, p. 437.
35. *Guardians of the Dynasty (Maryknoll, N.Y.: Orbis Books, 1977), p. 134.*
36. *Ibid.*, p. 55.
37. Selser, pp. 162-163, 167-168.
38. *Augusto C. Sandino: El pensamiento vivo*, Tomo 2, pp. 336, 341.
39. *Ibid.*, p. 377.
40. *Ibid.*, p. 380.
41. *Ibid.*, p. 373.
42. *FRUS*, 1934, Vol. V, p. 528.
43. *Ibid.*
44. *Ibid.*, pp. 530-531, 555.
45. Quoted in Selser, p. 174.
46. *FRUS*, 1934, Vol. V, p. 556.
47. *Ibid.*, pp. 540, 556.
48. *Ibid.*, p. 542.
49. *Ibid.*, pp. 555, 556.
50. Millett, pp. 169, 171-172, and *FRUS*, 1935, Vol. IV, p. 844.
51. Millett, p. 169.
52. *FRUS*, 1935, Vol. IV, pp. 855-859.
53. *Ibid.*, pp. 872-873, 883.
54. *Ibid.*, p. 881; *FRUS*, 1936, Vol. V, p. 826; and Millett, pp. 178-180.
55. Millett, p. 197.
56. *Ibid.*, p. 198.
57. *Ibid.*, pp. 196, 199, 200.
58. *Ibid.*, p. 213.
59. *FRUS*, 1955-1957, Vol. VII, p. 211.
60. Translated back from Spanish as quoted in Carlos Fonseca, Obras, Tomo 2, *Viva Sandino* (Managua: Editorial Nueva Nicaragua, 1982), p. 165.
61. *FRUS*, 1955-1957, Vol. VII, pp. 227 (footnote), 230, 238.
62. James D. Rudolph, ed., *Nicaragua: a country study*, Foreign Area Studies, The American University (Washington, D.C.: US Government Printing Office, 1982), p. 35; and Richard R. Fagan, *Forging Peace: The Challenge of Central America* (New York, A Pacca Book, 1987), p. 61.
63. Rudolph, pp. 81, 84, 89.
64. *Ibid.*, pp. 82, 85, 90.
65. Millett, pp. 235-244 *passim*.
66. *America and the World*, 1978, Vol. 57, No. 3, Richard R. Fagan, "The Carter Administration and Latin America: Business as Usual?", pp. 661-662.
67. Quoted in Peter Kornbluh, *Nicaragua: The Price of Intervention* (Washington, D.C.: Institute for Policy Studies, 1987), p. 15.
68. *American Foreign Policy 1977-1980* (Washington, D.C.: US Government Printing Office, 1981), p. 1317.
69. *Ibid.*, p. 1319.
70. Quoted in Kornbluh, p. 16. Somoza secretly taped his conversations with US officials and published them in *Nicaragua Betrayed*, written with Jack Cox.
71. *Ibid.*
72. Quoted in Christopher Dickey, *With the Contras: A Reporter in the Wilds of Nicaragua* (New York: Simon & Schuster, 1985), pp. 47-48.
73. Quoted in Kornbluh, p. 16.
74. "Hemisphere Relations: Everything is Part of Everything Else," *Foreign Affairs, America and the World 1980*, Vol. 59, No. 3, p. 622.
75. William I. Robinson and Kent Norsworthy, *David and Goliath: The U.S. War Against Nicaragua* (New York: Monthly Review Press, 1987), p. 40.
76. *Packaging the Contras: A Case of CIA Disinformation* (New York: Institute for Media Analysis, 1987), pp. 5-6.
77. Bob Woodward, *Veil: The Secret Wars of the CIA 1981-1987* (New York: Pocket Books, 1987), p. 111; and Kornbluh, p. 19.

78. "U.S. Security and Latin America," in Robert S. Leiken and Barry Rubin (eds.), *The Central American Crisis Reader* (New York: Summit Books, 1987), p. 513.
79. Quoted in Paul E. Sigmund, "Latin America: Change or Continuity?" *Foreign Affairs*, Vol. 60, No. 3, *America and the World 1981*, p. 630.
80. Republican Party: Platform (1980), in Leiken and Rubin, p. 515.
81. Quoted in Roy Gutman, *Banana Diplomacy* (New York: Simon and Schuster, 1988), pp. 66-67, 70.
82. *Ibid.*, p. 74.
83. "Central America: From Quagmire to Cauldron?" *Foreign Affairs*, Vol. 62, No. 3, *America and the World 1983*, p. 663.
84. Cited in Gutman, p. 115; and Kornbluh, p. 55.
85. Robinson and Norsworthy, pp. 45-46.
86. *Ibid.*, pp. 49, 73-74; and Kornbluh, p. 48.
87. Robinson and Norsworthy, pp. 100-101; and Kornbluh, pp. 49-51.
88. *Op. cit.*, p. 56.
89. *Ibid.*, pp. 60-62.
90. Kornbluh, pp. 139-141.
91. *Op. cit.*, p. 144.
92. *New York Times*, February 22, 1985.
93. Quoted in Christopher Dickey, "Central America: From Quagmire to Cauldron?", p. 660 (footnote).
94. *New York Times*, May 3, 1987.
95. April 8, 1984 and April 23, 1984.
96. *New York Times, November 29, 1984.*
97. General Assembly, Provisional Verbatim Record, A/42/PV.30, p. 27.
98. Booklet *Nicaragua: The Cost of U.S. Aggression (Managua: Dirección de Información y Prensa de la Presidencia de la República de Nicaragua, March 15, 1985), pp. 15-17.*
99. Paper, *Nicaragua: Los Costos Económicos de la Agresión Imperialista 1980-1985* (Managua: Presidencia de la República, February 17, 1986), p. 6.
100. Quoted in the *New York Times*, December 14, 1988.

Central and Southern Africa

1. Jean Van Lierde (ed.), La Pensée Politique de Patrice Lumumba (Paris: Présence Africaine, 1963), p. 230.
2. *Ibid.*, pp. 198-199.
3. Stephen R. Weissman, *American Foreign Policy in the Congo 1960-1964* (Ithaca, N.Y.: Cornell University Press, 1974), p. 55.
4. Weissman, p. 56.
5. Quoted in Waldemar A. Nielsen, *The Great Powers and Africa* (New York: Praeger Publishers, 1969), p. 134.
6. Van Lierde, p. 266.
7. *Official Records of the Security Council*, Supplement for July, August, September 1960, p. 12.
8. *Alleged Assassination Plots Involving Foreign Leaders*, An Interim Report of the Select Committee to Study Governmental Operations With Respect to Intelligence Activities (Church Committee), U.S. Senate (Washington, D.C.: U.S. Government Printing Office, 1975), p. 57.
9. Madeleine G. Kalb, *The Congo Cables* (New York: Macmillan, 1982), p. 27.
10. Van Lierde, p. 257.
11. Van Lierde, p. 257-258.
12. *Official Records of the Security Council*, p. 40.
13. *Op. cit.*, p. 53.
14. *Ibid.*, p. 54.
15. *Official Records of the Security Council*, p. 45.
16. *Alleged Assassination Plots...*, p. 58.
17. *Ibid.*
18. *Ibid.*, pp. 55-56.
19. Quoted in Weissman, pp. 79-80.
20. *Alleged Assassination Plots...*, p. 15.
21. *Ibid.*, p. 16.
22. Quotes and other information are from Weissman, pp. 89-91.
23. *Alleged Assassination Plots...*, p. 17.
24. Quoted in Richard D. Mahoney, *JFK: Ordeal in Africa* (New York: Oxford University Press, 1983), p. 47.
25. Quote and other information from Weissman, pp. 95-98.
26. *Alleged Assassination Plots...*, p. 17.
27. *Ibid.*
28. *Ibid.*, p. 62.
29. *Ibid.*
30. *Ibid.*, p.63.
31. *Ibid.*, pp. 27-32.
32. *Ibid.*, p. 48.
33. *Ibid.*
34. *Ibid.*, p. 49.
35. *Ibid.*
36. *Ibid.*, pp. 49-50.
37. Quoted in Mahoney, p. 77.
38. Quoted in Weissman, p. 110.
39. Quoted in Weissman, p. 106.
40. Quoted in Kalb, p. 275.
41. Mahoney, p. 87.

42. April 26, 1966, quoted in Weissman, p. 149.
43. Quoted in "The CIA and U.S. Policy in Zaire and Angola" by Stephen Weissman, in Ellen Ray, William Schaap, et al.(eds.), Dirty Work II (Secaucus, N.J.: Lyle Stuart, 1979), p. 189.
44. Weissman, American Foreign Policy in the Congo 1960-1964, p. 205.
45. Ibid., p. 206 and passim.
46. Ibid., pp. 213, 227-229, 239.
47. Ibid., p. 240.
48. Crawford Young and Thomas Turner, The Rise and Decline of the Zairean State (Madison, Wisconsin: University of Wisconsin Press, 1985), p. 53.
49. April 21, 1990.
50. Quoted in Basil Davidson, In the Eye of the Storm: Angola's People (Garden City, N.Y.: Anchor Books, 1973), p. 290.
51. John Stockwell, In Search of Enemies: A CIA Story (New York: W.W.Norton & Co., 1978), p. 115.
52. Robert Kennedy And His Times (New York: Ballantine Books, 1978), p. 606.
53. Thomas J. Noer, Cold War and Black Liberation (Columbia: U. of Missouri Press, 1985), p. 85.
54. Davidson, pp. 212-214.
55. Noer, pp. 78-79.
56. Ibid., pp. 79-80.
57. Ibid., pp. 80-81.
58. Ibid., p. 99.
59. Victor Marchetti and John D. Marks, The CIA and the Cult of Intelligence (New York: Dell Publishing Co., 1974), pp. 155-156.
60. Davidson, p. 240 and Wilfred Burchett, Southern Africa Stands Up (New York: Urizen Books, 1978), p. 30.
61. Op. cit., p. 261.
62. Ibid., p. 221.
63. Ibid., p. 241.
64. Mohamed A. El-Khawas and Barry Cohen (eds.), The Kissinger Study of Southern Africa: National Security Study Memorandum 39 (Westport, Connecticut: Lawrence Hill & Co., 1976), p. 93.
65. Ibid., p. 97.
66. Ibid., p. 105.
67. Ibid., p. 106.
68. Ibid., p. 47 and William Minter, King Solomon's Mines Revisited (New York: Basic Books, 1986), p. 234.
69. Stockwell, p. 67.
70. Ibid., p. 67-68.
71. Arthur Jay Klinghoffer, The Angolan War: A Study in Soviet Policy in the Third World (Boulder, Colorado: Westview Press, 1980), p. 44.
72. Stockwell, pp. 54-55 and Raymond L. Garthoff, Détente and Confrontation: American-Soviet Relations from Nixon to Reagan (Washington, D.C.: The Brookings Institution, 1985), pp. 509-510.
73. Stockwell, p. 206.
74. El-Khawas and Cohen, p. 183.
75. Op. cit., pp. 187-188.
76. Op. cit., p. 83.
77. Op. cit., p. 164.
78. Speech by Fidel Castro, April 19, 1976, in Fidel Castro Speeches (New York: Pathfinder Press, 1981), p. 92.
79. Wilfred Burchett, pp. 86-87.
80. Ibid., p. 92.
81. Op. cit., p. 216.
82. Ibid.
83. Ibid., pp. 229-231.
84. United Nations Security Council, Document S/16198 of 7 December 1983, White Paper on Acts of Aggression by the Racist South African Regime Against the People's Republic of Angola 1975-1982, p. 12.
85. William J. Pomeroy, Apartheid, Imperialism, and African Freedom (New York: International Publishers, 1986), p. 40.
86. El-Khawas and Cohen, pp. 188-189.
87. Op. cit., p. 256.
88. Ibid., pp. 256-257.
89. Ibid., p. 275.
90. Op. cit., p. 311.
91. Ibid., pp. 312-313.
92. "South Africa: Strategy for Change," Foreign Affairs, Vol. 59, No. 2, Winter 1980/81, pp. 326-327, 345, 346, 349.
93. Covert Action Information Bulletin, Number 13, July-August 1981, pp. 37-38.
94. Ibid., pp. 38-39.
95. Ibid., p. 40.
96. Ibid.
97. Ibid., pp. 40-41.
98. Ibid., p. 41.
99. White Paper on Acts of Aggression..., p. 14.
100. Ibid., pp. 27-29.
101. Report of the Special Committee Against Apartheid, UN General Assembly, Official Records: Fortieth Session, Supplement No. 22 (New York: United Nations, 1986), pp. 43-44.
102. Gerald J. Bender, James S. Coleman, Richard L. Sklar (eds.), African Crisis Areas and U.S. Foreign Policy (Berkeley: University of California Press, 1985), pp. 137-138.

103. *Covert Action Information Bulletin*, Number 13, July-August 1981, pp. 28-29, and Dan O'Meara, "Destabilization in Southern Africa: Total Strategy in Total Disarray," *Monthly Review*, April 1986, p. 60.
104. Bender *et al.*, p. 141.
105. Colin Legum, *The Battle Fronts of Southern Africa* (New York: Africana Publishing Co., 1988), p. 290.
106. *Children on the Front Line* (New York: United Nations Children's Fund, March 1987), p. 18.
107. *New York Times*, July 10, 1988.
108. *New York Times*, December 23, 1988.
109. Interview by Margaret A. Novicki, *Africa Report*, September- October 1989, p. 17.
110. Current Policy No. 1217, "National Reconciliation Efforts for Angola", United States Department of State, Bureau of Public Affairs, Washington, D.C.
111. From the text of the Freedom Charter, published in *Intercontinental Press*, New York, November 18, 1985, p. 690.
112. El Khawas and Cohen, p. 107.
113. US Department of Commerce, *Survey of Current Business*, various issues 1969 through 1977; US Department of Commerce, *Statistical Abstract of the United States*, 1971, p. 771, and 1978, p. 879; Christopher Coker, *The United States and South Africa, 1968-1985* (Durham, N.C.: Duke University Press, 1986), p. 98.
114. Ann and Neva Seidman, South Africa and U.S. Multinational Corporations, (Westport, Conn.: Lawrence Hill & Co., 1977), pp. 113, 115-116.
115. Seidman, pp. 108-109; Ann Seidman and Neva Makgetla, Transnational Corporate Involvement in Africa's Military Buildup, United Nations Centre Against Apartheid, Notes and Documents 35/78, October 1978, pp. 10-11.
116. Quoted in Seidman and Makgetla, p. 5.
117. Coker, p. 107.
118. Resolution 392 (1976) of 19 June 1976.
119. *Op. cit.*, p. 265.
120. Study Commission of U.S. Policy Toward Southern Africa, *South Africa: Time Running Out* (Berkeley: University of California Press, 1981), p. 249.
121. *Op. cit.*, pp. 326-327, 344, 349.
122. UN Security Council Resolution 554 (1984) of 17 August 1984.

123. *Report of the Special Committee Against Apartheid*, UN General Assembly, Official Records: Forty-First Session, Supplement No. 22 (New York: United Nations, 1986), p. 14.
124. *New York Times*, February 13, 1990.
125. *Ibid.*

Soviet Union: 1946-Early 1990

1. *FRUS*, 1946, Vol. I, pp. 1160-1165.
2. *Ibid.*
3. Michio Kaku and Daniel Axelrod, *To Win A Nuclear War: The Pentagon's Secret War Plans* (Boston: South End Press, 1987), pp. 31-32.
4. *Memoirs 1925-1950*, p. 294.
5. *Ibid.*, p. 558.
6. *Ibid.*, p. 549.
7. *Ibid.*
8. *Ibid.*, p. 550.
9. *Ibid.*, p. 554.
10. *Ibid.*, pp. 294-295.
11. *FRUS*, 1946, Vol. I, pp. 1167-1168.
12. *Ibid.*, p. 1170.
13. From text of report as given in Appendix A, Arthur Krock, *Memoirs: Sixty Years on the Firing Line* (New York: Funk & Wagnalls, 1968), p. 425.
14. *Ibid.*, p. 477.
15. *Ibid.*, p. 478.
16. *Ibid.*
17. *Ibid.*, p. 481.
18. *Ibid.*, p. 482.
19. *Present at the Creation: My Years in the State Department* (New York: W.W. Norton & Co., 1969), p. 218.
20. *Ibid.*, p. 219.
21. *Op. cit.*, pp. 288-289.
22. *Memoirs 1925-1950*, p. 316.
23. *Ibid.*, p. 317.
24. Richard B. Morris, *Great Presidential Decisions: State Papers That Changed the Course of History* (New York: Harper & Row, Perennial Library, 1973), pp. 429-435.
25. *Greece and Turkey: Some Military Implications Related to NATO and the Middle East*, Prepared for the Special Subcommittee on Investigations of the Committee on Foreign Affairs by the Congressional Research Service, Library of Congress (Washington, D.C.: U.S. Government Printing Office, 1975), p. 1.
26. George Kennan, *American Diplomacy 1900-1950* (New York: New American Library, Mentor Books, 1951), p. 92.

27. *Ibid.*, pp. 98-99.
28. *Memoirs 1925-1950*, pp. 358, 362.
29. *The Man Who Kept the Secrets: Richard Helms and the CIA* (New York: Alfred A. Knopf, 1979), p. 24.
30. Book IV, Final Report of the Select Committee to Study Governmental Operations with Respect to Intelligence Activities (Church Committee), U.S. Senate (Washington, D.C.: U.S. Government Printing Office, 1976), p. 26.
31. Thomas H. Etzold and John Lewis Gaddis, eds., *Containment: Documents on American Policy and Strategy, 1945-1950* (New York: Columbia University Press, 1978), NSC 20/1, p. 190.
32. William Colby and Peter Forbath, *Honorable Men: My Life in the CIA* (New York: Simon and Schuster, 1978), p. 104.
33. *Ibid.*, pp. 90-91.
34. Book IV, Final Report, Church Committee, p. 29.
35. Victor Marchetti and John D. Marks, *The CIA and the Cult of Intelligence* (New York: Dell Publishing Co., 1974), pp. 174-175.
36. David Alan Rosenberg, "American Atomic Strategy and the Hydrogen Bomb Decision," *Journal of American History*, Vol. 66, No. 1, June 1979, p. 68; and Michio Kaku and Daniel Axelrod, p. 50.
37. Quoted in Fleming, Vol. I, p. 396.
38. *Dropshot: The United States Plan for War with the Soviet Union in 1957* (New York: Dial Press, 1978), pp. 19-20.
39. *Containment*, p. 362.
40. Quoted in Peter Wyden, *Day One: Before Hiroshima and After* (New York: Warner Books, 1985), p. 350.
41. *Memoirs 1925-1950*, pp. 471, 473.
42. NSC 30, September 10, 1948, in *Containment*, pp. 340-341.
43. Acheson, p. 349; and Rosenberg, p. 84.
44. *War and Peace* (New York: Macmillan Co., 1950), p. 115.
45. *Memoirs 1925-1950*, pp. 407-408.
46. NSC 20/4 of November 23, 1948, *Containment*, p. 207.
47. Anthony Cave Brown, p. 1.
48. *Ibid.*, pp. 22, 24, 159.
49. *Ibid.*, pp. 22-23.
50. *Ibid.*, p. 165.
51. *Containment*, pp. 385, 386, 393.
52. *Ibid.*, p. 413.
53. *Ibid.*, p. 391.
54. *Ibid.*, p. 401.
55. *Ibid.*, pp. 401-402.
56. *Ibid.*, pp. 432-433.
57. *Ibid.*, pp. 435-436.
58. *Ibid.*, pp. 422-423.
59. *Op. cit.*, p. 375.
60. *Ibid.*, p. 378.
61. Quoted in Townsend Hoopes, *The Devil and John Foster Dulles* (Boston: Little, Brown and Co., 1973), pp. 127, 198, 203, 290.
62. Quoted in Fleming, Vol. II, pp. 682, 684.
63. *Op. cit.*, p. 287.
64. *Mandate for Change* (New York: Signet Books, 1963), p. 603.
65. *Ibid.*, p. 606.
66. Hoopes, p. 295.
67. (New York: W.W. Norton & Co., 1969), pp. 2-5.
68. *Ibid.*, pp. 42, 117.
69. *Ibid.*, pp. 145, 159, 190.
70. *Ibid.*, pp. 111 (Italics in original), 140.
71. (New York: Harper & Row, 1959), p. 31.
72. *Ibid.*, p. 60.
73. *Ibid.*, p. 33.
74. *Ibid.*, p. 63.
75. (New York: Pantheon Books, 1986), pp. 59, 111, 132.
76. *Ibid.*, p. 60.
77. Robert Scheer, *With Enough Shovels: Reagan, Bush and Nuclear War* (New York: Random House, 1982), p. 217.
78. *Ibid.*, pp. 215, 219.
79. *Ibid.*, pp. 216, 221.
80. *Ibid.*, p. 221.
81. *Ibid.*, pp. 220-221.
82. Hoopes, pp. 468, 493-496, 502.
83. Fleming, Vol. II, pp. 1003-1004.
84. *A Thousand Days: John F. Kennedy in the White House (Boston: Houghton Mifflin Co., 1965), pp. 359-364.
85. *Ibid.*, pp. 359-363.
86. *Kennedy* (New York: Harper & Row, 1965), p. 726.
87. Schlesinger, p. 893.
88. *Ibid.*, p.895.
89. Sorensen, p. 730.
90. Morris, pp. 462-465.
91. *Op. cit.*, p. 727.
92. *Op. cit.*, p. 910.
93. Sorensen, p. 745.
94. Schlesinger, p. 910.
95. *White House Years* (Boston: Little, Brown and Co., 1979), p. 124.
96. From his Posture Statement, quoted in John Newhouse, *Cold Dawn: The Story of Salt* (New York: Holt, Rinehart and Winston, 1973), pp. 66-67.
97. *Op. cit.*, p. 66.
98. *Ibid.*, p. 69.
99. Johnson, pp. 479-480.

100. *De Gaulle: A Political Biography* (New York: Simon and Schuster, 1966), p. 329.
101. *Soviet Foreign Policy*, ed. A.A. Gromyko and B.N. Ponomarev (Moscow: Progress Publishers, 1981), Vol. 2, 1945-1980, p. 415.
102. *The Ostpolitik of the Federal Republic of Germany* (Cambridge, Mass.: MIT Press, 1978), pp. 65, 66.
103. *People and Politics: The Years 1960-1975* (Boston: Little, Brown and Co., 1976), p. 90.
104. Kissinger, White House Years, p. 126.
105. From the passage given in Kissinger, *White House Years*, p. 1477.
106. Quoted in Garthoff, p. 30.
107. *The Real War* (New York: Warner Books, 1981), p. 16.
108. *Ibid.*, p. 290.
109. *White House Years*, pp. 129, 134.
110. *Ibid.*, p. 129.
111. *Ibid.*, p. 128.
112. *The Price of Power* (New York: Summit Books, 1983), p. 147.
113. Henry Kissinger, *Years of Upheaval* (Boston: Little, Brown and Co., 1982), pp. 258, 292, 1175.
114. *Op. cit.*, pp. 127-128.
115. *Ibid.*, p. 150.
116. Based on texts of the agreements given in *Detente and Defense: A Reader*, ed. Robert J. Pranger (Washington, D.C.: American Enterprise Institute for Public Policy Research, 1976), pp. 114-124.
117. Garthoff, p. 193.
118. *Ibid.*, p. 194.
119. *White House Years*, pp. 821, 1143; and *Years of Upheaval*, p. 237 (Italics in original).
120. *Detente and Defense*, p. 123.
121. Gerald R. Ford, A Time To Heal (New York: Harper & Row, 1979), p. 218.
122. *White House Years*, p. 1232.
123. *Years of Upheaval*, pp. 250, 985, 996-997.
124. *Years of Upheaval*, p. 996.
125. William G. Hyland, *Mortal Rivals: Superpower Relations From Nixon to Reagan* (New York: Random House, 1987), p. 105.
126. Garthoff, p. 417 and Kaku and Axelrod, pp. 176-182.
127. *The Memoirs of Richard Nixon* (New York: Warner Books, 1978), Vol. 2, p. 606.
128. *The Dynamics of Detente: How to End the Arms Race* (New York: W.W. Norton & Co., 1976), pp. 144-145.
129. Quoted in Garthoff, pp. 524-525.
130. Quoted in Ford, p. 373.
131. December 26, 1976, as quoted in Scheer, p. 54.
132. *New York Times*, April 4, 1977.
133. Cyrus Vance, *Hard Choices*, p. 28; and Zbigniew Brzezinski, *Power and Principle*, p. 150.
134. Jimmy Carter, *Keeping Faith: Memoirs of a President* (New York: Bantam Books, 1982), p. 218 and Brzezinski, p. 154.
135. *Op. cit.*, p. 808.
136. *Op. cit.*, pp. 806-807.
137. *Ibid.*, p. 809.
138. Vance, pp. 418, 424.
139. Brzezinski, pp. 146, 149.
140. *Op. cit.*, p. 850.
141. *New York Times*, March 18, 1978.
142. *Op. cit.*, pp. 189, 318.
143. Vance, p. 84.
144. Brzezinski, p. 180.
145. *New York Times*, March 2, 1978.
146. Vance, p. 78.
147. Brzezinski, p. 207.
148. *Ibid.*, p. 211.
149. *Op. cit.*, p. 102.
150. *New York Times*, June 8, 1978.
151. *New York Times*, June 12, 1978.
152. Brzezinski, p. 415.
153. *Ibid.*, p. 323.
154. *New York Times*, August 9, 1978.
155. Vance, p. 131.
156. Brzezinski, p. 341.
157. Garthoff, p. 733.
158. Brzezinski, p.456.
159. Garthoff, p. 828.
160. Brzezinski, p. 348.
161. Carter, p. 263.
162. Carter, pp. 263-264.
163. Brzezinski, pp. 346-352; and Vance, p. 358.
164. Vance, p. 362.
165. Garthoff, p. 843.
166. *Ibid.*, p. 847.
167. February 1, 1980.
168. Brzezinski, p. 459.
169. Quoted in Alexander M. Haig, Jr., Caveat: Realism, Reagan, and Foreign Policy (New York: Macmillan Publishing Co., 1984), pp. 102-103.
170. From text of speeches given in Strobe Talbott, *The Russians and Reagan* (New York: Vintage Books, 1984), pp. 104 and 116-117.
171. August 14, 1981.
172. Haig, pp. 104-105, 108.
173. *New York Times*, August 17, 1980.
174. "Is SDI Technically Feasible?" *Foreign Affairs*, Vol 64, No. 3, America and the World 1985, p. 454.
175. Quoted in Scheer, p. 171.
176. "The Harsh Decade: Soviet Policies in the 1980s," Vol. 59, No. 5, Summer 1981, p. 1016.

177. "Buildup and Breakdown," Vol. 62, No. 3, *America and the World 1983*, p. 588.
178. "The Rise, Fall and Future of Detente," Vol. 62, No. 2, Winter 1983/84, p. 371.
179. Strobe Talbott, *Deadly Gambits: The Reagan Administration and the Stalemate in Nuclear Arms Control* (New York: Alfred A. Knopf, 1984), pp. 46-48.
180. *Ibid.*, p. 247.
181. "As a European Saw It," Vol. 62, No. 3, *America and the World 1983*, pp. 521, 529.
182. "The Public Mood: Nuclear Weapons and the U.S.S.R.," Vol. 63, No. 1, Fall 1984, pp. 33, 37, 44, 46.
183. Michael Mandelbaum and Strobe Talbott, Reagan and Gorbachev (New York: Vintage Books, 1987), p. 40.
184. Strobe Talbott, *The Russians and Reagan* (New York: Vintage Books, 1984), p. 70.
185. From text of speech given in Talbott, *The Russians and Reagan*, p. 131.
186. "Foreign Policy Under Reagan II," Vol. 63, No. 2, p. 222.
187. *Ibid.*, pp. 229, 230.
188. "New Realities and New Ways of Thinking," Vol. 63, No. 4, Spring 1985, pp. 706, 708.
189. *Op. cit.*, p. 223.
190. *Op. cit.*, p. 157.
191. August 27, 1987.
192. August 10, 1987.
193. *New York Times*, August 24, 1987.
194. *New York Times*, December 12, 1987.
195. *Pravda*, December 15, 1987.
196. *New York Times*, December 11, 1987.
197. *New York Times*, December 20, 1987.
198. *New York Times*, December 20, 1987 and January 5, 1988 and *New York Times Magazine*, January 17, 1988.
199. *New York Times*, December 4, 1987.

200. "American Foreign Policy: The Bush Agenda," *Foreign Affairs*, Vol. 68, No. 1, *America and the World 1988/89*, p. 211.
201. *Ibid.*, p. 216.
202. "East-West Relations," Vol. 68, No. 3, Summer 1989, p. 1.
203. Remarks by the President at the Coast Guard Academy, White House press release, May 24, 1989.
204. *New York Times*, November 23, 1989.
205. December 4, 1989.
206. *Ibid.*
207. All quotes from *New York Times*, February 11, 1990.

Conclusion

1. Quoted in Peter Wyden, *Day One: Before Hiroshima and After* (New York: Warner Books, 1985), p. 167.
2. *Memoirs*, Vol. I, p. 419.
3. Quoted in David Alan Rosenberg, "American Atomic Strategy and the Hydrogen Bomb Decision," *The Journal of American History*, June 1979, p. 76.
4. McGeorge Bundy, *Danger and Survival: Choices About the Bomb in the First Fifty Years* (New York: Random House, 1988), p. 255.
5. March 15, 1990.
6. Quoted in Bundy, p. 234.
7. Quoted in Fleming, Vol. II, pp. 741, 742, 776.
8. Eisenhower, *Mandate for Change: 1953-1956*, p. 603.
9. Bundy, pp. 328 ff.
10. *Op. cit.*, pp. 726-727.
11. *Ibid.*, p. 726.
12. Quoted in Bundy, p. 537. See also p. 541.
13. Quoted in Bundy, p. 538 (Italics in original).
14. *New York Times*, February 3, 1990.
15. March 9, 1990.
16. "America without the Cold War," *Foreign Policy*, Number 78.
17. "America's New Course," *Foreign Affairs*, Vol. 69, No. 2.

INDEX